Pro Football Championships
Before the Super Bowl

SHERMAN. WASHINGTON

Pro Football Championships Before the Super Bowl

A Year-by-Year History, 1926–1965

JOSEPH S. PAGE

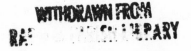
Rapides Parish Library
411 Washington St.
Alexandria, LA 71301

McFarland & Company, Inc., Publishers
Jefferson, North Carolina, and London

LIBRARY OF CONGRESS CATALOGUING-IN-PUBLICATION DATA

Page, Joseph S.
Pro football championships before the Super Bowl :
a year-by-year history, 1926–1965 / Joseph S. Page.
p.   cm.
Includes bibliographical references and index.

ISBN 978-0-7864-4809-8
softcover : 50# alkaline paper ∞

1. Football — United States — History — 20th century.
2. American Football League — History — 20th century.
3. National Football League — History — 20th century.   I. Title.
GV954.P345   2011   796.33209730904 — dc22   2010043875

British Library cataloguing data are available

On the cover: Washington Redskins quarterback Sammy Baugh (33)
tackled by the Chicago Bears defense during the NFL championship
game at Wrigley Field on December 12, 1937 (Associated Press)

Manufactured in the United States of America

*McFarland & Company, Inc., Publishers
Box 611, Jefferson, North Carolina 28640
www.mcfarlandpub.com*

I am lovingly and with deep, heartfelt appreciation dedicating this book to two people and a game. The people are Tom and Marjorie Page, my parents. The game is, of course, football. I owe much of what I am and what I have today to my parents and football.

My dad taught me a great deal about football and about life, about drive and determination and about how to treat others. He had been a player of some note at Vanderbilt University right after the war and he had a lot to share. He never missed one of my games until my own days at Vanderbilt when I was lucky to suit up at all and his frequent business travel would not always permit. For all of this and so very much more, thanks, Pop.

My mom had watched my dad, my uncle, and my brothers play for years before me. She made it to all my games too, but she had the added tasks of driving to and from practice for many years and the thankless chore of getting grass stains, blood, sweat, and that dreaded New Jersey swamp mud out of uniforms. Thank you, Mother.

Football taught me about life. It taught me about physical conditioning, mental and physical toughness, it taught me about drive, restraint, and a lot about myself. It taught me not to quit. It made me a better person. I have had success as a person, as a student, as an athlete, and in the business world, but it all started with my dad, my mom, and football. I will always love and appreciate them all and I will never, ever forget.

Table of Contents

Acknowledgments

It's generally difficult to know where to start with the acknowledgments when writing a book. So many people help along the way, and you want to make sure that you thank each one of them adequately. While that is no different with this book, the first thank-you goes, without hesitation, to sportswriter Jerry Izenberg, who many years ago wrote a book called *Championship*. I bought a copy of that book when I was no more than ten or eleven, at a school book fair, and never have I invested another 75 cents so wisely. That book was the inspiration for this collection of championship game stories. I have read *Championship* many times. Its cover is battered and taped, the glued backing all but disintegrated, and its pages worn, but I still own that same copy, and it has traveled the world with me — repeatedly landing on all six of the inhabitable continents of the earth, as I've worked on this book. As much as I love the book, I always thought that Jerry should have started with the 1932 indoor final, so several years ago I undertook to write that chapter myself. I did, and then I kept going, and the result is now in your hands. So to Jerry Izenberg, a heartfelt thank-you for many years of terrific stories and for the inspiration.

I have discovered that writing a book is a lot of work and a lot of fun, but also a collaborative effort. While the author is fully engaged, many different people step in and help throughout the process. My family have edited and listened to me ramble on about Bronko Nagurski, Glenn Presnell, Red Grange, Sammy Baugh, Charley Conerly, single plays in games that occurred seventy years ago, football in general, and the 1920s and 1930s. They and my friends have been interested and supportive throughout the process. Librarians across the country, and far too numerous to remember, have helped me access material. Of those, I especially want to thank librarians Tracey Howerton, Sally Raye, and Pat McGee at the Nashville Public Library; librarians Deirdre Schmidel, James Lewis, Willis Taylor, and Susan German at the Newark Public Library, librarians at the New York Public Library; Francis and Lou and company; Mary Plazo of the Akron–Summit County Public Library; Lynn Sullivan of the Omaha Public Library; Matt Waechter, the Information Services Specialist at the Pro Football Hall of Fame; Barbara Scheibel at the Onondaga County Public Library in Syracuse, New York; Melissa and the librarians at the Saint Paul, Minnesota, Public Library; Sam and the librarians at the San Francisco Public Library; librarians at the Minneapolis Central Hennepin County Library; George Rugg of the Special Collections Department of the Hesburgh Libraries at the University of Notre Dame. I would also like to say a word of thanks to author Bob Carroll, who encouraged me as I began writing this book several years ago, and who gave me a great deal of feedback on the very early chapters; Andy Piascik; Rubin and Annette Ratkin — Rubin, thank you more than I can say for sharing over ninety years of memories of New York sporting events and venues, including many at the Polo Grounds and Yankee Stadium; David and Ellen Levy; Robin Rose; Sandy Reagan of Sandra Reagan Photography in Nashville; former game participants Herb Rich and Bill Wade, whose stories I was fortunate to hear over the years; and my family, friends and colleagues who have been very patient and put up with me during the writing of this book.

Introduction

Time in professional football today seems to be measured only in Roman numerals. Ever since the National Football League's Green Bay Packers and the American Football League's Kansas City Chiefs, the 1966 professional titlists, met in the Los Angeles Memorial Coliseum in January 1967, the championship history of professional football has been summed up in just two words: "Super Bowl." It is almost as if the decades of championship contests that came before, never happened. The recent fiftieth anniversary of the 1958 Colts-Giants overtime championship served to remind fans that title game history did not simply start on that sunny, mid–January day in southern California in 1967. But with the passing of that anniversary, we returned to our fascination with the glitz and hoopla surrounding the modern championship contest. The Super Bowl, with its neutral site, warm-weather venues, multi-million dollar commercials, and lavish half-time extravaganzas, is certainly a bigger-ticket event than its earlier brethren. But don't tell the thousands of players, coaches, fans, and officials who watched or participated in those earlier contests that the Super Bowl is in any way more important.

The pre–Super Bowl history of professional football is rich in wonderful stories of the gladiators who slugged it out in the arena for the right to be called champion. From the first attempts at determining a title holder on the field of play in 1926, to the 1965 title contests waged in the snow and mud in Green Bay and on a sun-drenched field in San Diego, in the final pre–Super Bowl championship contests, legendary tales of gridiron struggles filled the airwaves, newspapers, dens, barber shops, and other venues where sports fans gathered. These are fascinating stories that bear telling and deserve to be remembered alongside of those from the Super Bowls.

The tales are those of contests waged indoors on pint-sized fields and circus straw; tales of battling snowstorms and bitter winds; tales of frozen fields and sneakers. The stories tell of heroes like an aging Y.A. Tittle, valiantly fighting to win his first championship on one good leg; of Frank Filchock fighting to prove his innocence in the wake of a gambling scandal; of Johnny Unitas and his Baltimore Colts refusing to give up against the vaunted Giants defense. The heroes were sometimes stars like Red Grange, Sammy Baugh, Otto Graham, and Bronko Nagurski; sometimes unsung like Jim Doran, Bucko Kilroy, and Gene Filipski; and sometimes diminutive equipment men like Abe Cohen, who never stepped foot on the field. This book looks at those great games and at those who played in them or made them possible.

1926 AFL — The First Championship Games

1926 AFL Championship Game #1 — Philadelphia Quakers (13) vs. New York Yankees (10)

November 25, 1926 — Yankee Stadium, New York City — 22,000
Weather Conditions: Cold, low 30s, gray skies.
Field Condition: Firm.

By all estimations, Red Grange was the biggest name in football in the mid–1920s. His exploits at the University of Illinois were legendary. His grueling but highly successful professional debut and barnstorming tour with the Chicago Bears in 1925 had made him rich and helped raise the National Football League's profile from what amounted to minor-league status to something greater. Grange and his manager Charles C. "Cash and Carry" Pyle had done a great service for the league, but they had been well paid for Grange's contribution. In 1926, however, the pair determined that the league should continue to show its gratitude by granting them a National Football League franchise in New York City. While some owners were warm to the idea of Grange as a draw in New York, Tim Mara, owner of the Giants, the existing league franchise in Gotham, felt differently. Mara personally disliked Pyle, but more practically, he knew that a second league franchise in New York would hurt his fledgling Giants at the gate. When the league turned Pyle and Grange down, the pair announced the formation of the first American Football League.

The first AFL started with great optimism, but by mid-season, the pain of economic reality had set in, and in the end, the league was a complete financial flop, in which eight of the nine squads lost money. The AFL was competing head-on with the 22-team NFL. The war between the leagues for talent, and the fight for fan bases in cities across the country, caused distress in the financial picture for most squads. While the New York Yankees drew respectable crowds, Pyle was spending money trying to keep the weaker AFL clubs alive. The Yankees were Grange's squad, and they were supposed to be the class of noteworthy circuit. In reality, they were becoming also-rans in a financially strapped confederation. "Apart from a crumbling league, the Yanks were facing the indignity of coming in second to the Philadelphia Quakers."[1]

As the season entered the home stretch, New York (8–3–0) was just behind Philadelphia (6–2–0) in the standings. One of Philadelphia's losses was a 23 to 0 trouncing by New York, at the close of October; so the race for the league title came down to two late November

3

games between the high-scoring Yankees and the defensively strong Quakers. In a move to strengthen their offense for a championship run, Philadelphia acquired former Lafayette College star halfback Doc Elliott from the Cleveland Panthers, setting the stage for a Thanksgiving weekend showdown.

The Quakers and Yankees squared off in front of 22,000 fans on Thanksgiving Day in Yankee Stadium in the first of a two-game, home-and-home series to determine the league championship.

The Quakers started the scoring in the first quarter with a drive that was capped by two five-yard runs by Al Kruez that put the ball in deep in Yankee territory. Finally, the New York defense stiffened and held, forcing Kruez to kick a 35-yard field goal, putting Philadelphia up 3–0.

"At the start of the second quarter two passes, one from Grange to Hubert, gained 9 yards, and another from Tryon to Baker, brought the ball to the 18-yard line. Continuing the aerial attack, Tryon made 9 yards on a pass from Baker, but the Quakers here checked the drive and took the ball on downs."[2] The Yankees defense, in turn, held Philadelphia, forcing a punt. Kruez's kick was poor, again giving the Yankees good field position, but New York again failed to move the ball. An exchange of punts ensued in what appeared to be settling into a defensive battle. Finally, after the Yankees got the ball back for a third time, the offense began to click. Aided considerably by a 15-yard penalty against the Quakers, New York regained possession at the Philadelphia 25. Grange picked up 7 yards around left end, but the Quaker defense then held firm, forcing a field goal. Tryon's 24-yard kick was successful and the game was knotted at 3.

In the third period, the Yankees made a 30-yard advance, but were stopped and forced to punt.

Robinson set up another Philadelphia score when he recovered Baker's fumbled punt on the New York 30-yard line. The Yankee defense refused to bend on the ensuing possession, bringing up a fourth-down situation. The Philadelphians determined to try the field goal. When Scott knelt to hold the ball on the 42-yard line, few thought Kruez could make it. But the big Penn man shot a low liner straight over the bar. Kruez's kick put the Quakers back on top 6–3 with his second field goal of the afternoon.

Tryon ran back Philadelphia's kickoff to give the Yankees good field position for their next drive. New York combined runs and a strong passing attack to move the ball downfield in a drive that began late in the third period. The successful possession would prove costly, however. It was on this drive that Grange went down with an injury and was "helped bruised and shaken from the field."[3] Grange was mediocre during the first half, throwing a couple of passes and picking up a few yards on end runs, but in the third period, he began to come alive. Early in the quarter, he broke loose for a 20-yard gain, he made one pass reception, and later, he picked up 14 yards around left end, but it was on this play that he injured his hip and was forced to leave the game.

Grange's replacement was George Pease, who led the league in touchdown passes. The former Columbia star wasted no time in moving his club by shooting a 26-yard pass to Tryon. After setting the tone, Pease continued his pinpoint passing by finding Pooley Hubert, Red Maloney, and Tryon on a series of completions that moved the Yankees to the Philadelphia 16-yard line as the third period came to an end.

On the first play of the final quarter, Pease slipped through the line unnoticed and caught a pass from Baker, advancing the ball to the 3. On the next play, Eddie Tryon dashed around left end and legged out a touchdown. Just as Tryon crossed the goal line, he was met by a horde of Quaker defenders and pushed back, but the score stood. Tryon's point-after kick put the Yankees back on top 10–6.

New York's lead was, however, short-lived. After the ensuing kickoff, Philadelphia began a sustained drive that terminated in the end zone. Quarterback Johnny Scott connected on two 10-yard aerial completions to get the drive moving. It was then, with just over five minutes remaining in the contest, that the Quakers' diminutive Charley "Pie" Way caught a 20-yard strike from Scott and then proved that he was the fastest man on the field. The former Penn State star blew by the New York defenders for the final 20 yards and a touchdown, restoring the Philadelphia lead. Kruez tacked on the extra point and the score stood at 13–10 in favor of the boys from the City of Brotherly Love.

In the final minutes of the game, the Yankees went to the air in desperation, but each time, the Philadelphia defense rose to the occasion, helping to secure the Quakers' lead, the win, and the game.

The star of the contest for the Yankees was former Colgate star Eddie Tryon, who scored all of New York's points that afternoon, putting across a touchdown, an extra point, and a field goal. Al Kruez scored seven points for Philadelphia and put the Quakers ahead twice in the first three quarters with field goals from placement. Tryon led the AFL in scoring in 1926 with 72 points and Kruez was fourth with 34. The Philadelphia defense also shone brightly as they were regularly found in the New York backfield.

"Twenty-two thousand fans watched Philadelphia win and Grange get his hip hurt. Two days later, the teams faced off in Shibe Park with twenty thousand watching Grange sit on the bench. The Quakers won and secured the title."[4]

Scoring

	1	2	3	4	Totals
Philadelphia Quakers	3	0	3	7	13
New York Yankees	0	3	0	7	10

1st Quarter: Philadelphia — FG — Al Kruez — 35 yards. 2nd Quarter: New York — FG — Eddie Tryon — 24 yards. 3rd Quarter: Philadelphia — FG — Al Kruez — 42 yards. 4th Quarter: New York — TD — Eddie Tryon 3-yard run (Tryon kick); Philadelphia — TD — Charley "Pie" Way 20-yard pass from Johnny Scott (Kruez kick)

Starting Lineups

Philadelphia Quakers		New York Yankees
George Tully	Left End	Red Maloney
Century Milstead	Left Tackle	Frank Kearney
Butch Spagna	Left Guard	Paul Minick
Karl Robinson	Center	Hal Griffen
Saville Crowther	Right Guard	Bill Oliver
Bull Behman	Right Tackle	Dick Hall
Whitey Thomas	Right End	Paul Goebel
Johnny Scott	Quarterback	Red Grange
Doc Elliott	Left Halfback	Roy "Bullett" Baker
Adrian Ford	Right Halfback	Eddie Tryon
Al Kruez	Fullback	Pooley Hubert

(*Substitutions:* **Philadelphia** — Ends: Charley "Pie" Way; Backs: Bob Dinsmore, Doc Elliott. **New York** — Ends: Art Coglizer, Larry Marks; Guards: Leo Kriz, Mike Michalske; Center: Steve Schimitisch, Backs: George Pease)

Head Coaches: Philadelphia: Bob Folwell; New York: Ralph Scott.
Game Officials: Referee: R.L. Lynch (St. John's Brooklyn); Umpire: H.E. Von Kersberg (Harvard); Head Linesman: E.A. Hastings; (De Witt Clinton); Field Judge: (unknown).

TEAM STATISTICS (No information available.)

1926 AFL Championship Game #2 — New York Yankees (6) vs. Philadelphia Quakers (13)

NOVEMBER 27, 1926 — SHIBE PARK, PHILADELPHIA — 22,000
WEATHER CONDITIONS: GRAY SKIES, MID–20S, BITTER COLD WIND GUSTS
FIELD CONDITION: FIRM, DRY

With the season series tied at one win apiece, the league championship came down to this final game between the rival squads. A Quakers win would end any discussion about who was the champion, but a Yankee win, coupled with a victory over the Chicago Bulls the following week, could still make good Pyle's guarantee of a title for his club.

Despite freezing temperatures and bitter cold wind gusts that swirled through the stadium, another good crowd of 22,000 showed up at Philadelphia's Shibe Park to take in the rubber match. Should the Quakers lose, they would fall into an interesting three-way tie for first place with the Yankees and the Chicago Bulls. The still-injured Grange was in uniform, but sat on the Yankees' bench wearing his team sweater and unable to play for New York.

The Yankees got off to a good start after a poor punt by Al Kruez gave New York the ball at midfield. The Yankees moved the ball to the Quakers' 32-yard line, where they stalled under pressure from a tenacious Philadelphia defense. There Eddie Tryon attempted a field goal from placement, but the low kick was blocked at the line and recovered by the Quakers at their own 34.[5]

After several exchanges of punts, the Quakers were the first to draw blood. At midquarter, an Eddie Tryon punt bounced into the end zone for a touchback, giving Philadelphia possession of the ball at their own 20. "Scott circled the end for 5 yards. Elliott crashed the line for five more, and first down. Little Albert Kreuz of Pennsylvania contributed 2 yards and Elliott 3 more."[6] On third down, Scott completed a pass to Pease, but the Quakers were also aided by a clipping penalty that moved the ball 25 yards to the New York 31. Buoyed by their strong field position, the Quakers showed a little swagger as they called a hook-and-ladder play. Adrian Ford passed to Johnny Scott, who in turn lateraled to Tully, who then ran the ball to the New York 14. Ford then ran off tackle for 3 yards, and then gained 2 more to the left. On third down, Scott took the center pass from Karl Robinson and sprinted around right tackle with Ford leading the way. Ford seemed to be Scott's blocking back, but as the New York defenders began to close in on Scott, the former Lafayette College star lateraled to Ford. Ford took the ball on the run and began a footrace to the end zone with New York back Eddie Tryon, who was in his path. At the 2, Tryon dove at Ford in a vain attempt to save the touchdown, but he bounced off the Quaker's shoulder "as if he had collided with a runaway freight car."[7] Ford then tumbled over the goal line for the touchdown. Al Kruez was injured on the play and was replaced by former Princeton standout Bob Dinsmore, who drop-kicked the point after, putting Philadelphia up 7–0.

Later in the first period the wind caused another poor kick, giving the Quakers good field position near midfield. Scott then fired a rocket to Dinsmore, who took in the pass and raced unmolested to the New York 25-yard line, where he was finally corralled. Things were looking bright for another Quaker scoring opportunity, but on the next play Hubert intercepted Dinsmore's pass and the drive died at the New York 20.

New York could not move the ball and decided to punt out of trouble, but Hubert's kick was hurried and went out of bounds at the 27-yard line. Once again, the Quakers were on the verge of another score. But once again, they came away empty. After Scott and Elliott pounded away for a first down, the New York defense stiffened and held. Dinsmore attempted a drop kick for goal, but the kick was blocked and the Yankees took over on their own 25.

Tryon electrified the crowd by slipping off tackles for 25 yards before being brought down at midfield. New York's progress was checked at this point. After a short ground gain, Quaker defenders batted two passes down and the Yankees were forced to punt. Tryon booted a kick to the Philadelphia 28-yard line, where it was immediately downed. It was three and out for the Quakers as Scott booted the ball to George Pease. He took the ball at his own 23 and wound his way around several would-be tacklers as he moved the ball past mid-field. After an interference penalty and several short runs put the Yankees in scoring position, the defense braced and the Yankees were forced to try for another field goal. But once again, the kick was low and the Philadelphians took over at their 20. With less than a minute in the half, the clock was allowed to expire. The Quakers headed into halftime with a slim 7–0 lead.

Philadelphia's Tully kicked off to Hubert to start the second half. The Yankees' fullback got back to his own 40-yard line before he was stopped. After an exchange of punts, the second half was beginning to look like a repeat of the first. But suddenly, the Quakers came alive. After Johnny Scott's deep punt pinned the Yankees on their own 3, the Grangers chose, as was the custom of the day, to quickly punt out of trouble. The return punt carried to the New York 35. After Ford broke off tackle for 14 yards, the ball sat on the New York 21. Five more running plays by Elliott, Scott, and Dinsmore hammered the ball down to the 5, where the drive stalled, forcing a field goal attempt by Dinsmore. Standing on his own 15-yard line, Dinsmore booted the pigskin through the middle of the uprights and extended the Quaker lead to 10 points.

Much of the third quarter devolved again into a punting duel between Tryon and Dinsmore, as each team played for field position. Midway through the quarter, however, the Yankees found some life. Getting good field position at their own 46, the Yankees began a three-play series that ended in the Philadelphia end zone. On first down, Bullet Baker's pass fell incomplete, but on the next play, Larry Marks heaved a long forward pass that Art Coglizer pulled in and carried all the way to the Philadelphia 18, where three Quakers smothered him. Trying to stay in the air, Baker fired a first-down pass that missed its mark. Undeterred, Baker let go a second-down bullet to Pease, who broke free, scooped in the pass at the Philadelphia 10, and didn't stop running until he crossed the goal line for the Yankees' first score. Coglizer's try for the point after failed, leaving the New Yorkers down by four and in need of a touchdown to win.

Time and again, the Yankees moved the ball deep into Quaker territory, but each time, they came away empty and frustrated. Early in the fourth quarter, on second down, with just 13 yards to the goal, a New York forward pass fell incomplete in the end zone — a touchback under 1926 rules. Once, Dinsmore knocked down a fourth-down pass at the 11, rather than catching it, to give his team the ball at the 31. Another time, the Quaker defense simply overpowered and shut the New Yorkers down at the Philadelphia 29; and once, Pease missed on a 35-yard field goal attempt from placement.

After several more punt exchanges, time was beginning to run out, and the Yankees took the ball at their own 20-yard line after the final Quaker punt of the game. Desperately trying to make something happen quickly as both the clock and the daylight began to run out, the Yankees took to the air. On third down, the Dinsmore picked off a New York pass, running it back to the New York 22. After grinding out a couple of yards and burning valuable time, Dinsmore drop-kicked a 27-yard field goal to put Philadelphia up 13–6.

The Yankees, knowing that the next possession might well be their last, braced themselves for a harried, two-minute offense in hopes of tying the score and maintaining at least a partial claim to the championship. Tulley kicked off to Red Maloney, who snaked his way back to the Quakers' 49-yard line. Once again, the Yankees took to the air, but the results were no different. On second down and less than a minute to play, Kostos picked off an errant New York aerial and the game was over. The Philadelphia Quakers were the first and only champions of the first American Football League.

The Grangeless Yankees moved the ball up and down the field respectably, but due to sturdy defensive play by the Quakers, the New Yorkers were only once able to take advantage of scoring chances. "The Quakers presented an alert and sturdy defense, and an attack that had power and precision."[8] The *Public Ledger* went on to say, "Judging from their play against the Yankees, the Quakers thoroughly deserved their American League championship. Folwell's team displayed a splendid deceptive attack which had great power on the ground and fine accuracy in the air due in large measure to Scott's passing and the ability of the receivers, particularly Tully, who proved himself to be one of the best ends in professional football."[9]

The next day team president Leo Conway issued a challenge to the Frankford Yellow Jackets to play for the Philadelphia professional championship, and to the winner of the NFL title to play for the overall professional championship.[10] Frankford, as it turns out, eventually won the NFL crown. At the time of the Quakers' challenge, however, the Yellow Jackets were in the midst of a neck-to-neck title race with the Chicago Bears. Despite much anticipation among the public, players and press, they couldn't or wouldn't oblige.[11] The Quakers settled instead for a game against the New York Giants. While the Giants may not have been the best club in the NFL, finishing their season ranked seventh in the league, they were certainly game enough to defend their league's honor against the upstart Quakers, handily defeating the AFL champs 31 to 0.

SCORING

	1	2	3	4	Totals
New York Yankees	0	0	0	6	6
Philadelphia Quakers	7	0	3	3	13

1st Quarter: Philadelphia — TD — Ford —10-yard pass from Scott (Dinsmore kick). 2nd Quarter: None. 3rd Quarter: Philadelphia — FG — Dinsmore —15 yards. 4th Quarter: New York — TD — Pease — 14-yard pass from Baker (kick failed) Philadelphia — FG — Dinsmore — 27 yards

STARTING LINEUPS

New York Yankees		Philadelphia Quakers
Red Maloney	Left End	George Tully
Frank Kearney	Left Tackle	Century Milstead
Paul Minick	Left Guard	Butch Spagna
Hal Griffen	Center	Karl Robinson
Bill Oliver	Right Guard	Saville Crowther
Dick Hall	Right Tackle	Bull Behman
Paul Goebel	Right End	Whitey Thomas
George Pease	Quarterback	Johnny Scott
Eddie Tryon	Left Halfback	Doc Elliott
Roy "Bullett" Baker	Right Halfback	Adrian Ford
Pooley Hubert	Fullback	Al Kruez

(*Substitutions:* **New York**—Tackles: Mike Michalske, Backs: Larry Marks, Art Coglizer. **Philadel-phia**—Ends: Joe Kostos, Backs: Bob Dinsmore, George Sullivan, Charley Way.)

Head Coaches: Philadelphia: Bob Folwell; New York: Ralph Scott.
Game Officials: Referee: M.J. Morris (Ansonia), Umpire: G.R. Vierling (Cudahy), Head Linesman: Edward L. Bader (Penn), Field Judge: Ed Bennis

TEAM STATISTICS

New York Yankees		Philadelphia Quakers
7	First Downs	8
/239	Total Offense Plays/Yards	/171
	Rushing Attempts	
121	Rushing Yardage	101
20	Pass Attempts	10
4	Pass Completions	6
20.0	Completion Percentage	60.0
118	Passing Yardage	70
1	Interceptions	2

1926 AFL — The NFL Challenge

1926 AFL-NFL Challenge Game — Philadelphia Quakers (AFL) (0) vs. New York Giants (NFL) (31)

DECEMBER 12, 1926 — POLO GROUNDS, NEW YORK CITY — 5,000
WEATHER CONDITIONS: GRAY SKIES, SNOW SHOWERS, COLD,
TEMPERATURES IN THE MID–20S, PERIODIC WIND GUSTS.
FIELD CONDITION: MOSTLY FROZEN WITH PATCHES OF MUD AND
ICE, LIGHT DUSTING OF SNOW

In a strange sort of early Super Bowl, staged in New York's Polo Grounds, 40 years before Vince Lombardi's Packers demolished the American Football League IV champion

Chiefs 35–10, the NFL's seventh-place squad crushed the visiting American Football League I champions 31–0, on a cold, snowy day in Gotham.

The first AFL started with great optimism, but in the end, the league was a complete financial flop. In a monument to poor planning, AFL founder C.C. Pyle allowed three New York City–area clubs to join his circuit. The three AFL clubs, along with the existing NFL Giants, severely strained the drawing power of all four clubs. This not only hurt his league, but the presence of three AFL elevens in the New York area also hurt the Giants. In just their second year of existence, the Giants were themselves looking to secure a loyal fan base. The presence of the Yankees, the Brooklyn Horsemen, and the Newark Bears caused the Giants to lose a then-whopping $40,000 in 1926.[i]

With Red Grange in their backfield and a large population base from which to draw, the New York Yankees hosted large crowds at Yankee Stadium. The Philadelphia Quakers also drew respectable crowds, but the other seven AFL teams drew poorly, and by mid–November, only the Yankees, the Quakers, the Chicago Bulls, and the Los Angeles Wildcats completed their schedules. The NFL squads also suffered heavy losses. Of the 31 clubs in the two leagues in 1926, only 12 remained in 1927.

The Quakers won the 1926 AFL title, by defeating the Yankees in a home-and-home playoff over Thanksgiving weekend. Although the Yankees were AFL runners-up, Giants owner Tim Mara was anxious to prove his team's superiority over the AFL and specifically, over Grange's Yankees. He challenged New York's AFL franchise to a December 12 contest at the Polo Grounds, for the mythical "championship" of New York City, but he could not agree to terms with Pyle. Pyle responded to Mara's offer by stating that Grange's Yankees would have loved to meet the Giants on the gridiron, but all possible dates were booked for 1926. Pyle wrote, "On the date you name, we play the Chicago Bulls at Chicago and immediate [sic] thereafter start our Southern and Western tours."[2] Pyle ended his letter by proposing that the teams schedule a home-and-home series of games in 1927.

Not to be deterred in his quest to defeat the AFL, Mara turned to the league champion Quakers, offering a chance at another payday for both financially strapped franchises. The Quakers' president, Leo Conway, had been trying to schedule an intracity contest with the NFL's Frankford Yellow Jackets, as well as putting forth a standing offer for a game with whoever would eventually win the NFL crown. The Quakers quickly accepted Mara's offer, and the game was set for December 12 at the Polo Grounds in New York.

The Quakers' 1926 squad featured a strong lineup, including both established NFL veterans and collegiate stars. Four Quakers were named as All-Pros: Bull Behman (T), Al Kruez (B), Century Milstead (T), and George Tully (E). The 6'4", 220-pound Milstead, who played his college ball at Wabash and Yale, had played for the 1925 Giants, and would return to the squad in 1927 after the AFL folded.

December 12 proved cold and snowy and the field at the Polo Grounds presented a challenge to the grounds crew. The groundskeepers managed to clear the field of most of the snow, but with the white stuff still falling, a light dusting continually clung to the turf. Under that thin coating lurked the twin demons of ice and mud. "Two-thirds of the playing surface was covered with snow, one-sixth of it was two inches deep in mud and water, while the remaining one-sixth was a sheet of ice."[3]

The first half was mostly a defensive struggle, with the Quakers offense unable to move the ball past midfield and the Giants managing only a first-quarter field goal from captain Jack McBride.

In the third quarter, the Giants put together a sustained drive with McBride and

Jack Hagerty rushing for four first downs and delivering the ball to the Philadelphia 5-yard line. McBride then got the call and responded by bulling his way through the Quakers' line to the end zone, only being stopped by a snow bank piled up at the back line of the end zone.

Soon after McBride's tally, the New Yorkers again took possession of the ball and immediately went back to work moving it downfield. Long runs by Hagerty, Walter Koppisch, McBride and Hinky Haines set up the Giants' second touchdown, as Hagerty skated across the goal to give the Maramen a 17-point lead.

As the second half wore on, the weather continued to deteriorate. The Quakers had trouble hanging onto the ball, and the Giants had no trouble converting Philadelphia turnovers into points. At the end of the third session, the Giants pinned the visitors down on their own 5-yard line with a deep punt. McBride then stepped in front of a Sullivan pass at the 15, and ran it back to make the score 24–0 in favor of the New Yorkers.

In the fourth quarter, the Quakers picked off a Giants pass, only to have New York end Tillie Voss return the favor just three plays later. Voss, however, put an exclamation point on his pick by running it 35 yards into the end zone for the game's final score. After McBride's fourth extra-point kick of the day, the Giants led 31–0.

The stars of the contest were Jack McBride, who kicked a field goal in the first half and scored two touchdowns and all four extra points in the second half, and the Giants' Jack Hagerty and Tillie Voss, each of whom hit pay dirt once. The New York defense played beautifully, stifling the American League champions and allowing them only one first down for the entire game.

As lopsided as the score was, it could have been worse. The Giants came within a hair's breadth of three more scores: the Quakers' defense held the New York second team at the Philadelphia 1-yard line, and two touchdowns were called back by penalties that happened far from the play. In the first instance Hagerty ran back a kick for 65 yards and an apparent touchdown, and in the second, it was McBride streaking for 52, but both runs were made null by penalties.

New York's legendary right guard Al Nesser and the Quakers' right tackle Joe Kostos from Bucknell got involved in a fistfight as McBride went over for his second touchdown. Both players were ejected from the game.[4]

While the Giants were leveling the Quakers, the Chicago Bulls and the New York Yankees squared off on an icy field in Comiskey Park for the last American Football League regular season game. The Yankees won, 7–3. As the final gun sounded the end of the contest, the league was no more.

Scoring

	1	2	3	4	Totals
Philadelphia Quakers (AFL)	0	0	0	0	0
New York Giants (NFL)	3	0	14	14	31

1st Quarter: New York — FG — McBride. 2nd Quarter: None. 3rd Quarter: New York — TD — McBride 5-yard run (McBride kick). New York — TD — Hagerty run (McBride kick). 4th Quarter: New York — TD — McBride 15-yard interception return (McBride kick) New York — TD — Voss 35-yard interception return (McBride kick)

Starting Lineups

Philadelphia Quakers (AFL)		New York Giants (NFL)
George Tully	Left End	Tillie Voss
Century Milstead	Left Tackle	Steve Owen
Saville Crowther	Left Guard	Doc Alexander
Karl Robinson	Center	Riley Biggs
Butch Spagna	Right Guard	Al Nesser
Jerry Fay	Right Tackle	Babe Parnell
Whitey Thomas	Right End	Mickey Murtagh
Johnny Scott	Quarterback	Mike Palm
Doc Elliott	Left Halfback	Cowboy Hill
Adrian Ford	Right Halfback	Jack Hagerty
Bob Dinsmore	Fullback	Jack McBride

(*Substitutions:* **Philadelphia**—Tackles: Joe Kostos, Guards: Bill Coleman, Center: Charlie Carton, Backs: Charley Way, George Sullivan, Al Kreuz. **New York**—Guards: Joe Williams, Backs: Hinky Haines, Walter Koppisch, Kid Hill, Tex Grigg)

Head Coaches: Philadelphia: Bob Folwell; New York: Dr. Joseph Alexander.
Game Officials: Referee: W.G. Crowell (Swarthmore), Umpire: Tom Thorpe (Columbia), Head Linesman: Ed Bader (?), Field Judge: Jack Reardon (New Hampshire).

Team Statistics

Philadelphia Quakers (AFL)		New York Giants (NFL)
1	First Downs	
	Total Offense Plays/Yards	
	Rushing Attempts	
	Rushing Yardage	
	Pass Attempts	
	Pass Completions	
	Completion Percentage	
	Passing Yardage	
1	Interceptions (Return Yards)	1 (35)
	Sacks/Yards Lost	
	Kickoff Returns—Yards	
	Punts	
	Punting Average	
	Punt Return Yards	
	Had Blocked	
	Fumbles/Lost	
	Penalties	
	Penalty Yards	

1932 NFL — In from the Snow and the Cold

1932 NFL Championship — Portsmouth Spartans (0) vs. Chicago Bears (9)

DECEMBER 18, 1932 — CHICAGO STADIUM, CHICAGO — 11,198
WEATHER CONDITIONS: INDOORS. (OUTSIDE: SINGLE DIGITS, SNOWY, WINDY)
FIELD CONDITION: LOOSE DIRT, STRAW, TAN BARK.

The 1932 National Football League title was won in what will probably always rank as the strangest playoff game in league history. With the Chicago Bears and the Portsmouth Spartans tied for first place in the single-division NFL, a one-game playoff was added to the end of the schedule to determine a league champion. The contest was actually counted as the final regular-season game for both teams. As such, the results were recorded into the official regular season standings and dropped the loser into third place. Although not officially counted as such, this was in many respects the first NFL championship game, and thanks to bitter cold temperatures and a heavy snowstorm, it occurred under very odd and very noteworthy circumstances. Forced indoors by the severe weather, the Bears and Spartans played a contest that fostered profound changes in the game of football.

The Quagmire

Since the league's inception, no end-of-season championship contest had ever been played. Instead, the league's owners and its executive committee had decided league champions by consensus based on the final regular season percentage standings. While won-loss percentage seems a reasonable criterion on which to decide a championship, the picture got a bit cloudy when the team with the highest winning percentage had fewer wins than one of the runners-up. By 1932, this had happened in 5 of the 13 official league seasons.

During the NFL's early days, teams controlled their own scheduling, with few conditions placed on equity of schedules or number of games played. As such, teams were at liberty to schedule as many or as few games as they wanted with whomever they chose. In 1927, for example, the Philadelphia-based Frankford Yellow Jackets played a grueling 18-game league schedule, the league champion New York Giants played 13 games, the runner-up Green Bay Packers played 10, the Dayton Triangles went 1–6–1, and the Buffalo Bison team was winless in their 5 league contests. It was also common to schedule games against non-league opponents, but these were, of course, not counted in the standings.

In 1921, a won-loss percentage tie at the top in the final standings made the vote by the league owners more of a necessity than a confirmation. The result of the vote was to install the Chicago Staleys (later Bears) as champions over the Buffalo All-Americans, even though both teams had 9 wins versus 0 losses. Year in and year out, the league encountered this problem, but given the loose and unstructured nature of each team's schedule, it was difficult to determine any undisputed champion. Understandably, this never left a very good taste in many people's mouths. To this day, fans of the Pottsville Maroons claim that the 1925 championship was rightfully theirs.

Periodically there had been scant talk of strengthening the league through more regulated scheduling and a post-season championship contest, but little had come of it. The Bears had been involved in three such quagmires, finishing in 1921 as champions over Buffalo, but in 1924 and 1926 as runners-up.

The vagaries of the loose scheduling had denied the Portsmouth Spartans a shot at a title in 1931 when the Green Bay Packers had refused to meet them on December 13 in the season finale game in Portsmouth. The Packers argued that the game was only tentatively scheduled and no formal contract was signed so they were free to choose not to play. Both teams had played 14 games and the Packers' 12–2 record was a full game better than the Spartans' 11–3. Had the game been played and a Portsmouth victory occurred, both teams would have been knotted at 12–3 and tied for first place. Obviously, it was in Green Bay's interest to avoid the game, though not necessarily in the league's. NFL president Joe Carr, still not realizing the wisdom of holding an annual title contest, accepted the Packers' argument, thus giving the league and Green Bay another disputed championship and missing for yet another year a great opportunity to present to the fans a championship contest. The Portsmouth fans' bitterness was summed up by Bob Hooey of the *Columbus State Journal*, who opined that the Packers were afraid to play the Spartans with their crown endangered, stating, "Such is the way of cheese champions."[1] But the desire and pressure for a true playoff game was building. The Spartans did score a bit of a moral victory during the 1932 regular season when they soundly defeated Green Bay 19–0 on December 4 at Universal Stadium in Portsmouth. The victory helped knock the Packers out of title contention that year. Perhaps the *Portsmouth Times* expressed it best in their Monday headline "Spartans Trounce Green Bay 19–0: Purple Gets Sweet Revenge."[2]

The 1932 season had in general been somewhat crazy. As the season opened, the Packers, behind the passing of Arnie Herber and the legs of Johnny Blood McNally and Clarke Hinkle, were the favorites to win a fourth straight league title. As if preordained, Green Bay carried a 10–1–1 record into the final two weeks of the season, their only blemishes being a scoreless tie with the Bears on September 25 and a 6–0 loss to the New York Giants on November 20. But the Packers, with their destiny in their own hands, promptly lost their last two games, first to the Spartans and then to the Bears, creating something of a statistical nightmare.

The Bears got off to a strange start at 0–1–4, posting three scoreless ties in their first three games, but they then went on to win six of their next seven, finishing their stated schedule at 6–1–6. Through 13 games, the Bears' defense had only given up a niggardly 44 points while their offense tallied a sound 151. Chicago finished up the regular season with a 6–0 win over the Giants and a 9–0 defeat of the Packers.

The Spartans, after an unimpressive 1–1–2 start, went unbeaten over the next seven games, including home and road ties with the Bears in November and the December 4 drubbing of the Packers. They wound up their regular schedule at 6–1–4.

The Packers, despite their 10 wins, finished with a .769 winning percentage due to their 3 losses, while the Spartans and Bears each with 6 wins and 1 loss, were statistically tied at .857 and in first place. The difficulty lay in the ties. The Spartans had 4 and the

Bears 6. Since ties did not count in figuring a team's won-loss percentage in 1932, the standings were tight among the top three teams.

Even the Spartans' and Bears' face-to-face records were not helpful in determining superiority as the two teams had played to 13–13 and 7–7 ties in their regular-season encounters. In the first meeting, the Bears tied the game on a deception play with a touchdown pass to All-Pro receiver Luke Johnsos. After the previous play, Johnsos had pulled up lame and limped towards the Chicago sideline, but he stopped short and lingered inconspicuously at the edge of the playing field, remaining eligible and unnoticed by the Portsmouth defenders. As the play commenced, Bears quarterback Carl Brumbaugh took a quick drop back and heaved a long pass to the uncovered Johnsos, who had sprinted full-out down the sideline. Johnsos was wide open when he pulled the pass in and streaked untouched into the end zone. The second meeting, at Universal Stadium in Portsmouth, evolved into a ground war in which the Spartans' Glenn Presnell and the Bears' Bronko Nagurski each provided a touchdown for the day's only scores.

Today's rules for counting ties, in which each tie counts as a half win, half loss, would have given Green Bay the title with a .750 percentage, with Portsmouth finishing second at .727, and Chicago third at .692, but this was 1932 and ties counted for nothing in the standings. Clearly, league scheduling and the accounting of tie games had to be addressed. On December 13, 1932, The *Milwaukee Journal* ran an article highlighting the problems of the current system and considered several alternatives for counting tie games. Interestingly, the *Journal* also reported, "The Packers have packed away their white flannels, Johnny Blood [McNally] has bought himself a ukulele, and the club has left Green Bay on the first lap of its journey to Hawaii."[3] All things considered, the Packers didn't fare too badly. They traveled to Hawaii for two exhibition games. The first was against the University of Hawaii varsity squad on Christmas Day, and the second was against a team of island all-stars on New Year's Day. While the Packers may not have won the league championship in 1932, they certainly won the "Weather Bowl." Honolulu weather is certainly more hospitable in December than either Chicago or Green Bay!

Finally, rearing its ugly head yet again was the factor of loose scheduling. Adding to the statistical quagmire was the varied number of games that each team played. In 1932, the Packers scheduled 14 regular-season league games, the Bears 13, and the Spartans 11.

The Solution

To resolve the matter of a league champion, it was agreed that the Spartans and the Bears would meet in Chicago on Sunday, December 18, in a one-game playoff. The contest would be counted as the final regular-season game for both teams. As such, the results would be recorded into the official regular-season standings and would drop the loser into third place behind Green Bay. Portsmouth's great tailback Glenn Presnell recalled years later, "It wasn't like the Super Bowl is today. It counted in the standings and we got our regular per game salary. I got $175 and was happy to get it during the Depression."[4]

The Bears were charter members of the League, having started out as the Decatur Staleys in 1920. They were a big-city team full of big names and a big reputation. They had one league championship to their credit already and were anxious to make it two.

After several years as an independent club, the Portsmouth franchise joined the NFL in 1930 and had a storied, though short-lived history. Rooted in the tradition-rich football heritage of southern Ohio, the Spartans were always a tough and competitive team and the Portsmouth fans were strong supporters, but Portsmouth was a small-market franchise. After just four league seasons, the promise of larger gates beckoned from elsewhere. The Spartans were to leave southern Ohio in 1934 for Detroit, where they would be rechristened the Lions. In December 1931, the Spartans had been denied the opportunity to play the Packers for the title. In December 1932, they were anxious to right that wrong.

Despite their similar records, and the two ties in their earlier, face-to-face encounters, the Bears were heavy favorites to win the game. This was due in part to Chicago's stingy defense that had racked up seven shutouts during the regular season; in part to their offensive power, which was bolstered by such legendary players as Bronko Nagurski and Harold "Red" Grange; and in large part to the fact that Portsmouth would have to play without the services of All-Pro back Earl "Dutch" Clark, the league's leading scorer and, along with Presnell, one of the team's two best players. Clark was already working in his off-season job, as head basketball coach for his alma mater, Colorado College. Clark would be coaching his basketball squad against Wyoming on Saturday and would be unable to make it to Chicago in time for Sunday's kickoff. The Portsmouth management had appealed to college president Charles C. Mierow to allow Clark to play and had even arranged for an airplane to fly him from Wyoming to Chicago in time for the game, but Mierow refused to consent.[5] The Portsmouth squad was, however, undaunted and its attitude may best be summed up by Spartan back "Father" Lumpkin, who declared, "We can beat the Bears, anytime, anywhere — even without Dutch Clark."[6] Despite this bravado, Lumpkin was no doubt whistling past the graveyard. The Spartans would certainly feel the loss of Clark. Both teams would feel the effect of the weather.

Although it was early in the season, the Chicago area had already been experiencing a tough winter. Shortly after the Bears' victory over the Giants on December 4, a heavy snow began falling and didn't let up for three days. On Wednesday, the residents of the Chicago area began to dig out. With a possible championship on the line, Bears owner and coach George Halas called out the work crews to clear Wrigley Field in time for the Packers' visit on Sunday, December 11. The snow was piled high against the stands and the turf was frozen, but the field at game time was playable. Five thousand hearty souls braved the blowing snows and bitter air to watch the contest. During the game, the snow resumed and Chicago's notorious winds blew in from Lake Michigan, making the low single digit temperature almost unbearable. By the 2nd quarter the field had become an icy mess and the gusting wind was wreaking havoc on the flight of both passes and kicks. Neither team was able to put up points, though the visitors came the closest. Shortly before the half, Green Bay's Arnie Herber fumbled on the Chicago 1, frustrating a Packer scoring chance.

The game remained scoreless until the fourth quarter, when Tiny Engebretsen put the Bears up 3–0 with a 24-yard field goal. The field goal was set up by Herber's second fumble of the day. Soon after, Bronko Nagurski skated 56 yards across the frozen turf for the final score of the day. The game wound up 9–0 as Red Grange's kick for the point after touchdown failed.

With a 9–0 victory over Green Bay in the Bears' back pocket and Portsmouth's equal won/loss percentage, one more game was necessary to break the tie at the top of the standings. After considering their options, league officials decided that the Bears would host the game at Wrigley Field on December 18. Chicago was the obvious site for the game. With attendance down throughout the league due to the Depression, both teams could use the money that a big crowd and a game for the league championship would generate.

The Weather

Anticipation about the game began to grow, but it was almost as if the weather gods were laughing at the helpless humans as they responded with a third blizzard in less than two weeks. As if on cue, the storm clouds gathered once again. During the week before the game, an arctic front ripped through Chicago, dumping more snow and sub-zero temperatures on the Windy City. It would take great effort for Wrigley Field to be readied one more time, but even if the surface could be made playable, would the fans brave the elements? Portsmouth's All-Pro back Glenn Presnell recalled, "The snow was waist deep when we arrived in Chicago and the wind was bitter. There was no way we could practice outside."[7] The league considered postponing the contest, but delaying the game to the next week would not have guaranteed more playable conditions and would have also placed the game on Christmas weekend, risking greatly diminished gate receipts. As a result, on Friday, at the urging of Bears owner George Halas, it was decided that the game would be moved from frigid, snow-covered Wrigley Field to the warm confines of Chicago Stadium, home of the National Hockey League's Black Hawks. Halas spoke with Bill Veeck, Sr., about a single-game release for the Bears from a contract obligating them to play all home games at Wrigley Field. Due to the extreme conditions, Veeck, owner of the ballpark, agreed to release them for this one game. The game time was rescheduled for 8:15 P.M.[8]

The idea of playing a football game indoors was not entirely new. The Bears and the cross-town rival Chicago Cardinals had played an indoor exhibition game in 1930, and New York's Madison Square Garden had hosted two series of professional games between teams from Pennsylvania, New York, and New Jersey in December of 1902 and December of 1903. In both cases a round robin series of games were played on abbreviated fields and makeshift playing surfaces. The New York games were played on some 500 loads of dirt spread and steamrolled on the Garden floor. These attempts had met with varying degrees of measured success. Given this history, Halas was anxious about the indoor game, but he knew that his options were limited. He would be lucky to draw 1000 paying customers to the frozen icebox on West Addison and Waveland Avenues.

The new Chicago Stadium, located at 1800 West Madison Street across from the current United Center, had opened in March 1929. It was, at the time, the largest indoor sporting arena in the world, with seating for approximately 20,000 spectators. The Bears/Cardinals exhibition game there had met with some success and Halas felt that, while not ideal, it would be suitable for this game and certainly better than playing outside. Though the game was played in front of 11,198 warm, grateful patrons, the tight confines of the indoor venue presented some interesting logistical problems.

The game was played on a makeshift field that, including the end zones, was 80 yards long. The floor of the arena was covered with the same dirt surface that had hosted a circus the week before. In his autobiography Halas states, "The Salvation Army had sponsored a circus there so the concrete floor had a thick covering of what the management described as a very swell brand of dirt."[9] What Papa Bear did not state is that being left over from the circus gave the six-inch layer of dirt, straw, and tanbark the aromatic qualities of a stable. Chicago's All-Pro guard Joe Kopcha recalled that the things he most remembered about the game were "the smell of elephant dung from the circus and that I hurt my shoulder in the last two minutes of the game," as well as receiving a $246 bonus for winning.[10]

In addition to the short playing field, each end zone was shorter than the regulation 10 yards and the end zone corners were rounded. Only 45 yards wide, the field was about 8 yards narrower than normal, and it was encroached upon by the sideboards of the hockey rink, adding a new element of danger to sideline runs.

To address the problems presented by the warm but tight confines of Chicago Stadium, several rule adjustments were agreed upon. Some of these had positive, lasting effects on the future of the game.

Since nothing could be done to increase the physical length of the field, several attempts were made to do so virtually. It was agreed that as the offensive team crossed midfield they would be backed up 20 yards; thus the field, while physically 60 yards from goal line to goal line, was virtually 80 yards long.

Because the hockey rink's sideboards were only a few feet from the field, the teams had for the first time the option of centering the ball towards the middle of the gridiron on plays ending within 10 yards of the sidelines. Under the existing rules in 1932, the ball was placed for the next play wherever it was downed. On runs that ended out of bounds, the ball was put back into play one yard in from the point where the ball carrier went out. It was therefore obvious to everyone to which side the next play would be run. This clearly gave defenses a leg up and created significant handicaps for the offense. It also had a major role in holding down scoring, as teams often wasted a play just trying to get the ball closer to the center of the field. According to the temporary rules put in place for this game, when the ball carrier went out of bounds or was tackled within 10 yards of the sidelines, the offensive team had the choice of lining up one yard from the sideline or having the ball spotted 10 yards in towards the center of the field before the next play. If team chose to center the ball, it cost them a down, but both teams saw the obvious benefit and typically surrendered the down for field position. The new rule was a success with coaches, players, and fans because it opened up the game, allowing for more frequent long runs from scrimmage and more offensive play-calling options. Because of its popularity in this game, the new inbound spotting rule *sans* the down loss would be adopted for all league and college games the next year.

Several other temporary rules were put into place that affected the kicking game. The goal posts were moved up to the goal line. Field goals were not allowed. Punts that hit the ceiling or rafters were counted as touchbacks — this happened twice. Only one punt was caught and returned all night. Another was caught and downed and the rest "landed in the mezzanine, balcony, and adjacent territory." The United Press reported, "One punt knocked the 'Bl' out of the Black Hawks hockey sign,"[11] while another hit the organ. Touchbacks were returned to the 10- instead of the 20-yard line. Kickoffs were initiated from the 10-yard line. In another attempt to "lengthen" the field, the ball was moved back 20 yards after each kickoff return. Many of the rule changes generated excitement and the game was a popular success.

The Game

George Halas worked diligently to get word of the game out and advance press helped to fill the arena to about two-thirds of capacity. The atmosphere in Chicago Stadium was charged with curiosity and anxiousness. The Spartans were clad in their purple jerseys with gold numbers, and the Bears in their white jerseys with navy-colored numbers and navy and orange piping on the sleeves. As the teams went through their pregame warm-ups, Portsmouth guard John Wager remembered, "It was real exciting. The place was jammed and the fans were almost on top of the field."[12]

As the game began, the underdog Spartans battled the Bears valiantly. Both teams had to adjust their game plans for the unique dimensions of the field. Presnell recalled the smaller-than-usual playing field: "We were handicapped by the small field because you could pull your defense in. There were no long runs, and it was difficult to pass because the field was so confining. Any kind of zone defense stopped everything except short passes."[13]

Both teams failed several times on scoring threats. In the first quarter, the Bears, starting on their own 10, began to hammer away at the Portsmouth defense. With Nagurski and Grange leading the way, Chicago drove deep into Portsmouth territory, but an incomplete pass into the end zone — a touchback under 1932 rules — gave the Spartans the ball. Portsmouth powered the ball to the Bear 14 on runs from backs Johnny Cavosie, Glenn Presnell, and Leroy "Ace" Gutowsky, but missed scoring on an incomplete pass in the end zone from Presnell to fullback Lumpkin. The Bears responded with a 15-yard pass from Molesworth to Luke Johnsos, and their devastating ground attack responded with runs from Grange, Nagurski, and halfback Dick Nesbitt, who led the team to the Portsmouth 10. There, the Bears offense stalled on yet another incomplete pass into the end zone, and the Spartans took over on downs. Just before the quarter ended, Chicago's Bill Hewitt intercepted a pass at the Portsmouth 19, but a minute later Presnell repaid the Bears in kind by intercepting a Nagurski pass to end yet another scoring threat.

For much of the second quarter the ball was traded back and forth with neither team showing much sustained offense. During one Chicago drive, Grange, after a fifteen-yard run, was temporarily knocked out of the game by the hard-hitting Spartans defense. In the final minutes of the second quarter Portsmouth's Cavosie picked off a pass from Chicago's John Doehring and returned it ten yards to the Bear 6-yard line. Short gains on runs by Presnell and Gutowsky advanced the ball to the 2, but then the Bears' defense held. Unable to try for a field goal, Portsmouth turned the ball over to Chicago on downs, again coming away empty-handed. Presnell remembers that series: "Our favorite play was a fake end run where I would plant my foot and cut off tackle. We ran that on fourth down. Just as the hole opened up, I tried to plant my foot, slipped and fell. If we had scored then it might have been a different game."[14] One can only speculate that had field goals been allowed, the score at halftime might well have been 6–3 in favor of Portsmouth.

The Associated Press reported that the third quarter was "largely a punting duel between Cavosie and Nesbitt. George Corbett, who went into the game as a substitute for Grange, provided stirring runs for the Bears, but did not get within scoring distance."[15] As the period ended, the game was still knotted at zero. Heading into the final period, the specter of yet another inconclusive tie ball game loomed.

With 11 minutes left in the fourth quarter, Chicago's Dick Nesbitt leapt high in the air to intercept an errant pass from Lumpkin and returned it 10 yards to the Spartan seven, where he was tackled out of bounds. The ball was brought in 10 yards and Chicago was charged with a down, making it second and goal. On the strength of a six-yard Nagurski run, the Bears advanced to the 1-yard line. On third and goal the Portsmouth defense keyed on Bronko and dropped him for a one-yard loss. With the Bears facing fourth and goal from the 2, Nagurski took a handoff from Carl Brumbaugh and headed for the line. As the Spartans' defenders clustered to halt the powerful Bears fullback, he stopped, backed up a couple of steps and tossed a low, sharp touchdown pass to Grange, who had just returned to the game and was standing alone in the end zone.

Presnell recalls, "In those days the rules were that you had to be five yards back to pass. He took the ball and started into the line. Of course, we thought he was going to plunge with it. Then he jumped up and threw what we called a flea flicker over the line to Grange. He wasn't anywhere near five yards back, and they wouldn't call it."[16]

Portsmouth disputed the score, with head coach George "Potsy" Clark furiously arguing that Nagurski had not been five yards behind the line of scrimmage when he threw to Grange.

"I lined up as usual, four yards back," said Nagurski of the play. "Red went in motion. The ball was handed to me by our quarterback, Carl Brumbaugh, and I took a step or two forward as though to begin the plunge everyone expected. The defenders converged and there was no way I could get through. I stopped, moved back a couple of steps, and Grange had gone around and was in the end zone, all by himself. I threw him a short pass. He was falling down but he caught it."[17] Grange recalls, "Actually, I was on my back. Someone had knocked me down, but I caught the ball and held on to it."[18]

The game officials did not uphold the protest, with referee Bobby Cahn ruling that Nagurski had obeyed the five-yard rule. The touchdown stood. Paul "Tiny" Engebretsen kicked the extra point through the wooden uprights and into the mezzanine, making the score Bears 7, Spartans 0.[19] After the game, Spartan defender John Wager, who had a unique perspective on the play, insisted, "Potsy was right. I know because I had hold of Nagurski's legs when he threw the ball."[20] Halas believed that the play would revolutionize football. It would prompt the league owners to make a rule change during the off season, allowing the ball to be thrown from anywhere behind the line of scrimmage. "We hoped the new rules would open up the game," Halas said. "I believe the record shows we were right."[21]

On the next Portsmouth possession, the Bears defense and two 5-yard penalties held the Spartans deep in their own territory, forcing fourth down and a kicking situation. The punter, Faye "Mule" Wilson, standing behind his own goal line, fumbled an errant long snap from center Clare Randolph, and it sailed past him and out of the Spartans' end zone for a safety. That would end the scoring for the day. As the game ended the Chicago Stadium scoreboard read: Bears 9, Spartans 0.

The *Portsmouth Times* sportswriter covering the game, Lynn A. Wittenburg, unhappy with the outcome and with the controversy over the Nagurski/Grange touchdown ruling, ran a sour-grapes headline referring to the "Sham Battle on Tom Thumb Gridiron."[22] In his article, he called the game "a synthetic show." Chicago fans, however, enjoyed pointing out that even had the Bears' touchdown been disallowed, the final score would have been Chicago 2, Portsmouth 0!

Bears owner George S. Halas, who had experienced all of the oddities of the first years of the NFL, stated, "I don't think anything could compare with the game. The only thing not ridiculous about the whole mess was that we won the game."[23]

The Aftermath

When the Bears and the Spartans met indoors during a blizzard on a cramped, fragrant field in Chicago Stadium to decide the 1932 championship, a new era in the NFL was about to begin. While the showdown was a last-minute idea and its temporary rules were born of necessity, the game's legacy to football has been immeasurable. While Portsmouth supporters may have been less than pleased with the result and the contest may have been, in Halas' words, "ridiculous" and a "mess," the game captured both the league's and the public's attention and it brought about many long-lasting and successful changes to the NFL.

Several of the temporary ground rules put into effect because of the small indoor field, and supposedly for that game only, had great appeal. The league rules committee, aware that pro games could be dull, low-scoring contests, began to consider changes that would make games and the entire season more interesting to the average fan. The committee, led by its president George Halas and by Boston Redskins owner George Preston Marshall, saw benefits to keeping some of the rules. They pushed for permanent adoption of the rules that moved the goalposts forward, allowed forward passes from anywhere behind the line of scrimmage, and created inbound lines or hash marks 10 yards in from each sideline, between which the ball would be spotted before each play. The NFL owners and officials at the next league meeting in Pittsburgh in February 1933 adopted these rule changes. The changes resulted in a more open and higher-scoring game that provided more excitement for the fans. As Potsy Clark said, "Nagurski will pass from anywhere, so why not make it legal!"[24]

Marshall also saw the advantages of more regulated scheduling and of splitting the league into two divisions with an annual championship game between the winner of each division. He reasoned that two divisions would lead to more teams remaining in the running for the lead later into the season and therefore generate more fan interest. He had also seen the interest the Bears-Spartans game had garnered and believed that an annual contest between the two division leaders to determine a clear-cut league champion would be popular with the public. Marshall's arguments prevailed, and divisional play and a one-game playoff were voted in. In the first official game, on December 17, 1933, in Chicago's Wrigley Field, the Bears defeated the New York Giants by a score of 23–21 in an exciting seesaw battle that was decided on the final play. While other NFL championship games over the years have certainly been grander and more exciting, it would be hard to top the 1932 title contest for either its significance or its uniqueness.

SCORING

	1	2	3	4	Totals
Portsmouth	0	0	0	0	0
Chicago	0	0	0	9	9

1st Quarter: None. 2nd Quarter: None. 3rd Quarter: None. 4th Quarter: Chicago — TD — Grange — 2-yard pass from Nagurski (Engebretsen kick). Chicago — Safety — Team — Portsmouth snap from center goes out of end zone.

STARTING LINEUPS

Portsmouth Spartans		Chicago Bears
Bill McKalip	Left End	Luke Johnsos
Ray Davis	Left Tackle	Bill Buckler
Maury Bodenger	Left Guard	Zuck Carlson
Clare Randolph	Center	Okie Miller
Ox Emerson	Right Guard	Joe Kopcha
George Christiansen	Right Tackle	Lloyd Burdick

Harry Ebding	Right End	Bill Hewitt
Leroy "Ace" Gutowsky	Quarterback	Keith Molesworth
Glenn Presnell	Left Halfback	Harold "Red" Grange
John Cavosie	Right Halfback	Dick Nesbitt
Roy "Father" Lumpkin	Fullback	Bronko Nagurski

(*Substitutions:* **Chicago**—George Corbett for Grange; Carl Brumbaugh for Molesworth; John Doehring for Nesbitt; Paul Franklin for Nagurski; Gil Bergerson for Carlson; Paul Engebretsen for Buckler; Bert Pearson for Kopcha; George Trafton for Miller; Johnny Sisk for Nesbitt. **Portsmouth**—John Wager for Bodenger; Bob Armstrong for Ebding; Fay "Mule" Wilson for Cavosie; Buster "Gran" Mitchell for McKalip.)

Head Coaches: Portsmouth: Potsy Clark; Chicago: Ralph Jones.
Officials: Referee: Bobby Cahn (New York); Umpire: G.A. Brown (Kankakee); Head Linesman: Meyer Morris (Rock Island).

Team Statistics

Portsmouth Spartans		Chicago Bears
5	First Downs	8
/126	Offensive Plays/Yardage	/184
/97	Rushing Attempts/Yardage	/156
12	Pass Attempts	16
2	Pass Completions	3
17 percent	Completion Percentage	19 percent
29	Passing Yardage	28
3( )	Interceptions (return yards)	5( )
	Punts	
43	Punting Average	43
	Punt Return Yards	
	Fumbles/Lost	
6	Penalties	3
45	Penalty Yards	15

1933 NFL—Number One

1933 Championship New York Giants (21) vs. Chicago Bears (23)

SUNDAY, DECEMBER 17, 1933—WRIGLEY FIELD, CHICAGO—26,000
WEATHER: GRAY, FOGGY, OVERCAST, MISTING RAIN. MID–30S.
FIELD CONDITION: WET AND SLICK FROM THE MIST, BUT REASONABLY FIRM.

On Sunday, December 17, the first official NFL championship game was played as the Western Division champion Chicago Bears hosted the Eastern Division champion New York Giants. A crowd of 26,000 fans sat in chilly Wrigley Field. The cold, gray, and wet day with its low-hanging mist was a marked improvement over the conditions that had driven the Bears and Spartans indoors for the first unofficial game for the championship at Chicago Stadium just a year before.

The Bears won the new Western Division with George Halas back at the helm. After three years off the sidelines, Papa Bear returned, replacing Ralph Jones as head coach. The Bears responded by winning their first six games of the season. Over the next three weeks, however, they slipped, losing on November 5 to the Boston Redskins 10–0, tying the Philadelphia Eagles 3–3 on the 12th, and losing to the Giants 3–0 on the 19th. But the Bears righted their ship and finished the season with four more wins, posting a 10–2–1 record.

The Bears had a fully balanced team with a backfield that still boasted a freight train by the name of Bronko Nagurski, as well as Johnny Sisk, Jack Manders, Keith Molesworth, and a slower, but still very capable Red Grange. The Bear receivers were Bill Hewitt, Bill Karr, and Luke Johnsos, with Grange always representing a considerable threat. Red only caught three passes all year, but he averaged 25 yards per catch, more than enough to force opposing defenders to keep an eye on him throughout the game. The Chicago line featured tackles George Musso and Link Lyman, both of whom weighed over 250 pounds, and guards Joe Kopcha and Zuck Carlson. All-purpose veteran lineman Bill Buckler filled in at guard, tackle, and end. Ookie Miller had ably replaced the recently retired George Trafton at center.

Nagurski, with his power running, had bulled his way to 533 rushing yards during the season and as usual seemed unstoppable. Before the game, Giants coach and right tackle Steve Owen was asked how he planned to stop Nagurski. He replied with a degree of resignation, "With a shotgun as he comes out of the dressing room."[1]

The Giants got off to an unimpressive 4–3 start in the 1933 campaign, but came on to win their last seven in a row to post an 11–3–0 record, more than doubling the win total of any other team in the new Eastern Division. The additions of back and kicker Ken Strong from the newly defunct Staten Island Stapletons and rookie passer Harry Newman of Michigan strengthened the Giants' already talented backfield. Multitalented Newman rushed for 452 yards and passed for almost 1,000 more. Bo Molenda and Stu Clancy both added significant rushing numbers. On the pass receiving end, Strong, Dale Burnett, Ray Flaherty, and Red Badgro made a formidable corps from which Newman could choose a target.

The New York line was anchored by center Mel Hein. Len Grant and Tex Irvin started at the tackles and Butch Gibson and John Cannella started at guard.

While not at capacity, the crowd was good. Anticipation was running high as fans began settling into their seats and the teams took the field to warm up. The visiting Giants wore their colorful red and blue jerseys with white numbers while the host Bears were clad in orange jerseys with navy numerals and the familiar trio of navy stripes on the sleeves.

As the game started, both teams drove deep into their opponent's territory, but were slowed by stiffening defenses. The Giants moved to the Bear 15, but came away with no points. That drive produced one of the more interesting plays of the game when New York center Mel Hein reported eligible. "This was a play we had to alert the officials about ahead of time," recalled Hein. "We put all the linemen on my right except the left end. Then he shifted back a yard, making me end man on the line, while the wingback moved up on the line on the right. Harry Newman came right up under me, like a T-formation quarterback. I handed the ball to him between my legs and he immediately put it right back in my hands — the shortest forward pass on record." Newman then dropped back, drawing in the Chicago defenders on a pass rush. Hein then hid the ball and took a walk towards the end zone. "I was supposed to fake a block and then just stroll down the field waiting for blockers, but after a few yards I got excited and started to run and the Bear safety, Keith Molesworth, saw me and knocked me down. I was about fifteen yards from the goal, but we never did score on that drive."[2]

Later in the period, with the Bears on their own 12-yard line, Molesworth quick-kicked, catching New York's Newman, playing safety on defense, flatfooted. The kick was long and didn't stop rolling until it reached the New York 18. Strong then kicked out to just past midfield, but Molesworth returned the ball to the Giants' 42-yard line. Nagurski then faked a pass and swept around end to the Giants' 26. Chicago halfback Gene Ronzani then slashed off right tackle to push the Bears to the Giants' 15. New York's defense then bent but did not break over the next three plays, in which Chicago netted only eight yards. The Bears had to settle for a 16-yard Jack Manders field goal. The Bears now led 3 to 0.

Early in the second period, Ronzani tossed the ball 17 yards to Molesworth, who cut his way to the Giant 29. Again, the Giants' defense stiffened and Chicago was forced to settle for a field goal. Manders kicked another from 40 yards out to make the score 6 to 0 in favor of the Bears.

Soon thereafter, the Giants got possession of the ball deep in their own territory and began a drive that would cover more than 80 yards in just four plays and put them on the scoreboard for the first time that afternoon. After picking up 23 passing yards in the first two plays of the series, the Giants turned to halfback Kink Richards. Richards gained 30 yards running off left tackle to set up a 29-yard Harry Newman to Red Badgro touch-down pass. Ken Strong kicked the extra point and the Giants led 7–6 as the half began to wane.[3]

The Bears missed a third opportunity to score just before the half ended. With the Chicago offense driving, Grange broke free on a 17-yard gallop around left end, advancing the ball to the Giants' 9. Again, the New York defense rose to the occasion and held. The Bears attempted yet another field goal, but this time "Automatic" Jack Manders was not so automatic and the kick failed.

In the third quarter, the Bear offense again marched downfield, but sputtered. Grange took a punt from Strong and ran it back 22 yards to the Giants' 46.[4] After a 15-yard scamper by Ronzani and a Molesworth to Brumbaugh pass brought the ball deep into New York territory, the Bears stalled at the New York 15. Again, they called on Manders, who responded with a 28-yard field goal, his third of the day. With that kick, the Bears regained the lead 9–7.

The Giants quickly responded. Newman, primarily on passes to Burnett, Richards, and Max Krause, moved the team 60 yards downfield, setting up the second New York tally. On the drive, Newman completed seven consecutive passes; the final one in that march was a strike to Krause, who was driven out of bounds at the Chicago 1-yard line. On first and goal from the one, the Bears held, but on second down and only the eighth play of the drive, Krause made the 1-yard plunge into the end zone. Another successful point after kick by Strong moved the Giants back into the lead at 14–9.

Now the Bears came roaring back. It only took them six plays to score. The Chicago offensive series started slowly and the Bears faced a third down and long on their own 25. They set up in a punt formation, but faked the kick as punter George Corbett threw a pass to a wide-open Carl Brumbaugh for a 67-yard pickup to the Giants' 8. The Giants' defense began to hold and the next two plays yielded very little. On third and goal, the Bears returned to Nagurski up the middle. With shades of the 1932 title game, Nagurski again took the ball, pulled up short of the line of scrimmage and lobbed an 8-yard pass to Bill Karr in the end zone. Manders converted and the Bears led again 16–14 as the third quarter was drawing short.

Following the Bears' kickoff, the Giants again came rolling back. With Strong and Newman leading the way, the New Yorkers, starting on their own 26, went on the attack. With lightning speed, Newman completed four straight passes to end the third quarter with the Giants threatening at the Chicago 8-yard line.

On the first play of the final period, the Giants lined up in the box formation about 15 yards from the left sideline. With Newman in position several yards behind Mel Hein, the Giant play caller took the pass from center and handed the ball to Strong, who took off in a dead run and swept to his left. As Strong was about to be met by a swarm of Bear defenders, he reversed field and flipped the ball back to a surprised Harry Newman. As Newman ran toward the right sideline, scrambling to make something of this play, he too began to draw a horde of Chicago defenders. Continuing the impromptu nature of this broken play, he wheeled, surveyed his options and saw Strong now all alone in the left corner of the Chicago end zone. Newman reared back and tossed the ball across the field to his teammate for the tally. After the score, Strong tossed his helmet aside, kicked his almost automatic extra point, and again in this seesaw battle of titans, the Giants led — this time by a score of 21–16.

With the clock winding down, the Bears needed another touchdown and they needed it quickly. A disastrous 8-yard punt by Strong gave them the ball at the New York 47-yard line, and the Bears had the break they needed. After a short gain on a pass from Molesworth to Brumbaugh, the Bears again looked to the Bronk. On two carries by Nagurski, the big man moved them down to the Giants' 33. On the next play Bronko headed toward the Giants' line, but again pulled up and tossed the ball, this time over the middle to the hel- metless Bill Hewitt, who was streaking from left to right across the field. Hewitt took off downfield for 14 yards, but as he was about to be met by Giant defender and former AAU hurdle champion Dale Burnett, Hewitt lateraled to his right into the waiting hands of Bill Karr.

As Karr caught the ball, he looked downfield and saw only Ken Strong and 19 yards between him and the end zone. The 19 yards was easy, but Strong was a concern. The former New York University star was a proven veteran and a terrific all-around player who instinc- tively cut down the angle on Karr to block him from the goal line. It looked like the Bear right end would be tackled short of the goal, but suddenly, and seemingly from out of nowhere, Chicago halfback Gene Ronzani came up big with a devastating block that elim- inated Strong from making the play. Karr stampeded into the end zone untouched. This time Brumbaugh converted the point after and the Bears led again 23–21.

In the game's waning moments, the Giants were driving again and had one last chance to take the lead. On the final play of the game, Newman found a Giant receiver on a des- peration pass that covered 28 yards. The receiver pulled in the pass, broke into the open and was on the move with only Red Grange between him and the Giants' second world championship. Complicating the issue for Grange, however, was he fact that Giants center Mel Hein was trailing the play in position to accept a lateral if Grange caught the Giants' receiver. But Grange, universally known for his running skills, was equally adept on the defensive side of the ball. While always a strong defender, Red began to concentrate more heavily on those skills after his devastating 1927 knee injury. "I didn't play at all in 1928," recalled Grange, "In fact, that injury erased most of my running ability. I was just an ordinary ball carrier after that. I did develop into a pretty good defensive back, however."[5] His abilities as an open-field tackler really paid off this afternoon. The Galloping Ghost reacted instantly, grabbing the runner around the chest and smothering him high so that no lateral was possible. The two were rolling to the ground when the final gun sounded the ending of the game. Grange made the game-saving tackle to secure a 23–21 win and another championship for the Bears.

But whom did Grange tackle? Many, including Grange, recall it was Giant wingback Dale Burnett, but Hall of Famer Red Badgro claimed to his dying day (July 13, 1998, at age 95) that it was he. Catching the first touchdown pass in the first official NFL championship game wasn't enough for Morris "Red" Badgro. It always bothered him that, unable to get past Grange, he failed to score on the last play of the game. His obituary in the *Seattle Times* referred to a 1994 interview with the *Valley Daily News*, now the *South County Journal*, in which even 60 years later, Badgro was greatly animated in describing his frustration at coming up short after catching the last pass of the game and turning toward the goal line. "If I had gotten by Red Grange, I would have scored," he said. "Grange had me around the middle ... his arms were around the ball, and I couldn't get rid of it," he said. "If I get by him, we win the game.... I wish I had [the ball] again."[6]

Grange recalled it this way: "I was alone in the defense and Burnett was coming at me with somebody on the side of him. I instinctively went for the ball. I tackled Dale high so he could not lateral, for if he had, Hein could have scored. The game ended on this play."[7]

Badgro also recalled, "On the last play of the game I caught a pass, and the only person between me and the goal line was Red Grange. I planned to lateral to a teammate who was running just behind me — it was Hein or Dale Burnett — but Grange grabbed me around the arms and upper body and I couldn't. It was the perfect tackle, and that's why Grange is heralded as one of the great defensive backs of that era."[8] Grange sensed the lateral was coming and his quick thinking was critical. "Red Grange saved the game,"[9] recalled Giants owner Tim Mara. George Halas said, "That play Grange made was the greatest defensive play I ever saw."[10]

The game was a resounding success. It had everything that the league fathers could have hoped for: two strong teams, exciting plays, a stellar performance by Bronko Nagurski that included not just his punishing runs that netted 65 yards, but a late touchdown pass. The gods on Olympus could not have granted a better end to the game than the last-minute, game-saving tackle by arguably the game's greatest legend, Red Grange.

According to the Associated Press, "The game was a brilliant display of offensive power and the 30,000 chilled spectators hardly knew from one minute to the next when either team would break out with a scoring play."[11]

The contest was exciting down to the final seconds. The score, the statistics, the teams on paper, all were even. After the Bears drew first blood on Manders' 16-yard kick, the lead changed hands six times. The Giants had 13 first downs to the Bears' 12. The Bears had 311 total yards to the Giants' 307. New York's Harry Newman completed 14 of 20 passes for an impressive 208 yards and 2 passing touchdowns. Chicago's Jack Manders also had a notable game, scoring 10 points on three field goals and an extra point kick.

SCORING

	1	2	3	4	Totals
New York	0	7	7	7	21
Chicago	3	3	10	7	23

1st Quarter: Chicago — FG — Manders —16 yards. 2nd Quarter: Chicago — FG — Manders — 40 yards. New York — TD — Badgro — 29-yard pass from Newman (Strong kick). 3rd Quarter: Chicago — FG — Manders — 28 yards. New York — TD — Krause —1-yard run (Strong kick). Chicago — TD — Karr — 8-yard pass from Nagurski (Manders kick). 4th Quarter: New York — TD — Strong — 8-yard pass from Newman (Strong kick). Chicago — TD — Karr —19-yard lateral from Hewitt after a 14-yard pass from Nagurski (Brumbaugh kick)

STARTING LINEUPS

New York Giants		Chicago Bears
Red Badgro	Left End	Bill Hewitt
Len Grant	Left Tackle	Link Lyman
Denver Gibson	Left Guard	Jules Carlson
Mel Hein	Center	Okie Miller
Tom Jones	Right Guard	Joe Kopcha
Steve Owen	Right Tackle	George Musso
Ray Flaherty	Right End	Bill Karr
Harry Newman	Quarterback	Carl Brumbaugh
Ken Strong	Left Halfback	Keith Molesworth
Dale Burnett	Right Halfback	Gene Ronzani
Bo Molenda	Fullback	Bronko Nagurski

(*Substitutes:* **New York:** Kink Richards (B), Cecil "Tex" Irvin (T), Stu Clancy (B), Glenn Campbell (E), Max Krause (B), John Cannella (T). **Chicago:** Jack Manders (B), Red Grange (B), Ray Richards (T), John Sisk (B), George Corbett (B), Bert Pearson (C), Richard Stahlman (E).)

Head Coaches: New York: Steve Owen; Chicago: George Halas.
Game Officials: Referee: Thomas Hughitt (Buffalo); Umpire: Bobby Cohn (Chicago); Head Linesman: Robert Karch (Columbus); Field Judge: Dan Tehan (Cincinnati).
Players' Shares: Chicago: $210.34; New York: $140.22

TEAM STATISTICS

New York Giants	Chicago Bears	
13	First Downs	12
45/307	Offensive Plays/Yardage	66/311
25/99	Rushing Attempts/Yardage	50/161
20	Pass Attempts	16
14	Pass Completions	7
.700	Completion Percentage	.438
208	Passing Yardage	150
1 (13)	Interceptions (return yards)	1 (11)
13	Punts	10
28.6	Punting Average	39.8
59	Punt Return Yards	58
0/0	Fumbles/Lost	0/0
3	Penalties	7/8
15	Penalty Yards	40

1934 NFL — MVP: Abe Cohen

1934 NFL Championship — Chicago Bears (13) vs. New York Giants (30)

SUNDAY, DECEMBER 9, 1934 — THE POLO GROUNDS, NEW YORK — 35,059
WEATHER CONDITIONS: 9° F., MOSTLY CLOUDY.
FIELD CONDITION: OVERNIGHT SLEET AND RAIN LEFT THE
SURFACE FROZEN, ROCK HARD, AND ICY.

On December 9, the New York Giants were hosting the Chicago Bears in the second NFL Championship contest. An impressive total of 35,059 shivering fans huddled in the stands at Coogan's Bluff on that clear but cold New York day. Overnight sleet and rain had left the field frozen and the temperature at game time was a frigid nine degrees. Years later George Halas recalled, "When I went to mass it was 9 degrees, and the ground was freezing into a solid sheet of ice."[1]

The Giants (8–5–0) had dropped their first two games of the season to Detroit and Green Bay, then won five in a row, but finished the season with an unimpressive 3–3 record over their last six games. They had also dropped both regular-season contests to the Bears. Adding to their woes were injuries to star passer Harry Newman and All-Pro end Red Badgro.

The Bears had amassed an impressive 13–0–0 regular season record, but today they would be without the services of star guard Joe Kopcha and 1,000-yard rookie rushing sensation Beattie Feathers, who were both nursing injuries. But the Bears were, of course, deep with talent and were still heavily favored when they met the Giants in the frozen Polo Grounds.

As the Giants were preparing for the game, Coach Steve Owen went out to examine the field. He slipped. He returned to the locker room with an uneasy feeling. How were his men going to get any traction? How would they be able get any leverage on the massive Bears linemen?

With the Polo Grounds' field an icy mess, the Giants' captain and end Ray Flaherty suggested that the answer to the footing problem might be to secure sneakers. While a collegian at Gonzaga, Flaherty and his teammates had worn sneakers under similar conditions. With increased traction, his team had easily defeated their opponents.

Owen liked the idea, but was not sure that the Giants could obtain that many pair of sneakers on such short notice on a wintry Sunday. Calls were made to sporting goods stores across New York and New Jersey, but all were closed. In a 1985 *New York Times* interview, Wellington Mara, son of the Giants' owner Tim Mara, recalled, "Steve and my brother Jack tried to call A.G. Spalding's and Alex Taylor's, the two biggest sporting goods stores in New York at that time. But they were closed on Sunday."[2] It took them a few minutes to realize it, but the answer to the problem was standing in the Giants' locker room. Wellington Mara remembered, "We had a little fellow on the payroll named Abe Cohen, a sort of jack of all trades. Abe was a tailor by profession, and he also worked for Chick Meehan, who was a famous coach at Manhattan College. Steve Owen asked Abe to go to Manhattan College, to which he had access — he had a key to their equipment room and gym — and borrow the sneakers from the lockers of the basketball players and bring them back to the Polo Grounds for our players."[3]

The 5'2", 140-pound Cohen was talking to Giants trainers Gus Mauch and Charley Porter as they were taping players' ankles. When Owen saw him, he had an idea. He spoke with Mauch, Porter, and Cohen about the field and Flaherty's idea. Mauch, who was also the trainer at Manhattan College, said that there were sneakers in the school's fieldhouse. Owen asked Cohen if he could get into the Manhattan College equipment room. When Cohen replied that he could, Owen gave him round-trip cab fare for the journey and off Cohen went. His mission: to secure as many pairs of sneakers as he could find at the school. Cohen hailed a cab outside of the Polo Grounds, just as the 35,059 fans inside were settling into their frigid seats. He knew he must hurry, as time was his enemy.

The Giants' opening drive took them 55 yards, but then stalled. Ken Strong kicked a 38-yard field goal to put the Giants up 3–0. There was no further scoring in the first stave.

Early in the second quarter the Bears began make some noise. They took the lead when a 50-yard march sparked by Keith Molesworth resulted in the first Chicago points. The big play on the drive came on a pass that Giants right end Ray Flaherty almost intercepted. As Molesworth released the pass, Flaherty reached up and hit the ball with both hands, but instead of catching it, he deflected it into Bears halfback Gene Ronzani's hands. Ronzani then carried to the New York one-yard line. As the Associated Press reported, "With Keith Molesworth and the big nag, Bronko Nagurski, splitting the Giant line despite the glazed and slippery footing, ended with Nagurski going over from the two-yard line."[4] It was actually recorded as a 1-yard run, but regardless of the distance, the Bears now held the lead. Jack Manders converted to make the score Chicago 7, New York 3.

Another Bears drive in the second stalled on the 10 and Manders kicked a 17-yard field goal to put the Bears up 10–3 at the half.

Owen and the Maras couldn't help wondering, "Where were those sneakers?" About the time the Giants were emerging from the warmth of the Polo Grounds' locker room, Abe Cohen's cab was pulling up outside of the stadium. Abe hopped out of the cab and proceeded directly to the Giants' locker room with his blessed bundle of gym shoes. According to Wellington Mara, "Abe got in a taxi and went to Manhattan. I think he had to break into the lockers. At any rate, he got back around halftime of the game with nine or ten pairs of sneakers." Mara continued, "Some of the guys didn't want to put them on, but those who did had so much success that eventually most of our players put them on."[5]

Even with the improved footing, the Bears took advantage of a Ken Strong fumble and Manders again converted on a field goal, this time from 24 yards out. The Bears now led 13–3, but the Giants were about to unleash a 27-point onslaught that would leave the Bears awe-struck.

Toward the end of the third period, Strong ran back a Chicago kick for 25 yards to the Giant 30. Quarterback Ed Danowski then went to work shredding the Chicago secondary with passes to ends Ray Flaherty and Dale Burnett, then another to Flaherty, and then to Strong. Strong was all over the field, which was especially amazing since he had been removed from the game in the first half after badly twisting his left leg.[6] With New York now deep in Chicago territory, Danowski went to the air again and fired a 26-yarder to 206-pound end Ike Frankian. As the ball neared the receiver, Carl Brumbaugh stepped in front of Frankian and intercepted it on the Chicago six, but as he did so, Frankian stole the ball from him and raced over the goal line.[7] Strong converted the point after to pull the Giants to within 3. Afterwards, Brumbaugh blamed himself for the Bears' defeat because Frankian stripped him of the football on that crucial touchdown after he had apparently intercepted the pass near the goal line. He needn't have blamed himself alone, since the Giants picked on all of the Bears equally throughout the second half.

After an exchange of kicks, the Giants were ready to go back to work. The next Giant score came with the help of Columbia University head coach Lou Little. Little, a friend of Owen's, was watching the game. He got word to Owen that with the Giants' edge in footing, they could beat the Bears on quicker moves. He recommended sending Strong on a pass pattern off-tackle. Owen listened to his knowledgeable friend and the next play went to Strong. Off the line, the New York back feinted to his left, then cut back to his right. Just as Little had suggested, Strong sprinted past the Chicago defenders and caught a Danowski pass for a 42-yard touchdown. Strong then kicked the conversion and put the Giants ahead 17–13. Strong said later that, "Right then we knew it was over. We could move and they couldn't."[8]

The Giants then took advantage of a Bears' turnover as they intercepted a pass at midfield. Two minutes later, Strong scored again going to his left on an 11-yard reverse, a difficult play on a frozen field. The conversion failed, but the Giants now led 23–13.

Bo Molenda intercepted another Chicago pass and returned it 15 yards to the Bears' 21. With five minutes left to play, Danowski skirted around the right side of the line and into the end zone from the Chicago 9-yard line. Molenda kicked the conversion and the Giants led 30–13. They had scored 27 unanswered points.

Strong, Danowski, and Frankian "were the New York players strikingly responsible for this smashing upset, but these scoring athletes got plenty of cooperation from their team-mates, and the Giants played like inspired men to turn what seemed like certain defeat into a glorious victory."[9] At the final gun, hundreds of fans, overcome with the emotion of the Giants' unbelievable four-touchdown comeback, "burst through the Polo Grounds police barriers, engulfed the frozen field, and carried off splintered goalposts and bruised heroes of the New York Giants football team."[10] The Giants then sought the warmth of their locker room to celebrate their second league championship in seven years.

After the game, Nagurski commented, "They won it with the sneakers. They could cut back and we couldn't. We were helpless." Nagurski added, "We had to mince about. We were down more than we were up."[11] George Halas was still frustrated by the loss 39 years later when he stated in a 1973 interview, "It was particularly galling the way we lost in 1934, because it was just a freaky thing. We had practiced in the Polo Grounds the day before the championship game, and had no trouble. But that night, New York was hit by a terrible nor'easter — snow and sleet and wind and cold — and the next day the field was a solid sheet of ice."[12]

In the Giants' locker room, Strong, who played a terrific game and scored 18 points on two touchdowns, a field goal, and three points after touchdown, told reporters, "I'm no hero." Then, pointing at the diminutive Cohen, he continued, "There's your hero."[13]

This sentiment was reconfirmed in the following day's edition of the *New York American*, when reporter Lewis Burton compared Cohen's taxi ride to several heroic journeys of history. "To the heroes of antiquity, to the Greek who raced across the Marathon plain, and to Paul Revere, add the name of Abe Cohen."[14]

SCORING

	1	2	3	4	Totals
Chicago	0	10	3	0	13
New York	3	0	0	27	30

1st Quarter: NY Giants — FG Strong — 38 yards. 2nd Quarter: Chi Bears — TD Nagurski — 1-yard run (Manders kick). Chi Bears — FG Manders — 17 yards. 3rd Quarter: Chi Bears — FG Manders — 24 yards. 4th Quarter: NY Giants — TD Frankian — 28-yard pass from Danowski (Strong kick). NY Giants — TD Strong — 42-yard run (Strong kick). NY Giants — TD Strong — 11-yard run (Strong kick failed). NY Giants — TD Danowski — 9-yard run (Strong kick)

STARTING LINEUPS

Chicago Bears		**New York Giants**
Bill Hewitt	Left End	Ike Frankian
Link Lyman	Left Tackle	Bill Morgan
Bert Pearson	Left Guard	Butch Gibson
Eddie Kawal	Center	Mel Hein
Zuck Carlson	Right Guard	Potsy Jones
George Musso	Right Tackle	Tex Irvin
Bill Karr	Right End	Ray Flaherty
Carl Brumbaugh	Quarterback	Ed Danowski
Keith Molesworth	Left Halfback	Dale Burnett
Gene Ronzani	Right Halfback	Ken Strong
Bronko Nagurski	Fullback	Bo Molenda

(*Substitutions:* **Chicago** — Jack Manders (B), Luke Johnsos (E), Art Buss (T), Johnny Sisk (B), Joe Zeller (G), Ted Rosequist (T), Bernie Masterson (Q). **New York** — Jack McBride (B), Kink Richards (B), Bill Owen (T), Len Grant (T).)

Head Coaches: Chicago: George Halas; New York: Steve Owen.
Game Officials: Referee: Bobby Cahn; Umpire: G.H. Lowe; Head Linesman: George Vergera; Field Judge: O. Meyer.
Players' Shares: New York: $621.00; Chicago: $414.14

TEAM STATISTICS

Chicago Bears		**New York Giants**
10	First Downs	12
61/165	Total Offense Plays/Yards	49/276
46	Rushing Attempts	37
93	Rushing Yardage	173
15	Pass Attempts	12
6	Pass Completions	7
.462	Completion Percentage	.538
72	Passing Yardage	103
3	Interceptions	2
9	Punts	6
40.7	Punting Average	45.7
46	Punt Return Yards	12
5/0	Fumbles/Lost	5/2
4	Penalties	0
30	Penalty Yards	0

1935 NFL — The Lions Roar

1935 Championship — New York Giants (7) vs. Detroit Lions (26)

DECEMBER 15, 1935 — UNIVERSITY OF DETROIT TITAN STADIUM, DETROIT —15,000
WEATHER CONDITIONS: SNOW/RAIN MIX, 30°F., COLD WIND GUSTS,
TEMPERATURE DROPPING THROUGHOUT THE GAME RESULTING
IN 3" OF SNOW FALLING DURING THE FIRST HALF.
FIELD CONDITION: MUD, ICE, SNOW, FROZEN PATCHES OF MUD AND GRASS.

With the defending champion New York Giants coming to town, Detroit coach Potsy Clark worried about the Giants' much-vaunted passing game. Clark was anxious to keep the game on the ground and to take advantage of the Lions' speed and quickness. As if answering his prayers, two events took place to bring him his wish.

First, Giants receiver Dale Burnett would miss the game with an infected hand. Burnett, a former AAU hurdle champion and a dangerous open-field runner, had been a stellar performer all year and his being out of the lineup would deal a serious blow to the Giants' passing attack.

Second, on Saturday night, soon after it became apparent that Burnett would be scrubbed from the Giants' lineup, the skies opened up. It had already been raining in Detroit for several days, but on Saturday evening, a violent rainstorm drenched the city, and the field at the University of Detroit's Titan Stadium became a swamp. The rain kept up all night long, not stopping until early Sunday morning. Suddenly, the temperature dropped rapidly and just before noon, a snowstorm began.

Only 15,000 fans were in the stands on this cold and wet day. A mix of rain, sleet, and snow fell and the mid–December winds were bitter. Lion great Glenn Presnell recalled, "It was an awful day, as I remember. The field was muddy, and it was bitingly cold and windy. Then there was a snowstorm. They had the field covered before the game, but by the time it was half over, the mud was frozen and there were about three inches of snow on top of it."[1] Mel Hein of the Giants agreed, "It was an awful day, mud and snow and terrible winds."[2]

The Lions' backfield was strong. They still had backs Presnell, Ace Gutowsky, and Dutch Clark from the team's storied Portsmouth Spartans days. In addition, they had Ernie Caddel at halfback.

After the opening kickoff by New York's Ken Strong, the Lions took control. Ernie Caddel returned the kick to the Detroit 39-yard line. Starting with good field position, Detroit immediately began to drive downfield. Presnell at quarterback surprised the Giants by attempting a quick and short pass on first down. The pass fell incomplete to the frozen turf, but set a tone for the afternoon. On second down, Caddel gained 4 yards around left end. Presnell then went to the air again and connected with Frank Christiansen on a long play that ended up all the way down to the New York 32. Presnell then fired a pass to end Ed Klewicki. The ball bounced off Giant defender Ed Danowski and into Klewicki's hands for a 24-yard gain that put the Lions on the New York 8. Presnell charged ahead through the line for 3 yards. Then, on just the sixth play of the ball game, Gutowsky powered the final 5 yards for the first Detroit score just three minutes into the contest. Presnell's kick for try made the score 7–0.

On the ensuing kickoff New York's Elvin "Kink" Richards returned the ball 25 yards to just short of midfield. He gained 11 more on the first play from scrimmage as the Giants began to flex their muscles. Danowski connected on an 13-yard completion with Tod Goodwin and the Giants had a new set of downs on the Detroit 23-yard line. The Giants, however, would bog down here as the Lions' defense dug in. The next three plays netted nothing and Ken Strong stepped back to attempt a field goal. The kick was long enough, but wide, and Detroit took over at the their own 20-yard line.

The Lions took over, but almost immediately New York got another break when Giants left tackle Bill Morgan recovered a Detroit fumble on the Lions' 21. Once again, a golden opportunity, but once again, the Giants fell short. The Maramen only managed 8 yards on the possession and gave the ball up on downs within a stone's throw of the end zone.

The Lions could do little with the ball and punted out of trouble to the New York 31. Again, the Giants began to move the ball when Ken Strong went over left tackle for 13 yards. Danowski then dropped back to pass. He threw it deep, but off target, and Detroit's Frank Christiansen picked it off, returning the ball 30 yards to the New York 46.

Detroit did not squander their opportunity. Dutch Clark and Ernie Caddel gained the first 6 yards up the middle. On third down, Clark took the ball around the left side of the Detroit line, then cutting to his right behind superb blocking, he scampered 40 yards through the New York defense for a touchdown. Clark's conversion kick failed, but the Lions now led the mortified Giants 13–0.

As the second quarter dawned, the ball was wet and cold and getting harder to handle by the minute. Another New York miscue occurred when a punt was blocked and Detroit's Harry Ebding recovered the bouncing ball, advancing it 35 yards on his way to an apparent touchdown. Out of nowhere, Ebding lost the handle just 3 yards from the goal line and the ball bounded into and out of the Giants' end zone for a touchback. The Giants got a new set of downs on their 20.

The Giants lost Burnett's replacement at end when 6'0", 185-pound Tod Goodwin, a rookie from West Virginia, left the game with two broken ribs. Goodwin had already made catches for big contributions in the first period and his loss would sting. Still, the Giants were determined to tighten the score before the half.

Late in the period, the Giants began another drive with a Danowski to Walter Singer pass good for 17 yards. New York then decided that it was time to run. Behind the blocking of Johnny Dell Isola and Mel Hein, Giant backs Danowski and Kink Richards rammed the ball down the field through the heart of the Detroit defense. After the Giants carried the ball to the Lions' 10, Detroit's defense stiffened. The Giants were stopped four straight times, moving the ball only to the Lions' 4, and came away with nothing for their efforts. The half ended with the Lions ahead by 13 and the Giants demoralized.

As the second half began, the Giants were determined to finally make something happen. After the New York defense held Detroit on the home team's first possession of the third period, Ed Danowski returned a Detroit punt to the Lions' 46. Five minutes into the third quarter, the New Yorkers had terrific field position and a real chance to draw within a touchdown of their hosts. On the next play, Danowski slashed for four more yards off tackle, and with the Giants now on the Detroit 42, the ex-Fordham star threw a looping 11-yard pass to Strong. In the Detroit backfield, Gutowsky, intently watching the high arc, ran in and leaped high for the ball, barely touching it. Strong reacted quickly, followed the redirection off Gutowsky's fingertips, and reached out to pull in the deflected pass on a dead run. He covered the rest of the distance to the end zone untouched for a 42-yard touchdown strike. Strong also connected on the conversion. Now, only trailing by six, the Giants had renewed hope of making this a real battle.

In the final quarter, with the snow still falling and the wind strong, the Lions struck twice to put the game out of New York's reach. With only three minutes remaining, a quick kick attempt by New York's Danowski was blocked by Ed Klewicki and recovered at the Giants' 26 by Frank Christiansen. The Lions moved the ball inside the Giants' 2-yard line on middle runs by Caddel, Clark, and a slashing 12-yard gain by Parker. With the Giants massed in the middle of the line expecting another line plunge, "Ernie Caddel swept wide around the Giants' right end" and into the end zone untouched. After Dutch Clark's extra point, the Lions led 20–7.[3]

Buddy Parker then took over in the final minutes as he picked off a desperation pass from Danowski at the New York 32 and returned it to the Giants' 10-yard line. Caddell gained 4 yards up the middle on first down. Parker picked up four more on second and on third down, Parker added the final points of the game as he hammered across from the four. Parker's PAT kick failed and the final score stood at 26–7 in favor of the Lions.

The Giants' passing attack never got on track that afternoon. Faulty, haphazard, and desperate were the words used by sportswriter John Drebinger to describe the New York air game.[4] The losses of Burnett and Goodwin, a superb Detroit defense, and the absolutely miserable weather conditions combined to stymie Danowski and New York's aerial assault. Other than Ken Strong's 41-yard touchdown reception in the third quarter, very little was of great note. Mel Hein would recall years later, "We could never get it going. They beat us pretty soundly."[5]

Detroit, on the other hand, played well, took advantage of New York miscues and their inability to move the ball consistently, and did not seem hampered by the inclement weather. They got on track early and never really let up. The offense moved well, gaining 286 total yards. "A heavy field, spotted with pools of water, failed to slow the fast offense of the Lions."[6] The defense bent, but rarely broke, crushing the Giants each time they began to rally. It was a decisive victory for Potsy Clark's team over the defending champions. It was especially nice for the eight Lions who were holdovers from the 1931 and 1932 Portsmouth Spartans, who had come oh, so close to the championship.

SCORING

	1	2	3	4	Totals
New York	0	0	7	0	7
Detroit	13	0	0	13	26

1st Quarter: Detroit—TD—Gutowsky—5-yard run (Presnell kick). Detroit—TD—Clark—40-yard run (Clark kick failed). 2nd Quarter: None. 3rd Quarter: New York—TD—Strong—42-yard pass from Danowski (Strong kick). 4th Quarter: Detroit—TD—Caddel—2-yard run (Clark kick). Detroit—TD—Parker—4-yard run (Parker kick failed)

STARTING LINEUPS

New York Giants		**Detroit Lions**
Ike Frankian	Left End	Ed Klewicki
Bill Morgan	Left Tackle	John Johnson
Tom Jones	Left Guard	Regis Monahan
Mel Hein	Center	Clare Randolph
Steve Owen	Right Guard	Ox Emerson

Len Grant	Right Tackle	George Christiansen
Tod Goodwin	Right End	John Schneller
Ed Danowski	Quarterback	Glenn Presnell
Ken Strong	Left Halfback	Frank Christiansen
Kink Richards	Right Halfback	Ernie Caddel
Les Corzine	Fullback	Ace Gutowsky

(*Substitutions:* **New York** —Ends: Walt Singer, Gran Mitchell; Tackles: Cecil "Tex" Irvin, Jess Quatse; Guards: Bob Bellinger, Johnny Dell Isola, Bernard Kaplan; Centers: None; Backs: Harry Newman; Leland Shaffer, Max Krause. **Detroit** —Ends: Ray Morse, Harry Ebding; Tackles: Jim Steen, Jim Stacey; Guards: Sam Knox, Tom Hupke; Centers: Elmer Ward; Backs: Dutch Clark, Bill Shepherd, Buddy Parker, Charles "Pug" Vaughan, Tony Kaska.)

Head Coaches: New York: Steve Owen; Detroit: George "Potsy" Clark.
Players' Shares: Detroit: $300.00; New York: $200.00
Game Officials: Referee: Thomas Hughitt; Umpire: Bobby Cahn; Head Linesman: M.J. Meyer; Field Judge: Harry Robb.

TEAM STATISTICS

New York Giants		Detroit Lions
8	First Downs	13
?/194	Offensive Plays/Yardage	?/286
?/106	Rushing Attempts/Yardage	?/235
13	Pass Attempts	5
4	Pass Completions	2
.308	Completion Percentage	.400
88	Passing Yardage	51
2	Interceptions By	0
5	Punts	4
43	Punting Average	39
	Punt Return Yards	
2	Had Blocked	0
3–3	Fumbles-Lost	4–2
	Penalties	
15	Penalty Yards	25

1936 NFL — The First Neutral Site

1936 NFL Championship — Green Bay Packers (21) vs. Boston Redskins (6)

SUNDAY, DECEMBER 13, 1936 — THE POLO GROUNDS, NEW YORK — 29,545
WEATHER CONDITIONS — 36°F., 6 MPH, BRISK AND SUNNY.
FIELD CONDITIONS: GOOD, DRY.

When the Boston Redskins hosted the Green Bay Packers for the 1936 NFL championship, the contest was not held in Boston or Green Bay. The game was played in New York at the Polo Grounds due to lack of fan support in Boston. Redskins owner George

Preston Marshall was fed up with it and would move his team from New England to Washington, D.C., shortly after the season. This was the first and only championship in NFL history to be played at a neutral site until Super Bowl I in January 1967.

Marshall and the Boston press and fans had been at odds for some time. Much of the press lashed out at Marshall for his poor treatment of the fans when the Redskins, now a winning club, raised ticket prices from $1.75 to $2.25 just before the final home game with the Giants. Not everyone in the Boston press corps felt Marshall was unjustified in his actions. Paul Craigue of the *Boston Globe* wrote, "It's hard to feel any resentment against a guy who has stayed in there trying for five years and spent $100,000 in vain pursuit of a championship. Marshall would have been satisfied with an even break financially, and he went through a long siege without cracking."[1]

After meeting with NFL President Joe Carr, it was announced, "The decision to play the game in New York was reached following a canvass of the club owners involved and of the players of the two teams." Carr continued, "New York is not only the most centrally located spot, but the danger of bad weather appears less here than in any other spot, with the Polo Grounds offering the best equipment for inclement weather, with its covered stands and lighting system."[2]

As former Redskin great Cliff Battles recalled, "There is no other way to put it — they ran us out of town. Now we were homeless." Battles continued, "For our last game of the season, against the Giants, he moved us to the Westchester Country Club in suburban New York, where we practiced on a big polo field, and he moved the game itself to the Polo Grounds in New York. We won the Eastern title, then played Green Bay for the championship, and he put *that* game in the Polo Grounds. Can't you see the picture? We were the Foreign Legion of football — champs without a home field."[3]

The Redskins had nosed out the Pittsburgh Steelers by a game to take the Eastern Division title with an unimpressive 7–5 record, while the Packers and Bears had battled to respective 10–1–1 and 9–3 records.

After a week of rain, the weather was perfect on that December 13. It was bright and sunny and the thermometer read 36 degrees with a light breeze. The field had dried out in the morning sun and was in top condition. This was all good news for the Packers and their high-powered offense. In all, 29,545 fans ventured out to watch the two teams, both of whom were appearing in their first league championship contests. The Packers had won three consecutive league championships in 1929, 1930, and 1931 but they had won on regular-season winning percentage prior to the establishment of a league championship contest.

The Packers won the toss and elected to receive. After a Riley Smith kick to George Sauer, the Packers started with decent field position on their own 30-yard line. But it was four plays and out as the Packers could only manage 2 yards on the series. Cliff Battles returned Clarke Hinkle's punt to the Boston 40.

Boston began moving the ball well, with Battles gaining 18 yards on two carries and Irwin teaming up for 4 more. But on the fifth play from scrimmage, the Packers' Lou Gordon recovered Riley Smith's fumble on the Green Bay 48. On the play, Boston lost more than the ball; they also lost Battles to a shoulder injury. Just several minutes into the game, he was finished for the day. The former West Virginia Wesleyan star, who between runs, receptions, and pass attempts, had touched the ball an amazing 234 times during the regular season, was replaced in the lineup by back "Pug" Rentner.[4]

Three plays later, Arnie Herber dropped back and spotted Don Hutson loping along in the Redskin secondary. He let go the pass and led Hutson, who pulled it in for a 48-yard touchdown. Ernie Smith converted to give the Packers a 7–0 lead.

Despite this setback, the Redskins came bounding back a couple of series later with a sustained 78-yard drive that resulted in a two-yard touchdown plunge by Rentner on the first play of the second quarter. Riley Smith's conversion kick went wide, leaving Boston at a 7–6 deficit. It was Smith's first missed conversion in fifteen attempts.

After forcing a second-down punt by Clarke Hinkle, the Redskins, starting with great field position at their own 45, lost 7 yards on first down as linebacker George Svendsen dropped Rentner on the Washington 38. They gained two back on second down, but on third set up to punt. Riley Smith took the long snap, but instead of a kick, he passed to Malone for a 19-yard pickup and a first down on the Packer 41. The Redskins continued to drive down to the Green Bay 22. On fourth and six, Riley Smith lined up for a field goal try. The kick from the 30 was blocked by the Green Bay defense and recovered by Smith on the Packer 42, where Green Bay took over on downs.

On second down Arnie Herber attempted a long pass that was intercepted by Rentner on the Redskins' 21. He returned it 5 yards to the 26. The two teams then exchanged punts and turnovers (3 punts, 2 turnovers on downs, 1 fumble, 1 clock runoff) for the remainder of the half.

In the third quarter Riley Smith kicked off out of bounds. The second attempt was returned 17 yards to the 26 by Clarke Hinkle. With the Redskins concentrating heavily on Hutson, Herber hit Milt Gantenbein on a 13-yard strike. He then hooked up with Green Bay legend Johnny "Blood" McNally on a 52-yard strike to the Redskin 8. After Hinkle was held for no gain up the middle, Herber dropped back to pass again. While releasing the ball he was hit by Wayne Millner. As the ball fell to the ground, it was scooped up by Redskins right end Charley Malone and returned 90 yards for what appeared to be the go-ahead touchdown. While the Redskins celebrated, the officials huddled. The officials ruled that Herber's arm was moving forward when he was hit, and therefore the play resulted in an incomplete pass instead of a fumble, negating the touchdown. Herber, knowing that he was fortunate to get a second chance, wasted no time in setting up the score. On the next play he pitched the ball over the middle to left end Milt Gantenbein in the end zone to cap a 74-yard drive. Paul Engebretsen's conversion made the score a more comfortable 14–6.

To add to the Redskins' mounting troubles, standout center Frank Bausch was ejected from the game for fighting with Green Bay substitute center Frank Butler on the ensuing kickoff.

The remainder of the third quarter was again filled with uneventful punts and turnovers, the last of which were an interception of a Riley Smith pass by Packer quarterback Hank Bruder, and on the very next play, a fumble recovered by Boston's Charley Malone to end the period.

The fourth quarter began with the swarming Packer defense backing the Redskins up and forcing them to punt on third and 25 from their own 22-yard line. Green Bay lineman Lon Evans came rushing through a gap in the line and blocked Riley Smith's kick just as it was coming off the former Alabama All-American's foot. Clarke Hinkle recovered the ball at the Redskins' three.

After Boston tackle Jim Barber stopped Hinkle for no gain on first down, the Packers scored once more on a three-yard outside run by the diminutive Bob Monnett. After the point after touchdown by former Chicago Bear "Tiny" Engebretsen, the score stood at 21–6.

The Redskins didn't fold as Bob McChesney returned the ensuing kickoff 33 yards to the Boston 42. The Redskins then managed to squander their great field position. After connecting with McChesney for an 8-yard pickup on first down, Rentner was hit by 6'5", 230-pound Lou Gordon while attempting a pass on the next play. The ball squirted out and was recovered by Gantenbein. The Redskins also lost Rentner to injury on this play.

Green Bay, starting on the Boston 40-yard line, continued to move the ball effectively. After a 3-yard rush, Bob Monnett found Don Hutson on a quick pass for 13 more. On 1st and 10 from the 24, Monnett hit Gantenbein in the end zone, but the play was called back when "an anxious Green Bay tackle pulled out of the line before the ball was snapped."[5] The Boston defense then held Hinkle on fourth and three, and Green Bay turned the ball over on downs at the 15.

Boston took over, but once again could do little to move the ball as three straight passes netted only 2 yards. On fourth and eight from their own 17, Riley Smith dropped back to punt. Tackle Ernie Smith came crashing through the line and blocked the kick, which was recovered on the 14 by teammate Tony Paulekas. Paulekas, a lineman out of Washington and Jefferson College, was playing in his only year in the league.

On the first play of the series, Johnny Blood McNally gained 6-yards on a reverse around right end, but there the Green Bay offense stalled, not gaining another yard on the series. Monnett's fourth-down pass from the Redskin 8 fell incomplete in the end zone, giving Boston the ball on their own 20.

Boston's offense still couldn't find an answer to the Packer defensive riddle and were forced to punt on 4th and 10 from their own 20. A weak punt from Riley Smith went out of bounds at the Redskin 48, again affording the Packers great field position. But on 2nd down Monnett's pass was picked off by Pinckert, who raced up the right sideline for a 17-yard return to the Packer 43. Green Bay's defense again held and Boston was forced to punt.

Green Bay then kept the ball on the ground to chew up the clock. Hinkle, Monnett, and Johnston ran eight plays before turning the ball over to Boston at the Packer 40 on downs.

In the Redskins' final gasp, Riley Smith threw an incomplete pass to Malone on first down. On second down Smith was forced to run, gaining 7 yards. On third and three from the Packers' 33-yard line, Smith's pass fell incomplete on the ground as the final gun sounded. Green Bay had returned to the top of the heap and the Redskins were still without a home.

The Packers got off to a bit of a slow start early in the contest, but began to stir late in the first period when Hutson and Herber began to click. The Associated Press reported, "Waking up after going around in what closely resembled a trance during the first quarter, the passing powerhouse from the Midwest marched into the title yesterday with a 21 to 6 victory over the Boston Redskins, champions of the East."[6] Boston played a decent game and Rëntner filled in ably for Battles, but one has to wonder what Battles would have added to the game had he been able to continue for the full sixty minutes. "The Redskins rolled up most of their yardage and first downs in the first quarter and showed a high geared running attack and clever pass offensive."[7]

As Cliff Battles later observed, "The Packers beat us, and then Marshall moved the franchise to Washington. Boston's reaction, I suppose, was good riddance."[8]

SCORING

	1	2	3	4	Totals
Green Bay	7	0	7	7	21
Boston	0	6	0	0	6

1st Quarter: G.B.—TD—Hutson 48-yard pass from Herber (E. Smith kick). 2nd Quarter: Bos.—TD—Rentner 2-yard run (R. Smith kick failed). 3rd Quarter: G.B.—TD—Gantenbein 8-yard pass from Herber (E. Smith kick). 4th Quarter: G.B.—TD—Monnett ⅖-yard run (Engebretsen kick).

STARTING LINEUPS

Green Bay Packers		Boston Redskins
Milt Gantenbein	Left End	Wayne Millner
Ernest Smith	Left Tackle	Turk Edwards
Paul "Tiny" Engebretsen	Left Guard	Les "Swede" Olsson
George Svendsen	Center	Frank Bausch
Lon Evans	Right Guard	Jim Karcher
Lou Gordon	Right Tackle	Jim Barber
Don Hutson	Right End	Charley Malone
Hank Bruder	Quarterback	Riley Smith
George Sauer	Left Halfback	Ed Justice
Arnie Herber	Right Halfback	Cliff Battles
Clarke Hinkle	Fullback	Don Irwin

(*Substitutions:* **Green Bay**—Ends: Bernie Scherer, Herm Schneidmann; Tackles: Ade Schwammel, Champ Seibold; Guards: Walt Kiesling, Buckets Goldenberg, Tony Paulekas; Center: Frank Butler; Backs: Paul Miller, Bob Monnett, Joe Laws, Cal Clemens, Swede Johnston, Johnny "Blood" McNally. **Boston**—Ends: Sam Busich, Flavio Tosi, Bob McChesney; Tackles: Gail O'Brien, Vic Carroll, Steve Sinko; Guards: none; Center: Larry Siemering; Backs: Ernie Pinckert, Eddie Britt, Pug Rentner, Mark Temple, Edward Smith.)

Head Coaches: Green Bay: Earl "Curley" Lambeau; Boston: Ray Flaherty.
Players' Shares: Green Bay: $250.00/$540.00; Boston: $180.00/$400.00
Game Officials: Referee: W.G. Crowell; Umpire: Robert Cahn; Head Linesman: M.J. Meyer; Field Judge: William Holleran.

TEAM STATISTICS

Green Bay Packers		Boston Redskins
7	First Downs	8
67/232	Total Offense Plays/Yards	57/147
44	Rushing Attempts	34
71	Rushing Yardage	66
23	Pass Attempts	26
9	Pass Completions	7/6
.391	Completion Percentage	.269
161	Passing Yardage	81
2	Interceptions By	1
0/0	Sacks/Yards Lost	2/12
10	Punts	11
37.6	Punting Average	35
27	Punt Return Yards	58
0	Had Blocked	2
2/1	Fumbles/Lost	5/2
3	Penalties	3
15	Penalty Yards	25

1937 NFL — Enter Sammy Baugh

1937 Championship — Washington Redskins (28) vs. Chicago Bears (21)

SUNDAY, DECEMBER 12, 1937 — WRIGLEY FIELD, CHICAGO — 15,878
WEATHER CONDITIONS: 15°F., SNOW FLURRIES, 12 MPH WIND
FIELD CONDITION: FROZEN FIELD COVERED WITH ICE AND SNOW PATCHES.

On December 12, 1937, the Chicago Bears played host to the Washington Redskins for the National Football League championship game.

The Redskins were playing in their second straight championship game, but much had changed in a year. On December 11, 1936, as the Redskins readied themselves for their contest with the Green Bay Packers, the team hailed from Boston, they were looking for a home, they would make a "home" appearance in New York's Polo Grounds, and a young man by the name of Sam Adrian Baugh was still on the campus of Texas Christian University. The Packers defeated the wandering, Baugh-less Redskins 21–6.

The 1936 Redskins boasted a strong ground attack behind the running of future Hall of Fame halfback Cliff Battles and his backfield mates Riley Smith and Ernie Pinckert. The Redskins, however, needed to balance their attack with a strong passer, and they found him in the long, lean Texan. In his first year, Baugh led the league with a record 81 completions. The Redskins ran the double-wing formation and were able to get as many as four receivers downfield quickly. With Baugh's precision arm, Washington was able to pick apart most defenses. Coupled with Battles's league-leading 874 rushing yards, and a measurably more supportive fan base in Washington, the Redskins were back in the championship game and ready for their Western Division opponent.

The Bears were 9–1–1 and were strong behind the running of Bronko Nagurski, Jack Manders, and Ray Nolting, who continually ground out yardage behind the power blocking of Danny Fortmann and Joe Stydahar.

The 15,878 in attendance at Wrigley Field braved the bitter 15-degree game-time temperature. Wrigley was covered with ice and snow. The hard, slippery surface left players bruised, bloodied, dazed, and staggered. Baugh recalled that the surface was "the worst field I ever saw. The field had been torn up the previous week, and it froze solid with jagged clods sticking up. I've never seen so many people cut up in a football game."[1] The Bears were in their navy jerseys with orange trim and the Redskins in burgundy jerseys with gold trim and logo on their sleeves.

Washington won the coin toss and elected to kick with the wind at their backs due to the persistent gusts. Bronko Nagurski fielded Turk Edwards's kick on the Chicago 1-yard line. Nagurski slipped on the icy field, but recovered to return the ball to the Bears' 33, where he was knocked out of bounds by Baugh.

On the strength of runs by Nagurski and Ray Nolting, the Chicago offense moved the ball to the Redskins' 46, but then stalled and were forced to punt. Nolting's kick went out of bounds on the Washington 7-yard line.

On the first play from scrimmage, Baugh dropped back and, standing in his own end zone, fired an 8-yard strike to Cliff Battles, who broke free and ran it out to the Chicago 49. It was the first of his 17 completions and a 358-yard passing day. But after being pushed, the Bears' defense then held and forced a Redskin punt.

On their next possession, Washington drove 46 yards to the Bears' 7, where Battles took the ball from Baugh and scored on a weak side reverse. With a Riley Smith kick, the Redskins led 7–0.

The Bears wasted no time in coming back with Bronko Nagurski, Edgar "Eggs" Manske, and Jack Manders leading the way. Starting from their own 28, Chicago began a 72-yard drive to the Washington goal line. On second and eight from their own 30, Masterson let go a low pass to Eggs Manske that the Bears' end reached down and gathered in at his shoetops. Manske's forward motion caused him to stumble and fall at the Redskins' 40-yard line, but no defender made contact as he got to his feet and bolted another 21 yards to the 19, where Baugh finally caught him. On first down Bronko Nagurski, playing in his last game until 1943, swept around right end for a 9-yard pickup to the 10, where he was brought down by Cliff Battles. On the next play Manders took the handoff and bolted through a massive hole behind right guard for the touchdown. Manders then converted to tie the game at 7.

On the kickoff, Manders kept up his heroics as his kick sailed out of the end zone for a touchback. Baugh took over on his own 20 and began to move the ball effectively. Baugh kept the ball on second down and gained 12 yards on a rush up the middle. He followed this up with completions to ends Chuck Malone and Wayne Millner. On first down from the Redskins' 47, however, Baugh's next pass was picked off on the Redskins' 49 by second-year end George Wilson of Northwestern. The interception proved costly.

From the 49, Manders ran off guard first to the left, then to the right, to pick up 9 yards. After Ray Nolting smashed up the middle for 3 yards and the first down, Masterson passed to Manders, who caught the pass on the 25 and glided into the end zone behind a crushing block on Battles by Wilson. Battles claimed clipping, but to no avail, and the play stood. Manders then converted and Chicago led 14–7 with 35 seconds remaining in the 1st quarter. Manders had scored all the Bears' points so far on two touchdowns and both extra points.

The 2nd quarter was scoreless as the two teams traded the ball back and forth on punts, interceptions, and fumbles. Jack Manders continued to have his name called on the PA system as he picked up two fumbles, made one interception, and missed on field goal attempts of 37 and 41 yards.

Sammy Baugh left the game on the first play of the second Washington possession of the quarter after faking a pass and rushing up the middle for 17 yards. He was hit hard and wouldn't return until the second half.

Washington held the Bears on the final possession of the second quarter and the Bears were forced to punt. As the 56-yard kick by Chicago's Beattie Feathers bounced in the Redskins' end zone, the half ended.

To start the second half, Jack Manders kicked off to second-year Colgate grad Don Irwin, who accepted the ball at his own 10 and returned it 20 yards, giving Washington decent field position to start the 3rd period.

Baugh, back in the lineup after being shaken up late in the 2nd quarter, began to move the Redskins down the field. Irwin was held for no gain at left tackle on first down, but Baugh then connected with end Wayne Millner for 9 yards. Irwin gained 6 over tackle for a first down at the Redskins' 45. Baugh's first-down pass was dropped by Millner. On second down, Baugh tried Millner again.

Only a minute and 13 seconds into the second half, Baugh found his target at the Bears' 35. Millner, who was running a crossing pattern, caught the ball on a dead run and sprinted into the end zone to complete the 55-yard touchdown strike. Smith converted, knotting the score at 14. The Redskins were running the double-wing, which enabled Washington to quickly flood the Bears' secondary with 4 receivers. Although Chicago adjusted in the second half by dropping a lineman and using six defensive backs, Baugh continued to pepper the Bruins with a steady aerial bombardment. But again, the Bears came storming back.

Manders returned Turk Edwards's kickoff 19 yards to the 23 as the Bears took over. The Bears moved downfield this time on a 13-play, 73-yard drive. Three backs led the way. Bronko Nagurski, playing in his final game before a five-season retirement, gained 27 yards on three attempts, including a vintage Nagurski run in which he charged the middle of the line and bowled over several defenders for a 20-yard pickup. Manders gained 26 yards on three carries and Nolting 16 yards on two rushes. On the final play of the drive, Masterson, after faking a plunge toward the center of the line, found Manske on a 4-yard pass. Manske, in the end zone, fought his way in between Washington defenders Eddie Kawal and Riley Smith to pull in Masterson's pass and put the Bears back into the lead. After a Manders conversion Chicago led once again, 21–14.

Though the Bears led by a touchdown 6 minutes into the third quarter, the next 9 minutes were all Redskins. After Jack Manders's kickoff was returned to the Washington 22 by Riley Smith, Sammy Baugh went right to work. On the first play from scrimmage, Baugh hit Wayne Millner at midfield. Millner pulled in the pass and outran Manders and Nagurski on the icy field and into the end zone on a 78-yard pass completion. On that play, Sammy rolled to his right, and with Manske untouched and rushing hard on Baugh from his defensive end position, Slingin' Sam let go the strike to Millner, who had beaten his man deep. Smith then converted to tie the game at 21-all.

On the next Washington possession, the Redskins again moved the ball effectively. Fullback Don Irwin caught a pass for 7 yards and ran 5 times for 18 yards, including a key 1-yard pickup from punt formation on 4th and 1 to keep the drive alive. Baugh moved the Redskins ahead as wingback Ed Justice found himself on the receiving end of a 35-yard strike from Slingin' Sammy. Baugh deceptively looked one way at Malone, then wheeled and threw in the other direction to Justice. Riley Smith converted again and the Redskins led by a score of 28–21.

The Bears were not done, however, and drove deep into Redskin territory early in the fourth period. Back Ray Buivid hit Pug Rentner, who made a leaping catch at the Redskins' 23 for a 32-yard completion. But there the Redskins' defense stiffened and stalled the Bears' drive.

Washington then took over on downs at their own 23. Baugh then unholstered his golden arm and passed the Redskins to the Bears' 19. In rapid succession, Baugh connected with Justice for 23, Millner for 10, and Battles for 19. He then hit Millner for 5, but the ball spurted loose and was recovered by the Bears' Bill Conkright at the 14.

On first down, Keith Molesworth passed to Plasman for 35 yards. Baugh ran Plasman out of bounds at the Bears' 49, where a fight broke out when Plasman hit Baugh. Both benches cleared, but no penalties were assessed. On the next play, Masterson fired a long strike to 6'4" rookie end Les McDonald, who was brought down on the Redskins' 12 by Riley Smith. Runs by Nagurski and Manders pushed the ball to the 7. On 3rd and 5, Masterson was sacked by Malone for a 7-yard loss. On 4th and 12, Masterson's pass to Manders in the end zone fell incomplete, ending the Bears' threat.

The next Redskins possession was bizarre as the Bears' defense held and Baugh attempted a quick kick on 3rd and 13 from his own 28. The kick was blocked, but recovered by Washington tackle Bill Young for a 6-yard loss. On 4th and 19 from the 22, Baugh punted again. The ball was fumbled by Buivid on the Washington 41 and recovered by the Redskins' Millner. On the third play of the new series of downs, Cliff Battles burst through the left side for 9 yards, but then fumbled. The ball was recovered by Chicago's Ray Nolting at his own 42. From there Masterson attempted two passes, the first of which fell incomplete, the second of which was intercepted by Riley Smith on his own 30-yard line. He returned it 10 yards to the 40. From there, the Redskins handed the ball to Irwin, who was stopped for no gain as time ran out. George Preston Marshall had his first NFL crown.

In addition to the three touchdowns, Baugh was 18 for 33 and 354 passing yards. Milwaukee sportswriter Oliver Kuechle wrote, "It was easily one of the greatest passing performances in the history of the game."[2]

After the game, Millner, when asked by a sportswriter how he had managed to outrun the Bears' defenders so readily, responded, "You'd run fast too, if you had those big devils chasing you."[3]

SCORING

	1	2	3	4	Totals
Washington	7	0	21	0	28
Chicago	14	0	7	0	21

1st Quarter: Washington—TD Battles 7-yard run (R. Smith kick)—8:04. Chicago—TD Manders 10-yard run (Manders kick)—11:12. Chicago—TD Manders 37-yard pass from Masterson (Manders kick)—14:25. 2nd Quarter: None. 3rd Quarter: Washington—TD Millner 55-yard pass from Baugh (R. Smith kick)—1:13. Chicago—TD Manske 4-yard pass from Masterson (Manders kick)—5:56. Washington—TD Millner 78-yard pass from Baugh (R. Smith kick)—6:26. Washington—TD Justice 35-yard pass from Baugh (R. Smith kick)—14:06. 4th Quarter: None.

STARTING LINEUPS

Washington Redskins		Chicago Bears
Wayne Millner	Left End	Edgar Manske
Turk Edwards	Left Tackle	Joe Stydahar
Les Olsson	Left Guard	Dan Fortmann
Eddie Kawal	Center	Frank Bausch
Jim Karcher	Right Guard	George Musso
Jim Barber	Right Tackle	Del Bjork
Charley Malone	Right End	George Wilson
Riley Smith	Quarterback	Bernie Masterson
Sammy Baugh	Left Halfback	Ray Nolting
Ernie Pinckert	Right Halfback	Jack Manders
Cliff Battles	Fullback	Bronko Nagurski

(*Substitutions:* **Washington:** Centers: George Smith; Guards: Eddie Michaels, Vic Carroll, Eddie Kahn; Tackles: Chuck Bond, Bill Young; Backs: Ed Justice, Don Irwin, Max Krause. **Chicago:** Centers: Bill Conkwright, Frank Sullivan; Guards: Joe Zeller; Tackles: Russ Thompson, Milt Trost; Backs: Ray Buivid, Dick Plasman, Gene Ronzani, Les McDonald, Pug Rentner, Sam Francis, Keith Molesworth, Beattie Feathers, Bill Karr.)

Head Coaches: Washington: Ray Flaherty; Chicago: George Halas.
Players' Shares: Washington: $300.00; Chicago: $250.00
Game Officials: Referee: W.T. Halloran; Umpire: A.W. Cochrane; Head Linesman: Bobby Cahn; Field Judge: E.F. Hughitt.

TEAM STATISTICS

Washington Redskins		Chicago Bears
22	First Downs	14
9	First Downs Rushing	8
13	First Downs Passing	6
0	First Downs Penalties	0
75/520	Total Offense Plays/Yards	61/357
33	Rushing Attempts	31
122	Rushing Yardage	150
41	Pass Attempts	30
21	Pass Completions	8
51.2	Completion Percentage	26.7
398	Passing Yardage	207
3	Interceptions By	3
2/39	Sacks/Yards Lost	3/25
7	Punts	6
24.8	Punting Average	49.5
1/12	Punt Return/Yards	2/1/0
1	Had Blocked	0
3-	Kickoff Returns — Yards	3–75
4/3	Fumbles/Lost	3/1
1	Penalties	1
5	Penalty Yards	15

1938 NFL — The Gridiron Sport at Its Primitive Best

1938 Championship — Green Bay Packers (17) vs. New York Giants (23)

DECEMBER 11, 1938 — POLO GROUNDS, NEW YORK CITY — 48,120
WEATHER CONDITIONS: 31°F., CLOUDY WITH AN 8 MPH WIND.
FIELD CONDITION: FIRM, BUT SOGGY.

A record 48,120 fans filed into the Polo Grounds on this overcast but mild December 11. The kickoff was scheduled for 2:00 P.M. The Giants were clad in their royal blue jerseys, helmets and hose. The Packers wore their dark blue jerseys with gold numbers and shoulder strips, gold helmets, pants, and dark blue hose with double gold bands just below the calf.

The road looked rocky for the hometown Giants. The long season had taken its toll and they were badly bruised. Stars like All-Pro guard Johnny Dell Isola, back Leland Schaffer, and halfback and placekicker Ward Cuff led the brigade of walking wounded. The Giants had, however, defeated Green Bay 15–3 just three weeks earlier and routed the Washington Redskins 35–0 a week later.

Adding to the Giants' woes was the fact that the Packers were big, strong, talented, and reasonably healthy. With so many of the Giants ailing, much fell to the Giants' All-Pro center Mel Hein. But according to Arthur Daley's *New York Times* report, "Mel Hein was kicked in the cheekbone at the end of the second quarter, suffered a concussion of the brain that left him temporarily bereft of his memory. He came to in the final quarter and finished the game."[1]

Daley went on to say, "What a frenzied battle this was! The tackling was fierce and the blocking positively vicious. In the last drive, every scrimmage pile-up saw a Packer tackler stretched on the ground.... As for the Giants, they really were hammered to a fare-thee-well. The play for the full vibrant sixty minutes was absolutely ferocious. No such blocking and tackling by two football teams ever had been seen at the Polo Grounds. Tempers were so frayed and tattered that stray punches were tossed around all afternoon. This was the gridiron sport at its primitive best."[2]

After receiving Clarke Hinkle's opening kickoff, the Giants jumped out to a 9–0 lead in the first quarter. The first two scores came after the Giants blocked Green Bay punts.

After each team ran two uneventful series of downs, the Packers decided to punt on third and 11 from their own 11-yard line.

The Giants' Jim Lee Howell accounted for the first block as the big right end stormed through the Packer line and blunted Clarke Hinkle's punt from the Green Bay goal line. "The ball made a short arch straight up and when it came down,"[3] fullback Leland Shaffer grabbed it for New York on the Packer seven. The Giants offense then couldn't get going as they gained a single yard on two rushes and an Ed Danowski pass to Ward Cuff fell incomplete. On 4th and goal from the 6, Cuff lined up for a field goal. Danowski made a successful placement and Cuff was true on a 14-yarder, putting the hometown Giants up 3–0.

The second block came almost immediately. The Packers, starting from their own 22, could only move the ball 9 yards, presenting them with a punting situation on fourth and one from 31. This time Cecil Isbell dropped back to punt, but Jim Poole knocked it back with Howell recovering on the Green Bay 28.

With the Maramen back in possession, Tuffy Leemans went to work. Dodging a hard charging pass rush by guard Russell Letlow, Danowski found Tuffy on a 5-yard strike. Leemans then ran off left guard for 4 yards before being brought down by Cecil Isbell on the 19. On third and one, Leemans broke left for a 13-yard pickup. On first and goal from the six, Leemans again got the call as he skated to his left; he was hit by four defenders, but kept his feet and scored the first touchdown of the day to extend the Giant lead. Johnny Gildea missed the conversion wide to the left and New York led 9–0.

As Gildea set up for the kickoff, Curley Lambeau made 10 substitutions, leaving Buckets Goldenberg as the sole starter on the field.

The first quarter ended appropriately with a Green Bay punt by Arnie Herber after the Packers gained only 4 yards on the series following the Giants' second score.

Early in the second quarter, the Packers began a long drive that resulted in their first score of the game. After a Green Bay punt on first down from their own goal line, the Giants, with terrific field position at the Packers' 41, whittled away an opportunity to break the game open.

Paul "Tiny" Engebretsen got things going when he intercepted a New York pass and returned it to midfield. Leemans had thrown a low strike that was deflected by Bruder and caught by Engebretsen, who then fumbled out of bounds on the Packers' 49. Jankowski then picked up 12 yards on a reverse, moving the ball to the New York 39. After losing a yard and an incomplete pass, Arnie Herber covered the rest of the distance when he unloaded a 40-yard bullet down the middle of the field to end Carl Mulleneaux. Mulleneaux beat Leemans and pulled the ball in at the 1-yard line, rumbling into the end zone between the goal posts. Tiny Engebretsen made good on the PAT kick to bring the Pack to within 2 points. Tempering the Packers' excitement was the fact that Don Hutson reinjured his knee on the drive and was inactive for most of the rest of the game, returning only late in the 4th quarter during the Packers' final desperate drive.

The Maramen came right back two series later. With the Packers on the move, Mel Hein recovered a Jankowski fumble at midfield, and the Giants were off on their next scoring drive. Tuffy Leemans got things going, gaining 10 yards on three carries. Danowski then hit Len Barnum on a pass that the Giant rookie pulled in at the Packers' 22, but when he was hit by Hinkle, he fumbled out of bounds. The Green Bay defense argued furiously that Barnum never had possession, but referee Bobby Cahn refused to listen to the challenge.[4] Barnum then ran off tackle for another yard. From the 21, Danowski passed to end Hap Barnard, who pulled the ball in at the 2 and strode into the end zone. Ward Cuff converted, extending the New York lead to 16–7.

On the next series of downs the Packers came right back. After losing 3 yards on the opening play, Cecil Isbell hit left end Wayland Becker with a short spot pass. Becker juked into the clear and ran 66 yards down the sideline before being brought down from behind by Hank Soar on the New York 17. On the next play, Isbell spun his way for an 8-yard pickup. Green Bay then turned to their big back Clarke Hinkle, who smashed across the center of the line four times. On his fifth consecutive plunge, Hinkle followed right guard Paul Miller through the line and scored from inside the 1. Engebretsen kicked the conversion to cut New York's lead to 16–14.

At halftime, with the Giants in the lead, Curley Lambeau attempted to fire up his troops. It worked, as the Packers came out of the locker room on fire.

Cuff's second-half kickoff went to Joe Laws, who returned it 29 yards to the Packers' 32. On the first play from scrimmage, Johnny Dell Isola tackled Laws after a 4-yard gain, but was seriously injured. He was taken to St. Elizabeth's Hospital with a spinal injury. Two plays later, Bob Monnett broke off tackle for a 33-yard gain before finally being brought down by Jim Lee Howell. Alternating between Laws and Hinkle, the Packers moved the ball down to the Giants' 5, but there they stalled. After a 62-yard drive, Engebretsen's 15-yard field goal gave Green Bay their first lead of the day at 17–16.

New York's Jim Lee Howell returned the ensuing kickoff 19 yards to his own 39. The Giants then responded to Green Bay's field goal with a 61-yard drive in which Soar carried the ball seven times for 26 yards, half of which came on a 13-yard run for the Giants' first first down of the drive. He also caught two passes, one for 10 yards, and the other a 23-yard touchdown pass from Danowski, to help the New Yorkers regain the lead. On the play, Danowski dropped back, waited for Soar to cut to his left, and then fired a bullet pass that hit Soar on the 7-yard line. The Giant halfback made a leaping grab, going up between two defenders, and then bowled his way into the end zone, despite having Hinkle attached to his back. Cuff converted for his second PAT of the day. The Giants now led 23–17.

The Packers came storming back on runs by Isbell and Hinkle and an Arnie Herber pass to Isbell that gained 22 yards. Lambeau's men were on the move and threatening to regain the lead. The New York faithful held their collective breath. As the Packers lined up on third and five from the Giants' 33, Steve Owen was looking for his defense to stiffen once again. As the play began, Isbell took the ball and quickly surveyed the field. Under a steady rush, he fired a pass to Carl Mulleneux. As the ball neared its mark, Ed Danowski stepped in front of Mulleneux to make an interception and end the Green Bay drive.

The fourth quarter opened with Clarke Hinkle gaining 29 yards on three carries behind strong blocking led by 8-year veteran Hank Bruder. With the ball at the Giants' 40, the New York defense stiffened. After just missing Becker on a third down pass at the 2-yard line, Herber punted, but the result was an unreturned punt that Becker downed at the Giants' 2. As was common at the time, New York chose to play for better position and punted on first down from their own end zone. Danowski's kick was downed by Widseth on the New York 35.

Green Bay then went to work, with Herber trying a long pass that was broken up by Cuff at the goal line. After Janowski gained 1 yard off left tackle, Herber again set his sights on the end zone. He fired a missile intended for Monnett, but the Giants' defense again rose to the occasion as Danowski and Cuff double-teamed Monnett and safely batted the pigskin to the turf. On the next play, Herber connected with Becker at the 22. As Becker pulled in the ball and began to run, he was leveled by Cuff. The ball popped loose and was recovered by New York guard Kayo Lundy, ending yet another drive.

New York could do nothing on their next possession and punted. Again Green Bay started to move. With good field position at their own 40, Hinkle opened with a reverse up the left side that gained 3 yards. Herber then found Milt Gantenbein for a 13-yard completion, but Gantenbein was ruled an ineligible receiver on the play. Again, the Packers argued with the officials to no avail. The ruling helped end the Packers' drive and took the wind out of their sails yet again. The Giants took possession at the Green Bay 43.

On the next play, the Packers held Tuffy Leemans to no gain, but were assessed a 15-yard penalty for unnecessary roughness as they piled on after the whistle. Frustration was setting in.

The Packers' defense then settled down and held New York to no net gain for the next three plays. On fourth and ten at the Packer 28, Ward Cuff lined up for a 36-yard field goal attempt that if successful would move the Giants' lead to a more comfortable 9 points. The ball, however, missed its mark, and the record crowd stayed in their seats as the game remained too close to call.

Cuff's missed field goal gave the Packers new life. Opening their next possession, Isbell hit Scherer and Mulleneaux for gains of 19 and 6 yards respectively. Runs by Laws, Hinkle and Isbell drove the ball to the Giants' 42, but there the offense stalled and the Packers yielded the ball on downs. The already gray, overcast day was getting darker and the Polo Grounds' lights were turned on.

New York, at their own 42, once again put the ball in the hands of Hank Soar, who carried six consecutive times for 21 yards. More importantly, his carries burned up valuable time. On fourth and two from the Packers' 37, Danowski punted the ball out of the end zone.

With the touchback, Green Bay took over at their own 20. On the Packers' final possession, with the clock winding down, Herber dropped back to pass, but strong coverage and a hearty pass rush forced him to run the ball. He gained 16 yards, but the clock was still running. On 1st and 10 from the 36, Herber threw a 14-yard strike to Carl Mulleneaux, who lateraled to the recently reinserted Don Hutson. Hutson tucked the ball and wound his way to the New York 40, where he managed to get out of bounds to stop the clock. There was time for one last play. On the final play of the game, Herber called a pass play, sending all of his receivers deep in hopes of pulling off a miracle. He dropped back to search the horizon, but a vicious New York pass rush hurried Herber. Finding no one open and running for his life, the Green Bay quarterback let loose a pass to Paul Miller, but it fell incomplete on the soggy turf to preserve the Giants' victory.

The Packers won the statistical battle, but lost the war. They outgained the Giants 378 to 212 in total yards by more than doubling New York up in the aerial total. The Giants, battered and beaten, performed well and held on to the 23–17 score and their third league championship.

After the game, a clearly disappointed Curley Lambeau told reporters that he believed that Hutson, Monnett, and Herm Schneidman were ready to go at full speed. "With these men seemingly okay and Clarke Hinkle fully recovered from his leg injury by two weeks of rest, I was pretty sure we'd make up for that 15–3 trimming the Giants handed us last time. But I know differently now. Hutson not only wasn't in form, but having his ankle injured almost as soon as he entered made him practically useless for the remainder of the afternoon. Even when we did start clicking, the Giants were superior opportunists, making the most of our errors."[5]

The Giants' win made them the first team to repeat as winners of an NFL championship game. Their first win had also come on this same Polo Grounds field in 1934 in the famous "Sneakers Game."

SCORING

	1	2	3	4	Totals
Green Bay Packers	0	14	3	0	17
New York Giants	9	7	7	0	23

1st Quarter: New York — FG — Cuff 14 yards. New York — TD Leemans 6-yard run (Gildea kick failed). 2nd Quarter: Green Bay — TD — C. Mulleneaux 40-yard pass from Herber (Engebretsen kick) New York — TD — Barnard 21-yard pass from Danowski (Cuff kick). Green Bay — TD — Hinkle 1-yard run (Engebretsen kick). 3rd Quarter: Green Bay — FG — Engebretsen 15 yards. New York — TD — Soar 23-yard pass from Danowski (Cuff kick). 4th Quarter: None.

STARTING LINEUPS

Green Bay Packers		New York Giants
Wayland Becker	Left End	Jim Poole
Champ Seibold	Left Tackle	Ed Widseth
Russell Letlow	Left Guard	Johnny Dell Isola
Lee Mulleneaux	Center	Mel Hein
Buckets Goldenberg	Right Guard	Orville Tuttle
Bill Lee	Right Tackle	Ox Parry
Milt Gantenbein	Right End	Jim Lee Howell
Herm Schneidman	Quarterback	Ed Danowski
Cecil Isbell	Left Halfback	Hank Soar
Joe Laws	Right Halfback	Ward Cuff
Clarke Hinkle	Fullback	Leland Shaffer

(*Substitutions:* **Green Bay** — Ends: Don Hutson, Carl Mulleneaux, Bernie Scherer; Tackles: Frank Butler, Buford "Baby" Ray; Guards: Swede Johnston, Pete Tinsley, Paul Engebretsen, Leo Katalinas; Center: Okie Miller; Backs: Paul Miller, Hank Bruder, Ed Jankowski, Andy Uram, Dick Weisgerber, Arnie Herber, Bob Monnett. **New York** — Ends: Hap Barnard, Chuck Gelatka; Tackles: John Mellus, Frank Cope; Guards: Kayo Lunday, Pete Cole, Arthur "Tarzan" White; Centers: Cliff Johnson, Stan Galazin; Backs: Tuffy Leemans, Len Barnum, Bull Karcis, Kink Richards, Johnny Gildea, Dale Burnett, Nello Falaschi.)

Head Coaches: Green Bay: Earl "Curley" Lambeau; New York: Steve Owen.
Players' Shares: New York: $900.00 Green Bay: $700.00

Game Officials: Referee: Bobby Cahn (Chicago); Umpire: Tom Thorpe (Columbia); Linesman: Larry Conover (Penn State); Field Judge: J.L. Meyer (Ohio Wesleyan)

TEAM STATISTICS

Green Bay Packers		New York Giants
16	First Downs	13
65/378	Total Offense Plays/Yards	58/212
46	Rushing Attempts	43
164	Rushing Yardage	115
19	Pass Attempts	15
8	Pass Completions	8
42.1	Completion Percentage	53.3
214	Passing Yardage	97
1	Interceptions By	1
0/0	Sacks/Yards Lost	0/0
6	Punts	8
26.8	Punting Average	40.6
3/10	Punt/Return Yards	2/34
2	Had Blocked	0
3/66	Kickoff/Return Yards	4/56
3/20	Penalties/Yards Lost	2/10
4/2	Fumbles/Lost	2/1–0

1939 NFL — Curley's Perfect Packers

1939 NFL Championship — New York Giants (0) vs. Green Bay Packers (27)

DECEMBER 10, 1939 — WISCONSIN STATE FAIR GROUNDS, MILWAUKEE — 32,279
WEATHER CONDITIONS: 28°F., CLEAR & SUNNY, 35 MPH WIND GUSTS.
FIELD CONDITION: HARD, FIRM.

The Wisconsin State Fair Grounds in Milwaukee played host to the 1939 NFL championship game on December 10. A throng of 32,279 attended the game between the "hometown" Green Bay Packers and the New York Giants. The teams had met the year before with the Giants winning. The Pack was ready for the payback.

Lambeau moved the game from Green Bay's small City Stadium to Milwaukee with its larger stadium and charged $4.40 a ticket, a new high for pro football prices.

To help accommodate the large crowd — a gathering that set a record for the time — a new wooden grandstand was completed. Still, the complaint of the day was that the seats closest to the field, which were situated on the actual race track, were the worst in the house. The $3.30 seats were called "the worst gyp this town has seen in a long time" by *Milwaukee Journal* writer R.G. Lynch.[1]

Members of the press corps found the facilities to be lacking. The 35-mile-an-hour winds shook the press box situated on top of the grandstand. The players weren't satisfied with the accommodations, either. The Packers' locker room was a dismal space located atop the southern end of the grandstand. The room was small with a single, small window looking out over the grandstand.

This was a grudge game and it was played on a dry but cold and blustery day. The 35-mph gusts played havoc on the aerial and kicking game.

After winning the coin toss, the Giants chose to receive. Ward Cuff juggled Clarke Hinkle's kick at the 10, but then gained control and returned it 13 yards to the New York 23. From there, the Giants could do nothing and punted on fourth and six.

The Packers took over with good field position for their first possession of the day, but nearly turned their good fortune into disaster. On fourth and three, Hinkle's punt was blocked by Jim Poole and recovered by New York's Jim Lee Howell on the Packers' 44.

New York gained 9 yards on a rare 6-yard pass from Ed Danowski to blocking back Nello Falaschi and runs by Kink Richards and Tuffy Leemans, but that brought fourth and one from the Green Bay 35. After the Giants stalled, Ward Cuff attempted a 42-yard field goal. While a long kick, it was well within Cuff's range on a good day, but admittedly, this was not a good day. The heavy wind caught the ball and pushed it wide. It was the first of three that New York would miss that day.

After the teams traded punts, the Packers finally put up some offense. Starting with terrific field position at the Giants' 47, Green Bay methodically moved the ball downfield. Arnie Herber picked up 8 yards on the ground and then connected on three big pass plays. First, he hit Craig for 5. After Hinkle carried around left end for the first down on fourth and one, Herber connected with Don Hutson on the left sideline for a 15-yard pickup. After Hutson was brought down on the six, the New York defense stiffened and tackled Cecil Isbell for a one-yard loss. As the Giants readied themselves for another plunge, Herber dropped back, faked to Hutson, and then fired a 7-yard touchdown pass to right end Milt Gantenbein, whom he saw in the middle of the end zone behind defender Kink Richards. Paul Engebretsen connected on the point after and the Packers led 7–0.

On the final play of the first quarter, with New York's Jim Poole in hot pursuit, Herber let go a pass intended for Jacunski. The hurried pass was off target and Ward Cuff picked it off. He was immediately tackled by Jacunski on the Green Bay 37.

With Tuffy Leemans leading the way, New York started the second quarter with their first sustained drive of the afternoon. Leemans picked up 9 yards rushing and 6 passing to set up New York's second field goal attempt of the game. This time, second-year back Len Barnum attempted a 52-yarder that fell short.

For the rest of the half, the Packers' defensive line, led by tackle Bill Lee and end Larry Craig, stopped the Giants' offense cold. In turn, the strong Giant defense held the Packers in check in the second quarter. The only sustained drive by either team was ended by an interception by New York's Barnum on a pass from Herber to Hutson. The wind adversely affected both squads. Neither team scored again for the remainder of the first half.

In the third period, Green Bay began to pull away as Engebretsen connected on a 29-yard field goal to extend the Green Bay lead to 10–0.

On the third play of the next Giant possession, Milt Gantenbein intercepted a Danowski pass at the New York 38 and returned it 5 yards. The Packers took over on the Giants' 33-yard line.

On third and eight, Green Bay halfback Cecil Isbell swept wide on an end-around. Sizing up the situation, he saw that the Giants' secondary was closing on him and that Joe

Laws was now wide open, having gotten behind Tuffy Leemans, who had begun closing in on the run. Isbell pulled up and lofted a high, wobbly 26-yard pass to Laws, who pulled it in over his shoulder at the Giants' 5 and then easily ran the ball across the goal. Engebretsen converted again for his fifth point of the game to make the score Green Bay 17, New York 0.

Leemans again gave the New Yorkers decent field position by returning Hinkle's kickoff to his own 30 and then making two consecutive 6 yard runs, but save the one first down, the Giants couldn't cross midfield. Danowski's punt rolled into the end zone for a touchback and the Packers started out on their 20.

Things started out well for Green Bay as Laws hit the line at tackle for a 6-yard pickup. From there, it went downhill. Blunted runs and a 15-yard holding penalty pinned the Packers back on their own 10 for fourth and twenty. Hinkle, standing in his own end zone, waited for the long snap from center, but as soon as the ball was snapped, Johnny Dell Isola came charging in and partially blocked the kick, sending it crashing to the turf. Packer Milt Gantenbein recovered it on the Green Bay 16.

The Giants had possession with first down on the Packers' 16. The contest was nearing the end of the third quarter. There was still time to get back into the game, but there was no time to waste. On the first play from scrimmage, Ed Danowski, under a heavy rush, inexplicably threw a hasty pass. The ball fell short of its target and into the waiting hands of first-year Packer defender Charley Brock at the 9. He pulled in the errant pass and ran it back 5 yards. With a golden opportunity to score squandered, Green Bay took possession and ran out the clock on the third quarter.

The first part of the final quarter was largely a punting duel with both defenses tightening, but then the Packers began to pour it on. After Andy Uram returned a punt to the Green Bay 40, the Packers began to move. Uram gained 4 off right tackle on first down. On second, Arnie Herber passed long to Jacunski on the Giants' 33, where he pulled it in and raced for another 8 before finally being pulled to earth. The next two plays yielded a 6-yard loss on a sack by New York tackle Frank Cope and a Herber fumble that was recovered by the Packers' Mulleneaux. The fumble cost Green Bay another 5 yards. But on fourth and 18 from the Giants' 33, Ernie Smith kicked a 42-yard field goal to put Green Bay up 20–0.

The coup de grâce came a few plays later as Packers linebacker Bud Svendsen picked off a Barnum pass at the New York 30-yard line and returned it to the 15. Harry Jacunski then carried the ball to the Giant 1 on a double reverse. The next play, Eddie Jankowski powered over for the score. Smith converted, making the final score Green Bay 27, New York 0.

It got no better for the Giants as rookie replacement back Eddie Miller was intercepted on just the third play of the next series by Green Bay's Jimmy Lawrence. The Giants' only really sustained drive of the day came late in the final quarter when Hank Soar and Eddie Miller moved the ball from their own 47-yard line to the Green Bay 14 against the Packer reserves. On the final play of the game, Miller hit Leland Shaffer with a pass over the middle. Shaffer headed for the end zone in an effort to avoid the shutout, but he was tackled at the three-yard line. His effort to avoid the shutout had fallen nine feet short of the end zone.[2]

"The Packers whipped New York at its own fundamental game of blocking, tackling, plunging, and kicking. They were keyed into a perfect scoring machine that couldn't miss and when the final gun called a halt to the slaughter, they had compiled the most decisive victory in the seven-year history of the National League playoffs, 27 to 0."[3]

The Giants were pleased to get out of the Fair Grounds that day. They'd been beaten badly. Not only had they been shut out, but game statistics showed that the Packers had intercepted six New York passes. New York missed three field goals and were held to a mere 173 total offensive yards.[4]

Green Bay coach Curley Lambeau told the press after the game, "Everything worked to perfection. No matter who we sent in, they all performed like champions."[5]

SCORING

	1	2	3	4	Totals
New York Giants	0	0	0	0	0
Green Bay Packers	7	0	10	10	27

1st Quarter: Green Bay — TD — Gantenbein 7-yard pass from Herber (Engebretsen kick). 2nd Quarter: None. 3rd Quarter: Green Bay — FG — Engebretsen 29 yards. Green Bay — TD — Laws 31-yard pass from Isbell (Engebretsen kick). 4th Quarter: Green Bay — FG — Smith 42 yards. Green Bay — TD — Jankowski 1-yard run (Smith Kick)

STARTING LINEUPS

New York Giants		Green Bay Packers
Jim Poole	Left End	Don Hutson
Frank Cope	Left Tackle	Buford Ray
Johnny Dell Isola	Left Guard	Russell Letlow
Mel Hein	Center	Bud Svendsen
Orville Tuttle	Right Guard	Buckets Goldenberg
John Mellus	Right Tackle	Bill Lee
Jim Lee Howell	Right End	Milt Gantenbein
Ed Danowski	Quarterback	Larry Craig
Kink Richards	Left Halfback	Cecil Isbell
Ward Cuff	Right Halfback	Joe Laws
Nello Falaschi	Fullback	Clarke Hinkle

(*Substitutions:* **Green Bay** —Ends: Harry Jacunski, Al Moore; Centers: Charley Brock, Tom Greenfield; Guards: Pete Tinsley, Paul "Tiny" Engebretsen; Gust Zarnas; Tackles: Ernie Smith, Charlie Schultz; Backs: Hank Bruder, Ed Jankowski, Andy Uram, Dick Weisgerber, Arnie Herber, Frank Balazs, Jim Lawrence. **New York** —Ends: Chuck Gelatka, Will Walls, Harry "Jiggs" Kline; Guards: Kayo Lunday, Pete Cole, Doug Oldershaw; Tackles: Ox Parry, Ed Widseth; Backs: Len Barnum, Tuffy Leemans, Dale Burnett, Leland Shaffer, Al Owen, Hank Soar, Eddie Miller.)

Head Coaches: New York: Steve Owen; Green Bay: Earl "Curley" Lambeau.

Players' Shares: Green Bay: $850.00; New York: $650.00

Game Officials: Referee: W. Halloran; Umpire: E. Cochrane; Linesman: Tom Thorp (Columbia); Field Judge: Dan Tehan.

TEAM STATISTICS

New York Giants		Green Bay Packers
9	First Downs	13
59/173	Total Offense Plays/Yards	61/236
34	Rushing Attempts	51
79	Rushing Yardage	140
25	Pass Attempts	10
8	Pass Completions	7
32.0	Completion Percentage	70.0
94	Passing Yardage	96
3	Interceptions By	6

1/9	Sacks/Yards Lost	1/6
6	Punts	7
40.3	Punting Average	26.0
25	Punt Return Yards	25
0	Had Blocked	2
4/54	Kickoff Returns	0/0
1/0	Fumbles/Lost	2/0
5	Penalties	4
21	Penalty Yards	50

1940 NFL — The Wrath of the Bears

1940 Championship — Chicago Bears (73) vs. Washington Redskins (0)

DECEMBER 8, 1940 — GRIFFITH STADIUM, WASHINGTON, D.C. — 36,034
WEATHER CONDITIONS: CLEAR AND BRIGHT SKY, 39°F., WINDS AT 2 MPH.
FIELD CONDITION: DRY, FIRM.

The sun was bright and the afternoon warm as the Bears prepared to meet the Redskins at Washington's Griffith Stadium. It was a pleasant December 8.

Papa Bear George Halas had waited for this game all week. His players had waited too. The Bears were primed to get revenge over their longtime rivals, the Washington Redskins. The Bears had been upset by Washington in the 1937 title game. They had also lost to the Redskins just a couple of weeks earlier on a non-call of pass interference in the Redskin end zone on the final play of the game. With the game close, the Bears' great back George McAfee barreled his way all the way down to the 1-yard line after receiving a Bob Snyder pass. With the Bears out of time outs, McAfee lay on the turf feigning injury to stop the clock. Under the rules of the time, Chicago was penalized 5 yards for the additional clock stoppage. There was time for only two plays to be run. Both were passes knocked away by Washington defenders. On the final play, the Bears argued furiously that receiver Bill Osmanski had been interfered with by defender Frank Filchock. Halas was furious as he verbally blistered the referee all the way across the field. The official refused to hear the Bears' argument and the game ended in a 7–3 Washington victory.

After the game, flamboyant and opinionated Redskin owner George Preston Marshall, as ungraceful a winner as he was a loser, taunted the Bears. He told the press, "The Bears are a bunch of crybabies. They're front-runners. They can't take defeat. They are a first-half club. They're not a second-half team. The Bears are quitters."[1]

No doubt the Redskins' players and coaches cringed when they heard Marshall make these statements. No team, much less one as talented as the Bears, would take this lying down. As luck would have it, it was the Bears and Redskins who would meet in 1940 for the NFL championship.

To say that Halas and the Bears wanted this game would barely begin to touch the surface of their burning desire. Halas sent for long-time advisor Clark Shaughnessy to help the Bears prepare. Shaughnessy was the head coach of Rose Bowl–bound Stanford University and one of the game's great strategists. The Indians' coach spent long hours studying game films of both teams and discovered their weaknesses. To remedy the Bears' weak points and to exploit those of the Redskins, Shaughnessy proposed a new series of plays that included counters to take advantage of the Redskins' habit of shifting their linebackers to follow an offensive man-in-motion. "By the time we were done, we had a two-way game plan," said Halas, "One was perfectly fitted to the Redskins' defense we had just seen. We were quite sure they wouldn't change something that had worked so well for them. If they did, though, we had a more general plan to put in."[2] Shaughnessy also put in a new communications system for the Bears that week.

In the week before the game, Halas had the Bears' locker room walls covered with clippings of Marshall's comments. Pointing out the clippings, Halas told his team, "I hear that the Chicago Bears have no guts. It's what they tell me in the newspapers. Have a look for yourself."[3] The Bears' anger was building. Add to this that the Redskins were favored to win.

During that week, Marshall struck again. Meeting with the press, he stated, "The trouble with the league right now is that the strength is concentrated in the East. There's not much competition in the West. They're definitely inferior to our brand of football."[4] Papa Bear didn't need to point that one out; the Bears had all heard this comment loud and clear, and they were fuming.

The Bears continued to prepare for the game and all the while, they simmered. Hall of Fame Bear quarterback Sid Luckman recalled, "I've never experienced anything like it. There was a feeling of tension in the air, as if something tremendous was about to happen."[5]

On the train to Washington, Luckman recalled that the players barely spoke. They didn't play cards. Instead they read their playbooks, rested, and thought of Marshall's comments and of revenge. Luckman remembers, "We got to Washington and read the papers. They still called the Bears crybabies and front-runners. That made us even angrier."[6]

Redskins' back Andy Farkas described the scene at Washington's Griffith Stadium on the day before the game:

> Well, the day before the game, on Saturday, we went through a long workout. I guess it must have lasted three hours. We worked very hard. I remember I got dressed as quickly as I could so I could watch the Bears work out. I got back to the field just as they were coming out. I'll never forget it. They came out screaming and yelling, like a pack of wild Indians. I'd never seen anything like it. They took off down the field, like they used to in those days, and ran around the goalposts at the far end of the field and then came back and ran around the other goalposts. They were whooping it up all the way. I was standing near George Halas, and I heard him say to Hunk Anderson, his line coach, "My, but the boys are enthusiastic today." Then Halas turned to Anderson and said, "Okay, get 'em all inside. If they've got that kind of enthusiasm, I don't want 'em to lose it." So the Bears didn't work out at all, except for that one gallop around the field.[7]

On Sunday, Halas walked into the clubhouse with a series of articles containing the Marshall quotes. Luckman said, "He told us he had nothing to say. He just pointed to the Washington papers and said: 'This is what the people in Washington think about you. Gentlemen, we've never been crybabies. Here are the headlines. Go out and play the best football you can!'"[8]

The weather was sunny and mild as the team captains met with the game officials at midfield. The Bears won the coin toss and elected to receive. Ray Nolting took the opening kickoff on his own 3-yard line and returned it to the 25, where he was forced out of bounds. On the opening play from scrimmage, Ed McAfee gained seven yards on a fake reverse. So far an impressive beginning for the Bears, but on second and three, the fireworks really started.

The game had barely begun when the Bears' fullback Bill Osmanski took the ball off-tackle on the first play from scrimmage and rumbled 68 yards for the first Bears score on the day. It would not be the last. Jack Manders made the score 7–0 as he converted on the point after kick. The Bears sensed something good was happening. "When Osmanski scored that first touchdown, I just knew this was going to be our day," recalled Luckman. "We all felt it. On the sidelines, everybody was screaming to get more points on the board."[9]

The Redskins looked like they would come right back when Washington back Max Krause fielded Jack Manders's kickoff at his own 10 and returned it 51 yards to the Chicago 39. Krause, an eight-year veteran out of Gonzaga, was playing in his last NFL game and certainly went out with a bang.

Baugh began a Redskin drive that moved the ball to the Bears' 26 on runs by Johnson and Ed Justice. On third and eight, Baugh hurled a perfect pass to receiver Charley Malone, who was wide open on the Bears' five-yard line, but Malone dropped it. On fourth down, the Redskins' Bob Masterson attempted a 32-yard field goal that went wide.

Chicago took over on their own 20. It took the Bears 17 plays to move the ball the 80 yards to pay dirt as Luckman carried the ball over on a keeper from the 1-yard line. Snyder converted and the Bears led 14–0.

Lee Artoe's ensuing kickoff was deep and sailed out of the end zone for a touchback. Sammy again went to work, but the tough Bears defense kept up the pressure, causing a 6-yard loss on the first play of the possession followed by two incomplete passes. On fourth and 16 from their own 14, Baugh stepped back to punt. As the ball was centered, the Bears' defense came with all they could muster. George Musso, rumbling in like a freight train, got a hand on the ball, altering its flight and keeping it in Redskins territory. Luckman returned the ball 3 yards to the Washington 42.

On the very next play, Sid handed the ball to backup fullback Joe Maniaci, who thundered around left end and along the sideline for a 42-yard touchdown run. With a Phil Martinovich run for conversion, the score was now 21–0 and the rout was on.

The Redskins got a big break when Artoe's kickoff went out of bounds, giving Washington the ball at their own 45. With Frank Filchock in for Baugh, the Redskins' luck didn't improve. Again, Washington played four and out. Todd, punting during Baugh's absence, got off a short, 35-yard kick that Ed McAfee fielded at the Bears' 25 and returned 17 yards to the Bears' 42.

On 1st and 10, Luckman's lateral to Ray Nolting missed badly and rolled out of bounds at the Bears' 28. On second and 24, Luckman quick kicked the ball to the Redskins' 14, where Wilbur Moore returned it to the 20.

On 1st and 10 from the Redskins' 20, Filchock, looking to jump-start the offense, threw long to the speedy Wilbur Moore, but his pass was intercepted by Chicago rookie back Scooter McLean, who returned the ball to midfield. Again, the Bears' offense began moving the ball well, but on 1st and 10 from the Redskins' 16 the Bears made one of the few miscues they experienced all afternoon. McLean, whose interception set up this drive, played easy come, easy go when he fumbled away a handoff that was recovered by Washington end Bob McChesney at the 19.

Filchock and the Redskins seemed to have a renewed spirit after the turnover. On the ensuing possession, Filchock connected on 3 of 9 passes for 60 yards, including a leaping grab by Wayne Millner for 42. But to the dismay of the Washington faithful, Filchock's final two passes on the drive were broken up in the end zone as the Washington drive ended on the Bears' 18. Mr. McLean stepped in again to atone for his fumble and broke up the first of those passes.

Taking over at their own 18, Luckman and the Bears again got moving. On 3rd and 9 Chicago halfback Bob Swisher had got behind Filchock and pulled in Sid's pass for a 36-yard pickup to the Redskins' 45.

On the next play, McLean took the handoff around left end and gained 19 yards before being knocked out of bounds by Dick Todd, a second-year halfback out of Texas A&M. There the Chicago drive stalled, and on 4th and 8 on the Redskins' 24, Martinovich lined up for a 30-yard field goal attempt. The kick sailed wide and Washington took over on their own 20.

On 1st down Filchock dropped back to pass, but under heavy pursuit cut out of the pocket and gained 17 yards around left end. On 1st and 19 from his own 37 and again under heavy pressure, Frank let go a long pass that was almost picked off by Dick Plasman. On the next play, while aiming long for Wayne Millner, he was picked off by Ray Nolting on the Chicago 34. Nolting returned the interception 10 yards to the 44.

With good field position, Luckman began moving the Bears again, alternating runs between Nolting and Osmanski. On 3rd and 9 from the Washington 30, Sid found Ken Kavanaugh, who had beaten Farkas and Filchock in the end zone. Kavanaugh caught the 30-yard pass from Luckman to increase the Bears' lead. A Snyder kick made the score Bears 28, Redskins 0.

Filchock took Lee Artoe's long kickoff at his own goal line and returned it 25 yards. On 2nd and 10, Sammy Baugh returned to the game and immediately hooked up with Farkas for a 19-yard pass completion. Baugh continued to move the club with a series of passes. The highlight of the drive came on 1st and 15 from the Bears' 45, when Baugh, in the grip of a would-be tackler, threw long to Malone, who streaked in between Snyder and McLean and pulled the pass in at the Chicago 5. With the 1st quarter winding down, the Redskins finally looked ready to get on the scoreboard. But again, it was not meant to be. On the next play, Baugh's pass for Farkas was picked up off by Bill Osmanski as the half came to an end.

The second half began just as badly for the Redskins as the first. After Malone returned Artoe's opening kickoff 9 yards to the 34, Washington had decent field position. On the first play from scrimmage, however, the Redskins were called for holding and now faced 1st and 25 from their own 19. On the next snap, Sammy Baugh threw a flat pass for Johnston that was intercepted by Hamp Poole at the 15. Poole gathered in the ball and raced the remaining 15 yards into the end zone. With the conversion by Dick Plasman, the Bears led 35–0 and had scored on yet another turnover just 45 seconds into the second half.

The Redskins' desperation over the mounting score became evident on their next possession. After moving the ball effectively for 29 yards and facing a comfortable 3rd and 3 on their own 49, Baugh fumbled the long snap. Johnston raced back to pick up the bouncing ball, but he was dropped for a 16-yard loss as he attempted to run around right end. On 4th and 19 from his own 33-yard line Baugh, rather than punting, tried to make something happen, but his pass intended for Malone fell sterilely to the Griffith Stadium turf.

Chicago, taking over on downs deep in Redskins territory, wasted no time in striking again. Ray Nolting was the star of this two-play drive as he gained 10 on a reverse around right end, followed by a 23-yard touchdown run up the middle. Plasman missed this conversion, but the Bears led 41–0 just 4½ minutes into the second half.

Less than a minute later, George McAfee picked off a Zimmerman pass on the Redskins' 35 and headed for the end zone. He juked Pinkert at the 5 and coasted in for the score. Joe Stydahar converted to put the Bears up 48–0.

The Redskins, despite the overwhelming advantage by the Bears, held their heads up for one more sustained drive. Zimmerman returned Lee Artoe's kickoff to the Redskins' 33. Aided by rookie Bob Seymour's 3 rushes for 17 yards, Zimmerman completed 2 passes for 31 yards to give Washington a first down on the Bears' 16. There, however, the drive stalled as the Bears' defense stopped Seymour for no gain on first down and then kept up the heavy rush on Zimmerman, not allowing him to set up and get away clean passes. On fourth down, Dick Farman went into the end zone on a tackle eligible play, but Zimmerman missed the mark and the Redskins' hopes of a comeback lay as helpless as the incomplete pass.

The Bears went 4 and out on their next possession when, on 3rd and 4 from the their own 26, Ed McAfee took the handoff and headed towards left end. Suddenly he pulled up and lofted a pass to Dick Plasman, who was in the clear, but Plasman dropped an easy reception in one of the Bears' few miscues of the afternoon.

The game continued to deteriorate for the Redskins. On the second play of their next possession, Zimmerman had to chase an errant snap from center, falling on it for a 17-yard loss. Going from bad to worse, his pass in the flat on third down was picked off by Bulldog Turner at the 20 and returned for yet another Bears score. Maniaci's kick was blocked by second-year guard Clyde Shugart, but the score now stood at an imposing 54–0 with just over two minutes to play in the 3rd period.

As the 4th quarter began, frustration was turning to anger for the Redskins. After the defense held the Bears' Solly Sherman for no gain on a 2nd and 3 at midfield, Washington was penalized 15 yards for unsportsmanlike conduct when punches were thrown. Three plays later, the Bears scored on a 44-yard double reverse run from Sherman to Famiglietti to Clark. Famiglietti's kick failed, but Chicago was now up 60–0.

On the third play of the next series of downs, Frank Filchock was under heavy rush by the Bears' defense. Frank valiantly tried to evade the oncoming rush but was hit by the Bears' 6'3", 240-pound rookie guard Joe Mihal, and lost the ball. Chicago's Jack Torrance fell on the loose ball at the Redskins' 2. The 6'4", 285-pound Torrance went out with a flash, as this was to be his last NFL game.

It took the Bears one play to score yet another touchdown on the beleaguered Washington defense as Gary Famiglietti plowed over left guard to hit pay dirt. In yet another sign of the magnitude of the runaway, the officials asked the Bears to stop kicking extra points to save balls. The Bears complied and promptly passed for the extra point as Sherman hit Maniaci in the end zone for the Bears' 67th point of the afternoon.

The next Washington possession was no better as Maniaci struck again, intercepting Filchock on his own 32 and returning the ball 26 yards to the Redskins' 42.

The Bears' final sustained drive of the afternoon culminated in a 1 yard power play over right tackle by Clark. On the conversion attempt, Snyder's pass to Maniaci failed, leaving the score at 73–0 over the shell-shocked Redskins.

Though the scoring was finished, the payback was not. After 21 yards through the air on two completions to Wayne Millner, Filchock, on the drive's third play, dropped another pass into the waiting arms of the Bears' Joe Maniaci at the Chicago 20. Although Maniaci returned the ball 15 yards before lateraling the ball to Clark, the lateral was ruled illegal and the ball moved back 15 yards from the spot of the infraction.

From their own 20, with time winding down, Snyder pitched out to Famiglietti, who ran around left end for an 11-yard pickup and another first down. On the next play Snyder kept the ball and snuck two yards up the middle to burn the final seconds off the game clock. Mercifully for the Redskins, the game was over.

The Bears scored eleven touchdowns to break a league scoring record and rolled up over 500 yards in total offense. The Bears had 382 yards rushing to the Redskins' 22. The Bears completed 7 of 10 passes for 138 yards and had eight interceptions by seven different players, with three of the picks being returned for touchdowns.

After the game, Shirley Povich of the *Washington Post* wrote in response to the obvious question: "If you're wanting to know what happened to the Redskins yesterday, maybe this will explain it: The Bears happened to 'em."[10] On that sunny December afternoon, the Bears were the perfect football team. Everything they did was right, and after the first touchdown, everything the Redskins did was wrong.

Legendary play-by-play announcer Red Barber, who was calling the game for the Mutual Broadcasting Service, recalled, "The touchdowns came so quickly there for a while, I felt like I was the cashier at a grocery store."[11]

Sammy Baugh described that afternoon as: "The most humiliating thing I have ever had happen to me in a football game." Continuing, Baugh said, "There was a lot of stuff in the newspapers that Mr. Marshall had put in there about the Bears. I think any team would have beaten us that day. The team was mad at Mr. Marshall, because he said some awful things about the Bears."[12] Later he was asked if the game's outcome would have been any different if Masterson had made his first-quarter field goal try. Upon reflection, Sammy said, "Hell yes, the final score would have been 73–3."[13] The *New York Times* may have expressed it the best when they said, "The weather was perfect. So were the Bears."[14]

Scoring

	1	2	3	4	Totals
Chicago Bears	21	7	26	19	73
Washington Redskins	0	0	0	0	0

1st Quarter: Chicago — TD Osmanski — 68 yard run (Manders kick)—00:56. Chicago — TD Luckman —1-yard run (Snyder kick)—10:50. Chicago — TD Maniaci — 42-yard run (Manders kick)—12:25. 2nd Quarter: Chicago — TD Kavanaugh — 30-yard pass from Luckman (Snyder kick)—11:45. 3rd Quarter: Chicago — TD Poole—15-yard interception return (Plasman kick)—00:45. Chicago — TD Nolting — 23-yard run (Plasman kick failed)—4:25. Chicago — TD McAfee — 35-yard interception return (Stydahar kick)— 5:12. Chicago — TD Turner — 20-yard interception return (Maniaci kick failed)—12:56. 4th Quarter: Chicago — TD Clark — 44-yard run (Famiglietti kick failed)—4:47. Chicago — TD Famiglietti — 2-yard run (Maniaci pass from Sherman)— 6:15. Chicago — TD Clark 1-yard run (Snyder pass failed)—12:36.

Starting Lineups

Chicago Bears		Washington Redskins
Bob Nowaskey	Left End	Bob Masterson
Joe Stydahar	Left Tackle	Willie Wilkin
Danny Fortmann	Left Guard	Dick Farman
Bulldog Turner	Center	Bob Titchenal
George Musso	Right Guard	Steve Slivinski
Lee Artoe	Right Tackle	Jim Barber

George Wilson	Right End	Charley Malone
Sid Luckman	Quarterback	Max Krause
Ray Nolting	Left Halfback	Sammy Baugh
George McAfee	Right Halfback	Ed Justice
Bill Osmanski	Fullback	Jimmy Johnston

(*Substitutes:* **Chicago:** Ends: Dick Plasman, Ken Kavenaugh, Jack Manders, John Siegal, Phil Martinovich, Hamp Poole, Edgar Manske; Tackles: Ed Kolman, Joe Mihal; Guards: Al Baisi, Aldo Forte, Jack Torrance; Center: Frank Bausch; Backs: Bernie Masterson, Solly Sherman, Harry Clark, Bob Swisher, Ray McLean, Gary Famiglietti, Bob Snyder, Joe Maniaci, Jack Manders. **Washington:** Ends: Wayne Millner, Bob McChesney, Sandy Sanford; Tackles: Bo Russell, Bob Fisher, Mickey Parks; Guards: Clyde Shugart, Clem Stralka; Centers: Steve Andrako, Vic Carroll; Backs: Erny Pinckert, Bob Hoffman, Boyd Morgan, Frank Filchock, Roy Zimmerman, Wilbur Moore, Bob Seymour, Jim Meade, Dick Todd, Andy Farkas, Ray Hare.)

Head Coaches: Chicago: George Halas; Washington: Ray Flaherty.
Game Officials: Referee: William Friesell; Umpire: Harry Robb; Head Linesman: Irv Kupcinet; Field Judge: Fred Young.
Players' Shares: Chicago: $873.99; Washington: $606.25

TEAM STATISTICS

Chicago Bears		Washington Redskins
17	First Downs	17
62/529	Total Offense Plays/Yards	63/281
52	Rushing Attempts	12
382	Rushing Yardage	22
10	Pass Attempts	51
7	Pass Completions	20
70.0	Completion Percentage	39.2
138	Passing Yardage	226
8	Interceptions By	0
2/18	Sacked/Yards Lost	1/17
2	Punts	3
48.0	Punting Average	42.3
3/29	Punt/Return Yards	1/6
-	Had Blocked	-
1/0	Fumbles/Lost	0/0
7	Penalties	6
36	Penalty Yards	71

1941 NFL — Storm Clouds on the Horizon

1941 NFL Championship Game — New York Giants (9) vs. Chicago Bears (37)

DECEMBER 21, 1941 — WRIGLEY FIELD, CHICAGO — 13,341
WEATHER CONDITIONS: 47°F., SUNSHINE, LIGHT WINDS.
FIELD CONDITION: DRY, HARD, FIRM.

The temperature in Chicago on December 21, 1941, was a balmy 47 degrees. The weather in Wrigley Field, so often the scene of pitched, late-season battles in its icy, snowy, windswept confines, was calm. The Bears, fresh off their Western Conference playoff win the week before, were heavy favorites to defeat the 8–3 New York Giants. On such a beautiful early winter's day in Chicago it seems odd that only 13,341 patrons showed up for the game. Just a week before, almost 30,000 more had braved frigid temperatures to watch the Western Division playoff with the Packers. Several factors most likely added up to keeping the crowd small. Perhaps it was the stern reality that the nation was now a fortnight into a two-front war and football championships seemed a bit trivial. Perhaps the impending holiday season kept others busy. Perhaps many had seen last week's contest between the two 10–1–1 teams as the real championship game. Whatever the reasons, those who attended on the 21st were treated to a pretty good game — at least for three quarters.

Many believed that the Bears were even better than they had been the previous year when they had decimated the hapless Washington Redskins 73–0 in the 1940 championship contest. But this might well be the last time this crack squad would perform together — or at least for quite a while. It had been two weeks since the surprise attack on Pearl Harbor and the nation was at war. With the mobilization of troops, at least half of the participants in today's contest were facing an early call into America's armed forces.[1] The Giants, facing the same potential breakup of their squad, were not about to lie down. The New Yorkers hung tough and the game was played evenly for two and a half quarters with the score knotted at 9–9.

The Bears registered the first points when they stalled at the New York 7 during the first quarter. Bob Snyder booted a 14-yard field goal.

The Giants came right back on the leadership of Tuffy Leemans. The 29-year-old back out of George Washington, now in his sixth year with the club, threw a 23-yard pass on which Ward Cuff made a sensational catch. Leemans then rushed for 4 yards. The Giants' score came when Leemans fired a 27-yard pass to speedy back George Franck. Franck pulled the ball in and then raced over the goal line aided by big end Jim Poole's block on the Bears' safety. The conversion kick failed when Chicago's Johnny Siegel blocked Cuff's kick, but New York now led 6–3.[2]

As the third period ended, Chicago quarterback Sid Luckman moved his squad down to the Giants' 32, where the stout New York defense then halted the drive. Again, the Bears called on Snyder, who booted a 39-yard field goal to tie the game at 6.

After a Giants punt gave the Bears excellent field position at the New York 47, George McAfee and Bill Osmanski rushed for a combined for 29 yards. The Bears, once again stymied by the tough New York defense, called on Snyder's leg. Snyder responded with his third field goal of the half to put the Bears up 9–6.

The Giants' defense was strong throughout the first half. With a five-man front and a linebacking corps led by the hard-charging, 230-pound Mel Hein, they effectively shut down the powerful Bear attack. Unable to find the end zone, the Bears were held to three Bob Snyder field goals of 7, 39, and 37 yards. While held to three kicks, Chicago still went to the locker room at halftime with a tenuous 9–6 lead.

George Halas, less than pleased by his squad's performance, reportedly rebuked his team in the locker room at halftime, stating, "You people are supposed to be champions, but you're playing like bums."

Early in the 3rd quarter, the Giants were still a voice to be heard. Sparked by Francks's 34-yard blast into Bears territory, the Giants, with 1st and 10 on the Chicago 46, set their sights for the end zone. New York moved 10 yards closer on Cuff and Leeman plunges. After a 5-yard penalty on the Bears for offsides, the pair teamed up for 20 more as Cuff reigned in a Leemans pass on the five. There, the Bears' defense stiffened and held the Maramen. The best the Giants could do was draw even at 9 on a 16-yard Ward Cuff field goal. While New York was happy to even the score, it was the end of the scoring that day for New York.

With the inside game being well shut down by the Giants' line and linebackers Mel Hein, Len Younce, and Nello Falaschi, the Bears determined to open the outside to their backs. The Giants were beginning to show signs of fatigue and Halas knew that they would not be able to shut off the middle and cover the end game effectively for very long against the bruising Chicago offense. Poppa Bear began to send George McAfee, Hugh Gallerneau, and 230-lb. rookie fullback Norm Standlee to the outside, and he had Sid Luckman picked apart the Giant secondary with his precision passing. Soon the wheels fell off for New York.

After the Giants' kickoff, Chicago began a drive to regain the lead and put the game away. Standlee began the drive with 10- and 3- yard pickups to move the ball to the Chicago 43. Luckman then connected with Dick Plasman in Giants territory at the New York 34. End Johnny Siegal kept things moving as he made a great diving catch of a Luckman strike. Chicago's backs kept hammering away at the weary New York defense. Finally, the Bears scored when Standlee, powering over the Giants' Falaschi, bowled into the end zone from the 3. Snyder converted and Chicago took the lead 16–9. It was a lead they would not relinquish for the rest of the day.

The Giants still refused to yield as Leemans led New York downfield. During that drive, however, linebacker Danny Fortmann picked Leemans off at the Bears' 32 and ended the drive.

McAfee, McLean, and Standlee moved the ball to the Giants' 7, where Standlee carried over for the score. Joe Maniaci kicked the extra point to make the score 23–9 as the 3rd quarter came to an end.

The Bears' linebacking corps struck again on the next Giants possession. With the final quarter getting underway, Clyde "Bulldog" Turner intercepted a New York pass and was brought down on the Bears' 46. The Chicago drive began as Standlee and McAfee gained 15 yards on the ground. Luckman then hit Standlee with a completion at the Giants' 23. After losing 5 yards on a holding penalty, Luckman threw long to McLean at the 5. The pass was ruled complete as New York's Chet Gladchuk was called for interference. McAfee scored on a burst up the middle after an interference call had given the Bears a first and goal on the Giants' 5. Artoe then kicked the extra point. The Bears now led 30–9.

In the game's waning seconds, a lateral attempt by New York's Hank Soar to back Andy Marefos went awry. Chicago's Ken Kavanaugh tacked on the final touchdown after scooping up the fumbled lateral and racing 42 yards to pay dirt. For old times' sake, Ray McLean drop-kicked the PAT to make the score 37–9 in favor of the Bears. That's the way the scoring ended as the Giants, game competitors for two and a half quarters, were simply worn down by the Chicago juggernaut.

The final game statistics were telling. They showed the Bears piling up 182 yards by passing and 207 yards by plunging, the bulk of it by George McAfee and Norman Standlee. Compared with this, New York gained only 73 yards by passing and 80 yards on the ground. The Bears also more than doubled the Giants in first downs, 20 to 8.[3]

After dismantling their second straight championship game opponent, this edition of the Monsters of the Midway seemed unbeatable. But the storm clouds of the Second World War would take their toll on the mighty Bears' roster, as it would all rosters throughout the league. Soon this terrific Bears squad would begin to part ways as Uncle Sam called them to a higher purpose. One Bear and one Giant from today's game would go to war and not return. Chicago back Young Bussey and New York end John Lummus would give their lives in the service of their country before the war was over.

SCORING

	1	2	3	4	Totals
New York Giants	6	0	3	0	9
Chicago Bears	3	6	14	14	37

1st Quarter: Chicago — FG — Snyder 14 yards —10:34.0 New York — TD — Franck 31-yard pass from Leemans (Cuff kick failed)—12:40. 2nd Quarter: Chicago — FG — Snyder 39 yards — 0:44. Chicago — FG — Snyder 37 yards — 9:58. 3rd Quarter: New York — FG — Cuff 17 yards — 4:25. Chicago — TD — Standlee 2-yard run (Snyder kick)—7:48. Chicago — TD — Standlee 7-yard run (Maniaci kick)—13:05. 4th Quarter: Chicago — TD — McAfee 5-yard run (Artoe kick)—10:55. Chicago — TD — Kavanaugh 42-yard fumble return (McLean kick) 14:51.

STARTING LINEUPS

New York Giants		Chicago Bears
Jim Poole	Left End	Dick Plasman
John Mellus	Left Tackle	Ed Kolman
Kayo Lundy	Left Guard	Danny Fortmann
Mel Hein	Center	Clyde Turner
Len Younce	Right Guard	Ray Bray
Bill Edwards	Right Tackle	Lee Artoe
Jim Lee Howell	Right End	John Siegal
Nello Falaschi	Quarterback	Sid Luckman
George Franck	Left Halfback	Ray Nolting
Ward Cuff	Right Halfback	Hugh Gallarneau
Tuffy Leemans	Fullback	Norman Standlee

(*Substitutions:* **New York**—Ends: Dick Horne, Will Walls, John Lummus; Center: Chet Gladchuck; Guards: Ben Sohn, Doug Oldershaw, Orville Tuttle; Tackles: Tony Blazine, Frank Cope; Backs: Howard Yeager, Hank Soar, Dom Principe, Kay Eakin, Len Eshmont, Clint "Red" McClain, Leland Shaffer, Andy Marefos. **Chicago**—Ends: Ken Kavenaugh, Hamp Pool, Bob Nowaskey, George Wilson; Centers: Albert Matuza, Bill Hughes; Tackles: Joe Stydahar, John Federovich, Joe Mihal; Guards: Aldo Forte, George Musso, Al Baisi, Hal Lahar; Backs: Bob Snyder, Ed McAfee, Bill Osmanski, Ray McLean, Bob Swisher, Joe Maniaci, Gary Famiglietti, Harry Clark, Young Bussey.)

Head Coaches: New York: Steve Owen; Chicago: George Halas.
Players' Shares: Chicago: $430.94; New York: $288.70.
Game Officials: Referee: Emil Heintz; Umpire: John Schommer; Head Linesman: Charles Berry; Field Judge: Chuck Sweeney.

TEAM STATISTICS

New York Giants		Chicago Bears
8	First Downs	20
/153	Total Offense Plays/Yards	/389
	Rushing Attempts	
80	Rushing Yardage	207
15	Pass Attempts	19
3	Pass Completions	11
20.0	Completion Percentage	57.9
73	Passing Yardage	182

0	Interceptions By	3
/5	Sacks/Yards Lost	/12
5	Punts	2
37.7	Punting Average	53.5
124	Punt Return Yards (KO)	36
2/2	Fumbles/Lost	3/1
3	Penalties	9
31	Penalty Yards	80

1942 NFL — The Redskins' Revenge

1942 NFL Championship Game — Chicago Bears (6) vs. Washington Redskins (14)

DECEMBER 13, 1942 — GRIFFITH STADIUM, WASHINGTON, D.C. — 36,006
WEATHER CONDITIONS: 15°F., OVERCAST, 12 MPH WINDS.
FIELD CONDITION: HARD, FIRM.

Washington's Griffith Stadium hosted the 1942 NFL Championship game as the Eastern Division champion Redskins squared off against the unbeaten Chicago Bears. George Halas had accepted a commission as a lieutenant commander and rejoined the Navy in 1942. When he left, he put his Bears in the hands of co-coaches Heartley "Hunk" Anderson and Luke Johnsos.[1] The Bears coasted through the regular season, easily dispatching each of their opponents. The Rams and Cardinals had come the closest to upending the Bears, but each lost by 14 points. Even on the road this afternoon, the Bears were the odds-on favorite to handily defeat the Redskins. But it was not to be. The 36,006 fans who took an afternoon's break from the seriousness of the war sensed an upset was in the air. Many had witnessed the 73–0 shellacking the Bears had given the Redskins two years earlier on this very field. They were ready for an upset and they would not go home disappointed.

The Redskins had had a terrific year themselves, losing only once during the regular season, a 14–7 defeat at home at the hands of the New York Giants on September 27. Washington had avenged that loss by turning that score around in New York on November 15. After dispatching the Lions 15–3 in front of a small crowd in Detroit, the Redskins brought their 10–1 record home for a championship rematch with their archrivals, the Chicago Bears and a chance to avenge the 73–0 loss from 1940. According to Redskin lineman Clyde Shugart, "We really wanted to get even with the Bears," Shugart said. "We hated them because of that tremendous score they ran up. Of course, we never liked them anyhow."[2]

Once again, Sammy Baugh and Sid Luckman, the two top passers in the league, were lining up against one another on the championship pitch. But for all of the vaunted offensive firepower on both sides of the ball, the first quarter was scoreless. The only real offensive burst at all came from Chicago's Ray Nolting, who gained 18 yards on a quick opener and followed that up with an 11-yard reception on a pass from Luckman. The closest either team came to posting any points was Lee Artoe's 45-yard field goal attempt that fell short. The Bears' defense would account for the first points of the game early in the second quarter.

That score came on a fumble recovery as Washington halfback Dick Todd pulled in a Baugh pass at the Chicago 44; he was hit immediately and fumbled. Chicago tackle Lee Artoe recovered the loose ball at the Chicago 48 and rumbled 52 yards for a touchdown. Artoe's conversion missed, but a minute and a half into the second quarter, the Bears now led 6–0.

After the Bears' kickoff, the Redskins found themselves first and ten on their own 28. In a play for field position no longer seen today, Sammy Baugh quick kicked and sent the ball 61 yards to the Chicago 11. The ploy worked. Though the Bears' Bill Osmanski ran for 32 yards on 6 carries, due to a Chicago holding penalty and a 4-yard loss, the Bruins never advanced the ball past their own 35-yard line. On 2nd and 8 from the Chicago 35, Luckman dropped back and threw long for former Columbia teammate John Siegel. The ball was picked off by Washington back Wilbur Moore at the Redskins' 44 and returned to the Bears' 42-yard line.

After the interception, Slingin' Sammy put it in high gear. On the third play from scrimmage, Baugh airmailed a 39-yard touchdown strike to Wilbur Moore, who pulled it in over Bears' defender John Petty and fell across the goal line to tie the game at 6. Bob Masterson's kick made the score 7–6 Redskins.

Masterson kicked off to the Bears' multi-talented halfback Scooter McLean, who returned the ball to the Chicago 29-yard line. There he was knocked out of bounds, but on the third play of that series, Luckman's pass for end George Wilson was intercepted by Cecil Hare at the Bears' 42. There have only been three men to play in the NFL with the last name Hare, but as luck would have it, two played for the Redskins in the early 1940s. Cecil and Ray were brothers who played at Gonzaga and then together with the Redskins in the early 1940s.[3]

Dick Todd carried on both first and second down for gains of 2 and 10 yards. Passes by Baugh to Cifers and Masterson then moved the ball to the Bears' 14, but there the Chicago defense tightened. On first and ten on the 14, Baugh's pass to Cifers was broken up by John Siegel. On second down, Joe Stydahar stopped Ray Hare at the line of scrimmage for no gain. On third down Baugh's pass into the end zone was knocked down by Maznicki. On fourth and ten, Baugh dropped back and launched a strike to Masterson in the south corner of the end zone, but McLean stepped between Masterson and the pass and knocked it away, thus ending the Redskin threat.[4]

The Bears killed time for the final seconds of the period and the half ended as Luckman's fourth down punt rolled safely out of bounds at midfield. The score remained 7–6 Redskins.

Entering the third period, the game was still tight, but Washington back Andy Farkas was about to begin a remarkable drive. The Washington possession began at the Bears' 43, where Farkas was tackled after receiving Luckman's punt. Hugging the ball closely to his number 44, he carried the ball on nine of the eleven plays of the Redskins' possession and gained 38 yards as the Redskins scored on a drive that seemed to sap the fight out of the Bears. Farkas scored the insurance touchdown on a one-yard plunge through the Chicago line. While he fumbled in the end zone, the officials ruled that the ball had broken the plane of the goal before coming loose and the touchdown stood. Masterson again converted on the PAT, making the score 14–6.

Twice in the fourth period the Bears threatened, but came away empty. Shortly after the quarter began, Chicago had moved the ball deep into Washington territory. On second and eight from the Redskins' 11, Maznicki rolled to his right and lobbed a pass into the end zone that was intercepted by Baugh, who downed it for a touchback, ending the Chicago threat.

Late in the game, Chicago put together another drive that started at their own 20. Canadian Charlie O'Rourke, in for Luckman, started things off quickly with two pass completions to McLean of 29 and 17 yards. The ball was now at the Redskins' 38. O'Rourke, under heavy pressure, fired a completion to end Bob Nowaskey, who was wrestled to the ground by Baugh at the two. The Redskins were then penalized half the distance to the goal for calling an illegal time out.

With first and goal from the Redskins' 1-yard line, things looked good for the Bears, but on first down Bill Osmanski ran into a burgundy wall as tackle Willie Wilkin and linebacker Dick Farman dropped him for a half yard loss. On second down Hugh Gallarneau barreled his way into the end zone over right guard, but the play was called back when the Bears were penalized for an illegal man in motion. On second and goal at the six, the Bears called again on Osmanski, who ground out three tough yards over left guard. On third down Osmanski was dropped for a 1-yard loss by tackle Dick Farman. On fourth and four O'Rourke passed into the end zone, but the ball bounced off Osmanski's outstretched fingertips, ending the Bears last-ditch effort.

Washington's defense did a great job containing Luckman. He completed just 5 of 12 passes for a net of zero yards. Sid threw 2 interceptions and never converted a big play. Boston College alum Charlie O'Rourke was the Bears' passing leader as he stepped in for Luckman in the fourth quarter and completed 4 of 6 passes for 119 yards, including the near miss by Osmanski in the end zone.

Chicago shut down Baugh reasonably effectively by holding him to 8 completions in 16 attempts for 84 yards, 1 touchdown and 2 interceptions. The Redskins' rushing leader was Andy Farkas, who gained 46 of Washington's 103 rushing yards. Bob Seymour added 34 to help balance the Washington attack.[5] They and their teammates felt they had at least partially settled a score with George Halas and the Bears. Due to the wartime manpower shortages, "it was not the same Chicago team which had humiliated Washington 73–0 in their last title meeting. And Sammy Baugh had not gained his own personal revenge against the stubborn Chicago defenders. But George Halas, on leave from the Navy, was there to see it and so was Redskin owner George Preston Marshall."[6] The Redskin locker room was a jubilant place that afternoon, not simply from the joy and satisfaction of winning a league championship, but also from the feeling that a huge monkey had been lifted off the team's back. While the score was close, the Redskins had ruined the Bears' shot at a perfect, undefeated season, and there was definitely satisfaction in that.[7]

SCORING

	1	2	3	4	Totals
Chicago Bears	0	6	0	0	6
Washington Redskins	0	7	7	0	14

1st Quarter: None. 2nd Quarter: Chicago — TD — Artoe 52-yard fumble return (Artoe kick failed) — 1:22. Washington — TD — Moore 39-yard pass from Baugh (Masterson kick) 8:56. 3rd Quarter: Washington — Farkas 1-yard run (Masterson kick) 7:25. 4th Quarter: None.

STARTING LINEUPS

Chicago Bears		Washington Redskins
Ed Kolman	Left End	Bob Masterson
Bob Nowaskey	Left Tackle	Willie Wilkin
Danny Fortmann	Left Guard	Dick Farman
Clyde Turner	Center	Ki Aldrich
Ray Bray	Right Guard	Steve Slivinski
Lee Artoe	Right Tackle	Bill Young
George Wilson	Right End	Ed Cifers
Sid Luckman	Quarterback	Ray Hare
Ray Nolting	Left Halfback	Sammy Baugh
Hugh Gallarneau	Right Halfback	Ed Justice
Gary Famiglietti	Fullback	Andy Farkas

(*Substitutions:* **Chicago** —Ends: John Siegal, Hamp Pool; Tackles: Joe Stydahar, Al Hoptowit; Guards: Chuck Drulis, Len Akin, George Musso; Center: none; Backs: Charlie O'Rourke, Harry Clark, Frank Maznicki, Ray McLean, John Petty, Bill Osmanski. **Washington**— Ends: none; Tackles: Ed Beinor, Fred Davis; Guards: Clem Stralka, Clyde Shugart; Center: none; Backs: Cecil Hare, Wilbur Moore, Dick Todd, Bob Seymour.)

Head Coaches: Washington: Ray Flaherty. Chicago: Heartley "Hunk" Anderson, Luke Johnsos.
Game Officials: Referee: Ronald Gibbs; Umpire: Carl Brubaker; Head Linesman: Charles Berry; Field Judge: Chuck Sweeney.
Players' Shares: Washington: $965.89; Chicago: $637.56

TEAM STATISTICS

Chicago Bears		Washington Redskins
10	First Downs	10
56	Total Offense Plays/Yards	49
38	Rushing Attempts	36
102	Rushing Yardage	104
18	Pass Attempts	13
5	Pass Completions	8
44.4	Completion Percentage	38.5
66	Passing Yardage	119
3	Interceptions By	2
6	Punts	1
42.0	Punting Average	52.5
13	Punt Return Yards	5
1/1	Fumbles/Lost	1/1
4	Penalties	4
47	Penalty Yards	26

1943 NFL — Bronko's Back!

1943 NFL Championship Game — Washington Redskins (21) vs. Chicago Bears (41)

DECEMBER 26, 1943 — WRIGLEY FIELD, CHICAGO — 34,320
WEATHER CONDITIONS: HIGH 20S, COLD, WIND GUSTS,
INTERMITTANT SUNSHINE AND CLOUDS.
FIELD CONDITION: HARD, FIRM.

December 26 was the date of the 1943 league championship game between old arch-rivals the Washington Redskins and the Chicago Bears. The game was played in Chicago's Wrigley Field in front of 34,320 fans. The sun on that post–Christmas Monday was bright, but the brilliance of the sun did little to stem the cold in Chicago. Wrigley Field was like an icebox.

The Redskins were led by quarterback Sammy Baugh and running backs Andy Farkas, Wilbur Moore, Ray Hare, Frank Seno, Bob Seymour and ends Joe Aguirre and Bob Masterson. The defense was sound, but overall, the Redskins were fortunate to be a good team in a mediocre division in 1943. The team had finished the regular season in a tie for the Eastern Division lead with the New York Giants. Both teams posted 6–3–1 records and a playoff was necessary on December 19 to determine an opponent for the Western champion Bears. In a quirk in scheduling, the Redskins and Giants met in the final two games of the season, both of which New York won, knotting the teams atop the NFL East. In the playoff — the third meeting of the bitter rivals in three weeks — the Redskins demolished the Giants 28 to 0. Farkas, bruised, scraped, and battered from the battle, told the press after the playoff that the Redskins were tired of the criticism they had received over the two weeks' previous losses to the Giants. "All of us played like hell because we knew we just had to win this one. Our linemen went out there with blood in their eyes and stopped 'em cold."[1]

The Bears had posted an 8–1–1 record behind the leadership of quarterback Sid Luckman. The team led the league in running, passing, and scoring. Luckman was ably supported by halfback Harry Clark, who had a career year, gaining 556 yards rushing and 535 yards through the air to lead the league with 1,091 offensive yards. Clark also gained 484 yards on kickoff and punt returns to give him 1,575 all-purpose yards on the season. It was the only time in his seven-year career that he would put up numbers anywhere near that level, but in 1943, he was tops. The Bears' supporting cast also included backs Gary Famiglietti, Dante Magnani, and Ray Nolting, who were the other big ground gainers, and Nolting, Hampton Poole, Jim Benton, and George Wilson, who assisted Luckman by air. Despite this impressive array of firepower, the Bears faced manpower shortages.

The Bears had been so depleted of manpower due to the war by 1943 that Halas, himself now serving in the South Pacific as a lieutenant commander in the United States Navy, had cabled co-coaches Hunk Anderson and Luke Johnsos, instructing them to contact Bronko Nagurski in Minnesota and ask him to come out of retirement. The Bronk had left football five years earlier, but had stayed in decent condition as a professional wrestler and by working on his farm. He was, however, 35 years old and fairly broken up from years on the gridiron. Nagurski, while attempting to enlist in the Army in 1942, was told by the doctor who was giving him his pre-induction physical, "Mr. Nagurski, I have already found six reasons to flunk you from military duty. I think it's time to stop counting."[2] Nagurski rejoined the Bears as a tackle and linebacker. He would not line up at fullback until the final game of the regular season. The Bears were playing the Cardinals in Comiskey Park and trailing 24 to 21 in the third quarter. Nagurski had been taking a few handoffs during practice the week before and Johnsos told him, "Why don't you go in and see what you can do? We're going no place this way."[3] Bronko did and proceeded to gain 84 yards on 16 carries and a touchdown to help lead the Bears to a 35–24 victory and the Western Division title.

Lieutenant Commander Halas was home on leave from the Navy and was visiting his team in the clubhouse prior to the game when Anderson and Johnsos told all of the press and visitors to clear out. "We've got a football game to play today. Everybody needs to clear out. That means you, too, George." Halas smiled and was only too happy to oblige.[4]

The game started slowly as the Redskins took possession of the ball early, but could not move it. In the first few minutes of the game, Washington's Sammy Baugh lofted a high, spiraling 44-yard punt that was caught and returned by Sid Luckman. Luckman started at his own 30 and headed up the left sideline when Baugh approached, ready to make the tackle. In the process, Sammy took a knee to the head and was out like a light. He was helped to the Washington bench, where he would remain for much of the game.

After a scoreless first period, the Redskins struck first. Late in the first period, George Cafego's 21-yard pass to Joe Aguirre was ruled complete due to a pass interference call. The completion moved the ball to the Chicago 3. On the very first play from scrimmage of the second quarter, fullback Andy Farkas drove the final one yard into the end zone. After a Bob Masterson kick, Washington took a 7–0 lead.

The lead, however, proved short-lived as Sid Luckman, playing in his final game before reporting for active duty in the Merchant Marine, went to work. Four straight completions including a 29-yard strike to Ray McLean got the Bears well downfield. Luckman then found Harry Clark on a screen pass that the Bears' halfback, behind a host of blockers, ran 31 yards for a touchdown. Clark ran the final yards with Washington back Ray Hare holding on to his waist. Bob Snyder's point after kick tied the score at seven.

Just before the half, the Bears put together an 8-play, 70-yard drive to take the lead. Luckman gained 39 yards on two carries. He hit Clark and Dante Magnani for pass completions and Bronko Nagurski picked up 19 yards on runs. On the final play of the drive, Nagurski, playing in the final game of his illustrious career, thundered over the goal line from the three for his last league touchdown. Bob Snyder again kicked the conversion and the Bears led at the half, 14–7. They would never look back.

Shortly after the touchdown, the Bears were surprised to see Redskins owner George Preston Marshall sitting on their team bench. End George Wilson walked over to Bears general manager Ralph Brizzolara and said, "I think that's Marshall sitting on the bench." Looking over at the man in the large hat and ankle-length raccoon coat who was sitting on the Bears' bench, Brizzolara confirmed that it was indeed the Redskins' owner. He immediately yelled at Marshall to get off the Bears' sideline and had him escorted by police off the field. Marshall then found an empty seat near the field. Halas, who was upstairs watching from the press box and having a good laugh at Marshall's antics, decided to get in on the fun. He prompted an usher to ask Marshall for his ticket. When the Redskins' owner could not produce one for that seat, he was again asked to leave.

Later, Marshall, finally back in his box, complained that he had only gone down on the field to visit with the Bears' players and coaches at halftime.[5] "You can say for me that Brizzolara is not a gentleman. And I'll never speak to him again."[6] After the game, Brizzolara claimed that Marshall had "snuck up on the Bears bench" and he fumed, "That's the lowest way there can be of trying to win a game, to sneak down to our bench, apparently to steal the instructions we're giving our players. Yes, we threw him out — not invited him out."[7] Both Marshall and Brizzolara were fined $500 for conduct unbecoming officials of the National Football League.

Sid Luckman opened the third quarter with two touchdown passes to Dante Magnani. The first was a pass in the flat for 36, the second a screen that Magnani carried for 64 yards. Snyder connected on the first conversion, but missed the second as the Bears opened up a sizeable 27–7 lead.

Washington managed another touchdown on an 17-yard pass from Sammy Baugh to Andy Farkas, and Masterson again connected on the point after to bring the score to 27–14. Baugh had been examined by the Redskins' physician and trainer and it was determined that his head was clear enough to return to the game.

Luckman went back to work, throwing two more touchdowns. The first was a 29-yarder to Jim Benton to cap a 56-yard drive. After that score, an onside kick gave the Bears possession again on their own 47. On third down on the Washington 40, Nagurski bulled over the line for a first down to keep the drive alive. Two plays later, Luckman threw 16 yards to Harry Clark for Clark's second touchdown of the day. Snyder connected on both touchdowns to increase the Chicago lead to 41–14.

Baugh hit Joe Aguirre late in the contest for a 26-yard score in which Aguirre also kicked the PAT, but the game ended right then, with the Bears celebrating a 41–21 victory and another league championship.

It had been a tough, brutal game. Harry Clark, who had caught two Luckman passes for touchdowns, had been battered all day, but played through several small injuries. Redskin tackle Joe Pasqua had to be helped from the field. Sammy Baugh was helped off after being hit on the first play of the game. He missed most of the game. And Bears guard Jim Logan wound up in Masonic Hospital.[8]

Luckman threw for five touchdowns on the day to set a new playoff record, breaking Baugh's six-year-old league mark. Baugh's record three had come in 1937 at the expense of the Bears. On the day, Sid went 14 for 26 for 276 yards. Baugh even connected with Bronko Nagurski in the final period for a 9-yard pickup. Baugh completed 7 of 11 for 106 yards, while backup George Cafego hit on 3 of 11 for another 76. The Bears outrushed Washington 168 yards to 45. Luckman was also on the receiving end of two interceptions in the third period.

Coach Hunk Anderson raved about the Bears' line. "That line of ours really rose to the occasion. Better even than the Green Bay game."[9]

The Bears needed Nagurski to grind out yardage and gain crucial first downs to keep their drives alive. At least five times during the contest the Bears were faced with fourth-down situations in which the Bronk was called upon. Each time, he delivered. In his final league game, Nagurski ran the ball eleven times for 34 yards and a touchdown — not a lot of yards, but when he got them, they were crucial. Bronk also caught one pass from Luckman for 9 yards.

It had been a long year for Nagurski. He had played well and done more than was asked of him. He said that he had played again "because George Halas wanted me to." After the game he was asked by reporters if he'd be back in 1944 for one more year. He said no, that he was retiring again. "It's not a game for 35-year-old men," he said. "After all, I can't go on taking care of George Halas all my life."[10]

SCORING

	1	2	3	4	Totals
Washington Redskins	0	7	7	7	21
Chicago Bears	0	14	13	14	41

1st Quarter: None. 2nd Quarter: Washington — TD — Farkas 1-yard run (Masterson kick) — 0:02. Chicago — TD — Clark 31-yard pass from Luckman (Snyder kick) — 2:23. Chicago — TD — Nagurski 3-yard run (Snyder kick) — 12:57. 3rd Quarter: Chicago — TD — Magnani 36-yard pass from Luckman (Snyder kick) — 2:59. Chicago — TD — Magnani 66-yard pass from Luckman (Snyder kick failed) — 11:33. Washington — TD — Farkas 17-yard pass from Baugh — (Masterson kick) — 13:44. 4th Quarter: Chicago — TD — Benton 29-yard pass from Luckman (Snyder kick) — 3:30. Chicago — TD — Clark 16-yard pass from Luckman (Snyder kick) — 11:50. Washington — TD — Aguirre 26-yard pass from Baugh (Aguirre kick) — 12:02.

STARTING LINEUPS

Washington Redskins		**Chicago Bears**
Bob Masterson	Left End	Jim Benton
Lou Rymkus	Left Tackle	Dom Sigillo
Clyde Shugart	Left Guard	Danny Fortmann
George Smith	Center	Clyde Turner
Steve Slivinski	Right Guard	George Musso
Joe Pasqua	Right Tackle	Al Hoptowit
Joe Aguirre	Right End	George Wilson
Ray Hare	Quarterback	Bob Snyder
Frank Seno	Left Halfback	Harry Clark
George Cafego	Right Halfback	Dante Magnani
Andy Farkas	Fullback	Bob Masters

(*Substitutions:* **Washington** —Ends: Alex Piasecky, Ted Lapka; Tackles: Willie Wilkin; Guards: Joe Zeno, Al Fiorentino, Tony Leon; Center: Ken Hayden; Backs: Sammy Baugh, Bob Seymour, Wilbur Moore, Billy Joe Gibson, Frank Akins, Leo Stasica. **Chicago**—Ends: Hamp Pool, Connie Mack Berry; Tackles: Bill Steinkemper, Al Babartsky, Fred Mundee; Guards: Tony Ippolito, Jim Logan; Center: Al Matuza; Backs: Ray McLean, Sid Luckman, Gary Famiglietti, Bronko Nagurski, Doug McEnulty, Ray Nolting, Joe Vodicka.)

Head Coaches: Washington: Arthur "Dutch" Bergman; Chicago: Heartley "Hunk" Anderson, Luke Johnsos.
Players' Shares: Chicago: $1,146. 87; Washington: $765.78.
Game Officials: Referee: Ronald Gibbs; Umpire: John Kelly; Head Linesman: Charles Berry; Field Judge: Edward Tryon.

TEAM STATISTICS

Washington Redskins		**Chicago Bears**
11	First Downs	14
46/232	Total Offense Plays/Yards	54/455
24	Rushing Attempts	27
50	Rushing Yardage	169
22	Pass Attempts	27
10	Pass Completions	14
45.8	Completion Percentage	55.6

182	Passing Yardage	286
0	Interceptions By	4
5	Punts	5
40.8	Punting Average	32.0
204	KO/Punt Return Yards	87
1/0	Fumbles/Lost	0/0
3	Penalties	9
35	Penalty Yards	81

1944 NFL — A Hidden Jewel

1944 NFL Championship Game — Green Bay Packers (14) vs. New York Giants (7)

DECEMBER 17, 1944 — POLO GROUNDS, NEW YORK — ATTENDANCE: 46,016
WEATHER CONDITIONS: MID 30S, CLEAR AND MILD.
FIELD CONDITION: MUDDY FROM THE WARM SUN THAWING THE FROZEN TURF.

Curley Lambeau won his sixth — and final — championship with the Green Bay Packers as his Western Division champs defeated the New York Giants 14–7 in the title game in New York on December 17. The game was described by Bob Considine of the INS as "a bruising intersectional playoff game."[1]

Like the other teams around the league, the Giants and Packers were mostly made up of a patchwork of servicemen on leave, returning retirees, and defense industry workers, but the Packers had Don Hutson. They also had a great fullback in Ted Fritsch and a big, strong line made up of Baby Ray, Buckets Goldenberg, Charley Brock, and Larry Craig.

The Giants had the league's best back in Bill Paschal, and they also had a big line with veteran Mel Hein, Frank Cope, Len Younce, and 2nd Lt. Al Blozis, on a weekend leave from the U.S. Army. In addition to Hein, the Giants had coaxed Ken Strong out of retirement, as well as former Packer star Arnie Herber, who was old and gray, but could still sling the pigskin.

While the war had put the game in perspective, it was still a great diversion for an afternoon from the steady diet of war news for the 46,016 fans who were in attendance at the Polo Grounds that day.

Green Bay finished the season at 8–2–0 after tearing out of the gate at 6–0. Their winning streak had come to an end at the hands of the Bears in a 21–0 trouncing on November 5 in Wrigley Field. Thinking they had righted their ship after a 42–7 routing of the Rams in Cleveland, the Pack experienced another meltdown, this time 24–0 to the Giants at the Polo Grounds on November 19. Their regular season ended in Comiskey Park with a 35–20 win over the hapless Card-Pitt combine, who were well on their way to a winless 0–10 season.

New York led the league with an 8–1–1 regular season, and despite their decisive victory over these Packers just a month earlier, they were considered the underdogs in the championship contest. This was due in part to the fact that the Giants were faced with a serious ankle injury to Paschal, the league's leading ground gainer. Prior to the game, they were unsure as to whether or not he could go at all. While he suited and played, Paschal's running that day was a shadow of what it had been all season long. He ran the ball two times for a total of four yards. Paschal carried the ball "for a mere three plays in the opening half and one in the second stanza and his absence was costly."[2] He was hurting so badly during the third period that he had to come out of the game for good. His biggest impact came as a decoy in the backfield. Though he was injured, the Packers had to key on him just in case. Without Paschal in the game, the Packers easily bottled up the New York ground game, holding them to a mere 24 yards rushing in the first half.[3]

The Giants, on the other hand, had to key on the healthy and always dangerous Hutson. While it was necessary, their overcompensating for Hutson may have cost them the game. The Giants often double- and triple-covered the perennial All-Pro receiver. While Hutson only caught two passes this afternoon, his mere presence on the field had a tremendous impact on the outcome of the game.[4]

To complicate matters for the New Yorkers, they also lost starting quarterback Len Calligaro on the third play of the game to a separated shoulder. Calligaro was a terrific lead blocker coming out of the backfield and his loss further stymied the Maramen's offensive power.

Neither team scored in the first stave, but Green Bay came alive after halfback Irv Comp returned a New York punt to midfield as the first period ended, and fullback Ted Fritsch pushed over two touchdowns before the half. On the first play of the drive, eleven-year veteran Joe Laws powered through the center of the line for 17 yards. Fritsch then followed up with his own 27-yard gain. With first and goal, the Giants' defense held for three plays. On fourth down Lambeau decided to go for the touchdown. Fritsch took the ball into the end zone on a 2-yard plunge behind a Buckets Goldenberg block. Hutson kicked the try successfully to give the boys from Green Bay a 7–0 lead.

The second score had a lot to do with Don Hutson. The drive started at their own 38 and moved along nicely before stalling just short of midfield. Green Bay faced third and three at the their own 46 when they looked to the long, lean Alabama All-American to keep the possession alive. The tough New York secondary had been all over Hutson so far and the Giants' pass rush had kept Irv Comp on his toes. Green Bay had completed just three of eleven passes to that point and the Giants had picked off three. This time, however, Hutson responded by beating Giant fullback Howie Livingston and catching a Comp pass for a 24-yard gain that put the ball on the Giants' 30.

Again, the New York defense showed resolve, holding the Packers to two yards on the next three plays. On fourth down, every eye in the stadium was once again on number 14. At the snap, Hutson broke to his right and virtually the entire defense went with him. With the Giants' defenders keying on Hutson, the 210-pound Fritsch was virtually unnoticed as he sprinted down the middle of the field. Fritsch found himself wide open at the 5-yard line, where he grabbed a 28-yard touchdown pass from Comp. Hutson then kicked the conversion to give the Pack a 14–0 lead as the teams headed to their locker rooms for halftime.

But the New Yorkers weren't about to give up without a fight. They played a strong second half. Late in the third period Howard Livingston cut in front of Hutson and picked off a Comp pass, returning it to his own 45. New York then mounted an inspired drive. The Packers helped the Giants' cause by getting flagged for pass interference, placing the ball on the Green Bay 42.

Herber then launched a 41-yard rocket to Frank Liebel that set up a first and goal situation at the Green Bay 1 as the third quarter ended. Comp had Liebel well covered on the play until he slipped on the wet and muddy turf and crashed to the ground, leaving Liebel free to pull in Herber's pass unmolested. A last-ditch effort by Joe Laws knocked him out of bounds just short of the end zone. New York halfback Ward Cuff took the ball up the middle and into the end zone on the first play of the fourth quarter. Forty-year-old Ken Strong kicked the conversion to tighten the score at 14–7, but the Giants would get no closer.

Green Bay began to play conservative football for the rest of the day. They were more concerned with pinning the Giants deep in their own territory and running out the clock than striving for another score. Respectable punting by Lou Brock and Ted Fritsch helped their cause.

Midway through the final quarter, the Maramen passed midfield on a pass from Arnie Herber to Frank Leibel that put the ball on the Green Bay 45. The drive came to a halt, however, when Herber fumbled on third down. He recovered the ball, but the muff forced a punt on the next play.[5]

The New York fans pleaded with their Giants to march down the field once more and the team responded with a final drive. Late in the fourth quarter, with the Giants on the move, Herber let go a deep pass, but Green Bay back Paul Duhart picked it off at the Packers' 20. It was to be the Giants' last gasp that afternoon.

"As usual, the game was decided 'up front,' where this time the edge went to the Packers. They hit harder, faster, more cleanly."[6]

While Herber's passes were a bit erratic and several of his throws were dropped, he had all in all a respectable day, completing 8 passes for 114 yards. But he also threw 4 interceptions: one went to Duhart, and the other 3 were picked off by 34-year-old all-purpose halfback Joe Laws. With Paschal and Calligaro injured, the Packers were able to key on Herber and they certainly knew the longtime Green Bay star's tendencies. At the end of the day it was simply too much for Herber to overcome as Laws feasted on Arnie's passes. Laws was also a force on offense as he gained an impressive 74 yards on 13 carries.

All in all, the game was pretty entertaining. It was close, with the Giants driving for the tying score in the closing minutes of the final quarter. The game had stellar defensive play and several exciting offensive drives. The contest also set a playoff record for gross receipts at $121,703.

On a sad note, it was Al Blozis's last game. He had played well enough in the contest to gain mention in the Monday newspapers. The day after the game, Blozis reported back to his infantry unit that was about to ship out for Europe. He was killed in action in the Vosges Mountains in northeast France near the town of Colmar on January 31, 1945, just 45 days after he had played in the championship game. Lt. Blozis was killed by a German sniper while searching for two of his men behind enemy lines. The two had failed to return from a reconnaissance mission that Blozis had sent them on earlier in the day and he heroically set about locating them. His grave in the St. Avold Cemetery in France is marked by a plain white cross. The simple inscription reads "Alfred C. Blozis 2 Lt 110 inf 28 div New Jersey Jan 31 1945."[7]

SCORING

	1	2	3	4	Total
Green Bay Packers	0	14	0	0	14
New York Giants	0	0	0	7	7

1st Quarter: None. 2nd Quarter: Green Bay — TD — Fritsch 1-yard run (Hutson kick) — 2:26. Green Bay — TD — Fritsch 28-yard pass from Comp (Hutson kick) — 13:43. 3rd Quarter: None. 4th Quarter: New York — TD — Cuff 1-yard run (Strong kick) — 0:03.

STARTING LINEUPS

Green Bay Packers		New York Giants
Don Hutson	Left End	O'Neal Adams
Buford "Baby" Ray	Left Tackle	Frank Cope
Bill Kuusisto	Left Guard	Len Younce,
Charley Brock	Center	Mel Hein
Buckets Goldenberg	Right Guard	Jim Sivell
Paul Berenzey	Right Tackle	Vic Carroll
Harry Jacunski	Right End	Frank Liebel
Larry Craig	Quarterback	Len Calligaro
Irv Comp	Left Halfback	Arnie Herber
Joe Laws	Right Halfback	Ward Cuff
Ted Fritsch	Fullback	Howie Livingston

(*Substitutions:* **Green Bay:** End: Ray Wehba; Tackles: Milburn "Tiny" Croft, Adolph Schwammel; Guards: Pete Tinsley, Glen Sorenson; Center: none; Backs: Lou Brock, Don Perkins, Paul Duhart. **New York:** Ends: John Weiss, Verlin Adams; Tackle: Al Blozis; Guards: Charles Avedisian, Frank Umont; Backs: Bill Petrilas, Bill Paschal, Carl Kinscherf, Joe Sulaitis, Hubert Barker, Ken Strong.)

Head Coaches: Green Bay: Curley Lambeau; New York: Steve Owen.
Players' Shares: Green Bay: $1,449.71; New York: $814.36.
Officials: Referee: Ronald Gibbs; Umpire: C.H. Brubaker; Head Linesman: Charles Berry; Field Judge: Eugene Miller; Timer: W. Friesell.

TEAM STATISTICS

Green Bay Packers		New York Giants
11	First Downs	10
/237	Total Offense Plays/Yards	/199
47	Rushing Attempts	27
184	Rushing Yardage	101
11	Pass Attempts	22
3	Pass Completions	8
27.3	Completion Percentage	36.4
74	Passing Yardage	114
4	Interceptions By	3
10	Punts	10
38.5	Punting Average	41.0
88	Punt Return Yards	31
0	Fumbles/Lost	0
4	Penalties	11
48	Penalty Yards	90

STATISTICS

Rushing GB — 47–184–3.9: Laws 13–72–5.5; Fritsch 18–59–3.3; Comp 7–42–6.0; Duhart 7–15–2.1; Perkins 2–(-)4–(-)2.0.

Rushing NY — 27–101–3.7: Cuff 12–76–6.3; Livingston 12–22–1.8; Paschal 2–4–2.0; Sulaitis 1–(-)1–(-)1.0.

Receiving GB — Hutson 2–46–23.0; Fritsch 1–28–28.0.

Receiving NY — Liebel 3–70–23.3; Cuff 2–23–11.5; Livingston 2–21–10.5; Barker 1–0–0.0.

Passing GB —11–3–74–3: Comp 10–3–74–3; L. Brock 1–0–0–0.

Passing NY (Herber) — 22–8–114–4.

Punting GB —10–38.5: L. Brock 6–36.8; Fritsch 4–41.0.

Punting NY (Younce) —10–41.0.

1945 NFL — Of Cold and Crossbars

1945 NFL Championship — Washington Redskins (14) vs. Cleveland Rams (15)

DECEMBER 16, 1945 — CLEVELAND MUNICIPAL STADIUM, CLEVELAND — 32,178
WEATHER CONDITIONS: GRAY SKIES, BITTER COLD, TEMPERATURES
IN THE LOW SINGLE DIGITS, HEAVY WIND GUSTS.
FIELD CONDITION: FROZEN, LIGHT PATCHES OF SNOW AND ICE.

On August 7, 1945, the Washington Redskins had journeyed to Cleveland, Ohio, to play the Rams in a preseason game. The war in Europe had ended three months earlier and the fighting in the Pacific was ending quickly. The dropping of the atomic bombs on Hiroshima and Nagasaki would make an armed invasion of the Japanese home islands unnecessary. The temperature in Cleveland hovered around 100 degrees.

Four months later, the war was completely over, and on the morning of December 16, the mercury in Cleveland hovered close to zero. Wind chill factors had not yet been introduced, but when the gusts came in off Lake Erie, suffice to say, it was bitter cold. The brutal wind whipping across the field would directly affect the outcome of the game.

A blizzard had covered Cleveland the previous week. More snow was predicted for game week. In an attempt to keep additional snow off and the heat in, the playing field at Cleveland's Municipal Stadium had been covered with a tarp and 9,000 bales of hay.

The Redskin marching band had made the trip from Washington to support their team as they squared off in the championship game against the Cleveland Rams. But it was so cold in Cleveland on that December 16 that the musical instruments froze, relegating the band to the role of spectators. The 8–2–0 Redskins were again led by Slingin' Sammy Baugh, who was coming off a terrific season in which he threw for 1,699 yards and 11 touchdowns against only four interceptions. Baugh had an unbelievable completion percentage of 70.3 percent. Rookie Steve Bagarus caught 35 of those passes for 517 yards.

But as good as Washington was in 1945, the Rams, for the first time in franchise history, were the team to beat in the NFL. They had posted a 9–1–0 record in 1945, but before this season, the Rams had never finished above .500. They joined the league in 1937 and were now in their eighth season of play. They sat out the 1943 season due to the manpower shortage created by the war. Not only were they short of players, but both of the Rams' owners (Dan Reeves and Fred Levy, Jr.) were called away on active duty. During this period of hibernation, Reeves bought out Levy.

Just after 6:00 A.M. on that dark Sunday morning, a large group of men began the task of removing the ground covering. It took hours of backbreaking work as they first shoveled off the new snow, rolled up the frozen tarp, and then removed the hay. On the thermometer, the temperature registered a frigid eight degrees below zero and the strong winds off Lake Erie chilled the grounds crew to the bone. By game time, much of the hay was piled up around the players' benches on each sideline, where it wound up insulating the players' legs against the cold.

It was a perfect day for staying home by the fireside, but no fewer than 32,178 eager fans assembled in the cavernous ballpark. Still, the frigid weather held down the crowd to less than half of Municipal Stadium's capacity of 77,569.

The cold temperatures, strong winds and frozen playing surface all played major roles in the outcome of the game. Getting much traction in football cleats would be difficult. Al DeMao, Washington's rookie center out of Duquesne, recalled, "From twenty yards into the end zone it was frozen like a sheet of ice." Curiously, before the game, Washington coach Dud DeGroot had agreed to a pact with the Rams' Adam Walsh not to wear the sneakers that the Redskins had brought along in case the field was frozen. The Rams had thought only to wear their cleats, which provided only marginal traction on the slick, rock-hard playing field. Apparently Abe Cohen wasn't available so Walsh, realizing his predicament, pleaded with DeGroot not to outfit his Redskins in the sneakers. In a singular moment of insanity, DeGroot agreed. It was a decision that may well have cost his team the game. Washington receiver Wayne Millner said later, "There's no doubt we would have won with the better footing."[1]

All week long, football fans had been talking about the game with a special emphasis on the match-up between two great passers, Cleveland's Bob Waterfield and Washington's Sammy Baugh. But the wind, so strong and erratic, not only froze the field and chilled the fans, it affected the aerial game as well.

The Rams took the field in their gold jerseys with royal blue trim, white pants, gold hose with three blue stripes, and gold helmets, while the Redskins' jerseys were burgundy with gold numbers. Burgundy helmets and hose, along with gold pants, finished the look.

The game was physical and on the opening play of the game, Washington rusher Frank Akins' gained 8 yards, but he suffered a broken nose when he collided with Rams linebacker Riley "Rattlesnake" Matheson.

Later in the first quarter, Cleveland started a drive on their own 21-yard line and drove downfield on the strength of three Waterfield to Jim Benton passes. The highlight was a 30-yarder that moved the ball to the Washington 14. The Redskin defense then kicked in, with Wayne Millner dropping halfback Fred Gerkhe for a 6-yard loss. The Rams bore down again, but fell short of pay dirt when the Jim Gillette was stopped five yards short of the goal. There the Redskins took over on downs.

On first down, the Redskins, in the custom of the day, decided to play for field position. Sammy Baugh dropped back in the end zone in punt formation, but he fumbled the snap. With Rams defenders swarming, he picked up the ball and aiming at the sidelines, intentionally grounded it. The penalty put the ball on the 2-yard line. On second down, Baugh fooled the Cleveland defenders, who expected another punt attempt. Instead of a kick, he attempted an unexpected pass from his own end zone to end Wayne Millner, who had run a crossing pattern and was open and streaking up the right flat. Millner recalled, "In the first quarter I managed to get into the clear. I could almost taste the touchdown as Sam started to throw the ball. But his pass never reached me."[2] As he let go the pass, a terrific gust of wind caught the ball and veered it into the goal post. At first, there was a great deal of confusion over how to rule on the play. The officiating crew consulted the rule book, "which clearly stated at that time that because the ball had not left the end zone, the play was ruled a safety. Two points for Cleveland."[3] According to the Associated Press, "The ball was at the height of its trajectory when it hit squarely against the goal post and bounced back into the end zone. Slingin' Sammy fell on it, but it went for an automatic safety and the two points that meant the game."[4] With the safety, Cleveland led by a score of 2–0 with 5:40 left in the 1st quarter. Later, Baugh, still frustrated by the event, remembered, "I had a damn touchdown. Wayne was clear out there, but I couldn't get as much on the ball as I usually did. We were going against the wind in that first quarter, and as soon as that ball left my hand, up came a gust and lifted it right into the crossbar. 'Damn!' I said as soon as that ball hit that post. I was upset about not completing the pass. I had no idea about a safety until the referee made the signal, but even then I was still more damn mad at missing a touchdown than at Cleveland getting two points."[5]

Shortly after the freak safety, Baugh received a blow to the ribs and the injury took him out of the game. He played only sporadically the rest of the day. Sammy's substitute was Frank Filchock, who filled in ably, throwing for 178 yards and two touchdowns.

At the midpoint of the second quarter, Washington center Ki Aldrich intercepted a Waterfield pass and returned it to his own 48. From there, the Redskins began to drive the ball downfield. A couple of hard runs and a roughing penalty against the Rams set up the first Washington score, which came on a 38-yard strike from Filchock to Steve Bagarus. Bagarus got by Waterfield, pulled in Filchock's pass at the twelve and sprinted across the goal line. A Joe Aguirre kick put the Redskins ahead 7–2.

Waterfield then went to work. Starting at their own 30, halfback Jim Gillette, who by himself tripled the entire Redskin ground total for the day, rushed twice, gaining 24 of his eventual 101 yards. Fred Gehrke added notable yardage on a run to the outside. Waterfield then connected twice through the air with Jim Benton, the second time on a 37-yard touchdown pass to regain the lead for Cleveland just before the half. A Waterfield conversion made the score 9–7 in favor of the Rams. The goal posts were once again friendly to the hometown Rams as the kick glanced off Washington tackle John Koniszewski's hand and into the crossbar, but it bounced upwards and through the uprights rather than deflecting away. Shortly afterwards, the teams retreated to the warmth of the locker rooms.

Waterfield picked up in the third where he'd left off before the half. After taking the opening kickoff he marched the Rams 81 yards for an insurance touchdown. A combination of ground and aerial strikes moved them into Redskin territory. He hit Benton to advance to their own 40. The rest of the series became the Jim Gillette Show as the Rams' halfback swept around left end three times to advance the ball to the Redskin 39. A penalty pushed the Rams back to the 44, but Waterfield was undeterred. On the next play he hit Gillette with a high toss down the middle that the 6'1" Virginian jumped over three defenders to pull in at the 14. The Rams' halfback then lumbered the rest of the way for the score. After the game Waterfield stated, "It was so cold I remember thinking at the time, 'How do these guys hold the ball?' I didn't have any trouble with the ball, but then I didn't have to catch it."[6] On the point after attempt, Waterfield's kick missed wide right and the score stood 15–7 in favor of Cleveland.

Later in the third, Filchock tried his best to get the Redskins back into the game. Rookie halfback Bob De Fruiter returned the kickoff 15 yards to the Washington 44. Steve Bagarus then caught a Filchock pass and ran all the way to the Ram 6-yard line before being caught from behind by halfback Fred Gehrke. On the next play Filchock, under heavy pressure, was sacked by Cleveland tackle Gil Bouley for an 11-yard loss. Washington made it back to the 9 on a shovel pass from Filchock to back Sal Rosato. The Redskins found the end zone for the final time that day when Filchock connected with Bob Seymour on an eight-yard pitch. Coupled with Aguirre's kick, the Redskins closed to within one point of the Rams at 15–14.

The fourth quarter was a back-and-forth duel in which possession changed eight times. After Washington center Ki Aldrich recovered a Pat West lateral, the Redskins took over on their own 24. Filchock continued his heroics as he fired a 44-yard rope to Dye at the Cleveland 31. The Rams' defense then held the Redskins to just 7 more yards over the next 3 plays, forcing a Washington field goal try. With the injured Baugh holding, Joe Aguirre set himself for the long 31-yard kick. With the Rams coming hard, the snap was clean, the set was right, and the kick long enough. The Municipal Stadium crowd held its collective breath. As the ball passed the uprights, referee Ronald Gibbs waved his arms furiously. No good. With the help of the gusting lake winds, the ball had sailed wide right. The Cleveland fans breathed again.

The Rams' offense took over, but again stalled and were forced to kick. Steve Bagarus fielded Waterfield's punt and wound his way up field to the Redskin 42-yard line. With the game in the closing minutes, Washington began what was to be their last-ditch effort to take the lead and the championship.

With the Redskins at midfield and driving, Filchock handed off to Bagarus, who took off on an end run to the right. Suddenly, he reversed field and swept across the open plain and down the left sideline with two Rams in hot pursuit. One of those Clevelanders was Waterfield, who dove fully extended and tripped Bagarus up with his left hand in what may well have amounted to a game-saving tackle. At this point the Redskins' drive stalled. Another Aguirre field goal try, this time from 31 yards out, failed, leaving the Redskins still down by a single point.

Washington was able to regain possession one last time, but on their first play from scrimmage Ram defensive back Albie Reisz picked off a Filchock pass. He returned it to the Redskins' 29, where Waterfield took a knee to burn the final seconds and protect the Rams' razor-thin lead.

The 1945 championship was in the books. The Cleveland Rams had won their first and only world championship. By the start of the 1946 season, Municipal Stadium would be the home of the AAFC Cleveland Browns and the Rams' home field would be the Los Angeles Coliseum.

Despite the loss, Frankie Filchock played wonderfully in relief of Baugh. He completed 8 of 14 passes for 178 yards and 2 TDs. In this one game he passed for more yardage than he did in the whole regular season. Slingin' Sam, who left after the first period, completed only 1 of 6 passes for 7 yards.

The game was Redskins coach DeGroot's last with Washington. He was dismissed by Marshall after the loss. Rumor has it Marshall fired him at halftime for his decision to have his players wear cleats rather than the sneakers they had brought with them from Washington.

The hero for the Rams was Bob Waterfield, who passed for 192 yards on 14 completions in 27 tries. He also threw 2 touchdowns and kicked an extra point. Other heroes were Jim Gillette, who ran for 101 yards on 17 carries, and Jim Benton, who caught 9 passes for 125 yards and 1 TD.

The Ram line also drew accolades. On both offense and defense, the line held true throughout the contest. Center Mike Scarry, guards Mike Lazetich and Riley Matheson, and tackles Eberle Schultz and Gil Bouley, yielded only 32 rushing yards to Washington backs.

Washington Post columnist Shirley Povich summed up the game nicely when he pointed out that "the goal posts have been the twelfth man in the Rams' lineup."[7]

SCORING

	1	2	3	4	Totals
Washington	0	7	7	0	14
Cleveland	2	7	6	0	15

1st Quarter: Cleveland — Safety — Automatic — Baugh's pass from inside of the end zone hit goal post. 2nd Quarter: Washington — TD — Bagarus 38-yard pass from Filchock (Aguirre kick). Cleveland — TD — Benton 37-yard pass from Waterfield (Waterfield kick). 3rd Quarter: Cleveland — TD — Gilette 53-yard pass from Waterfield (Waterfield kick failed). Washington — TD — Seymour 8-yard pass from Filchock (Aguirre kick). 4th Quarter: None.

STARTING LINEUPS

Washington Redskins		**Cleveland Rams**
Wayne Millner	Left End	Floyd Konetsky
Earl Audet	Left Tackle	Eberle Schultz
John Adams	Left Guard	Riley Matheson
Ki Aldrich	Center	Michael Scarry
Marvin Whited	Right Guard	Milan Lazetich
Joe Ungerer	Right Tackle	Gilbert Bouley
Doug Turley	Right End	Steve Pritko
Cecil Hare	Quarterback	Albie Reisz
Bob Seymour	Left Halfback	Steve Nemeth
Merle Condit	Right Halfback	Jim Gillette
Frank Akins	Fullback	Pat West

(*Substitutions:* **Washington** — Ends: Alex Piasecky, Joe Aguirre, Les Dye; Tackles: Fred Davis, John Koniszewski; Guards: Ev Sharp, Al Lolotai, Elzaphan "Zip" Hanna, Clem Stralka; Center: Al DeMao; Backs: Steve Bagarus, Sammy Baugh, Bill deCorrevont, Frank Filchock, Sal Rosato, Dick Todd, Bob deFruiter. **Cleveland** — Ends: Raymond Hamilton, Howard Hickey, Jim Benton; Tackles: Leslie Lear, Rudolph Sikich, Roger Eason; Guards: Leonard Levy, Arthur Mergenthal; Centers: Robert deLauer, Roger Harding; Backs: Bob Waterfield, George Koch, Don Greenwood, Fred Gehrke.)

Head Coaches: Washington: Dudley DeGroot; Cleveland: Adam Walsh.
Players' Shares: Cleveland: $1,469.74; Washington: $902.47.
Game Officials: Referee: Ronald Gibbs; Umpire: Harry Robb; Head Linesman: Charles Berry; Field Judge: William Downes.

TEAM STATISTICS

Washington Redskins		**Cleveland Rams**
8	First Downs	14
3	- Rushing	9
4	- Passing	4
1	- Penalty	1
54/214	Total Offense Plays/Yards	65/372
34	Rushing Attempts	38
35	Rushing Yardage	180
20	Pass Attempts	27
9	Pass Completions	14
45.0	Completion Percentage	51.9
179	Passing Yardage	192
2	Interceptions By	2
7	Punts	8
36.0	Punting Average	38.0
5/67	Punt Return Yards	5/34

2/58/29	Kickoff Returns/Yards/Avg.	3/38/12.7
/1	Fumbles/Lost	/1
5	Penalties	6
34	Penalty Yards	60

1946 AAFC — The Browns Take Center Stage

1946 All-America Football Conference Championship Game
New York Yankees (9) vs. Cleveland Browns (14)

DECEMBER 22, 1946 — MUNICIPAL STADIUM, CLEVELAND — 41,181
WEATHER CONDITIONS: 31°F., SNOW FLURRIES.
FIELD CONDITION: CHIEFLY CLEARED OF SNOW, BUT FROZEN; SNOW RINGED THE
FIELD WHERE PILED UP AFTER A 5" SNOWFALL ON FRIDAY AND SATURDAY.

An impressive 41,181 fans braved the cold and snow flurries on December 22, 1946, to attend the first AAFC championship game at Cleveland's Municipal Stadium. Just a year before, Clevelanders had come out in even worse conditions to watch the then–Cleveland Rams defeat the Washington Redskins on the same playing field for the NFL championship. This day, while still snowy, was 30 degrees warmer; so the attendance, while off, was still 9,000 better than the previous year. Snow had fallen in the Cleveland area for several days. An accumulation of 5 inches was measured on Friday and Saturday alone. The tarpaulin that had been covering the field was cleared of snow that was then piled up around the edge of the seats ringing the field. The field was clear, but frozen, and the persistent flurries would leave a dusting of snow on the field throughout the contest.

The Cleveland Browns, champions of the new league's Western Conference, squared off against the Eastern Conference champion New York Yankees. The two rivals had met twice during the regular season with both contests being played under sloppy conditions. After three quarters of close football, the Browns pulled away in the first game to win 24–7. In the rematch in New York two weeks later, the Browns eked out a win despite being outgained by more than 3 to 1 by the Yankees' single-wing offense.

The favored Browns came out passing behind quarterback Otto Graham. After completing his first pass to Dante Lavelli for a 20-yard pickup, Graham drove the Browns to the Yankees' 31. Cleveland looked ready to score when New York defensive back Eddie Prokop intercepted Graham's next pass near the line of scrimmage and returned it 38 yards to the Browns' 31.

Starting with excellent field position, New York continued to move the ball well as Ace Parker connected with Jack Russell at the 19 for a first down. A Spec Sanders run to the 7 was good for another, but the Cleveland defense held the Yankees at the four. Yankees kicker Harvey Johnson then kicked a 12-yard field goal to put New York up 3–0.

The Browns then started an 80-yard drive that gave them a first and goal at the New York 6. The drive started out with what appeared to be an 82-yard touchdown reception from Graham to Dub Jones, but the officials said that Jones stepped out on the Cleveland 35 and called the play back to that point. Graham, undaunted and pleased with a new set of downs, drove his team down to the Yankees' 6. There, the stubborn Yankee defensive unit would only surrender three more yards in three plays. On fourth and goal from the 3, Graham was dropped for a 13-yard loss and the ball went over to New York on downs. The Yankees still led 3–0 and the Browns knew they were in for a long afternoon.

The Browns broke into Yankee territory again in the second quarter. Lou Groza's 52-yard field goal attempt fell well short. Groza had sprained his left ankle and was having trouble planting his leg for kicks.

Late in the second quarter, Cleveland took possession after the versatile Graham returned an Ace Parker punt to his own 31. Behind Graham's golden arm, the Browns put together a 69-yard drive. Graham threw for 50 of those yards on 7 straight completions to Dub Jones, Mac Speedie, and Dante Lavelli. Those completions moved the ball in rapid fashion to the New York 12. Marion Motley then took over, first gaining 11 yards and then scoring on a 1-yard plunge. Groza converted, putting the Browns ahead 7–3.

At halftime the fans were treated to a festive show that included George Bud's Musical Majorettes, who sang "Santa Claus Is Coming to Town" and "White Christmas." Brown's mascot Tommy Flynn played Santa during the show.

A third quarter drive by Cleveland was started when Browns defensive end John Yonakor recovered an Ace Parker fumble at the New York 36. Three plays yielded only 6 yards and the possession ended in a second missed field goal by Groza, this one wide from 42 yards out.

The Yankees took over at the 20 and mounted a drive that took them 80 yards in 10 plays. Parker connected with Russell on three passes that gained half of the yardage on the drive. Sanders carried for the other half the yardage gained, carrying the ball over from the two on second and goal. Harvey Johnson's extra point attempt was blocked by Cleveland tackle Lou Rymkus and the score was 9–7 late in the third quarter.

On the next possession, the Browns threatened again when Motley broke through the line and into the New York secondary. After a 51-yard scamper, New York back Eddie Prokop finally caught from behind the speeding 238-pounder. When the drive stalled at the New York 12, Groza trotted out and promptly missed his third field goal attempt of the day. It clearly was not the AAFC scoring leader's day.

New York took over at their own 20, but went three and zero and were forced into a punting situation on fourth down. As Parker kicked the ball, Cleveland tackle Lou Saban got a hand on it and diverted the ball's path, giving the Browns the ball on the New York 32.

The Browns could only gain a couple of yards and attempted another field goal. Instead of the usually automatic Groza, Paul Brown tried another tackle, Chet Adams. Whatever kicking affliction Groza had contracted must have been contagious, because Adams missed, too, this time from 37 yards out. The score remained 9–7 in New York's favor.

As the middle of the fourth quarter approached, Cleveland started a drive at their own 26-yard line. Motley got things started as he carried for 9 yards on first down. From the 35, Graham dropped back and fired a pass to Edgar Jones, who made a shoe-level grab at the New York 42, good for a new set of downs. On second down, Graham fired a pass to Dante Lavelli, who corralled the bullet at the 39. He lateraled to Don Greenwood, who was brought down on the New York 34. On third down, Jones carried the ball for a 7-yard pickup to the 27. Graham then pitched wide to Tom Colella, who moved the ball to the 16. Though within three points of taking the lead, the Browns were not about to settle for another field goal try. They knew they could not count on the kicking game that day. From the 16, Graham found Dante Lavelli along the right sideline for a completion and the score. Groza returned to his kicking duties and this time he split the uprights to extend the Browns' lead to 14–9 with just 4 minutes remaining.

As the game wound down, New York, down by five points and the game still within reach, began to drive once more. Spec Sanders returned Cleveland's kickoff to the Cleveland 45. With excellent field position and a minute to play, the Yankees knew they had a chance.

Things did not start too well for the Yanks as a host of Cleveland defenders caught halfback Eddie Prokop in the backfield on first down for a 14-yard loss. On second down, Ace Parker connected with Perry Schwartz to regain the lost yardage and bring about a third and ten situation. Not great, but there was still a chance. The hopes of the New York faithful were dashed, however, on third down when Otto Graham picked off Parker's pass at the Cleveland 34. According to the Associated Press report, "Graham jumped between a pair of New Yorkers with such fury, he lost a part of his shirt — but he came up with the ball."[1] Cleveland then ran the ball three times and punted deep. New York had time for just one play, a Parker to Prokop pass that netted only 5 yards, and the game ended there.

The Browns were the champions. They finished the season with a 12–2 regular season record and a championship game win, and they had defeated the Yankees three times. During the game, Graham completed 16 of 27 passes for 213 aerial yards and Motley carried the ball 13 times for 98 yards. In the losing locker room, Ace Parker spoke of the Browns and told reporters, "They were a wonderful team."[2]

SCORING

	1	2	3	4	Totals
New York Yankees	3	0	6	0	9
Cleveland Browns	0	7	0	7	14

1st Quarter: New York — FG — H. Johnson — 12 yards — 5:31. 2nd Quarter: Cleveland — TD — Motley — 1-yard run (Groza kick) — 13:58. 3rd Quarter: New York — TD — S. Sanders 2-yard run (H. Johnson kick blocked) — 9:28. 4th Quarter: Cleveland — TD — Lavelli 16-yard pass from Graham (Groza kick) — 10:47.

STARTING LINEUPS

New York Yankees		Cleveland Browns
Jack Russell	Left End	Mac Speedie
Bruiser Kinard	Left Tackle	Ernie Blandin
John Baldwin	Left Guard	Ed Ulinski
Tom Robertson	Center	Mike Scarry
Chuck Riffle	Right Guard	Lin Houston
Nate Johnson	Right Tackle	Lou Rymkus
Bruce Alford	Right End	Dante Lavelli
Lloyd Cheatham	Quarterback	Otto Graham
Spec Sanders	Left Halfback	Edgar Jones
Lowell Wagner	Right Halfback	Don Greenwood
Eddie Prokop	Fullback	Marion Motley

(*Substitutions:* **New York** — Ends: Bob Masterson, Perry Schwartz, Harry Burrus, Mel Conger; Tackles: Roman Bentz, Darrell Palmer, Roman Piskor; Guards: Mike Karazin; Center: Lou Sossamon; Backs:

Harvey Johnson, Pug Manders, Ace Parker, Bob Morrow, Dewey Proctor, Bob Sweiger, Bob Perina. **Cleveland**— Ends: George Young, John Yonaker, John Harrington; Tackles: Len Simonetti, Chet Adams, Lou Groza; Guard: Bill Willis; Center: Frank Gatski; Backs: Cliff Lewis, Tom Colella, Lou Saban, Gene Fekete, Gaylon Smith, Ray Terrell.)

Head Coaches: New York: Ray Flaherty; Cleveland: Paul Brown.
Officials: Referee: Thomas Timlin, Umpire: Ernest (Tommy) Hughitt, Field Judge: Earl Gross, Head Linesman: Lou Goedon, Sideline Judge: Hal Slutz.

TEAM STATISTICS

New York		Cleveland
10	First Downs	18
49/146	Offensive Plays/Yardage	64/325
29/65	Rushing Attempts/Yardage	37/112
20	Pass Attempts	27
8	Pass Completions	16
40.0	Completion Percentage	59.3
81	Passing Yardage	213
1 (4)	Interceptions (return yards)	1 (16)
5	Punts	2
32.2	Punting Average	38.5
1/5	Punt Return Yards	5/20
3/77	Kickoff Return Yards	3/37
2/1	Fumbles/Lost	3/0
4	Penalties	5
20	Penalty Yards	25

1946 NFL — A Dark Day in Gotham

1946 NFL Championship — Chicago Bears (24) vs. New York Giants (14)

SUNDAY, DECEMBER 15, 1946 — THE POLO GROUNDS, NEW YORK CITY — 58,346
WEATHER CONDITIONS: OVERCAST SKIES, COLD, LOW 30S.
FIELD CONDITION: DRY, FIRM.

Two old rivals were set to square off for the league championship for the fourth time. Chicago and New York had each been in 7 championship tilts. In the 3 head-to-head contests, the Bears had won in 1933 and 1941, the Giants in 1934. The Giants were 2–5 in championship contests, while the Bears were 4–3.

With World War II now a year in the past, the economy and sports teams had begun to return to their prewar strength.

Betting had long been a mostly ignored part of professional game. Heavy betting was common during the early days when many denizens of small towns wagered that their home town team could whip their rivals. Many of the "home town" players were ringers who were paid an attractive wage in order to help secure a victory for their "home town" club. By the next week, they might well have adopted a new "home town" in order to pick up another payday. Roster hopping was a very common practice in pro football's early days, but evidence of players throwing games had not been evident. Even after baseball's 1919 Black Sox scandal, pro football seemed unaffected by any organized efforts to fix games. On Sunday, December 15, 1946, that would change.

According to Robert W. Peterson in his book *Pigskin*, "There was a buzz on the streets of New York because of the point spread favoring the Bears."[1] The spread, not reported in newspapers of the day, was reported to be anywhere from 10 to 14 points.

In the late afternoon on Saturday, December 14, Giants owner Tim Mara received a call from New York City Mayor William O'Dwyer. The mayor told Mara, "Something has happened that you should know about." He asked Mara to meet him at his office in City Hall immediately.[2]

His mind racing, Mara headed for the mayor's office from upstate Bear Mountain, where the team had been since Wednesday. With Mara were his sons Wellington and Jack and head coach Steve Owen. When the Mara contingent arrived, they were met by Mayor O'Dwyer and city police commissioner Arthur Wallender. Also joining the group was NFL commissioner Bert Bell.

Once everyone had arrived the mayor proceeded to inform them that a small-time, 28-year-old gambler named Alvin J. Paris had allegedly offered Giants tailback Frankie Filchock and backup fullback Merle Hapes $2,500 each to lose the game. Paris wanted the players to fix the game so the Bears would beat the spread and win by more than 10 points. The two players were key to New York's game plan. Filchock was a highly gifted passer, and Hapes, who was a first-round draft pick out of Ole Miss in 1942, became a pivotal player when New York starter Bill Paschal was injured. Paris apparently also offered to bet another $1,000 against New York for each player.

Stunned silence filled the air as the Maras and Owen digested the unbelievable news. An angry Owen apparently offered to obtain the full truth from Paris if the police commissioner would provide a private room with a locked door. After weighing the matter it was agreed that the game should be played that afternoon as scheduled, but not without consequences.

That evening, Filchock was scheduled to receive a Most Valuable Player award on a local radio show. While there, he received word to go to Gracie Mansion, the mayor's official residence, that evening. There he met Tim, Jack, and Wellington Mara, Steve Owen, Bert Bell, Mayor O'Dwyer, and Police Commissioner Wallender.

Filchock was escorted into a room. In another room down the hall sat Merle Hapes. Neither player knew the other was in the building. The mayor and police commissioner spoke repeatedly with each player, trying to get the full story behind the bribe attempt. Filchock continually denied even knowing about the fix offer and was excused shortly thereafter. The questioning of Hapes continued throughout the night. After he was released in the wee hours of Sunday morning, the police commissioner reported that Hapes admitted that Paris had indeed approached him, but denied accepting his offer.

League rules required that any player approached by a gambler regarding game tampering needed to report it immediately. Although he turned the gamblers down flat, Hapes did not report the attempt. For breaking that rule, league commissioner Bell determined that Hapes could not play against the Bears, but Filchock, who denied any knowledge of the attempted fix, was still ruled eligible. In a statement to the press, Bell said that Hapes was ineligible, but "Frank Filchock was permitted to play, because he was approached only by innuendo. That wasn't quite clear to the commissioner's listeners and he failed to explain."[3] Neither player was charged with a criminal offense.

Based solely upon his word, Filchock was allowed to play, but in truth, he too had been approached by Paris. Like Hapes, he spurned the gambler's offer, but he wanted to play in the game so he lied about his knowledge to Mayor O'Dwyer, Commissioner Wallender, Bell, Mara, and Owen. He was determined to play as hard as he could to clear his name.

"Paris called himself a salesman, but police said he was a bookmaker and a front man for a 'vicious' New Jersey gambling syndicate that had dabbled in trying to 'fix' college sports."[4] Phone taps on Paris's home line revealed conversations between the gambler and a New Jersey bookie named Moish that proved Hapes's side of the story to be true. These came to be known as the "Al and Moish tapes." Paris admitted to having met the players at a cocktail party on November 23. He said that he first mentioned the plan to them at the party, and several times thereafter, but each time, the players refused Paris's offer. Paris was charged with attempted bribery of a participant in a professional game. Conviction was punishable by up to five years in prison and a $10,000 fine.[5]

Giant fullback Hank Soar later said that the team was taken to Bear Mountain, New York, on the Wednesday before the game. They were told that it was to isolate the players from being bothered by fans seeking autographs and tickets to Sunday's game. Soar recalled thinking, "That's bullshit. I know there's something wrong here. First thing Sunday morning, somebody called and said, 'Did you hear what's going on? Filchock and Hapes are in the soup. Some guy says they want to sell the game.'"[6]

New York Center Lou DeFilippo recalled the atmosphere in the Giants' locker room before the game: "We were shaken to the roots just to hear about it. There was a big to-do, and we didn't know what the hell was going on. The whole team was shaken up."[7]

The Rev. Benedict Dudley addressed the team before his pregame prayer in the Giants' clubhouse. He told the players, "It's up to you to restore the faith of the fans in pro football."

By game time on Sunday the news had hit the papers and Filchock was greeted by a chorus of boos from the New York crowd as he emerged from the Giants' clubhouse in center field. But in the first quarter, Filchock bore down and went to work, determined to win the game and clear his name. Adding to his host of problems, Filchock's nose was broken early in the first quarter. He would be hampered by great pain, swelling and blood for the remainder of the afternoon, but he was determined not to stop.

Turnovers were to trouble the Giants all afternoon. The first came as New York was driving early in the first quarter. Giants back George Franck fumbled as he was being brought down after a short gain and Chicago linebacker Ed Sprinkle recovered to end the New York possession.

On the ensuing Chicago drive, Luckman connected with Sprinkle on a pass that moved the Bears to the New York 23. The next play netted two more yards on the ground. On second and eight, Luckman went back to the air. The Bears got on the scoreboard on a 21-yard toss from Sid Luckman to Ken Kavanaugh. Frank Maznicki converted on the PAT kick to put the Bears in the lead 7–0.

Later in the first, the Bears' Dante Magnani intercepted a Filchock pass on the Giant 19-yard line and sailed unmolested into the end zone for the second Chicago score. It was on this play that Filchock broke his nose. Ed Sprinkle, known as a devastating tackler, was playing right end for Chicago and leveled Filchock. Sprinkle recalled, "I got around my blocker and hit Filchock from the blind side as he was just throwing a pass. Dante Magnani was playing defense, and the ball went up in the air; he caught it and practically walked in, but Filchock stayed in the game."[8] Again, Maznicki converted to make the score 14–0 in favor of the visitors.

Late in the first quarter, Filchock had the Giants moving as he connected on two long passes. The first went to Jim Poole for first-down yardage. Two plays later, Frank threw a 38-yard touchdown pass to Frank Liebel. Longtime veteran Ken Strong's extra point brought the Giants to within 7 points of the Bears.

The second period was strictly a punting duel as both defenses stiffened and refused to give up ground. As the first half came to an end, Chicago led 14–7.

The defensive trend continued well into the second half, but late in the third quarter, the Maramen got a break when Jim Lee Howell recovered a Bill Osmanski fumble on the Chicago 20. The Giants then moved the ball 15 yards in 2 plays, and finally Filchock, desperately avoiding a fierce Chicago rush, hooked up with Giant back Steve Filipowicz on a 5-yard pass for the Giants' second score of the afternoon. Strong converted once again and with just three seconds remaining in the third period, the score was knotted at 14–all.

The precious December sunlight began to wane late in the third quarter and at the break between periods, the lights at the Polo Grounds were turned on. Sid Luckman put the Bears back into the lead on an uncharacteristic run from scrimmage. With the ball on the Giants' 19-yard line, Luckman and Halas decided to call "97 Bingo, keep it." The misdirection play appeared to be a sweep to the left side by halfback George McAfee, but instead of a handoff, Luckman kept the ball and, hiding it behind his hip, bootlegged to the right side, away from the play. By the time the Giants' defenders discovered the deception, Luckman was well across the 10 and it was too late to recover. He scored easily for his only touchdown of the 1946 season. Luckman recalled, "I faked to George McAfee on a run around left end. They feared that play and overshifted to the left side of our offensive line." Ed Sprinkle remembered, "Everybody pulled and went to the left, and Sid did a bootleg. Everybody chased McAfee. I was playing offensive right end, and was alone blocking for Sid. It was pretty open, and he ran it in. He was a good runner." "It was the easiest 19 yards of my life," recalled Luckman.[9]

Frank Maznicki's PAT boot put the Bears up to stay, 21–14. In an interesting twist, Luckman, who ran infrequently, led both teams in rushing that day, gaining 81 yards in 4 attempts.

The Bears added a 26-yard Frank Maznicki field goal late in the game to bring the final score to 24–14. The Bears' 10-point win was one less than the gamblers needed to cover the spread. Filchock had played his heart out, determined to clear his name by playing hard and winning. His team lost, but he kept the gamblers from beating the spread. He could rest comfortably knowing at least that.

The game was especially physical. "Halfback Frank Reagan was manhandled so badly by Chicago's bruising Bears that he was rushed to the hospital at halftime, with a fractured nose. Halfback George Franck also got sent to the hospital — banged-up shoulder. Halfback Frank Filchock played almost the entire game with a broken nose."[10] These injuries virtually depleted New York's running game for the rest of the contest. With Paschal on the sidelines in street clothes, and Reagan and Franck being treated at St. Elizabeth's Hospital, a halfback of Hapes's quality was sorely needed that afternoon.

Filchock wound up the day going 9 for 26 in passing attempts for 128 yards and two touchdowns. Even with the allegations and his broken nose weighing heavy on his mind,

Filchock, seeking vindication to clear his name, played a gritty game. He threw two touch-down passes to send the game into the fourth quarter tied 14–14. Despite his two touchdown passes, Filchock was picked off six times that afternoon. Few people found this cause for much alarm as he was always noted for his high interception percentage. But his extra effort and playing through the pain of his broken nose was enough to convince many of his innocence. Steve Owen was quoted after the game as saying, "It choked you up knowing how hard that boy was trying."[11]

Owen added, "The situation caused the Giants to play that much harder, but there's no use denying they were greatly disturbed and there wasn't much we could do with Filipowicz playing fullback without one day's practice. Steve did all right, but it wasn't enough."[12]

At Paris's trial, Filchock admitted his foreknowledge of the fix. He testified that both he and Hapes turned down the offer. Since they intended to play the game honestly, they saw no reason to mention the bribe offer to the team, the league, or the police. The players had then determined to put it out of their minds. "I just forgot about it after saying no to Paris's proposition. I wouldn't even think of doing anything dishonest in football."[13]

Regardless of the fact that neither player accepted anything from Paris, both Filchock and Hapes were suspended by Bell the following April for "acts detrimental to the welfare of the National League and of professional football."[14] Bell stated, "This suspension prevents the employment of Hapes or Filchock by any club in the National Football League as player, coach, or in any capacity whatsoever."[15] Bell eventually lifted the suspensions of Filchock and Hapes in 1950 and 1954, respectively.

After his suspension, Hapes returned to Mississippi and took a job teaching and coaching football at a local high school. He was never again associated with the NFL, but his playing days were not quite over. In 1953, he was induced to make a two-year comeback with the Hamilton Tiger-Cats of the Canadian Football League. Filchock headed north as well, and continued his professional career by playing and coaching in the CFL. After his suspension was lifted, Filchock played briefly for the 1950 Baltimore Colts before returning to Canada, where he played through 1953. He continued to coach in Canada, and in 1960 was named the first head coach of the AFL Denver Broncos. The two players remained forever linked by the scandal and both maintained their innocence. Citing the trial judge's pronouncement that the two players were not accomplices, but merely the unfortunate victims of circumstance, Filchock stated that the suspensions were unfair and that the two had been "dealt one off the bottom of the deck." Ironically, the two died within a month of each other in June and July 1994.[16] Filchock died on June 20 and Hapes on July 18.

Paris was determined to be the front man for three more highly placed gamblers. At his trial he testified against Harvey Stemmer, David Krakauer, and Jerome Zarowitz, who were known sports fixers with well-established criminal records. Stemmer was already serving time and had managed to orchestrate the attempted fix from prison. The three were convicted on conspiracy and bribery charges. Paris was found guilty of two counts of bribery and spent 9 months in prison.

SCORING

	1	2	3	4	Total
Chicago Bears	14	0	0	10	24
New York Giants	7	0	7	0	14

1st Quarter: Chicago — TD — Kavanaugh 21-yard pass from Luckman (Maznicki kick). Chicago — TD — Magnani 19-yard pass interception return (Maznicki kick). New York — TD — Liebel 28-yard pass from Filchock (Strong kick). 2nd Quarter: None. 3rd Quarter: New York — TD — Filipowicz 5-yard pass from Filchock (Strong kick). 4th Quarter: Chicago — TD — Luckman 19-yard run (Maznicki kick). Chicago — FG — Maznicki 26-yard kick.

STARTING LINEUPS

Chicago Bears		**New York Giants**
Ken Kavanaugh	Left End	Jim Poole
Fred Davis	Left Tackle	DeWitt Coulter
Rudy Mucha	Left Guard	Bob Dobelstein
Clyde "Bulldog" Turner	Center	Chet Gladchuck
Ray Bray	Right Guard	Len Younce
Mike Jarmoluk	Right Tackle	Jim White
George Wilson	Right End	Jim Lee Howell
Joe Osmanski	Quarterback	Steve Filipowicz
Dante Magnani	Left Halfback	Dave Brown
Hugh Gallarneau	Right Halfback	Howie Livingston
Bill Osmanski	Fullback	Ken Strong

(*Substitutions:* **Chicago**: Ends: Walt Lamb, Jim Keane, Ed Sprinkle; Tackles: Walt Stickel, Ed Kolman; Guards: Aldo Forte, Pat Preston, Chuck Drulis; Centers: Stu Clarkson, John Schiechl; Backs: Frank Maznicki, George McAfee, Don Perkins, Hank Margarita, Sid Luckman, Tom Farris, Dick Schweidler, Ray McLean. **New York:** Ends: John Mead, Don McCafferty, Frank Liebel; Tackles: Frank Cope, Phil Ragazzo, Vic Carroll; Guard: Bill Edwards; Center: Lou DeFilippo; Backs: Hank Soar, Pete Gorgone, George Franck, Frank Filchock, Frank Reagan, John Doolan.)

Head Coaches: Chicago: George S. Halas; New York: Steve Owen.
Players' Shares: Chicago: $1,975.82; New York: $1,295.57.
Officials: Referee: Ronald Gibbs; Umpire: Carl Brubaker; Field Judge: William Grimberg; Head Linesman: Charles Berry; Timer:

TEAM STATISTICS

Chicago Bears		New York Giants
10	First Downs	13
62/245	Total Offense Plays/Yards	59/248
40	Rushing Attempts	33
101	Rushing Yardage	120
22	Pass Attempts	26
9	Pass Completions	9
40.9	Completion Percentage	34.6
144	Passing Yardage	128
6/84	Interceptions/Return Yards	2/10
7	Punts	4
41.4	Punting Average	31.7
2/1	Fumbles/Lost	3/2
9	Penalties	6
112	Penalty Yards	70

1947 AAFC — The Browns Repeat

1947 All-American Football Conference Championship Game — Cleveland Browns (14) vs. New York Yankees (3)

DECEMBER 14, 1947 — YANKEE STADIUM, NEW YORK CITY — 61,879
WEATHER CONDITIONS: COLD, 32°F.
FIELD CONDITION: ICY, FROZEN FIELD.

The second All-American Conference championship was played on December 14, 1947. The contest again pitted the Eastern Conference champion New York Yankees against the Cleveland Browns, champions of the Western Conference. The Browns were looking to make it two in a row, while the Yankees were looking for a measure of revenge after a close loss to these same Browns in last year's championship contest.

The 12–1–1 Browns and the 11–2–1 Yankees had played twice in the 1947 regular season. The teams had tied once and the Browns had beaten New York in the next game.

The championship game was played in a frigid Yankee Stadium. "A thermometer that hovered near the freezing mark kept the crowd down to 61,879."[1] The snow had been removed from the frozen playing surface and sat piled up in a ring around the field.

Backs Orban "Spec" Sanders and Claude "Buddy" Young led Coach Ray Flaherty's New Yorkers. Sanders had rushed for an amazing 1431 yards in 1947, the most of any professional at that time. In doing so, Sanders became the only 1000-yard rusher in AAFC history. He also scored 19 touchdowns that year. The speedy Young, a rookie out of Illinois, had been impressive all season and complemented second-year back Sanders. New York was, however, concerned about Sanders, who had injured his ankle in the final league game the week before. He would play that day, but would he be effective?

Cleveland's high-powered offense was led by Otto Graham, who led all AAFC passers with 2,753 yards, the bruising 235-pound Marion Motley, end Mac Speedie, and back Edgar Jones.

An explosive game was anticipated between the two high-octane offenses. The teams had played two offense-oriented battles earlier in the season. The first game, played in front of more than 80,000 fans in Cleveland Municipal Stadium in early October, was a wild battle won by the Browns in a second-half spurt, 26–17. The second game ended in a 28–28 tie in front of 70,000 Yankee Stadium fans in late November. Neither team lacked in offense. Despite this, the icy playing surface made getting much footing difficult and neither squad could get much going offensively. Subsequently, the squads punted back and forth to each other for most of the first period.

Late in the first quarter, the Browns began to come alive. Cleveland started a drive on their own 32-yard line. The key play in the series came when Cleveland's massive, 232-pound fullback Marion Motley broke out on a 52-yard gallop. He appeared touchdown bound as he broke through the Yankees' line at the 35, but he was finally brought down on the New York 13-yard line by Yankees end Harmon Rowe.

The drive was almost for naught as New York's Bruce Alford picked off Otto Graham's pass on the next play. Fortunately for Cleveland an interference call nullified the play and the Browns gained another chance. After two runs gained only 4 yards, Mac Speedie caught an 8-yard pass from Graham at the 1. Graham then scored from the 1 on a quarterback sneak with two minutes remaining. The 68-yard drive was capped off by Lou Groza's extra point kick that gave Cleveland a 7–0 lead.

The Yankees mounted a drive in the second quarter led by fullback Buddy Young and half back Spec Sanders. After Young ran the kickoff to the New York 32, Young and Sanders drove the ball down to the Cleveland 6, but there the Yankees' offense stalled. New York had to settle for a 12-yard field goal by Harvey Johnson. The score now stood at 7–3.

Cleveland threatened twice more before the half ended, but each drive ended in a rare missed field goal attempt by Lou Groza. At halftime the Browns were up by four.

As the third quarter was coming to a close, Cleveland's interception king Tom Colella swiped a Spec Sanders pass and returned it 12 yards to the New York 41. Taking advantage of the turnover, Graham drove the Browns down the field. On the first play from scrimmage, Motley bolted through the middle of the line for 16 yards before finally being brought down on the 25. Graham then hit on passes to Lewis "Mickey" Mayne and Dub Jones. Mayne's reception went for 8 yards and Graham's connection with Jones gave the Browns a first down at the New York nine. Jones then carried twice, moving the ball to the four. With the ball resting 12 feet from the goal line, Graham faked handoffs to Motley and Mayne before handing it to Jones, who took it in for the score untouched. In a unique situation, Lou Saban, not Lou Groza, kicked the extra point to bring the score to 14–3.

The Yankees would drive deep into Cleveland territory twice more, threatening to score. The first drive took them all the way to the Browns' 19 before they lost the ball on a Buddy Young fumble. The second drive reached the 29-yard line, but an unnecessary roughness call pushed New York back to the Cleveland 44, taking the Yankees out of scoring position.[2]

The fourth quarter was a defensive struggle with both teams trading punts. Neither team tallied any points and the final score remained 14 to 3 in favor of the Browns.

The contest was disappointing to the Yankees and their faithful, who believed their team would defeat the Browns this time around. They sat in the cold, frustrated as they watched Sanders, hobbled by his ankle injury, fail to score or throw for a touchdown for the first time in the last 19 games. Sanders was held to 40 yards rushing on 12 carries. Restricted in his ability to run, Sanders played mostly a passing role, but even there he only completed seven of 17 attempts. The fans also were frustrated as they watched the usually reliable Buddy Young slowed by the frozen turf. While he gained 69 yards, they were unimportant to the game's outcome. Young also fumbled twice. New York only crossed the midfield stripe three times all day.

The Cleveland victory produced some notable performances. Graham completed 14 passes in 21 attempts for 112 yards on the day. The game was devoid of big-yardage passing plays, with the Browns opting for shorter aerial gains due to the slippery field.[3] Graham connected with Mac Speedie for four catches for just 25 yards, and Dante Lavelli and Dub Jones for three each for 37 and 31 yards respectively. Graham's other four completions were scattered among three receivers for only 19 yards more. Motley gained 109 yards on 13 carries. Punter Horace Gillom, whose accurate and long punts kept the Yankees mired in poor starting field position, was a true hero on the afternoon.[4]

The game was the Browns' fifth victory over the Yankees, against one tie and no losses, in the two-year history of the league. The score could easily have been more lopsided as twice the Browns lost a touchdown when Jones stepped out of the end zone while trying to catch a pass from Graham.

SCORING

	1	2	3	4	Totals
Cleveland Browns	7	0	7	0	14
New York Yankees	0	3	0	0	3

1st Quarter: Cleveland — TD — Graham 1-yd run (Groza kick) — 13:00. 2nd Quarter: New York — FG — H. Johnson 12-yards — 4:14. 3rd Quarter: Cleveland — TD — E. Jones 4-yard run (Saban kick) — 10:04. 4th Quarter: None.

STARTING LINEUPS

Cleveland Browns		New York Yankees
George Young	Left End	Jack Russell
Lou Groza	Left Tackle	Bruiser Kinard
Ed Ulinski	Left Guard	Roman Bentz
Lou Saban	Center	Lou Sossamon
Bill Willis	Right Guard	Dick Barwegan
Chet Adams	Right Tackle	Nate Johnson
John Yonakor	Right End	Bruce Alford
Otto Graham	Quarterback	Lloyd Cheatham BB
Cliff Lewis	Left Halfback	Spec Sanders TB
Tom Colella	Right Halfback	Bob Sweiger WB
Marion Motley	Fullback	Buddy Young

(*Substitutions:* **Cleveland** — Ends: Mac Speedie, Dante Lavelli, Horace Gillom; Tackles: Chet Adams, Roman Piskor, Ernie Blandin, Len Simonetti; Guards: Lin Houston, Bob Gaudio, Weldon Humble; Center: Mo Scarry, Frank Gatski, Mel Maceau; Backs: Tony Adamle, Ermal Allen, Dub Jones, Lew Mayne, Ray Terrell. **New York** — Ends: Van Davis, Roy Kurrasch; Tackles: Vic Schleich, Darrell Palmer; Guards: Joe Yackanich, Charley Riffle; Center: Paul Duke; Backs: Harvey Johnson, Bob Kennedy, Eddie Prokop, Dewey Proctor, Harmon Rowe, Harry Burrus.)

Head Coaches: Cleveland: Paul Brown; New York: Ray Flaherty.

Officials: Referee: Thomas A. Timlin (Niagra), Umpire: George Holstrom (Muhlenberg), Field Judge: George Vergara (Notre Dame), Linesman: William H. Ohrenberger (Boston College), Sideline Judge: Titus Lobach (Franklin & Marshall)

TEAM STATISTICS

Cleveland		New York
17	First Downs	13
12	By Rushing	8
4	By Passing	5
1	By Penalty	0
54–212	Offensive Plays — Yardage	51–284
33–172	Rushing Attempts -Yardage	33–123
21	Pass Attempts	18
14	Pass Completions	7
67.0	Completion Percentage	38.9
112	Passing Yardage	89
1—13	Interceptions (return yards)	0—0
5	Punts	6
45	Punting Average from scrimmage	36
4–27	Punt Return Yards	3–14
2–1	Fumbles-Lost	3–2
7	Penalties	3
45	Penalty Yards	21

1947 NFL — This One's for Charlie

1947 Championship — Philadelphia Eagles (21) vs. Chicago Cardinals (28)

DECEMBER 28, 1947 — COMISKEY PARK, CHICAGO — 30,759
WEATHER CONDITIONS: CLEAR, COLD, 28°F., PERIODIC LIGHT BREEZE.
FIELD CONDITION: FROZEN, FIRM, SLIPPERY.

It was Chicago in late December. What else can be said but that it was cold and the field was frozen? Cardinals tackle Chet Bulger recalled, "It was bitter cold. When you play in Chicago that late in the year, it's a penetrating type of cold."[1] Cardinal fans didn't care. They were excited to be playing for the championship. The cross-town Bears owned the Windy City. The Bears had played for the league championship in 10 of the last 16 seasons. This season, however, the good denizens of the South Side could claim the city laurels.

This was the first trip to the championship game for both franchises. The Cardinals were declared league champions in 1925, but the years since had been lean. Their opponents, the Philadelphia Eagles, had long been league doormats. But since the end of the war, both teams had built top-notch squads.

The Cardinals had put together a terrific backfield made up of triple-threat back Charlie Trippi from Georgia, Elmer Angsman, strong-armed Missouri passer Paul Christman, full-back Pat Harder from Wisconsin, and former Pitt All-American Marshall Goldberg. Their coach was longtime NFL veteran Jimmy Conzelman.

Despite the success on the field, it had been an emotionally taxing year in some ways. Sadly, Cardinals owner Charles Bidwell, the architect of this contender, who had suffered with his team since 1932, had died in April.

The Cardinals had also experienced tragedy on October 24, when rookie punting specialist Jeff Burkett was killed in the crash of a United Airlines flight. Burkett, a three-sports star at LSU, was flying back to Chicago from Los Angeles after an emergency appendectomy that had forced him out of the Rams game several days earlier. He was leading the league in punting with a 47.4-yard average on 11 kicks at the time of his death.

The Eagles had all-everything back Steve Van Buren out of LSU. Van Buren had set a new league record for rushing yards in a season, breaking Beattie Feathers' 1934 mark by four yards. Complementing Van Buren, they had Tommy Thompson at quarterback, fullback Joe Muha, and a strong line anchored by center Alex Wojciechowicz. Philadelphia coach Earle "Greasy" Neale had starred in the league as a player and coach since the 1920s. He had coached the Providence Steam Roller to the championship in 1928.

While the weather was respectable for Chicago in late December, the field was still frozen, making footing an issue. Vince Banonis remembered, "The field was hard as cement. Jimmy Conzelman had the foresight to make sneakers available and they really helped. That gave us a lot of traction."[2] Eagles end Jack Ferrante recalled in 1979, "Comiskey was like a skating rink."[3]

The Eagles opted for well-honed cleats on their football shoes. The *Green Bay Press Gazette* reported, "They had filed the cleats on their shoes to razor sharpness."[4] The Cardinals were made aware of the cleat sharpening by a Comiskey Park clubhouse attendant who had been in the Eagles' dressing room prior to the game. The Cardinals, who won the coin toss and elected to receive, said nothing until the game started. Chicago coach Jimmy Conzelman remembered later, "Right after the kickoff one of our men grabbed an official and pointed to one of the Eagles. The official looked at the player's shoes and walked off a 5-yard penalty. We did the same thing on the next play and the next."[5] In the opening minutes of the game, the Eagles were penalized repeatedly for illegal equipment when the officials objected to the sharpness of Philadelphia's too-well-honed cleats. Neale and trainer Freddie Schubach complained that the cleats were legal, but referee Tom Dowd (Bill Downes) would have none of it and the penalty stood.[6] Conzelman added, "Well, pretty soon Greasy called the players off the field and they changed the shoes right there."[7] The Eagles then followed the Cardinals' lead and donned sneakers. Thompson missed four plays as he was forced to change his footwear. The Eagles claimed that the penalties and loss of traction cost them dearly. Coach Neale said after the game, "It won't show in the final score, but at the start of the game we were penalized five yards for illegal equipment when we could have made a first down, and that cost us plenty."[8]

Midway through the first quarter, Charlie Trippi ran off tackle on a quick opener, breezed past the Philadelphia linemen, juked past defensive back Russ Craft, and scampered 44 yards for the game's first score. Fullback Pat Harder kicked the conversion to put Chicago up 7–0.

The Eagles had massed their defense up front to stop Christman and the passing game. It worked because Christman completed only 3 of the 14 passes he attempted that afternoon, but the price they paid was letting the Cardinal backfield run wild.

Early in the second quarter, Elmer Angsman went 70 yards for the second Cardinals score. He too scored on the same off tackle play Trippi had scored on earlier. Angsman carried an Eagle defender with him for the final three yards.

Philadelphia battled back just before the half. From his own 30-yard line, quarterback Tommy Thompson lofted a 53-yard strike that found teammate Pat McHugh on the Cardinal 17. McHugh pulled in Thompson's pass and scampered the final 17 yards to complete a 70-yard touchdown play. Cliff Patton kicked the PAT to bring the Eagles to within 7 points. The half ended with the Cardinals in front 14–7.

Both teams struggled offensively on their first possessions of the second half. The Eagles began heading downfield early in the third period with Thompson moving the ball through the air with greater ease. After arriving at the Chicago 27, Thompson went to the skies again, but this time with disastrous effects. Stepping in front of the Thompson aerial at the 14, Cardinal linebacker Buster Ramsey intercepted and returned the ball 42 yards to the Philadelphia 34. In just seconds, Ramsey had turned the tide, snuffing out the Eagles' scoring chance and setting up his Cardinals with a terrific opportunity to drive home points. The Cardinals, however, came up short as well, wasting a golden chance. The ball went over to the Eagles.

It was now halfway through the third quarter and the Eagles were once again stalled by the Cardinals' defense. On fourth down, the Eagles were forced to kick the ball away. Chicago's Trippi then struck again as he collected the Philadelphia punt by Joe Muha on his own 25 and returned it 75 yards to extend the Cardinals' lead. Trippi eluding several tacklers with his quick-motion style, zigging and zagging across the field. He stumbled on the Eagle 30 and again at the 22, but both times, he regained his balance and with the Eagles swarming hot on his heels, continued racing downfield. As he neared the goal line he picked up a blocker in Chet Bulger and finally crossed into the end zone. Harder's conversion kick made the score 21–7 in favor of Chicago.[9]

Not ready to lie down, the Eagles mounted a 73-yard drive that was sparked by the Philadelphia passing game. Thompson set up in a sort of shotgun formation that released his backs from their blocking assignments and sent them as receivers downfield. The big play was a 20-yard gainer from Thompson to Ferrante to get the ball to midfield. The ball was soon resting on the Chicago six. Three runs for short yardage advanced the ball to the one, and on fourth down, Neale and Thompson decided to forsake the field goal and sent Steve Van Buren on a successful one-yard touchdown plunge. Patton again converted to narrow the Cardinals' lead to 21–14.

In the 4th quarter the teams again traded scores, but the Eagles could not close the gap enough to garner the win. In a sloppy first possession, Trippi was forced to recover his own fumble and Christman was intercepted. Fortunately for the Cardinals, Philadelphia was equally sloppy and penalties kept the Eagles' field position in check.

The first score of the final period was a repeat of the first score of the second. After being pinned deep in the shadows of their own end zone by a Joe Muha quick kick, the Cardinals found lightning in a bottle. Elmer Angsman once again took a handoff on a quick opener and raced 70 yards for his second touchdown of the day. McHugh had the last chance to catch him. He was in hot pursuit for 30 yards and finally dove at his legs to try to stop Angsman, but his effort ended in frustration. He missed the churning legs of the Cardinal back by inches and landed hard on the frozen field, reduced to a spectator as he watched Angsman sprint into the end zone for the score. Harder's fourth PAT kick of the day put Chicago up 28–14. Angsman's run helped him set a new league championship game record with 159 yards in just ten carries to break Bill Osmanski's 109, set with the 1940 Chicago Bears.

The Eagles put up a last-ditch effort as they drove to the Cardinal 1 on the strength of Thompson passes. From there, halfback Russ Craft battled over for the score. Patton converted for the third time, bringing the score to 28–21, but that was as close as they would get. Chicago's Babe Dimancheff returned the ensuing kickoff 46 yards to the Cardinals' 47. Conzelman instructed his offense to keep the ball on the ground and burn as much time as possible. Twelve straight running plays did just that, and as the final seconds ticked away, the gun sounded and the Cardinals were crowned league champions for the first time since 1925.

After the game, Greasy Neale blamed it all on the footing. The Associated Press quoted Neale as saying, "We did everything but beat them. We had our defensive men all set, but they just couldn't recover on the slippery field when Angsman and Trippi set sail."[10]

Conzelman, who had just won his second league title as a coach, countered that his team's delayed smashes through line had kept Philadelphia's defense off balance. "They were delayed smashes that kept Philadelphia entirely off guard and left their secondary badly faked out of position," stated Conzelman.[11] The Cardinals believed that they could run on the Eagles' 8-man line, and by the end of the game, they had proven to the world that they were right.

After the game, Violet Bidwill, widow of the Cardinals' late owner, noted sadly as she fought back tears of joy and sorrow, "It's just too bad that Charlie couldn't see this."[12] Somehow, you've got to believe that he did.

Scoring

	1	2	3	4	Totals
Philadelphia	0	7	7	7	21
Chicago	7	7	7	7	28

1st Quarter: ChiC — TD — Trippi — 44-yard run (Harder kick). 2nd Quarter: ChiC — TD — Angaman — 70-yard run (Harder kick). Phil — TD — McHugh 53-yard pass from Thompson (Patton kick). 3rd Quarter: ChiC — TD — Trippi — 75-yard punt return (Harder kick). Phil — TD — Van Buren —1-yard run (Patton kick). 4th Quarter: ChiC — TD — Angsman — 70-yard run (Harder kick).   Phil — TD — Craft —1-yard run (Patton kick).

Starting Lineups

Philadelphia Eagles		Chicago Cardinals
Jack Ferrante	Left End	Bill Blackburn
Vic Sears	Left Tackle	Dick Plasman
Cliff Patton	Left Guard	Lloyd Arms
Alex Wojciechowicz	Center	Vince Banonis
Bucko Kilroy	Right Guard	Ham Nichols
Al Wistert	Right Tackle	Stan Mauldin
Pete Pihos	Right End	Jack Doolan
Pat McHugh	Quarterback	Paul Christman
Steve Van Buren	Left Halfback	Red Cochran
Bosh Pritchard	Right Halfback	Marshall Goldberg
Joe Muha	Fullback	Walt Rankin

(*Substitutions:* **Philadelphia:** Ends: Neil Armstrong John Green, Larry Cabrelli, Hal Prescott; Tackles: Jim Kekeris, Otis Douglas, Jay MacDowell, Roger Harding; Guard: John Wyhonic; Center: Vic Lindskog; Backs: Ernie Steele, Russ Craft, Ben Kish, Allie Sherman, Tommy Thompson. **Chicago:** Ends: Joe Parker, Mal Kutner, Bill Dewell; Tackles: Joe Coomer, Chet Bulger, Bill Campbell; Guards: Plato Andros, Buster Ramsey, Ray Apolskis; Center: Bill Blackburn; Backs: Ray Mallouf, "Babe" Dimancheff, Bill DeCorrevont, Elmer Angsman, Pat Harder, Charlie Trippi.)

Head Coaches: Philadelphia: Earle Neale; Chicago: Jimmy Conzelman.
Players' Shares: Chicago: $1,132.00; Philadelphia: $754.00
Game Officials: Referee: William Downes; Umpire: Harry Robb; Head Linesman: Dan Tehan; Field Judge: Harry Haines; Back Judge: Carl Rebele.

Team Statistics

Philadelphia Eagles		Chicago Cardinals
22 (10/r, 11/p, 1pen)	First Downs	11 (8/r, 2/p, 1pen)
/329	Offensive Plays/Yardage	/311
37/60	Rushing Attempts/Yardage	39/282
44	Pass Attempts	14
27	Pass Completions	3
61.4	Completion Percentage	21.4
297	Passing Yardage	54
3 (45)	Interceptions (return yards)	2 (11)
8	Punts	8
34.5	Punting Average	32.0
4/10	Punt Return Yards	4/150
2/0	Fumbles/Lost	2/1
7	Penalties	10
55	Penalty Yards	97

1948 AAFC — Perfect

1948 All-American Football Conference Championship Game — Buffalo Bills (7) vs. Cleveland Browns (49)

DECEMBER 19, 1948 — MUNICIPAL STADIUM, CLEVELAND — 22,981
WEATHER: 33°F., SNOWY, FRIGID COLD BREEZES OFF LAKE ERIE.
FIELD CONDITION: PATCHY SNOW, FROZEN.

Never before had a team from a major professional football league finished an entire season and the post-season undefeated. Today, in the wintry confines of Municipal Stadium, the Cleveland Browns were determined to do just that. The Chicago Bears had come close in both 1934 and 1942, but each year they had dropped the league championship game.

The 1948 Browns recorded a perfect 14–0 regular season record led by Otto Graham and fullback Marion Motley. The golden-armed Graham passed for 2,713 yards while the powerful Motley ground out 964 yards overland, both remarkable amounts for the era. The team was so strong on both sides of the ball that Coach Paul Brown called them "the best team I've ever coached."[1]

The disappointing crowd of 22,981 was probably due to several factors: weak competition for the Browns, the feeling that the real championship games had already been played, and the snowy, cold weather that was accentuated by persistent breezes off of Lake Erie. "Snow fell most of the morning then subsided at noon. It began again late in the second quarter and continued intermittently throughout the remainder of the game."[2]

After two seasons as the cream of the Eastern Division, the New York Yankees had slipped to a weak 6–8 record in 1948. They gave way to the almost equally mediocre Buffalo Bills and Baltimore Colts. Both teams finished with 7–7 records, forcing a one-game playoff that the Bills won in come-from-behind fashion. Trailing 17–7 in the fourth quarter, the Bills mounted a comeback to defeat rookie quarterback Y.A. Tittle and the Colts 28–17.

With the East settled, the Browns made ready to host the championship tilt. Cleveland was an overwhelming favorite to decimate their visitors. For most, it was a foregone conclusion, the only question was how decisive the Browns' victory would be.

Many felt that the real championship contests were played on November 14 and 28, when the Browns had squared off with their Western Division rivals, the San Francisco 49ers. By rights, the 49ers were the obvious choice to suit up against the Browns for the championship contest. They had finished the regular season with a 12–2 record. The 49ers dispatched their rivals in the twelve victories by no fewer than 10 points and by as many as 41. The two losses came in those two November contests at the hands of the Browns. Both were closely-fought contests won by the Browns by 7 and 3 points, respectively.

The Bills were anything but bereft of talent; they were simply inconsistent and unbalanced. The offense boasted the league's leading scorer in two-time All-League halfback Chet Mutryn, two of the league's leading ground gainers in Mutryn and Lou Tomasetti, and the number four passer in the league in George Ratterman, and Al Baldwin was the league's second-rated receiver. Even with this talent, Buffalo head coach Red Dawson had a challenge trying to slow down Cleveland's offensive juggernaut with the Bills' porous defense that generally allowed as many or more points than the offense generated.

The first half was fairly evenly played, but Cleveland began to chip away at Buffalo. The Browns' defense struck first as Tommy James picked off a Buffalo pass at midfield and returned it 30 yards to the Bills' 20. In six plays, the Cleveland offense moved the ball down to the 3. With just ten seconds remaining in the first quarter, Edgar "Special Delivery" Jones carried the ball over the goal line to start the day's scoring. Lou Groza added the point after and the Browns were on top 7–0.

Early in the second period, Cleveland end George Young scooped up a Rex Bumgardner fumble and scrambled 18 yards for the Browns' second touchdown. Again, Groza converted and the score stood at 14–0.

At halftime Buffalo desperately searched for an answer to the Cleveland Browns before the game got out of hand. Cleveland came out of the locker room after the half, ready to put the game away. Just minutes into the third quarter, James again picked off a Ratterman pass, returning it to the Buffalo 21. Otto Graham connected for 12 yards with Dante Lavelli and then passed the final 9 yards to Edgar Jones for the score. Groza's kick put Cleveland up 21–0.

Later in the third period, Lou Rymkus recovered Don Schneider's fumble at the Buffalo 42. On the ensuing drive, Cleveland's blistering 340-pound fullback Marion Motley bolted 29 yards on a trap play for Cleveland's fourth touchdown. Groza gained his fourth point on the day as the Browns padded their lead to 28–0.

Hoping for a spark, Buffalo replaced the limping Ratterman at quarterback with backup Jim Still. Still delivered. After driving for one first down, Buffalo was forced to punt. Still kicked the ball away, but a roughing-the-kicker penalty gave the Bills a new set of downs. On first down, Still hit Bumgardner on a 25-yard pass that put the ball on the Cleveland 28. After a 3-yard running play, Still passed to Bill O'Connor, who gained another first down before being brought down on the Cleveland 10. Still and Al Baldwin then connected on a 10-yard touchdown pass to put the Bills on the scoreboard. Graham Armstrong's point after kick narrowed the score to 28–7.

On the ensuing kickoff Dub Jones returned the ball 46 yards to the Buffalo 34. Jones then carried for 3 yards from scrimmage to put the ball on the 31. On second down, Graham handed off to Motley, who bolted through the Buffalo defense for a 31-yard touchdown run. Groza widened the score, which now stood at 35–7. Only 48 seconds had elapsed on the scoreboard clock since Buffalo had registered their seven.

The next Cleveland score came after Tom Colella, AAFC interception leader in 1946 and 1947, picked off yet another Buffalo pass. Starting on their own 40, Graham drove the Browns downfield. Ollie Cline ran for 20 yards and Motley for 25 to bring the ball to rest at the Bills' 5-yard line. Motley then carried across goal for his third touchdown of the day. Groza made the tally 42–7 in favor of the Browns.

The coup de grâce came with just over three minutes remaining in the contest, when linebacker Lou Saban intercepted a Still pass and returned it 39 yards for Cleveland's seventh touchdown of the afternoon. Once again, Groza added the extra point to make the final score 49–7.

Cleveland held Buffalo's talented offense to 170 yards. Motley carried 14 times for 133 yards, more than the entire Buffalo offense. "Buffalo crossed midfield only four times and only twice under its own power."[3]

As lopsided as the score was, the Browns had not played one of their better games of the season. It had taken them longer to put the Bills away than most people had expected. They had turned the ball over four times. Despite these miscues, the Browns came out on top and proved that they were the top team in the AAFC for the third year in a row. Coach Paul Brown, still anxious to prove his team's mettle against the NFL, stated, "If the National Leaguers think they are better, we're ready to play them, anytime, anyplace."

SCORING

	1	2	3	4	Totals
Buffalo Bills	0	0	7	0	7
Cleveland Browns	7	7	14	21	49

1st Quarter: Cle — TD E. Jones — 3-yard run (Groza kick) — 14:50. 2nd Quarter: Cle — TD Young — 18-yard fumble return (Groza kick) — 3:25. 3rd Quarter: Cle — TD E. Jones — 9-yard pass from Graham (Groza kick) — 2:02. Cle — TD Motley — 29-yard run (Groza kick) — 10:35. Buf — TD Baldwin — 10-yard pass from Still (Armstrong kick) — 14:50. 4th Quarter: Cle — TD Motley — 31-yard run (Groza kick) — 0:44. Cle — TD Motley — 5-yard run (Groza kick) — 9:44. Cle — TD Saban — 39-yard pass interception off Still (Groza kick) — 11:49.

STARTING LINEUPS

Buffalo Bills		**Cleveland Browns**
Alton Baldwin	Left End	Mac Speedie
Graham Armstrong	Left Tackle	Lou Groza
Harold Lahar	Left Guard	Ed Ulinski
Arthur Statuto	Center	Frank Gatski
Rocco Pirro	Right Guard	Bob Gaudio
John Kerns	Right Tackle	Lou Rykmus
William O'Connor	Right End	Dante Lavelli
George Ratterman	Quarterback	Otto Graham
Chet Mutryn	Left Halfback	Edgar Jones
Rex Bumgardner	Right Halfback	Dub Jones
Lou Tomasetti	Fullback	Marion Motley

(*Substitutions:* **Buffalo** — Ends: Vince Mazza, George Kisiday, Ed Balatti, Paul Gibson; Tackles: John Kissell, Jack Carpenter, Jerry Whalen; Guards: Edward King, John Wyhonic, Vince Scott; Centers: Ed Hirsch, Felto Prewitt, Jack Baldwin; Backs: Jim Still, Don Schneider, Alex Wizbicki, Achille Maggioli, Vic Kulbitski, Charles Schuette. **Cleveland** — Ends: George Young, John Yonakor, Horace Gillom, Frank Kosikowski; Tackles: Chet Adams, Forrest Grigg, Ben Pucci, Len Simonetti; Guards: Weldon Humble, Bill Willis, Alex Agase, Lin Houston; Centers: Lou Saban, Mel Maceau; Backs: Cliff Lewis, Tommy Colella, Tommy James, Tony Adamle, George Terlep, Billy Boedeker, Dean Sensenbaugher, Bob Cowan. Ara Parseghian, Ollie Cline.)

Head Coaches: Buffalo: Red Dawson; Cleveland: Paul Brown.
Officials: Referee: Samuel H. Giangreco; Umpire: George F. Holstrom; Field Judge: Hol Slutz; Linesman: William H. Ohrenberger; Sideline Judge: Titus B. Lobach; Alternate: George Vergara.

TEAM STATISTICS

Buffalo Bills		**Cleveland Browns**
13	First Downs	20
4	By Rushing	10
7	By Passing	8
2	By Penalty	2
69/167	Offensive Plays/Yardage	66/333
33/63/1.9	Rushing Attempts/Yards/Avg.	40/215/5.4

36	Pass Attempts	26
11	Pass Completions	11
30.6	Completion Percentage	42.3
104	Passing Yardage	118
1–2	Interceptions — Return Yards	5–80
6	Punts	3
42.5	Punting Average	32.7
0–0	Punt Returns/Yards	4–41
3	Kickoff Returns	2
51		66
3–3	Fumbles — Lost	6–3
7	Penalties	9
27	Penalty Yards	90
0/0	Field Goals/Attempts	0/1

1948 NFL — Snowbirds

1948 Championship — Chicago Cardinals (0) vs. Philadelphia Eagles (7)

SUNDAY, DECEMBER 19, 1948 — SHIBE PARK, PHILADELPHIA — 28,864
WEATHER CONDITIONS: 27°F., 5" OF SNOW ON THE GROUND — HEAVY SNOW
CONTINUED TO FALL THROUGHOUT THE GAME. SWIRLING WIND GUSTS. DARK, GRAY
OVERCAST. STADIUM LIGHTS TURNED ON PRIOR TO THE START OF THE GAME.
FIELD CONDITION: MUDDY IN SPOTS, FROZEN IN SPOTS, SNOW-COVERED, SLICK.

The Chicago Cardinals and the Philadelphia Eagles resumed their grudge match in the City of Brotherly Love. The Eagles were anxious to repay their Midwestern friends for their 1947 championship game loss. All seemed ready for a great game, but southeastern Pennsylvania provided some of the worst weather imaginable for a football game on that day. A tremendous winter storm left the field covered with several inches of snow and the yard markers, end zones, and sidelines virtually undetectable. At game time (1:30 P.M.), the snow was still falling hard and it would continue throughout the contest.

Cardinals center Vince Banonis recalled, "The ironic part of it was that the day before, it was very warm in Philadelphia. We practiced in our T-shirts. The next day we get up and there's a foot of snow on the windowsill."[1]

It had been another bittersweet season for the Cardinals. They had posted an 11–1–0 record, and according to many observers, they were even better than the 1947 squad. But once again, the specter of death visited the squad — this time right in their own locker room. After the team had defeated these same Eagles in Comiskey Park 21 to 14, tackle Stan Mauldin collapsed after his shower and died immediately, suffering a heart attack. The Cardinals dropped their game to the Bears the following week, but then ran the table, winning their next ten in a row to post the league's best record and beat out the Bears by one game in the Western Division.

The snow continued to fall in Philadelphia and Commissioner Bert Bell met with officials from both teams to determine whether or not to play the game or postpone it until the following week. The logistics for this seemed difficult. It was a week before Christmas; the Cardinals were already in town, and who knew whether a week's delay would ensure better weather? Cardinals coach and vice president Jimmy Conzelman stated that his team was there and ready to play. The conditions would affect each team equally. He saw no reason to delay. Eagles coach Earle "Greasy" Neale was for a postponement. He felt that better weather would provide a fairer test of the two teams, but the Eagles were ready whichever decision Bell made. The commissioner decided to proceed with the game.

Cardinals team captain Billy Dewell recalled, "If it wasn't for an unbelievable weather day, we could have beaten anyone. I remember Paul Christman looking out the window that morning at the hotel and then telling me, 'Don't look outside.'"[2]

The weather had amazingly little effect on the crowd as virtually all of the 37,000 seats in Shibe Park were sold in advance and 28,864 fans actually showed up. It did, however, affect the start time of the opening kickoff. Instead of warming up and kicking off at 1:30 P.M., the players were still busy helping the groundskeepers remove the heavy, snow-covered tarpaulin prior to warmups.[3] Ground crew estimated that 4 inches of snow covered the tarpaulin by game time. "The bad part about the field," continued Vince Banonis, "was that it was never shoveled during the night when it began snowing hard, so the tarp had all of this snow on it. Both teams had to help get the tarp off the field. During the game, it was tough to center the ball since the ball would get stuck in the mud."[4] Eagles fullback Steve Van Buren, who trekked across town by train and foot to get to the ballpark, recalled the players helping the grounds crew remove the tarpaulin. Rhetorically, Van Buren asked later, "Can you imagine players from the two teams doing that today before a Super Bowl?"[5]

Of course, as soon as the tarp came up, the field began to be covered with a layer of snow that blotted out all traces of yard markings. Ropes tied to stakes were employed along each sideline to mark the playing field. Bell ruled that while the yardage chains would be used on the sidelines to help demarcate "to go" distances, no measurements would be taken to determine first downs. Instead, the referee and field judges would make all final yardage and down determinations on the field. Marshall Goldberg remembers, "You couldn't even see the yard markers. The game should never have been played."[6]

After the tarpaulin was removed, the teams conducted abbreviated workouts, and at 2:00 P.M. the Eagles kicked off to their visitors from Chicago. Starting from their own 21-yard line, the Cardinals kept the ball on the ground and went three and out. The punt was returned to the Eagles' 37.

Eagles quarterback Tommy Thompson wasted no time in trying to catch the Cardinals off guard. On Philadelphia's very first play from scrimmage, Neale instructed him to call the "81 Special," an all-or-nothing pass play they had been practicing all week. Thompson, out of the shotgun, dropped back another step, set, and let go a bomb. He connected with Jack Ferrante at the Chicago 20, where two Cardinals defenders lost their footing and Ferrante glided untouched into the end zone. The Shibe Park faithful erupted in shouts of joy, but the excitement ended quickly as the officials called the play back, stating that Ferrante had lined up offside. Ferrante raced back screaming at the official, "Who? Who? Who was it?" The official responded deadpan, "You, and it wasn't even close."[7] The Eagles could not replicate their success and quickly stalled in the snow.

On their next possession, the Cardinals put together a sustained drive. Starting on their own 42, Chicago ran the ball six times. The foul weather and an injury to quarterback

Paul Christman forced Chicago to stay mainly on the ground all day. They would gain only 35 yards on 3 completions that afternoon. On this series, sparked mainly by Elmer Angsman's left-side runs of 6 and 14 yards, Chicago found themselves with a first down and the ball on the Eagles' 35-yard line. There the Philadelphia defense held tough, allowing the Cardinals only 5 more yards. On fourth down, Pat Harder attempted a 37-yard field goal. After clearing a spot where the ball would be placed, the ball was snapped and kicked, but it sailed up, but wide of the goal posts.

After the failed kick, the Eagles took over the ball on their own 20 and began a 40-yard drive into Cardinal territory. Leading the charge was Steve Van Buren, who picked up 25 through the line. On third and three, Tommy Thompson dropped back and let go an 18-yard pass to Pete Pihos. As Pihos drew a bead on the ball, Chicago defender Red Cochran stepped in front of him at the Cardinals' 22, picked off the pass and returned it 15 yards to the Chicago 37. The quarter ended on two more uneventful series of plays in which the teams traded punts.

The second quarter ran much the same way as the first. The teams traded the ball back and forth, resulting in 4 punts, 1 fumble, and 1 interception. The highlight of the period was when the Eagles, starting on the Chicago 34, drove the ball to the 8, where the Cardinals' defense stiffened and Cliff Patton missed on his first field goal attempt of the day.

Pat Harder kicked off to Philadelphia's McHugh to start the second half. McHugh, fielding the ball on his own 18, returned it 21 yards to give his team good field position at their own 39. On the third play from scrimmage, the usually sure-handed Van Buren gained 2 yards, but fumbled. The ball was recovered at midfield by Marshall Goldberg.

The Cardinals quickly moved into Eagle territory as Mallouf connected with Kutner for 11 yards on their final pass completion of the day. On the next set of downs, they were held just short of the first down and turned the ball over to Philadelphia on the Eagles' 31.

On a series of short runs and passes and a 15-yard penalty for roughing the passer, the Eagles penetrated to the Chicago 29. On fourth and one, Patton set up for his second field goal try of the afternoon, but the result was the same as the first as his 37-yard kick failed to register. The game remained scoreless.

The next two possessions for each team resulted in limited offense and punts. The final punt in this sequence was a booming, wind-aided 33-yarder by Philadelphia's Muha that went out of bounds at the Cardinals' 19. Chicago's Elmer Angsman then gained 2 yards off left tackle on each of the next two carries, setting up a third and six situation on their own 23. On the next snap, Ray Mallouf again handed off to Angsman, but this time with disastrous results. During the exchange, the ball was fumbled backwards and recovered on the Cardinals' 17-yard line by the Eagles' Bucko Kilroy. After the game, Cardinals coach Jimmy Conzelman, magnanimous in defeat, said of the play, "It was nobody's fault, just a mix-up on the handoff."[8]

On the final play of the third quarter, Philadelphia's Bosh Pritchard hit the left side of the line for a 6-yard pickup. Following a pair of 3-yard runs up the middle by Joe Muha and Tommy Thompson, the Eagles had a new set of downs and goal to go from the 5. Anxious not to let another scoring opportunity slip away, the Eagles turned to as much of a sure thing as they had — and sure-handed fullback Steve Van Buren got the call. On the next play, with the snow still coming down heavily, Van Buren took the handoff from Thompson, tucked the ball under his right arm and powered his way off right tackle into the end zone from the 5 for the score. As he crossed into the end zone, Van Buren lost his footing and fell forward, landing face first in the snow. As Van Buren's 200-pound frame came to rest, he lay on his stomach in the snow-covered end zone, cradling the ball. Al Wistert stood over him, patting him on the back, and the rest of the offense soon arrived. After congratulating Van Buren, the Eagles quickly got on their hands and knees to clear the snow off a patch of turf for Cliff Patton to attempt the PAT. With the snow cleared, Patton kicked the conversion to put the Eagles up 7–0. That ended the scoring for the day.

On the ensuing kickoff, Schwall provided some anxiety for the Philadelphia faithful as he gathered in Muha's deep kick at his own 5-yard line and returned it 20 yards, but nearly broke loose for a great deal more. That was as good as it got on that series as the Cardinals were forced to punt on fourth and one on their own 34. Mallouf's punt was noteworthy, as it traveled 52 yards and was blown dead at the Eagle 14.

With the ball deep in their own territory and a one-score lead, the Eagles' offense knew that they needed to move the ball and burn time. They proceeded to do just that. The first play was a sweep to the right by Pritchard that gained 11 yards, but was nullified by a holding call. It was now first and seventeen on their own 7. After a repeat to Pritchard gained only a yard and Van Buren was stopped for no gain on second down, Philadelphia knew that this third down was crucial. Needing 16 yards for a first down and a chance to retain the ball, Thompson and Neale looked to some diversion tactics to throw off the Chicago defenders. They repositioned Van Buren and sent halfback Joe Muha in motion. Thompson then faked a handoff to Van Buren, kept the ball, and, finding daylight in the middle of the line, reeled off a 17-yard run good for a first down. From here on in, the Eagles kept the ball on the ground, switching up runs between Van Buren, Thompson, and Pritchard and moving the pigskin to the Chicago 30. In all, they ran 15 plays, culminating in Patton's third field goal attempt of the day. Patton missed again as the slippery field and swirling wind wreaked havoc on the kicking game. In the contest, Patton hit on an extra point, but missed on field goal attempts from 12, 37, and 39 yards.

With a little over six minutes to play and the ball on their own 20, Chicago knew that it was time for a new tactic. Rookie Charley Eikenburg replaced Ray Mallouf. The results were not what Jimmy Conzelman had hoped for. On first down, Eikenburg's pass to Dewell was long. On second down, Eikenburg dropped back and was sacked for a 12-yard loss, and on third down, his deep pass was intercepted at the Chicago 42 by Ernie Steele, who was brought down immediately.

With 5:12 remaining in the contest, all the Eagles needed for their first championship was to keep control of the ball. But after losing yardage on the first two plays of the series, they found themselves deep in their own territory. Facing a third and 16 from their own 8-yard line, the Eagles needed a big play to ensure they kept control of the ball and the game. The Cardinals expected the ball to go to Van Buren, but instead Thompson faked a pitchout to the big back, kept the ball and scampered 17 yards for a first down. From there, the Eagles began to grind out more yardage. The Cardinals' defenders again received a steady diet of Van Buren, Pritchard, and Thompson. With two minutes to play, Van Buren's number was called and the big back did not disappoint as he broke loose for an 11-yard pickup to the Cardinals' 31. The Eagles held on and controlled the ball at the end of the game. As the final seconds ticked away, the Eagles were just 5 yards short of a second score, but they were content to simply hold the ball and let the clock run down. The final score was 7–0 in favor of the Eagles. The Philadelphia defense had shut down the Cardinals' potent backfield and the Eagles were league champions for the first time in franchise history.

The loss was bitter for the talented and favored Cardinals, who had experienced another emotional year as they again lost a teammate under tragic circumstances during the season. "It was a crime that we lost that game," stated halfback Red Cochran. "We had a much better ball club in '48 than in '47. We had beaten the Eagles twice going into that game. We were averaging thirty-three points per game and we were shut out, so you know something was wrong."[9]

Philadelphia made 17 first downs to the Cardinals' 7 and outrushed their visitors 225 to 96. Van Buren personally outrushed Chicago 98 yards to 96. Van Buren remembers, "It was sloppy, but not slippery. I could run okay, I just couldn't see far. It was snowing so hard, I couldn't even see the Cardinals' safety, Marshall Goldberg."[10] The passing game was fairly nonexistent for both teams, with the Cardinals going 3 for 11 and gaining 35 yards and the Eagles registering a mere 7 yards on 2 receptions and 12 attempts.[11]

SCORING

	1	2	3	4	Totals
Chicago	0	0	0	0	0
Philadelphia	0	0	0	7	7

1st Quarter : None. 2nd Quarter: None. 3rd Quarter: None. 4th Quarter: TD — Van Buren — 5 yard run (Patton Kick).

STARTING LINEUPS

Chicago Cardinals		Philadelphia Eagles
Red Cochran	Left End	John Green
Bob Zimny	Left Tackle	Jay MacDowell
Buster Ramsey	Left Guard	Duke Maronic
Vince Banonis	Center	Vic Lindskog
Plato Andros	Right Guard	Bucko Kilroy
Chet Bulger	Right Tackle	Al Wistert
Corwin Clatt	Right End	Neil Armstrong
Jerry Davis	Quarterback	Tommy Thompson
Charlie Trippi	Left Halfback	Ernie Steele
Elmer Angsman	Right Halfback	Russ Craft
Pat Harder	Fullback	Joe Muha

(*Substitutions:* **Chicago:** Ends: Mal Kutner, Bob Ravensberg, Bill Dewell, Sam Goldman; Tackles: Joe Coomer, Walt Szot, Dick Loepfe; Guards: Jake Colhouer, Ham Nichols, Ray Apolskis; Center: Bill Blackburn; Backs: Ray Mallouf, "Babe" Dimancheff, Vic Schwall, Marshall Goldberg, Charley Eikenburg. **Philadelphia:** Ends: Jack Ferrante, Dick Humbert, Pete Pihos; Tackles: Vic Sears, Otis Douglas, George Savitsky; Guards: Cliff Patton, Mario Gianelli; Center: Alex Wojciechowicz; Backs: Steve Van Buren, Bosh Pritchard, John Myers, Pat McHugh.)

Head Coaches: Chicago: Jimmy Conzelman; Philadelphia: Earle Neale.
Players' Shares: Philadelphia: $1,540.84; Chicago: $874.39.
Officials: Referee: Ronald Gibbs; Umpire: Sam Wilson; Field Judge: William F. McHugh; Head Linesman: Charles Berry; Back Judge: Robert C. Austin.

TEAM STATISTICS

Chicago Cardinals		Philadelphia Eagles
6	First Downs	16
3	- By Rushing	15
3	- By Passing	0
0	- By Penalty	1

/131	Offensive Plays/Yardage	/232
34/96	Rushing Attempts/Yardage	57/225
11	Pass Attempts	12
3	Pass Completions	2
27.3	Completion Percentage	16.7
35	Passing Yardage	7
2/20	Interceptions (return yards)	1/0
8	Punts	5
37.4	Punting Average	38.6
2/35	Punt Return Yards	2/22
3/2	Fumbles/Lost	1/1
4	Penalties	3
33	Penalty Yards	17
1	Field Goals Missed	3

1949 AAFC — Four for Four!

1949 All-American Football Conference Championship — San Francisco 49ers (7) vs. Cleveland Browns (21)

DECEMBER 11, 1949 — MUNICIPAL STADIUM, CLEVELAND — 22,550
WEATHER CONDITIONS: MID 20S, GRAY SKIES, COLD.
FIELD CONDITION: MUDDY, SLIPPERY.

Just two days after announcing a merger with the NFL, the All-American Football Conference held its fourth and final championship game. The Associated Press announced that a merger agreement had been reached between the two rival leagues on December 9. Knowledge of the agreement may have helped to keep fans away, as the crowd at Cleveland's Municipal Stadium was a disappointing 22,550. The weather also did not help. The skies were gray and threatening, the air cold, and the field was a mess — a mixture of mud and slush.[1]

On December 9, 1949, two days before what became the fourth and final AAFC championship game, the National Football League and All-American Football Conference announced a merger to take effect for the 1950 season. While it was called a merger and the "new" league was to be called the National-American Football League, the agreement was in reality an acceptance by the NFL of three AAFC teams and a dispersal of the remaining squads' players. The "merger" effectively ended the AAFC. Mercifully, the bidding war for players ended as well. The following March 3, Commissioner Bert Bell would announce that the "new" league he had touted in December would not be so new after all. Bell stated that on the advice of counsel and at the unanimous agreement of all 13 club owners, the 30-year-old NFL would continue to operate as it had, but with the addition of the three AAFC franchises.

The three teams from the AAFC that would merge into the NFL were the Cleveland Browns, the San Francisco 49ers, and the Baltimore Colts. The New York Yankees franchise was purchased by the owner of the NFL's New York Bulldogs, Ted Collins. Collins retained the right to all of the Yankees' players except six, who were assigned to the New York Giants. In addition to the Yankees, the Los Angeles Dons, the Chicago Hornets, and the Buffalo Bills were being discontinued. Inexplicably, the successful Buffalo Bills franchise was ignored in the merger, and their players were dispersed along with those of the other discontinued clubs.

The 49ers had traditionally provided stiff competition for the Browns. They had always played them tough and twice had beaten them in the four-year history of the league. San Francisco had finished second to the Browns in the Western Division in all three years that the league had two divisions. In 1949 the league was reduced to seven teams, after the Brooklyn Dodgers franchise merged with the New York Yankees. At that point it was decided to drop the divisions and let the top four teams compete in a playoff to determine a league champion. In the opening round, the first-place Browns played the fourth-place Buffalo Bills, defeating them 31–21. The 49ers, in second place behind Cleveland yet again, stopped the third-place Yankees 17–7 to put them into the league championship game for the first time.

Midway through the first quarter, Cleveland took over the ball and began a seven-play, 56-yard drive. The field at Municipal Stadium was a muddy, slushy mess, and the Browns' all-white uniforms were soon brown. The Browns struck first as Cleveland's Otto Graham hit end Mac Speedie on a 38-yard pass on which Speedie made a beautiful diving catch at the 49ers' 19. Marion Motley then moved the ball 10 yards, and four plays later, Edgar (Special Delivery) Jones scored the only touchdown of the first half on a 2-yard blast 7 minutes and 20 seconds into the first quarter. Lou Groza's PAT kick made it 7–0.

San Francisco threatened early in the second quarter as quarterback Frankie Albert moved the ball from their own 27 to the Browns' 24 on a nine-play drive. There they stalled and attempted a field goal, but Joe Vetrano missed a 41-yarder. The score was 7–0 at the half.

After receiving the second-half kickoff, the 49ers went three and out after netting just four yards on three carries. They were forced to punt. Graham then drove the Browns to the San Francisco 5 on the strength of receptions by Dante Lavelli and Dub Jones, but there the 49ers' defense held firm and the ball went over on downs. San Francisco was given another chance, but they fell short, again unable to move the ball past their own 30. Albert was again forced to punt.

In the third quarter, Cleveland's devastating fullback, Marion Motley, broke off tackle on a trap play and burst through the 49ers' defense, scoring the Browns' second touchdown on a 63-yard sprint. As the Associated Press reported, Motley's gallop was easily the most spectacular play of the game as he bolted through "the San Francisco backfield before anyone saw him, and he was going away as he crossed the goal line."[2] Groza's point after kick made the score 14–0.

In the waning minutes of the third quarter, the 49ers responded to Cleveland with a 74-yard drive that produced San Francisco's only points of the game. Just 14 seconds into the final period, the 49ers faced a fourth-down situation deep in Cleveland territory. With the snap of the ball, Frankie Albert dropped back and connected with end Paul Salata, who reached out, pulled the ball in and covered the remaining ground for a 23-yard touchdown pass. As he had done in all previous 49ers games, Joe Vetrano trotted onto the field and prepared for the point after. He then kicked his 107th consecutive extra point and preserved his record of having scored in all 56 San Francisco games. The score was now 14–7. There was still a chance that the 49ers could pull the game out and blemish the Browns' four-year dominance of the AAFC.

With San Francisco now within a score of tying the game, the Browns set in motion a drive designed to burn time and ideally to add some padding to their single-touchdown lead. The Browns returned the kickoff to their own 34-yard line. In an almost perfect eleven-play, 69-yard drive, the Browns accomplished both items when back Dub Jones plunged over the goal line from four yards out. Lou Groza's kick, which made the score 21–7 in favor of Cleveland, would prove to be the final point ever scored in an official AAFC game.[3]

The Browns had won their fourth straight championship and put an exclamation mark on their complete dominance of the AAFC. Paul Brown's juggernaut from Cleveland finished their four-year run with an overall record of 56–4–3. Two of those losses had come at the hands of these 49ers, but not today. In reflecting on San Francisco's defeat coach Buck Shaw said, "They had a weight advantage on the line and in the backfield, which was a heavy asset for a muddy field. We weren't covering close enough on Graham's sneaks either." After a moment he continued, "Aw hell, what's the use of analyzing? We just weren't good enough. You can't afford to make any mistakes against them. They're a great team."[4]

With the field a mixture of mud and slush, the game was remarkably error-free. Only one 5-yard offside penalty (on Cleveland) was called all afternoon and neither team lost the ball on a turnover. The Cleveland defense was again stout as they held the explosive 49ers offense to one touchdown and just 230 total yards. The powerful running game was held to 3.4 yards per rush, a full 2.1 yards below their season average. Frankie Albert was the big gainer for the 49ers, picking up 41 yards in five carries — much of this was impromptu as he scrambled away from the Cleveland pass rush. Fullback Joe Perry ran the second most for the Californians, gaining 36 yards on six attempts. San Francisco back Sam Cathcart from Santa Barbara State, who had gained 116 yards in the 49ers' previous appearance in Cleveland, was held to just 11 yards on 9 attempts on today's sloppy field.

Cleveland gained 217 yards on the ground versus San Francisco's 122 and completed passes for 128 yards to their opponent's 108. Marion Motley, aided greatly by his single 63-yard jaunt, was the leading ground gainer with 78 yards on eight carries. Edgar Jones ran the ball sixteen times for 63 yards and Otto Graham gained 62 on nine attempts.

After the game, Paul Brown, no doubt tired of being ignored and put down by NFL officials, stated, "I'd like nothing better than to play the National League champ as soon as possible."[5] Unfortunately for Brown and his team, they would have to wait nine months for that opportunity, but when it did come, they made the most of it. The Browns overwhelmed the defending NFL champion Eagles by a score of 35–10 in Philadelphia on September 16, 1950.

The AAFC would have one last hurrah on December 17, 1949, when the Browns squared off against the AAFC All-Star team in Houston, Texas, in the Shamrock Bowl. The game would be the last official function of the noteworthy and in many ways successful circuit that helped make the National Football League truly national in scope.

SCORING

	1	2	3	4	Totals
San Francisco 49ers	0	0	0	7	7
Cleveland Browns	7	0	7	7	21

1st Quarter: Cle: E. Jones 2-yard run (Groza kick) — 7:20. 2nd Quarter: None. 3rd Quarter: Cle: Motley 68-yard run (Groza kick). 4th Quarter: SF: Salata 23-yard pass from Albert (Vetrano kick). Cle: D. Jones 4-yard run (Groza kick).

STARTING LINEUPS

San Francisco 49ers		Cleveland Browns
Hal Shoener	Left End	Mac Speedie
Bob Mike	Left Tackle	Lou Groza
Homer Hobbs	Left Guard	Ed Ulinski
Bill Johnson	Center	Frank Gatski
Visco Grgich	Right Guard	Lin Houston
John Woudenberg	Right Tackle	Lou Rymkus
Alyn Beals	Right End	Dante Lavelli
Frankie Albert	Quarterback	Otto Graham
Len Eshmont	Left Halfback	Edgar Jones
Joe Perry	Right Halfback	Dub Jones
Norm Standlee	Fullback	Marion Motley

(*Substitutions:* **Cleveland**—Ends: George Young, Horace Gillom, John Yonakor; Tackles: Derrell Palmer, Forrest Grigg, Joe Spencer; Guards: Bill Willis, Alex Agase, Bob Gaudio, Weldon Humble; Center: Lou Saban; Backs: Cliff Lewis, Warren Lahr, Tommy James, Tony Adamle, Ed Sustersic. **San Francisco**—Ends: Paul Salata, Gail Bruce, Norm Maloney; Tackles: Ray Evans, Charley Quilter, Jack Carpenter; Guards: Don Clark, Bruno Banducci; Centers: Peter Wismann, Tino Sabuco; Backs: Sam Cathcart, Jim Cason, Don Garlin, Joe Vetrano, Lowell Wagner, Verl Lillywhite.)

Head Coaches: San Francisco: Buck Shaw; Cleveland: Paul Brown.
Officials: Referee: Thomas A. Timlin; Umpire: William A. Pritchard; Head Linesman: William H. Ohrenberger; Field Judge: Lloyd Brazil; Sideline Judge: Edward F. Fendt.

TEAM STATISTICS

San Francisco		Cleveland
14	First Downs	16
58/230	Offensive Plays/Yardage	58/345
33/122	Rushing Attempts/Yardage	41/217
25	Pass Attempts	17
9	Pass Completions	7
36.0	Completion Percentage	41.2
108	Passing Yardage	128
0	Interceptions By	0
6	Punts	4
44.0	Punting Average	43.0
23	Punt Return Yards	61
2/0	Fumbles/Lost	0/0
0	Penalties	1
0	Penalty Yards	5

1949 NFL — Are You Sure This Isn't Seattle?

1949 NFL Championship — Philadelphia Eagles (14) vs. Los Angeles Rams (0)

SUNDAY, DECEMBER 18, 1949 — LOS ANGELES MEMORIAL
COLISEUM, LOS ANGELES — 22,245
WEATHER: MID 40S, RAIN, THREE INCHES OF RAIN HAD FALLEN IN THE
DAY PRIOR TO THE GAME. THE OVERCAST AND RAIN CONTINUED
THROUGH THE FIRST HALF, SLOWING IN THE SECOND.
FIELD CONDITION: MUDDY AND SOAKED WITH THREE INCHES OF RAIN.

The Rams were back in the NFL championship game for the second time in five years, but this time they were representing their new home of Los Angeles. Rams owner Dan Reeves had never been satisfied with his team's success at the gate in Cleveland. Seeing the vast business potential in southern California, Reeves had forced a move from Cleveland prior to the 1946 season, much to the chagrin of his league ownership brethren. This was, however, the first year of the All-American Football Conference and the AAFC had already placed teams in Los Angeles and San Francisco. The NFL fathers knew that they could not simply cede the West Coast to the new circuit and grudgingly gave in to Reeves. Just months after winning their first NFL title, the Cleveland Rams packed up and headed west.

Clark Shaughnessy's 1949 Rams got off to a blistering 6–0 start, but lost in game seven to the Eagles and struggled through the remainder of their schedule. The Rams finished with an 8–2–2 record in 1949, eking out the Western Division crown from the 9–3–0 Chicago Bears. While the Rams only beat the Bears by percentage points in the standings, they did defeat the Bruins twice in head-to-head play. Veteran Bob Waterfield and rookie Norm Van Brocklin led the offense at quarterback. They were aided on the receiving end by Tom Fears, Bob Shaw, and Elroy "Crazy Legs" Hirsch.

The Philadelphia Eagles had rolled to an 11–1–0 record and an easy third straight Eastern Division crown behind the hard running of Steve Van Buren and Bosh Pritchard. Quarterback Tommy Thompson had made frequent targets of ends Jack Ferrante, Pete Pihos, and Neil Armstrong. The Eagle defense and its 5–2–4 defense had stopped their opponents' passing games cold.

In a rare turn of events, Los Angeles was hit by a rainstorm on December 17. It rained all night and it would not let up until well into the third period of the game. The storm deposited more than 3 inches of rain on the land of sunshine just in time for the first NFL championship game played west of Chicago.

Concerned about the effect the weather might have on the quality of play and, maybe more importantly, the game's attendance figures, Rams owner Dan Reeves and Eagles owner Jim Clark telephoned league commissioner Bert Bell requesting a postponement of the game for the following weekend. Reeves and Clark rang the commissioner asking, "Could we postpone the game? Conditions are impossible. The gate sale will be lost."[1] Bell, who had decided not to travel to California for the game, was still in Philadelphia. He stated that radio commitments made postponement impossible. Bell also mentioned that the league had television commitments with the Dumont Network and he did not want to pass up the opportunity to showcase his league on the new medium. An irate Reeves emerged from his office to address the waiting press. He stated, "The league commissioner, who is 3,000 miles away, informed us that radio commitments make the postponement impossible." The press, as amazed as Reeves and Clark, packed up their gear and got ready to report a soggy game.[2]

Reeves's and Clark's concerns over attendance were well justified, as only 22,245 patrons showed up for the game. Advance sales of 40,000 tickets during the week before the game gave Reeves hope of twice that many attending Sunday's championship tilt.

The Eagles gathered at the Bel-Air Hotel on the eve of the game for their pregame meeting. The Philadelphians had been acting overly confident all week. They had not taken practice seriously and refused to prepare adequately for the hometown Rams. The meeting was fairly routine as coach Earle "Greasy" Neale addressed his defending world champions, but the players still seemed sluggish and uninterested. As the meeting drew to a close, the Eagles' big tackle and field captain Al Wistert stood and addressed his teammates. In a stern tone he said, "Just a minute. You guys take a good look at yourselves. You're not ready for this game. Your attitude is plain lousy. You'd better get the lead out of your pants and grow up."[3] His words resonated with his Eagle teammates. They knew he was right.

By game time, Wistert's words had turned the lackadaisical Eagles into a team ready to give all to defend their championship. Despite the inhospitable weather and a muddy field, the Eagles' fullback Steve Van Buren lived up to his billing as tough and reliable ground gainer. Though he did not score that day, he ground out 196 yards on 21 carries, both championship game records. Again and again, Philadelphia gave the ball to Van Buren and time and time again, he'd respond with the yardage to keep a drive alive.

The teams took the field as the rain continued to pelt Los Angeles. The Rams wore gold jerseys with blue trim, white pants, and blue helmets with the gold ram's-horn logo. The Eagles wore white jerseys and pants with green numbers and trim and green and white helmets. In a short time, the mud made it hard to tell who was wearing what.

No one scored in the 1st quarter as the teams slogged through mud to a scoreless draw. The Rams were keying on Van Buren as the big back out of LSU ground out yardage for the Eagles.

Early in the 2nd the Eagles put together the only sustained passing attack of the day. On this drive Philadelphia passer Tommy Thompson threw for 58 of the 68 yards he would gain through the air for the day. First he hit end Jack Ferrante for gains of 11 and 16 yards. Thompson mixed in plunges of 2 and 3 yards by Bosh Pritchard and Steve Van Buren respectively. Thompson then took advantage of an injury to the Rams' Gabby Sims to go for a quick aerial strike. With star defensive back Sims out for a play, Thompson sent Pete Pihos deep between the Rams' Fred Gehrke and Jerry Williams. There the Eagles' end took a Thompson pass over his shoulder at the Rams' 15 and ran the rest of the way unmolested into the end zone for a 31-yard touchdown toss. Bucko Kilroy remembered later, "Pete made a great catch under any conditions. He had great hands to begin with and rarely dropped a ball. This one seemed to stick as soon as it hit his fingers, and he came down with it and with no one around him. He just turned and ran into the end zone. The Rams couldn't believe it. We had used a play that was supposed to be a specialty of theirs and had scored against them. All of that work trying to stop Van Buren had netted them zero."[4] Cliff Patton kicked the extra point to put the Eagles ahead 7–0. That was all the scoring in the first half.

By halftime Van Buren already had collected 121 yards on 13 carries, but his day was far from over. In the second half, he would carry the ball 18 more times for another 75 yards.

In the third period, with the Rams set to punt deep in their own territory, Rams center Don Paul snapped the ball high. Waterfield, who had kicked marvelously all day, was able to jump and corral the ball, but by the time he kicked it, Philadelphia's end Leo Skladany was on top of him. As soon as the ball left Waterfield's foot, Skladany blocked it, scooped up the loose ball on the 2-yard line, and rumbled untouched into the end zone for the Eagles' second score of the day. Again, Patton connected for the PAT to put Philadelphia up 14–0. That was the end of the scoring for the day, but with over a quarter to play, the game was far from over. Neale, looking to maintain possession and to keep the ball on the ground, turned to the ever-reliable Steve Van Buren to grind out yardage. Time and again, Thompson gave the ball to the sure-handed LSU alumnus, who would dig through the mud and rain for valuable yardage, as the Eagles put a wrap on their second straight NFL championship.

The downpour, the muddy field, and the persistent Eagles rush hampered the potent Rams passing attack. Waterfield and Norm Van Brocklin combined for 98 yards on the day in 28 attempts. The ground game was worse. All Ram backs combined for only 21 yards rushing. This gave the Rams only 119 yards total offense on the day. Los Angeles was able to cross the 50-yard line only twice and were unable to score.

The Eagles combined for 342 yards total offense, the lion's share of which belonged to Van Buren. The former LSU star gained 196 yards on 31 carries while continually giving the Eagles strong field position. During the game, Van Buren broke both the single and career championship game rushing marks, held by Elmer Angsman and Bronko Nagurski, respectively. Thompson completed 5 of 9 passes for 68 yards on the day.

The other unsung heroes of the day were the Philadelphia defenders, who held Los Angeles to only 21 yards rushing, the fewest in league playoff history. Drives to the Eagle 25 and 37 were the extent of the Los Angeles scoring threats for the soggy afternoon.

After the game, Coach Neale was addressing the press. When asked what made the difference in the game's outcome, he didn't hesitate to tell the reporters, "We won the world championship right there in the Bel Air Hotel, and Al Wistert is the guy who did it."[5]

SCORING

	1	2	3	4	Total
Philadelphia Eagles	0	7	7	0	14
Los Angeles Rams	0	0	0	0	0

1st Quarter: None. 2nd Quarter: Philadelphia — TD — Pihos 31-yard pass from Thompson (Patton kick). 3rd Quarter: Philadelphia — TD — Skladany 2-yard return of blocked LA punt (Patton kick). 4th Quarter: None.

STARTING LINEUPS

Philadelphia Eagles		**Los Angeles Rams**
Jack Ferrante	Left End	Tom Fears
Vic Sears	Left Tackle	Dick Huffman
Cliff Patton	Left Guard	Hal Dean
Vic Lindskog	Center	John Martin
Frank "Bucko" Kilroy	Right Guard	Ray Yagiello
Al Wistert	Right Tackle	Gil Bouley
Pete Pihos	Right End	Bill Smyth
Tommy Thompson	Quarterback	Bob Waterfield

Steve Van Buren	Left Halfback	Tom Kalmanir
Clyde Scott	Right Halfback	Verda "Vitamin T" Smith
John Myers	Fullback	Dick Hoerner

(*Substitutions:* **Philadelphia**— Ends: Neil Armstrong, Leo Skladany; Tackles: George Savitsky, Jay McDowell, Mike Jarmoluk; Guards: Mario Gianelli, John Magee, Walt "Piggy" Barnes, Duke Maronic; Centers: Alex Wojciechowicz, Chuck Bednarik; Backs: Frank Reagen, Frank Ziegler, Russ Craft, Bosh Pritchard, Jim Parmer, Pat McHugh, Joe Muha, Ben Kish. **Los Angeles**— Ends: Frank Hubbell, Don Currivan, John Zilly, Bob Shaw, Tom Keane; Tackles: Al Sparkman, Ed Champagne; Guards: John Finlay, Mike Lazetich; Centers: Fred Naumetz, Don Paul; Backs: Norm Van Brocklin, Fred Gehrke, Elroy Hirsch, Paul "Tank" Younger, Jerry Williams, George Sims, Gerry Cowhig.)

Head Coaches: Philadelphia: Earl "Greasy" Neale; Los Angeles: Clark Shaughnessy.
Players' Shares: Philadelphia: $1,094.68; Los Angeles: $739.66.
Officials: Referee: Ronald Gibbs; Umpire: Joseph Crowley; Field Judge: William F. McHugh; Head Linesman: Charles Berry; Back Judge: Robert C. Austin.

Team Statistics

Philadelphia Eagles		Los Angeles Rams
17	First Downs	7
70/342	Total Offense Plays/Yards	51/119
61	Rushing Attempts	24
274	Rushing Yardage	21
9	Pass Attempts	27
5	Pass Completions	10
56.0	Completion Percentage	37.0
68	Passing Yardage	98
1	Interceptions By	2
0/0	Sacks/Yards Lost	2/10
6	Punts	9
36.3	Punting Average	38.1
14	Punt Return Yards	17
0	Had Blocked	1
0/0	Fumbles/Lost	0/0
6	Penalties	4
40	Penalty Yards	25

1950 NFL — Look, Elmer, We've Got a Ball!

1950 NFL Championship — Cleveland Browns (30) vs. Los Angeles Rams (28)

DECEMBER 24, 1950— MUNICIPAL STADIUM, CLEVELAND — 29,751
WEATHER CONDITIONS: SNOW PILED HIGH IN A RING AROUND THE FIELD, OVERCAST, 28 MPH WINDS, WINTRY, 29°F.
FIELD CONDITION: FROZEN, HARD.

It was cold and bitter in Cleveland on this Christmas Eve afternoon. A persistent wind was blowing in off Lake Erie. The Rams, who had defeated the Redskins for the world championship here on an even colder day just five years before, were back in their old hometown to teach a lesson to the class of the All-American Football Conference.

The AAFC had been a source of irritation for the NFL and the Browns and their success had been a particular sore spot. The story began five years earlier when Rams owner Dan Reeves, recently back from the war, saw a gold mine waiting to be tapped on the increasingly populous West Coast. Shortly after winning the 1945 NFL championship, the Rams packed up their trophy and left the cold, snowy banks of Lake Erie for the warm, sunny climes of southern California. The Cleveland fans, understandably feeling jilted, wanted and felt they deserved a new team immediately. Attempts were made to secure a new franchise for Cleveland, but the NFL's appetite for expansion was not there; so Cleveland businessman Arthur B. "Mickey" McBride, who had built his fortune with a fleet of taxicabs, applied for a franchise in the upstart AAFC. Although they were unwilling to grant Cleveland a new franchise, NFL owners were irritated that McBride was throwing his lot in with the AAFC.

The NFL had battled the AAFC for talent and attendance for four long seasons until both leagues, battered, bruised, and financially wounded, agreed to a merger for the 1950 season. As it turned out, it was not really so much a merger as an absorption of the AAFC into the NFL. It was agreed that the Browns, along with the San Francisco 49ers and the lowly Baltimore Colts, would join the NFL in 1950. The remaining clubs (the Los Angeles Dons, New York Yankees, Chicago Hornets, and Buffalo Bills) were inactivated and their players placed in a special reentry draft for the NFL clubs to pick over the remaining talent.

Outspoken Washington Redskins owner George Preston Marshall stated, "The worst team in our league could beat the best team in theirs."[1] The Browns were out to prove once and for all that they deserved to be "in the club." It was as if they were carrying both their own reputation and that of their AAFC brethren on their shoulders as they entered their first NFL season.

In their first game as members of the NFL, the Browns had defeated the NFL champion Philadelphia Eagles by the overwhelming score of 35–10 in Philadelphia's Shibe Park. Cleveland coach Paul Brown and quarterback Otto Graham called such a perfectly orchestrated game that the score could easily have been more lopsided. Many in the NFL old guard claimed the victory was a fluke based on overdependency on the passing game. Brown answered these critics by refusing to call a pass in the rematch on December 3. The flightless Browns still defeated Greasy Neale's Eagles 13–7. The only real trouble the Browns had all season was with the New York Giants, who defeated them twice in the regular season and wound up with an identical 10–2 record in the American Conference. In a one-game playoff, the Browns edged the Giants 8–3. Now, after a highly successful inaugural NFL season, the Browns were ready to put to rest the AAFC's critics.

Three members of the Rams were holdovers from the team's days in Cleveland and had played in the frigid 1945 championship game. Quarterback Bob Waterfield, tackle Gil Bouley, and guard Mike Lazetich must have had flashbacks to that game when they trotted onto the Municipal Stadium playing field for the 1950 game. The snow was again piled high in a ring around the field, and while 20 degrees warmer, it was nonetheless a wintry Cleveland day with the frigid wind whipping in off the lake.

The Browns wore their white jerseys with orange and black trim, white pants and helmets; the Rams were clad in yellow jerseys with blue trim, white pants, and dark blue helmets with the now-familiar yellow ram-horns logo. Many of the Browns wore sneakers on the frozen turf.

Cleveland won the coin toss and elected to kick off, keeping the wind at their backs. Groza teed up the ball and kicked it deep to Los Angeles' dangerous Verda "Vitamin T" Smith. Smith was always a threat to break loose on a return. He had three touchdowns this season, but the Browns' coverage team brought him down on the Los Angeles 18-yard line.

The Rams lined up in the T-formation with Waterfield at quarterback and Smith, Glenn Davis, and Dick Hoerner rounding out the backfield. The always-dangerous Elroy Hirsch and Tom Fears lined up at the ends for Los Angeles.

On the first play from scrimmage, Rams quarterback Bob Waterfield, who had led the Rams to the championship in this same arena just 5 years earlier, threw an 82-yard touchdown strike to former Army All-American Glenn Davis to put Los Angeles up to an early 7–0 lead. After eluding Cleveland defenders Tommy James and Ken Gorgal, Davis caught the ball at the 45 and streaked the rest of the way down the sideline for the score. Just 27 seconds into the game, the Rams were prepared to show their dominance. Rams assistant Hamp Pool remembers, "That first play took advantage of their 5–3–3 defense. We sent a man in motion to the right and had our left end, Tom Fears, break inside. Our left half back, Glenn Davis, gave a first picture that he was going to block. The Browns' linebacker was supposed to cover Davis, but when he took his eyes off him to follow Fears, Davis sneaked out and took Waterfield's pass for the TD."[2]

The Rams kickoff was returned to the Cleveland 30 by the Browns' Ken Carpenter.

Graham, refusing to let the early Rams lead rattle him, led the way back for the Browns. In five plays he moved the Browns to the Los Angeles 31. Graham completed three passes to Dub Jones and Dante Lavelli, ran for a 22-yard gain, and then handed off for a short gain by Marion Motley. With the ball now resting at the Rams' 31-yard line, he hit receiver Dub Jones on a flareout pattern for a 31-yard touchdown strike. Lou Groza successfully completed the PAT kick, tying the score at 7 only three minutes into the game.

Now the Rams came roaring back. Smith was again stopped for a short return and the Rams started this drive at their own 19. After a 5-yard completion to end Tom Fears, Waterfield went to the well again, connecting with Fears on a 44-yard pass to put the Rams back in scoring position at the Cleveland 32. Los Angeles then went with the ground attack to secure a score. After gaining 13 yards over the next five plays, the Rams struck for a large gain that put them on the verge of another score. From the 19, Smith followed left guard Jack Finlay through the line for a 16-yard gain to give the Rams first and goal on the 3. On the final play of the drive, 6'4", 220-lb. fullback Dick Hoerner slashed his way over tackle and into the end zone. With the successful PAT, Los Angeles led 14–7 as the first quarter came to an end.

The offensive onslaught continued for the first four minutes of the second quarter. Cleveland returned the Los Angeles kickoff to the Rams' 35-yard line. The Browns drove down to the Rams' 21, aided by a pass interference call against Los Angeles defender Woodley Lewis and a 17-yard reception by Mac Speedie at the 26-yard line. Graham then threw 21 yards to Dante Lavelli, who was streaking towards the end zone. Lavelli pulled in the pass and, with the ball tucked tightly with both arms against his body, sprinted the remaining yards into the end zone to bring the Browns to within one point. Everyone in the stadium was sure of a tie score as Groza lined up for the PAT. Holder Tom James kneeled, waiting for the long snap, but when it came, it was high. James was able to get his fingers on it and knock it down. He recovered the ball and ran to his right, looking to improvise the score. He located teammate Tony Adamle in the end zone, but the pair couldn't quite connect and the ball bounced off Adamle's fingers and fell futilely to the ground. It was a rare miscue for the well-disciplined Browns.

After the spate of early scoring, the defenses stepped into the game and took over for the rest of the quarter. The Rams threatened twice, forcing drives to the Cleveland 7- and 8-yard lines. On the first, Waterfield connected on passes to Tom Fears and Elroy Hirsch and featured Dick Hoerner on delays, traps and even a Statue of Liberty play, to bring the ball to the Cleveland seven. They could get no closer as a holding penalty pushed the Rams back to the Browns' 26. Waterfield then underthrew Fears over the middle and the ball was intercepted by Cleveland defender Ken Gorgal at the 16. Gorgal took the low throw on the run and returned the ball to the Cleveland 49-yard line.

Graham and the Browns' offense could do nothing with the ball, losing twelve yards on three plays and being forced to punt it away. Standing on his own 30, Cleveland punter Horace Gillom took the snap from center, but the Rams were coming fast for the block. The normally reliable Gillom, who had punted 66 times in 1950 for a 43.2-yard average, hurried the kick and sent the ball a scant nine yards downfield, giving the Rams terrific field position.

Waterfield went back to work, hitting Fears and Hirsch for gains of ten and eight yards, respectively, but when he tried the Statue of Liberty play again, Cleveland defensive end Len Ford saw it coming and dropped Vitamin T Smith for a fourteen-yard loss. Los Angeles got back on track thanks to a reception by Fears and a personal foul against the Browns. On third and eight on the ten-yard line, Waterfield called keeper up the middle, but gained only two. Waterfield then set up for what should have been an easy 15-yard field goal try, but with the help of the wind, the ball went wide. Time ran down on the half and the clubs went into the clubhouses with the Rams clutching their tight 14–13 lead. The Browns, who had been thoroughly outplayed so far, were just glad to head into the warm locker room trailing by a single point.

Knowing that his squad was fortunate to be as close as they were on the scoreboard, Paul Brown knew that he must motivate his men quickly if they were to have any chance of winning this game. Whatever he told the Browns had the desired effect as Cleveland came out of the club house ready to play.

The Browns took the second-half kickoff and, starting at their own 27, immediately began to march downfield. They were without the services of receiver Mac Speedie, who had pulled a hamstring; he had gamely played the first half, but by halftime he could barely straighten his leg and was forced to sit out the remainder of the contest. Gillom replaced Speedie and made an immediate impact as he took a screen pass from Graham and bolted for a 29-yard pickup. In just four plays, the Browns were in scoring position. From the Rams' 39, Graham lobbed a pass over the outstretched fingers of Los Angeles defender Tom Keane and into the hands of Dante Lavelli, who scored the go-ahead touchdown. Groza connected for the point after and the Browns led for the first time 20–14.

Vitamin Smith returned Groza's kickoff to his own 29. Waterfield wasted no time in heading the charge back downfield as he passed for a first down on receptions by Smith and Fears. From the Los Angeles 45, Waterfield connected again with Smith on a 38-yard strike to the Cleveland 17. The Rams' quarterback then turned back to powerful fullback Dick Hoerner, who began battering the Browns' defenders, carrying the ball seven consecutive times. Finally Hoerner ended the 71-yard drive by scoring on a 1-yard plunge. Waterfield kicked the extra point and the Rams led again 21–20.

The Browns downed Woodley Lewis's kickoff in the end zone and began their next drive on their own 20. Graham called a pitchout to Marion Motley, who cut to the outside to his right behind several good blocks. He had gained 8 yards when the Ram defenders began to close on him. Determined to make more yardage, he cut back in an attempt to let his blocking regroup. It never did, and what started as a sizeable gain began to be a sizable loss. Motley continued to run behind the line of scrimmage, looking for daylight. At the 14, Los Angeles defenders Larry Brink and Jack Zilly caught the brilliant Cleveland runner, and then a horde of Rams descended on Motley and brought him down, knocking the ball loose. As the ball rolled loose, Brink scooped it up and sprinted into the end zone. With the extra point, the Rams increased their lead to 28–20. They had scored twice in twenty-one seconds. The Municipal Stadium crowd was in shock. In just minutes, the Browns' 20 to 14 lead had evaporated into a 28 to 20 deficit.

After the kickoff, the Rams' defense stiffened, and the Browns, demoralized and ineffective, ran three plays for five yards and were forced to punt. Again, Los Angeles began to move the ball, but when the Rams resumed the passing game, the Browns were ready. Cleveland defensive back Warren Lahr put some life back into his team when he picked off a Waterfield pass five minutes into the fourth quarter. Lahr's pick gave the Browns a renewed chance as he stopped what looked like a certain Rams scoring drive and brought the ball back to the Cleveland 35-yard line.

Los Angeles, knowing that Cleveland had to score twice, set their defense to foil the long pass. Brown and Graham saw this and immediately sent Lavelli on short, sideline routes. Five straight times he found Dante as the Browns moved the ball to the Rams' 43. Graham and his receiving corps were dangerous long or short. Paul Brown remembers, "The defenders couldn't afford to come up fast or Graham would have faked a quick one and thrown deep."[3] On fourth and one, Graham lowered his shoulders and gained three hard-fought yards.

The Browns continued to drive and moved the ball to the Rams' 14 on five runs and three more passes to Lavelli. One of the runs was a three-yard rollout by Graham to keep the drive alive on fourth down. Graham now had to consider how to score quickly. He knew that Los Angeles would be keying on Lavelli and Dub Jones, so he decided to go to Mac Speedie's replacement Rex Baumgardner. The Cleveland end took off downfield, but was quickly picked up by linebacker Fred Naumetz and defensive back Woodley Lewis. Although the coverage was tight, Baumgardner got a step on his defenders. Graham then let go a low and wide pass that Baumgardner reached down and pulled in off his shoe top before tumbling onto the frozen end zone turf. Groza's extra point cut the Los Angeles lead to just one point with half the period left to play. The anxious Municipal Stadium crowd went wild with hope and anticipation.

When the Rams took possession of the ball, they hoped for a sustained drive that would burn the clock and put the game away. Instead, the Browns, led by their excellent defensive end Len Ford, harassed Waterfield in the backfield, forcing a Los Angeles punt by Waterfield. Ford had been tormenting the Rams' backfield throughout the game, dropping Los Angeles runners for several big losses. Ford had a great deal of pent-up energy as he was playing for the first time in more than two months. He had been injured on October 15, suffering a fractured jaw and cheekbone when the Chicago Cardinals' Pat Harder slugged him in the face.

The Browns' offense was slowed once again by a tough Los Angeles defense, and Gillom stepped in to punt it away. This time he did, sending the ball 68 yards and putting the

Rams deep in their own territory to start the next possession. Waterfield was not comfortable with the one-point lead and he went to the air to try to keep the drive alive. The Cleveland defense then came through when Tommy Thompson made a diving interception of a Waterfield pass on the Los Angeles 47-yard line. The Browns had the ball back and there was still time, but the clock was beginning to become a factor.

Graham again went to the air, connecting for 22 yards to Jones, putting Cleveland well within Groza's kicking range. But with three minutes left to play, Graham made an uncharacteristic miscue. He reasoned that on this cold day, a 31-yard kick would be difficult for Groza. He determined to gain a first down and keep the drive going rather than try the kick now. Graham then called his own number, running a bootleg around left end. As Otto began to round the end of the line, he was leveled by Rams linebacker Mike Lazetich. Graham fumbled the ball and Lazetich recovered. Graham recalled, "I never saw the guy coming. I wanted to dig a hole right in the middle of that stadium, crawl into it and bury myself forever."[4] The quarterback continued, "I figured that fumble cost us the game."[5] As the dejected Graham trotted off the field, he remembered, "I got to the sidelines and wanted to hide, but Paul came over, put his arm around my shoulder and said, 'Don't worry. We'll get it back. We're going to win.'"[6]

Across the field, the Rams were still hoping for a time-consuming drive. With three minutes left on the clock, a first down would all but cinch the championship. They burned time between plays, they handed off to Hoerner up the middle twice for no gain, and then to Davis, who gained 6 yards off right tackle, but the desperate Cleveland defenders held their ground. It was three and out. Cleveland would indeed have one last chance. On fourth down, Waterfield punted a deep 54-yard kick to Cliff Lewis, who stood at the Cleveland 19. He caught the ball and returned it for 13 yards before going out of bounds. The Browns would start their drive on their own 32-yard line with 1:50 left on the game clock.

The Rams defenders were obviously as determined to stop the Cleveland drive as the Browns were to score. On the first play from scrimmage they flooded the backfield and looked to bottle up the Browns' quarterback. Under pressure, Otto looked downfield, but saw that all of his receivers were tightly covered. Graham deftly stepped out of the pocket, headed to his right and weaved his way through the Los Angeles defenders. As Otto broke free, he headed for the sideline and stepped out of bounds to conserve precious seconds after a 14-yard gain.

On the next play, Graham found Baumgardner open in the left flat for a 15-yard gain. The next play, a pass intended for Jones in the end zone almost ended in disaster as linebacker Fred Naumetz got a hand on the ball and almost had an interception that would have sewn up the championship for the Rams. While the Rams' defense kept up the pressure, Graham passed to Dub Jones at the 23 for 19 more yards. Graham, once again in his rhythm and with his confidence renewed, hit Baumgardner again for 12 more yards, putting the ball on the Los Angeles 11 with 45 seconds to play. Graham called time out and trotted over to strategize with his coach. Brown had been on the phones with assistant coach Blanton Collier, who was watching from the coaches' booth high above the field. He suggested that with 45 seconds and another time out left, the Browns might do well to run another play and gain a better angle on the kick. The Browns were in the open end of the stadium, where the crosswinds off the lake could wreak havoc with airborne footballs. On the sidelines, the Browns' brain trust debated a straight handoff up the middle to Baumgardner, but cold hands and the fear of a bobbled handoff ruled that out. "The ball had been marked on the left hash mark when Otto called a timeout, and this left a bit of an angle," recalled Collier.

Paul came to the phone and said, "What do you think?" I said, "Let's run Otto on a quarterback sneak to the right because of that wind, then kick it." He said, "Okay." I lived one hundred years for the next few seconds because all of a sudden it dawned on me, "You crazy nut! You have the ball down there now and you want to take a chance on someone fumbling it on this frozen ground just to move it in a little better position." That's all we would get, maybe just a little better position. But I had become so intent on that factor I forgot about the danger of handling the football in one more scrimmage situation.[7]

But Otto Graham did not forget. To improve their field position, Graham again lowered his right shoulder and ran with the ball firmly tucked against his torso, on a keeper straight up the middle for one centering yard. The ball was now lying directly in front of the goal posts and well within Groza's range.

With the game clock ticking off the final 30 seconds of the game, holder Tommy James dropped to one knee on the 16, Lou Groza set himself up for a chance at the lead. "The only thing I thought about was my own little checklist for kicking a ball," recalled Groza. "I didn't hear the crowd, I blotted out the distance, the time left, even the score. All I had to do was to kick the ball."[8] On the count, Cleveland center Hal Herring fired off a clean snap to James, who set the ball. Groza stepped forward and connected, sending the ball straight between the uprights for a 30–28 Browns' lead as the clock sank below 20 seconds.

As the final seconds ticked off the clock, the Rams made a desperate effort to move the ball into field goal range, but it was to no avail. Los Angeles' Jerry Williams took Groza's kickoff at his own 12-yard line and made a remarkable 35-yard run. Williams almost broke into the clear, but was caught at the Rams' 47. With time ticking away, Stydahar sent in Van Brocklin to air out a long pass. A reception in the end zone would mean a win, and one just short of the end zone would put the Rams in field goal range. At the snap, Van Brocklin dropped back seven yards and set up for a long pass. Ignoring the sharp pain from his broken ribs, the Dutchman fired a 55-yard sideline pass to Glenn Davis, but Warren Lahr was covering Davis closely. Lahr again snatched the ball for a Cleveland interception. He was immediately wrestled to the ground by Davis, who fought for the ball until the referee could sort through the mass of arms and legs. There were several moments of high anxiety for the Browns as the officials huddled to make the call. If Davis had joint control of the ball, the Rams would maintain possession, enabling a chip shot field goal try. Also, Lahr's momentum had carried him into the end zone. The Browns feared that the officials might rule either for a touchdown, giving the Rams the win, or for a safety, tying the game and giving the ball back to Los Angeles. "It was terrible," Graham said. "We didn't know what the referee was going to call."[9] Eventually, the referee signaled for the change of possession and the Browns were champions for a fifth straight year, but this time in a new league. The naysayers had finally been silenced. What more could they say?

Both teams had played well. They posted amazingly similar team statistics. Waterfield had a great day, completing 18 of 31 passes for 312 yards and the 82-yard touchdown to Davis. Graham was 22 of 33 for 298 yards and four touchdowns. Cleveland end Dante Lavelli caught 11 passes and scored twice.

The defensive star for Cleveland may well have been end Len Ford. Ford came to Cleveland after two seasons with the Los Angeles Dons, but played in only five games due to a broken jaw. After missing two months to the injury, he returned to the Cleveland lineup with immediate results. No one was getting around him and he seemed to be in the Rams' backfield as often as Waterfield. At one point, he dropped Smith for a 14-yard loss, sacked

Waterfield for 11 more, and then for good measure, he collared Davis on a sweep for 13. Ford would continue to help anchor the Cleveland defense throughout the 1950s.

In the locker room after the game, coach Paul Brown said, "I never gave up hope. I know this gang too well. I know they never quit. This is the greatest football team a coach ever had. There has never been a team like this one. There never was a game like this one. Next to my wife and my family, these guys are my life."[10]

SCORING

	1	2	3	4	Totals
Los Angeles Rams	14	0	14	0	28
Cleveland Browns	7	6	7	10	30

1st Quarter: Los Angeles — TD — Davis — 82-yard pass from Waterfield (Waterfield kick). Cleveland — TD — Jones — 31-yard pass from Graham (Groza kick). Los Angeles — TD — Hoerner — 3-yard run (Waterfield kick). 2nd Quarter: Cleveland — TD — Lavelli — 26-yard pass from Graham (Groza kick failed). 3rd Quarter: Cleveland — TD — Lavelli — 39-yard pass from Graham (Groza kick). Los Angeles — TD — Hoerner — 1-yard run (Waterfield kick). Los Angeles — TD — Brink — 6-yard fumble return (Waterfield kick). 4th Quarter: Cleveland — TD — Bumgardner — 19-yard pass from Graham (Groza kick). Cleveland — FG — Groza — 16 yards.

STARTING LINEUPS

Los Angeles Rams		Cleveland Browns
Tom Fears	Left End	Mac Speedie
Dick Huffman	Left Tackle	Lou Groza
John Finlay	Left Guard	Weldon Humble
Fred Naumetz	Center	Frank Gatski
Harry Thompson	Right Guard	Lin Houston
Bob Reinhard	Right Tackle	Lou Rymkus
John Zilly	Right End	Dante Lavelli
Bob Waterfield	Quarterback	Otto Graham
Glenn Davis	Left Halfback	Rex Bumgardner
Verda "Vitamin T" Smith	Right Halfback	"Dub" Jones
Dick Hoerner	Fullback	Marion Motley

(*Substitutions:* **Los Angeles** — Ends: Bob Boyd, Larry Brink, Bill Smyth, Elroy Hirsch; Tackles: Ed Champagne, Gil Bouley; Guards: Dave Stephenson, Stan West, Vic Vasicek, Mike Lazetich; Centers: Don Paul, Art Statuto; Backs: Woodley Lewis, "Deacon" Dan Towler, Jerry Williams, Paul Barry, Tom Keane, Tom Kalmanir, Ralph Pasquariello, Norm Van Brocklin, Paul "Tank" Younger. **Cleveland** — Ends: George Young, Jim Martin, Horace Gillom, Len Ford; Tackles: Darrell Palmer, Forrest Grigg, John Kissell, John Sandusky; Guards: Bill Willis, Abe Gibron, Alex Agase; Centers: Hal Herring, Tom Thompson; Backs: Ken Gorgal, Ken Carpenter, Emerson Cole, Tony Adamle, Warren Lahr, Tom James, Cliff Lewis, Dom Moselle, Don Phelps.)

Head Coaches: Los Angeles: Joe Stydahar; Cleveland: Paul Brown.
Game Officials: Referee: Ronald Gibbs; Umpire: Samuel Wilson; Head Linesman: Charles Berry; Field Judge: Lloyd Brazil; Back Judge: Norman Duncan.

TEAM STATISTICS

Los Angeles Rams		Cleveland Browns
22	First Downs	22
418	Offensive Yardage	414
106	Rushing Yardage	116
32	Pass Attempts	33

18	Pass Completions	22
58.3	Completion Percentage	66.7
312	Passing Yardage	298
1	Interceptions By	5
4	Punts	5
50.8	Punting Average	38.4
14	Punt Return Yards	22
0/0	Fumbles/Lost	3/3
4	Penalties	3
48	Penalty Yards	25

1951 NFL — How to Stop a Freight Train?

1951 NFL Championship — Los Angeles Rams (24) vs. Cleveland Browns (17)

DECEMBER 23, 1951— LOS ANGELES MEMORIAL COLISEUM, LOS ANGELES — 59,475
WEATHER CONDITIONS: GRAY, TEMPERATURES IN THE 30S.
FIELD CONDITION: CLEAR, FIRM, DRY.

The NFL Championship was returning to Los Angeles Memorial Coliseum for the second time in three years and this time the weather would cooperate by providing warm and dry conditions. The Rams would compete for the third time in three years, having dropped the first two decisions to the Eagles and Browns, respectively. Coming into the game today, the Rams had never defeated the Browns. With good weather and home field advantage, the Rams hoped that this was their year. Most of the championship-game record crowd of 59,475 fans hoped so, too.

Cleveland had proven to again be the class of the league, posting an 11–1 record, while the Rams finished with a less impressive 8–4 in the National Conference. To make it worse for the NFL old guard, the Browns' only loss had come in their season opener against fellow AAFC alumnus the San Francisco 49ers. Who could stop the Browns? Even the New York Giants, who had defeated the Browns twice in 1950, had lost two close contests in 1951.

Among the familiar faces of the veterans, the Rams sported 13 rookies on their roster. Among them were end and future Hall of Famer Andy Robustelli, who had replaced an injured Jack Zilly early in the season. Zilly never got his job back. Also in that crop of newcomers were ends Larry Brink and Norb Hecker. Robustelli, Brink, and Hecker would each play critical roles in today's game.

On October 7 these same two teams met at this same venue. 67,186 fans watched the Rams jump out to a 10–0 first-quarter lead, but the Browns came back, scoring 28 unanswered points to win 38–23. Back Ken Carpenter scored the first three touchdowns in the Cleveland onslaught, which was also aided by a 23-yard interception return for a touchdown by defensive back Warren Lahr, and by four Lou Groza PAT kicks.

Both teams were passing juggernauts. Cleveland's Otto Graham was still linking up with Dante Lavelli, Dub Jones, and Mac Speedie. Common wisdom was that the game would pivot on whose pass rush could keep the heaviest pressure on the opposing offense. Rams ends Larry Brink and Andy Robustelli would need to apply that pressure. To do so, they would have to get past formidable Cleveland tackles Lou Rymkus and Lou Groza.

The Browns took the opening kickoff and Lew Carpenter returned the ball to his own 23. Cleveland advanced to the Rams' 16 in just ten plays, but could get no further as the stout Los Angeles defense held firm. Needing seven yards on fourth down, Groza set up at the 23 for a field goal, but the kick went wide.

After a scoreless first quarter, the Rams finally got on the board on a 55-yard drive. Waterfield hit Verda Smith for 18 yards, and then threw a screen for 15 more to fullback Dick Hoerner. An interference call against Cleveland's Tommy Thompson at the 12 moved the Rams into scoring position. From there, Hoerner bulled his way for four more, Smith added one, and Dan Towler powered his way for 6 yards to the Cleveland 1. The scoring drive culminated in a 1-yard plunge by Hoerner. Waterfield's point after kick put the home team up 7–0, five minutes into the second period.

"Cleveland started another march after the next kickoff, got to the Rams' 40, but then Graham was spilled for consecutive losses of six and nine to his own 45, forcing Gillom to punt. Smith again signaled for a fair catch and the Rams started from their 17."[1] Waterfield started to move the Rams, but on third down and six, he threw a long pass down the middle to Elroy Hirsch that was intercepted by Cleveland defender Warren Lahr at the Browns' 45-yard line.

As Cleveland took over, Graham connected with Speedie for ten to the Rams' 45 for a first down. On the next three downs Graham threw incomplete passes, the last two of which hit Carpenter in the hands, but he couldn't hold on. On fourth down, Groza set up for a long field goal attempt. Remarkably, Lou hit from 52 yards, breaking the championship game record of 42 yards that was held jointly by the Giants' Ward Cuff (1938) and the Packers' Ernie Smith (1939).

Cleveland's defense held the Rams on their next possession and got the ball back to the offense with three minutes remaining in the half. Graham struck again before the break, to take a 10–7 lead into the clubhouse. On the drive, Otto completed three passes for 54 yards. Completions went to Speedie for 14 yards, Motley for 23, and Dub Jones for the final 17 yards of the drive. Groza added the extra point kick to extend Cleveland's lead to 3.

On the Rams' final possession before the half, Waterfield got the ball moving as he connected by air to Davis for 11 yards to the Los Angeles 31. Two more passes put the ball on the Browns' 23, but there, Cleveland's Tommy James intercepted Waterfield at the Cleveland 22 to end the half and prevent a Los Angeles score. Cleveland went into the locker room leading 10 to 7.

As the second half started, Cleveland got a break as Tommy Thompson hit the Rams' Dan Towler head-on in a run from scrimmage and caused a fumble. Cleveland's Hal Herring recovered the ball on the Browns' 36.

On second down from the Browns' 35-yard line, Graham called a pass. As the play unfolded, Rams ends Larry Brink and Robustelli converged on the great Cleveland quarterback as he dropped back and set up. The 240-pound Brink was the first to arrive and he hit Graham a lick, jarring the ball loose at the 30, where it bounced off the turf once and into Robustelli's hands. According to Robustelli, "I never got a really good grip on the ball because I just grabbed it off-balance and began to run. I stumbled as soon as I started, and it seemed I kept stumbling all the way down the field, trying to keep the ball in my grasp."[2] Robustelli "stumbled" for 28 yards before he was dropped from behind by Marion Motley. The Rams' offense took over at the Cleveland 2, and the first two plays on the drive yielded no yardage. Dan Towler got three straight calls. On third down, Deacon Dan powered over the goal line to put the Rams back on top by 3. Bob Waterfield's PAT kick made the score 14–10.

Graham was intercepted again on the Browns' next possession as Jerry Williams grabbed a long pass. But Graham, still determined to win his sixth straight championship, refused to yield. As he ran off the field, he was already thinking about the Browns' next opportunity. It came after the Cleveland defense again held the Rams and forced a punt.

Fighting their way to their own 48, the Browns were moving the ball well. On first down, Graham decided to go for it all. He fired a 52-yard pass for touchdown to a wide-open Mac Speedie, who was so far from the nearest defender that he trotted the final 20 yards into the end zone. The Rams, however, caught a huge break when the play was called back as Groza was called for holding on Robustelli. That ended the Cleveland drive. After the Browns' punt, the Rams' number 11, Norm Van Brocklin, trotted onto the field at quarterback. Stydahar decided to spell Waterfield and go with "The Dutchman" to attempt to gain another quick score as insurance against the powerful and lightning-quick Cleveland offense.

On his first drive at the helm, Van Brocklin moved the Rams downfield to the Cleveland one. The key play on this drive was a 48-yard strike to Tom Fears. At the one, the Browns' tenacious defense found its resolve and dug in. Over the next four downs, the Cleveland defenders pushed the Rams' offense back 17 yards. The highlight of the stand came on a fourth-down field goal fake on which the Browns dropped the always-dangerous Glenn Davis on a reverse.

The Browns took over at the 20, still looking for a way back into the lead. But the Los Angeles defenders, still guarding a tenuous seven-point lead, took advantage of another Graham miscue. Graham, again under heavy pressure, hurried a pass that was intercepted by Rams rookie defensive back Marvin Johnson at the Browns' 36. Johnson ran it back to the one.

Once again, the Rams could get no closer to the goal line. For a second time, the Browns' defenders, aided by two Rams penalties, held tough and pushed Los Angeles back to the 11. This time the Rams decided not to get fancy and Waterfield kicked a 17-yard field goal to extend their lead to 17–10.

Early in the fourth quarter, Graham led the Browns back on a ten-play, 70-yard drive. Anticipating that Graham would come out throwing, Stydahar pulled his linebackers and inserted seven defensive backs. Graham netted 34 yards himself on a sideline run. On one play, Graham dropped back to throw, saw his receivers well covered, and decided to run. With the Rams now back in their standard defense, the Browns continued to chip away the yardage. Ken Carpenter went 5 yards over right tackle into the end zone. Groza added the extra point to knot the game at 17 with just under eight minutes remaining in the game.

The Rams got the ball back at their own 24-yard line after the Browns' tying touchdown. After gaining only 3 yards on the first play of the series, Van Brocklin went to the air. On second and three he sent Fears to the left and down the sideline. He then made a cut to the center between Lewis and James. As Van Brocklin's pass came down, Fears caught it in mid-stride and easily outdistanced all defenders as he raced into the end zone to complete the 73-yard touchdown play. Remembering that play, then-Cleveland assistant Blanton

Collier said, "We knew he loved to throw long on those third-and-eights, third-and-tens. He never changed that style. I can see that ball coming off his hands and going through the air. Fears had run down the sidelines and made his cut. It looked like the pass might be overthrown, but Tom reached out and made a great catch as the ball came right down on his fingertips between Lewis and James."[3] With Waterfield's extra point kick, the Rams led by 7 points, 24–17.

It was now up to the defense to contain the high-octane Browns' offense that was seemingly always just one play away from a score. The bigger the challenge, the more determined they seemed. In the 1950 championship game against these same Rams, Graham had engineered a 71-yard drive in the final minutes of the game to pull out a victory. "There still were more than eight minutes to play when the Rams went ahead, and the belief was universal that the Browns would once more strike back as they always have done. But they didn't."[4]

On first down, Graham threw a pass directly into Ram defender Don Paul's hands. Paul tucked the ball in and bulled his way to the Browns' 14-yard line. The Cleveland defenders held their ground, forcing a field goal. Lineman Bill Willis ended the Rams' scoring threat by blocking Waterfield's field goal try from the 23. Cleveland's offense took over the ball with a first down on their own 38.

Again, Graham went to work with a series of short passes to Jones and Carpenter designed to limit the Rams' reaction time. This worked well at first, but the Rams quickly adjusted. On fourth and two from the Los Angeles 42-yard line, Graham threw a short flare pass to Jones, who caught the ball, but he was dropped immediately by rookie defensive back Norb Hecker for a 2-yard loss. From there on, the Rams' defense was superb, holding the Browns' offense at key junctures and quickly getting the ball back to their own offense. The game ended with the score still 24–17 in favor of the hometown Rams. In their excitement, the Los Angeles players carried their coach Joe Stydahar — all 275 pounds of him — off the field.

Waterfield was 9 of 24 for 125 yards and two interceptions. Van Brocklin completed four of six passes for 128 yards and a touchdown. Graham had a pretty good day, completing 19 of 40 passes for 280 yards and one touchdown. He also led all rushers with 43 yards on 5 carries.

Tom Fears had a big day with 4 catches for 146 yards. Mac Speedie led all Cleveland receivers with 7 catches for 81 yards.

Both teams' defenders were stars this afternoon. Time and time again both defenses rose to the occasion, stopping drives and putting up goal-line stands. Twice the Browns stopped the Rams at the 1-yard line.

In their account of the game, the Associated Press gave a glancing, yet poignant compliment and recognition of the Browns' dominance of professional football since 1946 when they said, "Los Angeles' spectacular Rams, with a tie breaking 73-yard pass play in the final quarter, captured the National League championship today from the Cleveland Browns in a battle that ended the visitors' five-year rule in professional football. The score was 24–17."[5] For a five-year rule to end, Messrs. Bell, Marshall, et al., it must have actually begun.

SCORING

	1	2	3	4	Totals
Cleveland Browns	0	10	0	7	17
Los Angeles Rams	0	7	10	7	24

1st Quarter: None. 2nd Quarter: Los Angeles — TD — Hoerner —1-yard run (Waterfield kick)— 5:44. Cleveland — FG — Groza — 52 yards —10:44. Cleveland — TD — D. Jones —17-yard pass from Graham (Groza kick)—12:30. 3rd Quarter: Los Angeles — TD — Towler — 2-yard run (Waterfield kick). Los Angeles — FG — Waterfield —17 yards. 4th Quarter: Cleveland — TD — Carpenter 5-yard run (Groza kick). Los Angeles — TD — Fears — 73-yard pass from Van Brocklin (Waterfield kick).

STARTING LINEUPS

Los Angeles Rams		Cleveland Browns
Tom Fears	Left End	Mac Speedie
Don Simensen	Left Tackle	Lou Groza
Dick Daugherty	Left Guard	Abe Gibron
Leon McLaughlin	Center	Frank Gatski
Bill Lange	Right Guard	Bob Gaudio
Tom Dahms	Right Tackle	Lou Rymkus
Elroy Hirsch	Right End	Dante Lavelli
Bob Waterfield	Quarterback	Otto Graham
"Deacon" Dan Towler	Left Halfback	Ken Carpenter
Paul "Tank" Younger	Right Halfback	"Dub" Jones
Dick Hoerner	Fullback	Marion Motley

(*Substitutions:* **Los Angeles** —Ends: Larry Brink, Norb Hecker, Tom Keane, Andy Robustelli, Bob Boyd; Tackles: Jim Winkler, Charley Toogood, John Halliday; Guards: Harry Thompson, Stan West, John Finlay, Bob Collier; Centers: Don Paul, Joe Reid; Backs: Glenn Davis, Verda "Vitamin T" Smith, Woodley Lewis, Jerry Williams, Tom Kalmanir, Norm Van Brocklin, Herb Rich, Marv Johnson. **Cleveland**— Ends: George Young, Len Ford, Bob Oristaglio, Horace Gillom; Tackles: Darrell Palmer, Forrest Grigg, John Kissell, John Sandusky; Guards: Tom Thompson, Bob Gaudio, Bill Willis, Lin Houston, Alex Agase; Center: Hal Herring; Backs: Rex Bumgardner, Emerson Cole, Tony Adamle, Warren Lahr, Tom James, Cliff Lewis, Don Shula, Harry Jagade, Carl Taseff.)

Head Coaches: Cleveland: Paul Brown; Los Angeles: Joe Stydahar.
Players' Shares: Los Angeles: $2,108.44; Cleveland: $1,483.12
Game Officials: Referee: Ronald Gibbs; Umpire: Samuel Wilson; Head Linesman: Charles Berry; Field Judge: Lloyd Brazil; Back Judge: Norman Duncan.

TEAM STATISTICS

Cleveland Browns		Los Angeles Rams
22	First Downs	20
69/325	Offensive Plays/Yardage	73/334
23/92	Rushing Attempts/Yardage	43/81
41	Pass Attempts	30
19	Pass Completions	13
46.3	Completion Percentage	43.3
280	Passing Yardage	253
5/47	Sacks/Yards Lost	0/0
3/76	Interceptions By (return yards)	2/0
5	Kickoff Returns	4
132	Kickoff Return Yards	21
4	Punts	5
37.3	Punting Average	43.4
13	Punt Return Yards	0
-1	Fumbles/Lost	-1
6	Penalties	5
41	Penalty Yards	25

1952 NFL — The Lions' Texas Connections

1952 NFL Championship — Detroit Lions (17) vs. Cleveland Browns (7)

DECEMBER 28, 1952 — CLEVELAND MUNICIPAL STADIUM, CLEVELAND — 50,934
WEATHER CONDITIONS: PARTLY CLOUDY, 30°F.
FIELD CONDITION: FIRM, DRY.

The Browns were heading to their seventh league championship game in seven years. They had won the first five, but dropped the sixth to the Los Angeles Rams. They were anxious not to let that happen again. They had met their championship game opponent, the Detroit Lions, only twice. Both games had come in 1952. The Browns topped the Lions in an exhibition game in August, but lost the regular season contest in October by a score of 17–6.

Going into this game, the Browns were hampered by injuries to half a dozen players. Most notably, halfback Dub Jones and end Mac Speedie were gimping around on damaged knees, and tackle and place kicker Lou Groza was nursing a rib injury. "Jones and Speedie had accounted for 105 of the Browns' 184 good passes and 1,562 of the 2,389 yards the Brownies gained by the air this season."[1] It was hoped that all would be ready to play, but only Groza was.

Detroit coach Buddy Parker, who had been a fullback on the Lions' only other championship team in 1935, had brought the team back by assembling a group of stalwart holdovers, castoffs from other teams, and some fine rookies, and turning them into a strong, cohesive unit. Parker inherited quarterback Bobby Layne, who arrived in the Motor City in 1950 after spending his rookie year on the bench with the Chicago Bears and a frustrating year on the turf with the hapless and soon to be defunct New York Bulldogs in 1949. Layne was a spark plug ready to energize the Lions. Now he just needed an engine to start. Enter Coach Parker.

Parker saw the huge potential in the fiery Layne. The tow-haired Texan looked like anything but an athlete off the field. He was never in great condition, sometimes even sporting a bit of a paunch. He was a notorious carouser and never believed in the concept of training rules. More than once, teammates told of practically being knocked over from the smell of liquor on his breath in the huddle. Bobby Layne was no role model off the field, but the man could win. He had a strong and quick throwing arm and a sharp mind, and he was an inspirational leader on the field. He was the consummate competitor and he wanted to beat his opponent whether on the gridiron, at the card table or playing at jacks. Layne's longtime friend and teammate Doak Walker said of his fellow Texan, "Bobby never lost a game in his life. Time just ran out on him."[2] And teammate Jim David, a cornerback, said of Layne, "Bobby just had a way. He got you there. Say what you want about him and how he lived his life, but he got you there."[3]

Parker also recognized the tremendous talent in former SMU halfback Doak Walker.

Walker had arrived in Detroit in 1950 and led the league in scoring as a rookie. Walker started out well, but would miss seven games during the 1952 regular season due to a leg injury. He was back for the championship game, however, and he would make a difference.

Parker went about assembling a supporting cast. One of his first moves was bringing fullback Pat Harder over with him from the Cardinals in 1951. Harder was a terrific blocking fullback and place kicker out of the University of Wisconsin who had played in the 1947 and 1948 championship games. He kicked four points after touchdown in the Cardinals' win over the Philadelphia Eagles in the 1947 game. Harder was considering retirement after the 1950 season, but Parker talked him into a few more years in Detroit.

To shore up the line, Parker also brought center Vince Banonis with him from Chicago. Banonis had played his college ball in Detroit and was happy to return. Parker also obtained end Bill Swiacki from the Giants, and guard Jim Martin from the Browns. Parker brought the retired Cloyce Box out of a one-year retirement to suit up at end. In 1952, he added back Earl "Jug" Girard from Green Bay.

Most of the first quarter was a defensive struggle with neither team able to move the ball effectively. Late in the quarter, however, the Lions got a break. Faced with fourth and long from their own 28-yard line, Cleveland was forced to punt. Horace Gillom, the league's leading punter, stood back on the Cleveland 20 awaiting the snap. Gillom took the center's pass and swung his usually reliable leg, making contact with the ball. As soon as the ball left his foot, it was obvious that something was wrong. The ball went uncharacteristically off the side of his foot and wobbled weakly out of bounds at midfield, giving the Lions great starting field position.

Layne trotted onto the field with his mind at work. He was sizing up the situation and determining how to turn this opportunity into a score. As the first quarter was ending, Layne connected with Box for a 10-yard pickup and followed that up with a bootleg around left end to gain 13 more as the quarter came to a close.

As the second frame began, Pat Harder fought his way forward for a solid gain to the Browns' 17-yard line, landing just inches short of another first down. Layne followed up with a quarterback keeper, gaining a yard and the first down. Layne then fired a line drive to Bill Swiacki good for 14 yards, giving the Lions first and goal at the Cleveland 2. A five-yard illegal procedure penalty pushed Detroit back to the 7, but Doak Walker quickly gained those 5 yards back to make it second and goal from the 2. On the next play, the eighth of the drive, Layne simply lowered his shoulder and charged up the middle to score. Harder's kick put the Lions on top 7–0.

The teams then settled in for trench warfare for the remainder of the half as both Layne and Graham were harassed by enemy defenders. No points were scored and tempers flared as the two sides fought a pitched battle for supremacy. Several times officials had to separate players who were shoving and wresting, and in the fourth quarter Cleveland's John Sandusky was ejected for landing a right to a Lion's jaw.

Cleveland took the second-half kickoff and began to move the ball downfield at a rapid pace. "They got to the 25, but on a second-down play, Graham aimed a pass at Carpenter, who made contact with the ball for an apparent first down on the 15. But he didn't hold it, the leather bounding into the hands of Jim David of the Lions."[4]

During the third quarter, the gimpy Walker briefly returned to the brilliant form that he had shown in his first two seasons in Detroit. The Lions had the ball on their own 33-yard line when Layne told Cloyce Box to go long. At the snap, Layne dropped back as if to pass. With the tall end lumbering downfield and Cleveland defenders Tommy James and

Bert Rechichar striding alongside, Layne handed off to Walker. The former SMU star slipped through the line between the guard and tackle slot and then cut hard to his left. Clear of the line traffic, Walker now looked downfield to see what roadblocks lay ahead, just in time to see Box throw a sweeping body block that leveled both James and Rechichar in one shot. With an open lane in front of him, Walker didn't slow down for 67 yards until he passed the goal line for his first touchdown of an injury-riddled season. Harder's kick made it 14–0 in Detroit's favor.

The Browns answered immediately with a 10-play drive that started on their own 22-yard line. Graham, who had been ineffective in the first half, gaining only 9 aerial yards on 10 attempts, returned to form. After a 15-yard penalty for shoving, Graham connected with end Dante Lavelli for gains of 9 and 11 yards, Pete Brewster for 22 and Ray Renfro for 8. Otto even carried for 12 yards himself. Harry Jagade powered the ball the last seven yards with Lion defenders Thurman McGraw and Don Doll hanging on. Lou Groza lined up for a successful point after kick and the Browns were back in the ball game at 14–7.

Detroit took the ensuing kickoff, but could do nothing with the ball and punted to Cleveland, pinning the Browns down on their own 17-yard line as the third quarter was winding down.

The Browns pushed the ball to midfield and threatened to tie the game after big Marion Motley rumbled 42 yards before being forced out of bounds at the Detroit 5. His momentum was so strong that he slid a full five yards downfield and into the goal line flag. But the drive stopped there. On first down, Motley was stopped in the backfield for a 5-yard loss by defensive back Don Doll, who flew into the Cleveland backfield untouched. It got worse on second down, when Graham dropped back to pass and was mobbed by the Detroit defense. Otto was sacked for a 12-yard loss. Graham kept the ball on third down, but gained only a yard. It was now fourth and goal from the 22. Everyone knew Graham would throw, and when he did, Detroit linebacker Dick Flanagan read the pass and deflected the ball to the turf. Detroit took over on downs.

The Lions again could not move the ball, and coming up short of first down yardage, they again were forced to punt. There were nine minutes left in the final quarter. Plenty of time to make up the seven-point deficit, but it was here that the bottom fell out for Cleveland. Browns halfback Ken Carpenter dropped back deep for Bob Smith's punt. The high kick came down easily, but the usually sure-handed Carpenter muffed the catch and the ball squirted away. Detroit's Jim Martin recovered at the Cleveland 24-yard line. A 15-yard personal foul penalty moved the Lions back to the 39. Over the next three plays, they gained ten yards, making it back to the 29, where Pat Harder kicked an insurance field goal to give the Lions a two-score advantage at 17 to 7.

But the mighty Cleveland Browns refused to lie down. On their next series of downs, which started on their own 15, the Browns moved the ball confidently downfield. After moving the ball to the Detroit 39, Graham connected with end Pete Brewster for 31 yards. The Lions' Jack Christiansen collared Brewster at the 8, saving the touchdown. Again, the Browns fell apart with first and goal. Graham threw three incomplete passes and drew a 5-yard penalty for delay of game. On fourth down, Graham threw a tipped pass that found Brewster in the end zone for what appeared to be a touchdown. Again, however, fate was not on the Browns' side as the officials determined that Ray Renfro had tipped the pass into Brewster's hands and no defensive player had touched it in between. The touchdown was thus nullified and the Lions took possession of the ball on their own 13-yard line. The game soon ended and the Detroit Lions were league champions for the first time in seventeen years.

The score was not one-sided and the game stats were not terrible, but they didn't tell the story. Graham finished the game with 191 yards passing on 20 out 34 completions. Respectable numbers, but he was only himself in spots. He missed badly on many of his incomplete passes and the team never really got moving consistently. "Though Graham was constantly bothered by the Lions' crashing ends and his receivers weren't getting clear, the Browns twice got close enough for Groza to try field goals. But both times Lou missed, once from the 44 and again from the 47."[5]

The Browns outgained Detroit on the ground, 229 yards to 199. Harry Jagade rushed for 104 yards and a touchdown and led all backs on the day. But for all of the good, when they needed a big play, the Browns went cold. In addition, the Browns were unquestionably hampered by the absence of Mac Speedie and Dub Jones.

"In short, it seemed as if this was the Browns' whole season wrapped up in 60 minutes of bristling action — injuries, errors and the inability to punch the ball over for those precious points when within shooting range of the end zone."[6] The Browns held the ball for almost twice as many plays as the Lions did. They outran and outpassed Detroit, gaining 126 more total yards than the Lions. Only twice did the Browns' defense allow the Lions to pass the 50-yard line under their own power. The other two times Detroit started with the ball on Cleveland's side of the 50.

Despite their lackluster showing, both Graham and Dante Lavelli set championship game records. Graham passed Bob Waterfield for passes attempted and Lavelli passed the Redskins' Wayne Millner by catching 19 passes in three games.

On the Lions' stat sheets, Doak Walker led Detroit with 97 yards rushing on 10 carries, 67 of which came on his third-quarter touchdown gallop.

Detroit did not play their best game of the season, but they did enough to win and took advantage of the several Browns miscues. Cleveland coach Paul Brown recognized the talent in the other locker room when he told reporters after the game, "I've been saying all along that Detroit had the best club in the league. I guess this proves it."[7]

SCORING

	1	2	3	4	Totals
Detroit Lions	0	7	7	3	17
Cleveland Browns	0	0	7	0	7

1st Quarter: None. 2nd Quarter: Detroit — TD — Layne — 2-yard run (Harder kick). 3rd Quarter: Detroit — TD — Walker — 67-yard run (Harder kick). Cleveland — TD — Jagade — 7-yard run (Groza kick). 4th Quarter: Detroit — FG — Harder 36 yards.

STARTING LINEUPS

Detroit Lions		**Cleveland Browns**
Bobby Layne	Quarterback	Otto Graham
Pat Harder	Fullback	Chick Jagade
Doak Walker	Left Halfback	Ray Renfro
Bob Hoernschemeyer	Right Halfback	Ken Carpenter
Cloyce Box	Left End	Pete Brewster
Lou Creekmur	Left Tackle	Lou Groza
Jim Martin	Left Guard	Abe Gibron
Vince Banonis	Center	Frank Gatski
Gus Cifelli	Right Tackle	John Sandusky
Dick Stanfel	Right Guard	Lin Houston

Leon Hart	Right End	Dante Lavelli
Jim Doran	Left Defensive End	George Young
Thurman McGraw	Left Defensive Tackle	Bob Gain
Les Bingaman	Middle Guard	Bill Willis
John Prchlik	Right Defensive Tackle	Jerry Helluin
Blaine Earon	Right Defensive End	Len Ford
Dick Flanagan	Left Linebacker	Walt Michaels
Jim Martin	Middle Linebacker	Tommy W. Thompson
LaVern Torgeson	Right Linebacker	Hal Herring
Yale Lary	Defensive Back	Tommy James
Jack Christiansen	Defensive Back	Warren Lahr
Jim David	Defensive Back	Bert Rechichar
Don Doll	Defensive Back	Don Shula

Head Coaches: Detroit: Buddy Parker; Cleveland: Paul Brown.
Game Officials: Referee: Tommy Timlin (Niagra), Umpire: Samuel Wilson (Lehigh), Linesman: Charlie Berry (Lafayette), Back Judge: James E. Hamer (California State Teachers), Field Judge: Lloyd Brazil (Detroit)

TEAM STATISTICS

Detroit Lions		Cleveland Browns
10	First Downs	22
44/258	Total Offense Plays/Yards	70/384
34	Rushing Attempts	34
199	Rushing Yardage	227
10	Pass Attempts	36
7	Pass Completions	20
70.0	Completion Percentage	55.5
68	Passing Yardage	191
1/7	Interceptions (Return Yards)	0/0
- 9	Sacks/Yards Lost	- 34
6	Punts	3
40.8	Punting Average	43.3
1/18	Punt Return Yards	6/18
2/39	Kickoff Returns/Yards	4/84
0/0	Fumbles/Lost	1/1
3/25	Penalties/Yards	7/65

1953 NFL — The Lions Repeat

1953 NFL Championship — Cleveland Browns (16) vs. Detroit Lions (17)

DECEMBER 27, 1953 — BRIGGS STADIUM, DETROIT — 54,577
WEATHER CONDITIONS: PARTLY CLOUDY, MID–30S.
FIELD CONDITION: FROZEN, HARD.

No one thought that Paul Brown could be beaten for three straight years in a championship game. The Los Angeles Rams had beaten Cleveland by a touchdown in 1951 and the Detroit Lions had knocked them off last year in Cleveland 17–7. Surely this was the year that Brown and Automatic Otto Graham would sit again at the top of the heap. Still, the fans in Detroit held out hope that their Lions could win their second straight championship.

This game, like the one in 1952, would be a tough defensive struggle. The Browns received the opening kickoff, but it was a rough start for Cleveland. On the game's second play, Detroit rookie linebacker Joe Schmidt leveled Graham with a savage hit. "On the next play Graham's arm was nicked by LaVern Torgeson as he was bracing himself to throw a pass."[1] The ball popped out of his hands and was recovered by big Les Bingaman at the Cleveland 13-yard line.

On first down, halfback Gene Gedman picked up seven yards off left tackle. The squads then slugged it out in the trenches for the next three plays, with the Lions gaining four more yards and a first down at the Cleveland two. Two plays later, after just 4:05 elapsed off the game clock, Doak Walker carried over the goal line on a one-yard plunge. He also kicked the extra point and the Lions took an early 7–0 lead.

Midway through the period, Detroit drove the ball to the Cleveland 26-yard line, but on third down, Layne was sacked for a 12-yard loss. Walker tried a field goal from 45 yards out, but the kick fell short.

The second quarter saw an exchange of field goals between Lou Groza and Walker. Groza's kick came early in the period after Detroit's Bob Hoernschemeyer fumbled a handoff and Cleveland's Len Ford recovered for the Browns on the Detroit six-yard line, but this glowing opportunity netted only three points. It was late in the opening chapter when Hoernschemeyer made his error and Cleveland's offense took over. Chick Jagade took a first-down pitchout from Graham and began to make his way around left end, but before he could turn the corner, he was dropped for a one-yard loss. Ken Carpenter gained that yard back as the gun sounded the end of the first quarter. On third down, the first play of the second period, Graham threw a pass to Dante Lavelli over the middle. It looked like a sure touchdown, but the sure-handed Lavelli slipped on the icy turf and the ball fell to the earth as the Cleveland faithful gasped. Enter Groza, who kicked the easy field goal to bring the Browns to within four points, 7–3.

Turnovers led to another score late in the second period when Detroit's Jim David picked off a Graham pass at the Detroit 44 and returned it 36 yards to the Cleveland 20. Detroit could manage only four yards in three plays, forcing a fourth-down field goal attempt. Walker's kick from 23 yards out helped the Lions to hold a 10–3 halftime lead. The field goal was almost unnecessary as Detroit quarterback Bobby Layne had found Walker on an apparent touchdown pass a few plays earlier. After signaling for the touchdown, the officials huddled and called the play back. "Since Layne had taken the snap from center and handed off to Walker, the Lions' quarterback became an ineligible receiver. The illegal pass also brought a 15-yard penalty and loss of the down, moving the ball back to the 30-yard line."[2] Following the ruling, Layne threw twice more, once for 10 yards to Cloyce Box, and the next throw fell incomplete. Walker then kicked from the 23, the Lions having picked up five yards on an offside against the Browns.

The Browns made a valiant attempt to come right back after Jagade returned the kickoff 29 yards to his own 49. The clock showed only a minute and a quarter remaining as George Ratterman stepped in at quarterback for Graham, who had apparently injured his throwing hand on a previous series of downs. Halfback Ray Renfro went off tackle for a yard. On second down, Ratterman was caught in the backfield and dropped for a 13-yard loss. On third down, Ratterman hit Jagade with a screen pass that was good for a 19-yard gain to the Detroit 44, but with just seconds on the game clock, the Browns had no time to get the ball any closer. Groza set up near midfield and kicked a long boot, but the ball sailed wide of the goal posts as the half ended. The score remained 10 to 3 in favor of Detroit.

The Browns did very little offensively in the first half, gaining only 71 yards. After the break, however, they began to move the ball. For the next 25 minutes, "it looked as if they at last had started to drop the parts of the puzzle of how to beat Detroit into place."[3]

On the third play after the intermission, Ken Gorgal intercepted a Bobby Layne pass and the Browns pushed over a score on an eight-play, 49-yard drive, with Harry Jagade ringing up the tally with a punch through the middle of the line. Groza's kick tied the score at 10.

The remainder of the third session became a defensive struggle as neither team threatened much. As the period began to wane, however, the Browns made some noise. Cleveland had pinned Detroit deep in their own territory, forcing a punt. As the ball came down at the Cleveland 41, Ken Carpenter was waiting. He pulled the ball in and returned it seven yards to the 48. Graham then stayed principally on the ground. Jagade went through the middle of the line twice, gaining eight and 14 yards. The Browns then called on Dub Jones, who gained 18 yards over guard, to advance the ball to the Detroit nine. It was Jagade again for two as the third quarter ended. The Lions' defense then held, giving up no more yardage on the next two plays. The first play was an incomplete pass that Renfro could not hold onto in the flat, and the second was a keeper by Graham who ran to his left trying to bull his way in to make the touchdown or at least center the ball for a field goal. He centered the ball, but gained no yardage. In came Groza for a 15-yard field goal attempt and the Browns went up by the score of 13 to 10.

Groza's kickoff was deep, landing near the goal line. Walker picked the ball up and attempted to run it out, but he never got any traction on the frozen turf and was downed on the Detroit five-yard line. The Lions clawed their way downfield over the next eleven plays, gaining 69 yards and moving the ball to the Browns' 26. But here the Browns' defense stiffened, forcing a field goal attempt by Walker, who misfired from the 33.

The Browns then came right back. Leaning on Jagade, who ran for 30 yards, the Browns moved the ball to the Detroit 33, where once again, Detroit's defense stiffened and forced a fourth down. Groza then stepped off the line and into the backfield to kick his third field goal of the contest from 43 yards out, increasing the Browns' lead to 16 to 10.

But the Lions weren't finished yet. No team led by Bobby Layne was ever finished before the clock read 0:00. The Lions got the ball back on their own 20-yard line with 4:10 left to play. In these closing minutes of the game, Layne calmly and coolly went to work. Layne went back to the air, moving the ball quickly and making most of the needed 80 yards on passes. Layne twice connected to Jim Doran for gains of 17 and 18 yards, and also fired one to Box for nine, before the big one to Doran for 33 and the winning points.

Layne masterminded the drive, passing successfully to Lions end Jim Doran for 17 and 18 yards putting the ball on the Cleveland 45. Doran had been an impressive receiver at Iowa State, but had seen mostly action on defense with the Lions due to Leon Hart's presence in Detroit. But when Hart had left the game early due to a severely sprained knee, Parker had pressed Doran back into service at offensive end. Showing no rust from his lack of offensive playing time, Doran stepped in and played the game of his life.

On third and ten on the Lions' 37, Doran cut across the center and grabbed a Layne pass while tearing through the Cleveland secondary for the first down and more as he streaked into Brown territory before being wrestled down at the Cleveland 45-yard line.

Layne then called a keeper and carved his way through the Browns' line for a first down on the Cleveland 33. With time winding down, Bobby called a timeout. Jerry Izenberg described the scene this way, "The Lions dropped into an exhausted semi-circle on the frozen ground; and Layne, his helmet beside him, his blond head easily discernible in the pack, told them in his Texas drawl, 'Listen, you just get me the time and I will get you into that All-Star game in Chicago next year.'"[4] Layne was referring to the College All-Star Game held each summer at Soldier Field, pitting the best recently graduated college stars against the NFL champions.

Doran told Layne in the huddle that he believed he could get past the Cleveland defenders on an up pattern and Layne listened. With just over 2 minutes remaining and the Browns' defenders in tight, Layne called for his receiver to go long. Off at the snap, Doran faked a block, then released quickly downfield, cutting inside, and getting behind Cleveland halfbacks Ken Konz and Warren Lahr. Having beaten his man, Doran looked back at Layne and saw the ball starting up on its arc and coming his way. Layne saw Doran break free and had lofted an easy 33-yard floater towards the goal line. Fully realizing that catching this ball meant winning the championship, Doran, digging for all he was worth, caught up to it, pulled the ball in and cradled it securely as he crossed the goal line to tie the contest at 16-all. Doak Walker kicked the point after and Detroit led 17–16.

Only 2:02 now remained as Detroit kicked off to the Browns. The Browns knew that they had to get downfield quickly and close enough for the strong and accurate leg of Lou Groza to put them back in the lead and sew up the championship. They set out to do just that, but the Lions' defense had other ideas. Ken Carpenter returned the ensuing kickoff 18 yards to the Cleveland 28. On the first play from scrimmage, Graham dropped back to pass, surveyed the field and let go a long pass. But today was to be Detroit's as Otto fell victim to an unlikely hero — Carl Karilivacz, an obscure 23rd-round draft choice out of Syracuse. The second-year Lion back read Graham's eyes and raced with outstretched arms towards the ball, picking it off and sealing the victory for his Lions.

All that remained now was for Layne to take a knee several times and the clock ran down to nothing. At the sound of the gun, the Detroit Lions were repeat champions of the league.

Doran told interviewers in the locker room after the game that the winning touchdown pass was set up after the Lions' bench noticed that Cleveland's secondary was pulled in close to bump and slow down the Lions' receivers running their pass routes. Doran stated, "I went out and faked a block and then cut around a Cleveland defender. I raced toward the end zone and when I looked up, there was the ball."[5]

SCORING

	1	2	3	4	Totals
Cleveland Browns	0	3	7	6	16
Detroit Lions	7	3	0	7	17

1st Quarter: Detroit — TD — Walker — 1-yard run (Walker kick). 2nd Quarter: Cleveland — FG — Groza — 13 yards. Detroit — FG — Walker — 23 yards. 3rd Quarter: Cleveland — TD — Jagade — 9-yard run (Groza kick). 4th Quarter: Cleveland — FG — Groza — 15 yards. Cleveland — FG — Groza — 43 yards. Detroit — TD — Doran — 33-yard pass from Layne (Walker kick).

STARTING LINEUPS

Cleveland Browns		**Detroit Lions**
Otto Graham	Quarterback	Bobby Layne
Chick Jagade	Fullback	Bob Hoernschemeyer

Ray Renfro	Left Halfback	Doak Walker
Billy Reynolds	RightHalfback	Gene Gedman
Pete Brewster	Left End	Dorne Dibble
Lou Groza	Left Tackle	Lou Creekmur
Abe Gibron	Left Guard	Harley Sewell
Frank Gatski	Center	Vince Banonis
Chuck Noll	Right Guard	Dick Stanfel
John Sandusky	Right Tackle	Ollie Spencer
Dante Lavelli	Right End	Leon Hart
George Young	Left Defensive End	Jim Cain
Don Colo	Left Defensive Tackle	Thurman McGraw
Bill Willis	Middle Guard	Les Bingaman
Derrell Palmer	Right Defensive Tackle	John Prchlik
Len Ford	Right Defensive End	Sonny Gandee
Tom Catlin	Left Linebacker	Joe Schmidt
Walt Michaels	Right Linebacker	LaVern Torgeson
Tommy James	Defensive Back	Yale Lary
Ken Konz	Defensive Back	Jack Christiansen
Warren Lahr	Defensive Back	Jim David
Ken Gorgal	Defensive Back	Bob Smith

Head Coaches: Cleveland: Paul Brown; Detroit: Buddy Parker.

Game Officials: Referee: Ronald Gibbs (St. Thomas), Umpire: Samuel Wilson (Lehigh), Back Judge: James Hamer (California State Teachers), Linesman: Dan Tehan (Xavier), Field Judge: Carl Rebele (Penn State)

TEAM STATISTICS

Cleveland Browns		Detroit Lions
11	First Downs	18
55/191	Total Offense Plays/Yards	67/293
36	Rushing Attempts	39
182	Rushing Yardage	129
16	Pass Attempts	26
3	Pass Completions	12
18.8	Completion Percentage	46.2
38	Passing Yardage	179
2/9	Interceptions (Return Yards)	2/48
3/29	Sacks/Yards Lost	2/15
4/70	Kickoff Returns/Yards	3/46
5	Punts	4
42.6	Punting Average	49.3
3/35	Punt Return/Yards	0/0
2/2	Fumbles/Lost	3/2
5	Penalties	4
50	Penalty Yards	49

1954 NFL — Goodbye, Otto

1954 NFL Championship — Detroit Lions (10) vs. Cleveland Browns (56)

DECEMBER 26, 1954 — CLEVELAND MUNICIPAL STADIUM, CLEVELAND — 43,827
WEATHER CONDITIONS: LOW 40S, CLEAR, ALMOST BALMY AFTERNOON.
FIELD CONDITION: EXCELLENT, FIRM.

There is only one way to describe Otto Graham's performance in the 1954 NFL Championship Game — miraculous. But for the fact that he was intercepted twice and that three of his twelve passes fell incomplete, perfect would have been an apt word.

The Browns had never beaten the Lions in any of the eight contests they had played since entering the league in 1950. They had dropped the last two championship contests to Detroit and even lost to the Lions right here in Cleveland the previous Sunday to close out the regular season. The Browns seemed snakebitten against the boys from the Motor City and entered the contest as 2-and-a-half-point underdogs. To many, the Browns were down for the count before the opening bell.

Detroit's Jack Christiansen took Lou Groza's opening kickoff at his own 1-yard line and returned it 16 yards to start the Lions' first offensive series at their own 17. Bobby Layne and the vaunted Lions offense took the field and did so with sudden impact. On the first play from scrimmage Layne handed off to Bill Bowman, who burst through a massive hole in the line and bolted 50 yards to the Cleveland 33. The faithful in Municipal Stadium let out a collective groan that filled the massive edifice, as it appeared that the Lions might well be on their way to their third straight league championship. On the very next play, however, light appeared out of the darkness as Lions back Carpenter fumbled and Cleveland tackle John Kissell picked up the ball at the 30.

Just when the Browns' fans were settling back and sighing a collective sigh, Detroit linebacker Joe Schmidt abruptly flipped the switch, turning off that light when he picked off Graham's first pass at the Cleveland 35. The Lions' offense barely moved the ball forward and Detroit had to settle for a field goal attempt. When the Lions' Doak Walker kicked successfully to put the Lions up 3–0, many in the stands at Municipal Stadium were thinking, "Here we go again!"

They soon had reason to hope again, however. On the ensuing kickoff, Billy Reynolds ran 46 yards to the Detroit 41. While the Browns initially stalled, a roughing the kicker penalty against Detroit tackle Gil Mains on Browns punter Horace Gillom, kept the drive alive.

Two plays later Graham, rolling to his right and throwing back across his body, connected with the speedy Ray Renfro at the eight on a 37-yard touchdown pass. Renfro, one of the fastest men in the league, had missed 6 weeks of the season due to a knee injury, but he was back on top of his game today. Going at full speed, Renfro lunged forward with fully outstretched arms. Almost falling forward, he pulled Otto's pass in and turned up the burners as he headed for the end zone and the score. Groza's kick put Cleveland up 7–3.

Cleveland's Don Paul then intercepted Layne at the Detroit 43-yard line and returned the ball to the Detroit 8. Graham threw an 8-yard touchdown strike over the middle to Darrell "Pete" Brewster, who leaped between two Lion defenders and came down twisting and turning for the final 2 yards and the score. Groza connected on his second point after of the day, and the Browns led 14–3. Graham, who had never thrown a touchdown pass in a championship game, now had two in one quarter.

With momentum now clearly on their side, the Browns continued to pour it on. After the Cleveland defense held the Lions on the next series of downs, Reynolds returned Jug Girard's punt 46 yards to the Detroit 12 and set up the Browns' third touchdown in the second quarter. The Browns moved the ball down inside the 1-yard line as the first quarter came to an end.

On the first play of the second session, Graham, leaping into the air past the out-stretched arms of Lion defensive back Jack Christiansen, snuck over on a 1-foot quarterback keeper to extend the Browns' lead. Groza's third PAT put Cleveland out front 21–3.

On the ensuing kickoff, Lou Groza booted the ball deep for a touchback. Starting on their own 20, the Lions came alive again with Lew Carpenter breathing life back into the team with a 52-yard bolt that set up Detroit's second scoring opportunity. Ultimately, Bill Bowman took the ball in for the final 5 yards. Walker's kick made the score 21–10.

Detroit's Bobby Layne was all play off the field, but all business while on it. After the Detroit kickoff, Layne began moving his Lions on what he hoped would be a drive to tighten the score. After gaining three on a first down run, Layne called for a second down pass. He took the snap from under center, but as he dropped back, Cleveland's big middle guard Mike McCormick tore through the Detroit front line and hit Layne a lick, stripping the ball out of his hands. Cleveland recovered on the Lions' 31-yard line.[1]

Renfro picked up 3 yards, Graham ran twice and passed once to Pete Brewster, and the Browns found themselves with first and goal on the Detroit 5. Pete touched the ball, which bounced from Carl Karilivacz to Renfro for a first down on the seven. On the next play, Graham rolled wide to his right on a bootleg, and instead of looking for a receiver, he immediately tucked the ball under his golden right arm. Avoiding the converging Cleveland defenders, he leaped into the air behind a Lou Groza block and tumbled into the end zone for six. Groza, whose block paved the way for the touchdown, then kicked the successful point after. The Browns now led 28–10.

As the second quarter was winding down, Walt Michaels intercepted a Layne pass, returning it to the Detroit 17-yard line. On the last play of the second quarter, Graham fired a low pass to Renfro, who was at the Detroit 2. Renfro reached down and caught the ball off his shoe tops while moving at full speed. He had to twist quickly to avoid the goal post, but the ugly play yielded another Cleveland touchdown. Groza connected for his fifth point after kick and the Browns took a commanding 35–10 lead.

Again the Lions came out firing, but the ever-present Michaels was again on the scene, recovering a Jug Girard fumble and ending the Detroit possession. The Browns let the clock run out on the first half taking a 35–10 lead into the clubhouse.

Graham and his Browns came out fighting in the second half, but the Lions were flat. Billy Reynolds took the second-half opening kick off back to the Cleveland 31-yard line. It took the Browns just six plays to find the end zone again. After connecting with Brewster on a 43-yard pass, Graham ran less than a yard for one more touchdown to make it 42–10.

The Browns scored two more meaningless touchdowns. Ken Konz stole two Layne passes, and both turnovers set up pile-on touchdowns for Cleveland. Two plays after the ensuing kickoff, Konz returned the first pick 18 yards to the Detroit 13. After Renfro ground out a single tough yard on first down, Fred "Curley" Morrison took a second-down pitchout from Graham and scored on a 12-yard blast for Cleveland's seventh touchdown. Groza's kick put the Browns up 49–10.

The third quarter ended with Detroit threatening on the Cleveland 10-yard line, but Len Ford, charging hard on a pass rush, leaped high into the air and pulled down a Layne pass. He rambled to the Lions' 45 before being brought down.

As the game grew late, the Lions began to grow frustrated with their weak performance, and inevitably, tempers flared. In the fourth quarter, Detroit lineman Charlie Ane, a second-year man out of Southern Cal, got into a fight with Cleveland's rookie defensive end Carlton Massey. Both men were ejected.[2]

After Konz's second pick, Chet "The Jet" Hanulak powered through the line and scored in the fourth quarter on a 10-yard jaunt. Once again, Groza converted the PAT and the final score was 56–10 in favor of the Browns. After a 3-year absence, the Cleveland Browns were on top of the heap. At the game's conclusion, jubilant Browns fans swarmed the field and tore down the goal posts.

While Layne passed for 177 yards on the day, he connected on less than 50 percent of his throws. The hard-charging Browns defenders and the ball-hawking secondary so confounded Layne that Tom Dublinski, a third-year backup out of Utah playing in his final game with the Lions, had to spell him for a while in the third quarter.

Paul Brown pulled Graham later to let the fans express their admiration for the only quarterback the franchise had ever known. While receiving a thunderous standing ovation, Graham left the field in the final minutes of the game to the sounds of the band playing Auld Lange Syne.

The Cleveland offense had been superb. After eight tries, they had finally defeated the Lions. Graham threw for three touchdowns and ran for three others. He completed nine of twelve passes for 163 yards and almost single-handedly defeated the Lions that day. The still-hurting Renfro gutted out a strong performance, catching five passes for 94 yards to lead all Cleveland receivers. He played a whale of a game in spite of his ailing knee that had him limping throughout the contest. Third-year left end Dorne Dibble led Detroit receivers with four receptions good for 63 yards.

The Browns' defense, which had been strong throughout Cleveland's eight-game winning streak, had harassed the normally calm Layne all afternoon long. Although he completed 19 passes, it was well less than half of the 44 attempts he launched, and six of those attempts fell into Browns defenders' hands. The Browns' defenders returned those interceptions for a total of 122 yards or better than 20 yards average per pick. Len Ford at end and halfback Kenny Konz grabbed two each. Adding to the turnover carnage, Cleveland defenders recovered three Detroit fumbles, with two of those resulting in Cleveland scores. Detroit's ground game fared no better. With the exception of two long runs from scrimmage — a 50-yard jaunt by rookie fullback Bill Bowman in the first quarter and a 52-yard dash by halfback Lew Carpenter in the second — the powerful Cleveland line kept the Lions' running game in check.

In the Detroit locker room the mood was a mixture of frustration and awe. "I saw it, but still hardly can believe it," Coach Buddy Parker, who never had lost to the Browns, said on the other side of the stadium. "It has me dazed."[3]

In the locker room after the game, Paul Brown called this the finest team he had ever coached and he had coached some very good ones on all levels. A satisfied and relaxed Otto Graham remarked to reporters, "Detroit has a helluva team, but they got the breaks in those two other championship playoffs. This time we got them."[4] Otto was ready to put football behind him. He was involved in numerous business ventures in and near Cleveland including life insurance and mail-order condiments, and he had recently opened a discount furniture and household appliances store with Cleveland Indians catcher Jim Hegan.[5]

While passing was the mainstay of both offenses this day, Carpenter and Bowman ran for 64 and 61 yards for the Lions, respectively, and Hanulak led the Browns with 44.

SCORING

	1	2	3	4	Totals
Detroit Lions	3	7	0	0	10
Cleveland Browns	14	21	14	7	56

1st Quarter: Detroit — FG — Walker — 36 yards. Cleveland — TD — Renfro — 35-yard pass from Graham (Groza kick). Cleveland — TD — Brewster — 8-yard pass from Graham (Groza kick). 2nd Quarter: Cleveland — TD — Graham —1-yard run (Groza kick). Detroit — TD — Bowman — 5-yard run (Walker kick). Cleveland — TD — Graham — 5-yard run (Groza kick). Cleveland — TD — Renfro — 31-yard pass from Graham (Groza kick). 3rd Quarter: Cleveland — TD — Graham —1-yard run (Groza kick). Cleveland — TD — Morrison —12-yard run (Groza kick). 4th Quarter: Cleveland — TD — Hanulak —10-yard run (Groza kick).

STARTING LINEUPS

Detroit Lions		Cleveland Browns
Bobby Layne	Quarterback	Otto Graham
Bill Bowman	Fullback	Maurice Bassett
Doak Walker	Left Halfback	Chet Hanulak
Lew Carpenter	Right Halfback	Billy Reynolds
Dorne Dibble	Left End	Pete Brewster
Lou Creekmur	Left Tackle	Lou Groza
Harley Sewell	Left Guard	Abe Gibron
Andy Miketa	Center	Frank Gatski
Jim Martin	Right Guard	Chuck Noll
Charlie Ane	Right Tackle	John Sandusky
Jug Girard	Right End	Dante Lavelli
Bob Dove	Left Defensive End	Carlton Massey
Bob Miller	Left Defensive Tackle	John Kissell
Les Bingaman	Middle Guard	Mike McCormack
Gil Mains	Right Defensive Tackle	Don Colo
Jim Cain	Right Defensive End	Len Ford
Joe Schmidt	Left Linebacker	Tom Catlin
LaVern Torgeson	Right Linebacker	Walt Michaels
Carl Karilivacz	Defensive Back	Tommy James
Jack Christiansen	Defensive Back	Ken Konz
Jim David	Defensive Back	Warren Lahr
Bill Stits	Defensive Back	Don R. Paul

Head Coaches: Detroit: Buddy Parker; Cleveland: Paul Brown.
Game Officials: Referee: Thomas Timlin; Umpire: Sam Wilson; Linesman: Dan Teehan; Field Judge: William McHugh; Back Judge: James Hamer

TEAM STATISTICS

Detroit Lions		Cleveland Browns
16	First Downs	17
73/331	Total Offense Plays/Yards	57/303

28	Rushing Attempts	45
152	Rushing Yardage	140
44	Pass Attempts	12
19	Pass Completions	9
43.2	Completion Percentage	75.0
195	Passing Yardage	163
2/14	Interceptions (Return Yards)	6/122
1/16	Sacks/Yards Lost	0/0
6/108	Kickoff Returns/Yards	3/85
6	Punts	4
41.3	Punting Average	43.0
0/0	Punt Return Yards	2/42
3/3	Fumbles/Lost	2/2
5	Penalties	4
63	Penalty Yards	40

1955 NFL — Goodbye, Otto ... Again

1955 NFL Championship — Cleveland Browns (38) vs. Los Angeles Rams (14)

DECEMBER 26, 1955 — LOS ANGELES MEMORIAL COLISEUM, LOS ANGELES — 87,695
WEATHER CONDITIONS: OVERCAST, 65°F.
FIELD CONDITION: DRY, FIRM.

Immediately after winning the 1954 league championship, Otto Graham made the announcement that many felt was sure to come — he was retiring. Although he had considered retiring before the 1954 season, he had decided to give it one more year. In retrospect, Graham was glad that he had. He was able to lead the Browns to one more title and wash away the bitter taste of three straight championship game losses, but now it was time to go. In his words, "That's the way to quit, go out on top."[1]

He was leaving the game after nine successful seasons, with six championship game wins in nine chances, and a host of records and honors in two leagues. As such, he was arguably still the league's most successful quarterback, but he was growing tired. The physical grind wasn't so bad, but the mental wear and tear were beginning to take their toll on him. Graham stated, "I hate that pre-game feeling and it gets worse and worse as the years go by." He also commented that being away from his family so much was another factor in his decision.[2] He was now retired and enjoying himself. Enter Paul Brown.

With the absence of their star quarterback, the 1955 preseason was a disaster. Cleveland stumbled through its exhibition schedule. Head coach Paul Brown tried several men under center, but with each the results were disastrous. In desperation, he picked up the telephone and called Graham. Out of loyalty more than desire, Otto agreed to ride to Cleveland's rescue one more time, but Otto made it clear that this one really would be his last season. Immediately, the results were outstanding. Graham led the team out of its preseason wilderness to the Eastern Division title and into the championship game against their old nemesis, the Los Angeles Rams.

The Rams had driven to the Western Division title with a pair of quarterbacks at the helm. The dual leadership was typical — Bob Waterfield and Norm Van Brocklin had long been platooned as the Rams' play callers, but now Waterfield was gone, replaced by the young Billy Wade out of Vanderbilt. The team had fought injuries all season long and was still hobbled. This and Cleveland's strength and vast experience caused odds makers to install the Browns as 5-point favorites. As usual, the Rams' leading receivers were Tom Fears and Elroy Hirsch. Hirsch, however, got a late start on his season. When Crazy Legs announced to the Rams' management that he would be reporting to training camp late because he had a conflict with the shooting of the film *Unchained*, new head coach Sid Gillman told Hirsch not to bother showing up at all. Gillman reconsidered his position when early season injuries depleted the receiver corps. When asked why he had changed his position and welcomed Hirsch back into the fold with open arms after so unceremoniously dismissing him in August, Gillman shrugged and said, "We're interested in winning football games, not arguments."[3]

A record crowd of 87,695 filled the Los Angeles Memorial Coliseum on game day. The weather that afternoon was pleasant, but the sun was blocked by a steel-gray overcast. NBC was on hand setting up their equipment and getting ready for the contest. This was the first championship game to be televised nationally.

The first Cleveland score came late in the first quarter after Browns defensive back Ken Konz stole a Van Brocklin pass at the Browns' 12 to break up a 56-yard drive and what looked to be a sure Los Angeles touchdown. Konz returned the interception to his own 24. Graham took advantage of this good fortune by driving Cleveland downfield at a rapid pace. When the drive stalled, Lou Groza stepped away from his place in the Browns' line and hit on a 26-yard field goal to put Cleveland up by a 3–0 score. It was a lead they would never relinquish.

Four minutes into the second frame, Browns defensive back Don Paul leaped into the air and stretched his fingers in front of a pass from Van Brocklin to Paul Quinlan. He tipped the ball and caught it on the way back down. Righting himself as he landed, he looked downfield at a wide-open field. Only Van Brocklin had a chance of catching him, but the Dutchman was known for the strength and accuracy of his arm, not the fleetness of his feet. Paul juked the quarterback and raced 65 yards on the return for Cleveland's first touchdown. Groza's conversion kick put the Browns up 10–0.

Los Angeles knew that it was time to get it moving before this game got out of hand. After receiving the ensuing kickoff, Van Brocklin got his offense busy immediately. Within a minute, Paul "Skeets" Quinlan stood in the end zone, clutching the ball and catching his breath after receiving a Van Brocklin strike and scampering 67 yards for the Rams' first score. Quinlan cut outside quickly, got behind his Cleveland defender Warren Lahr, and took Van Brocklin's pass on the dead run. By the time Lahr caught up with the little Texan, Quinlan was crossing the goal line.[4] Les Richter's point after kick brought the Rams to within 3 points of the defending champions and the Los Angeles fans began to rouse. Very soon, they would settle back down into their seats.

Graham was determined not to be denied his going-away present. Not being one to wait around for things to happen, he determined to go and get it for himself. After the taking the Los Angeles kickoff, the Browns' offense moved the ball to midfield. Konz made a second interception to set up Graham's 50-yard TD pass to Lavelli.

"Graham sent a flanker back and a spread end down the right end as decoys. The defense shifted to cover them."[5] With the defenders concentrating on the right side of the field, Automatic Otto hit his favorite target — Dante Lavelli — on a 50-yard touchdown strike, extending the Cleveland lead. Lavelli saw that his pattern, as prescribed by the play, was well covered by Los Angeles defenders, so he improvised. "When I went down and out, half the Rams were there waiting for me so I went the other way," Lavelli said. "I'm 30 yards wide open by myself, caught the touchdown, got in at the half, and Paul Brown says, 'Lavelli, you broke the pattern.' I says, 'Yeah, but we're up by 10-points.'"[6] Lou Groza added the point after, and with just 39 seconds left to play in the half the score stood 17–7.

But for a great defensive play, the score could actually have been worse. After another long Cleveland drive, Rams defensive back Ed Hughes stepped up and wrestled a pass away from Ray Renfro in the end zone to stop what looked to be a sure Cleveland touchdown.

In the third quarter, Ken Konz returned a punt 24 yards, setting up the next Cleveland score. It took Graham five plays to travel the 46 yards to the goal line. Otto himself carried the ball for the final 15 yards on a bootleg around right end. Groza's kick put the Browns up 24–7 midway through the quarter.

On the Rams' next possession Cleveland linebacker Sam Palumbo picked off a Van Brocklin pass and returned it 10 yards to the Los Angeles 36. After working the ball down to the 1, Graham kept the pass from center and plunged across the goal for pay dirt. Groza continued his perfection on the conversion and the game was now officially a rout, standing at 31–7.

As the fourth quarter hit the halfway point, the Browns were threatening again. Adding to their total, Graham connected with halfback Ray Renfro for a 35-yard strike and the final touchdown pass of his illustrious career. With Groza's fifth conversion of the day, the Browns led by an overwhelming score of 38–7.

Late in the fourth quarter the Rams scored a meaningless "make it look a little better on the scoreboard" touchdown. Halfback Ron Waller carried across from the 4 and Richter's conversion ended the scoring on the day with the final tally reading Cleveland 38, Los Angeles 14.

Deacon Dan Towler, who had missed most of the season with injuries, was the leading ground gainer for the Rams, gaining 64 yards, followed by Waller's 48. Cleveland's Ed Modzelewski gained 61 yards for the defending champions before being sidelined with injuries in the third quarter. His replacement, Maurice Bassett, didn't miss a beat, carrying for 49 yards in eleven tries and powering one of the Browns' late scoring drives.

The Rams' Skeets Quinlan led all receivers with 116 yards on 5 receptions. Van Brocklin had a marginal day, completing 11 of 25 passes for 166 yards. Those respectable numbers were, however, tempered by six interceptions. Backup Billy Wade was responsible for the seventh.

Graham, on the other hand, had a field day. He was 14 of 25 for 209 passing yards. He threw for two touchdowns and ran for two others. He led the team up and down the field like the field general he had always been — calm, cool, and unflappable. Looking back on his last game, Graham praised Paul Brown's willingness to listen to his players regarding offensive and defensive strategy. "We told him a spread offense would really murder them," Graham said, "and he agreed to put it in. We always took a great deal of pride in feeling that we were architects of that great victory."[7]

On August 26, 1955, Otto Graham was retired from professional football. On December 26, 1955, he had his seventh league championship ring. The man was genuinely amazing on a football field. "He's the greatest ever," Paul Brown said during a post-game press conference. When a reporter suggested that maybe he would try to get Otto to try it just once more in 1956, Brown responded genuinely, "No, I've imposed on him long enough."[8]

SCORING

	1	2	3	4	Totals
Cleveland Browns	3	14	14	7	38
Los Angeles Rams	0	7	0	7	14

1st Quarter: Cleveland — FG — Groza — 26 yards (12:38). 2nd Quarter: Cleveland — TD — Paul — 65-yard interception return (Groza kick). Los Angeles — TD — Quinlan 67-yard pass from Van Brocklin (Richter kick). Cleveland — TD — Lavelli — 50-yard pass from Graham (Groza kick). 3rd Quarter: Cleveland — TD — Graham — 15-yard run (Groza kick). Cleveland — TD — Graham — 1-yard run (Groza kick). 4th Quarter: Cleveland — TD — Renfro — 35-yard pass from Graham (Groza kick). Los Angeles — TD — Waller — 4-yard run (Richter kick.

STARTING LINEUPS

Cleveland Browns		Los Angeles Rams
Otto Graham	Quarterback	Norm Van Brocklin
Ed Modzelewski	Fullback	Dan Towler
Ray Renfro	Left Halfback	Ron Waller
Fred Morrison	Right Halfback	Skeet Quinlan
Pete Brewster	Left End	Tom Fears
Lou Groza	Left Tackle	Glenn Holtzman
Abe Gibron	Left Guard	Duane Putnam
Frank Gatski	Center	Bobby Cross
Harold Bradley	Right Guard	John Hock
Mike McCormack	Right Tackle	Charlie Toogood
Dante Lavelli	Right End	Elroy Hirsch
Carlton Massey	Left Defensive End	Paul Miller
John Kissell	Left Defensive Tackle	Bud McFadin
Bob Gain	Middle Guard	Don Paul
Don Colo	Right Defensive Tackle	Art Hauser
Len Ford	Right Defensive End	Andy Robustelli
Chuck Noll	Left Linebacker	Les Richter
Walt Michaels	Right Linebacker	Larry Morris
Don R. Paul	Defensive Back	Don Burroughs
Ken Konz	Defensive Back	Jim Cason
Warren Lahr	Defensive Back	Will Sherman
Tommy James	Defensive Back	Ed Hughes

Head Coaches: Cleveland: Paul Brown; Los Angeles: Sid Gillman.
Game Officials: Game Officials: Referee: Ronald Gibbs (St. Thomas); Umpire: Samuel M. "Mike" Wilson (Lehigh); Head Linesman: Cleo N. Diehl (Northwestern); Field Judge: George Rennix (Minnesota); Back Judge: James E. Hamer (California State Teachers)

TEAM STATISTICS

Cleveland Browns		Los Angeles Rams
17	First Downs	17
73/371	Total Offense Plays/Yards	54/259
48	Rushing Attempts	26
169	Rushing Yardage	116
25	Pass Attempts	28

14	Pass Completions	11
56.0	Completion Percentage	39.3
202	Passing Yardage	143
7	Interceptions By	3
3/41	Kickoff Returns/Yards	7/215
3	Punts	4
42.6	Punting Average	45
27	Punt Return Yards	9
0/0	Fumbles/Lost	1/1
5	Penalties	2
74	Penalty Yards	10

1956 NFL — Gene Filipski's Giant Day

1956 NFL Championship — Chicago Bears (7) vs. New York Giants (47)

DECEMBER 30, 1956 — YANKEE STADIUM, NEW YORK CITY — 58,836
WEATHER CONDITIONS: PARTLY CLOUDY, WINDY, BITTER COLD, 18°F.
FIELD CONDITION: FROZEN, FIRM, ICY IN SPOTS.

It had been eighteen long years since the New York Giants had worn the mantle of NFL champions. After defeating the Green Bay Packers in 1938, the Giants had experienced nothing but frustration at the championship level. Though they held the Eastern Division title in 1939, 1941, 1944, and 1946, each year had brought defeat in the big game. The Giants were ready to end the string of futility. The team was very good but was not seen as strong enough to win the crown from the Bears. Chicago was a pre-game three-and-a-half-point favorite and seemed to have a lock on the title. Their record was only one game better than the Giants, but they had a high-powered offense that had rolled up 363 points — 63 better than the second best team in the league, the Detroit Lions, and 99 better than the Giants. Chicago's offense had also gained over 4,500 yards rushing yards, and quarterback Ed Brown led the league in passing. New York, on the other hand, had one of the league's best defenses, yielding only 197 points to Chicago's 246.

Aside from genuine stars like backs Kyle Rote and Frank Gifford, and the young defensive phenom Sam Huff, the Giants were made up of a great many unsung starters and pickups from other teams. Quarterback Charlie Conerly had been in the league for eight seasons, but he had never made it to the championship game. Placekicker Ben Agajanian was an anomaly — he had lost the toes on his kicking foot in a childhood accident and didn't even kick for the team until the fourth game of the season, but he had been perfect since then. Defensive linemen Dick Modzelewski and Andy Robustelli were early-season pickups from the Steelers and Rams, respectively.

The Bears had lost a close one to Baltimore in week one and been blown out in week ten by the powerful Lions, but the only other blemish on their record was a November tie with these same Giants.

The Giants had played the powerful Monsters of the Midway to a 17–17 tie in November, and while many pundits thought the Bears would make short work of the New Yorkers, Giants coach Jim Lee Howell was a believer in his team. All during the week leading up to the final contest Howell reminded his boys that if they had tied this powerful Chicago team a month earlier, there was no reason they couldn't beat them this go-around. Howell made believers of his team. "When it came time to play the game," Howell later recalled, "we just opened the door and got out of the way."[1]

A sharp wind whistled out of the northwest, making it feel much colder than the 22-degree temperature, but 58,836 hardy fans showed up at Yankee Stadium to root on their Giants. Due to the frozen turf, "Howell called for Operation Sneakers before the game started, and the Bears stole the idea as the game progressed."[2]

The Maramen wasted no time in proving their readiness. Giants rookie Gene Filipski impatiently waited on the New York goal line for George Blanda's opening kickoff. It was windy and cold, and he was nervous. Momentarily the rookie wished that the ball would go to Jim Patton, New York's other deep man, but as if predestined, the deep, booming kick came down at the 7-yard line and into Filipski's hands. He began to run toward the middle of the field to be sure of making it to the 20. He did much more than that. Avoiding several would-be tacklers, the 5'10", 180-pound back took the opening kickoff 53 yards before finally being downed by Chicago defender John Mellekas at the Bears' 38.[3] Filipski was a classic example of the flawed player on the 1956 Giants. Expelled from West Point in the 1951 cheating scandal, Filipski had finished up at Villanova. While a moderately successful professional, he had the reputation of being a fumbler, but this time he held onto the ball and the Giants were on a roll.

It took New York only four plays to find the end zone. The first two plays from scrimmage yielded nothing, but on third and ten Frank Gifford beat Chicago's J.C. Caroline on a pass route by running directly at him, then pivoting sharply and snagging a pass from Giants' quarterback Charlie Conerly before Caroline could react, and cutting quickly up field. Caroline finally ran Gifford down at the Chicago 17. After that 21-yard gain, Conerly called for another pass in the huddle. When the Ole Miss alum got to the line and began barking out the count, however, he saw a shift in the Bears' defensive alignment. Immediately he called an audible changing the play at the line. Instead of a pass, halfback Mel Triplett got the ball and the touchdown after breaking loose on a smash-mouth run for 17-yards off left tackle. Triplett was moving so hard and so fast that he ran over umpire Mike Wilson, who found himself in the hard-charging Giants' path to the end zone. "I saw him," Triplett said later, "but I wasn't going to stop then."[4] Agajanian's kick from placement put the Giants up 7–0 almost within minutes of the opening kickoff.

The ensuing kickoff pinned the Bears down deep in their own territory. On the second play from scrimmage, Bears great Rick Casares fumbled and the ball was recovered by Robustelli on the Chicago 15. The Bears' defense held firm, but Agajanian's field goal increased the New York lead to 10–0 in less than ten minutes.

Later in the quarter, New York's Jim Patton intercepted an Ed Brown pass and returned it 28 yards to the Bears' 36-yard line. Again the Chicago defense stopped the Giants, but Ben Agajanian trotted onto the field and booted a long, but true, place kick for a 43-yard field goal that put the Giants up 13–0 at the end of the first quarter.

Chicago's Don Bingham took Don Chandler's kickoff up to his own 35, giving the Bears good field position to start the next possession. J.C. Caroline hit the line for 9 yards on two of the next three plays, but the Bears found themselves in a fourth and one situation. Desperately trying to make something happen and get back into the ball game, the Bears gambled. Ed Brown faked a handoff to Casares, giving the ball instead to Caroline. As the Bear halfback headed for a hole in the right side of the New York line, so did defensive back Emlen Tunnell, who hit Caroline with such force that he did not gain an inch. The gamble had failed, and the ball went over to the Giants at the Chicago 43. The New York offense wasted no time taking advantage of this gift. They covered the 43 yards in six plays with Alex Webster taking it in on a three-yard jaunt. Agajanian's conversion put the Giants up by 20.

The Bears finally caught a break when New York's star defensive back Emlen Tunnel fumbled a punt return and the Bears' John Mellekas recovered the ball on the New York 25-yard line. Rick Casares atoned for his earlier fumble by highlighting the five-play drive with a 9-yard gallop for Chicago's first points of the day. George Blanda kicked the conversion, and the Bears were on the board. Chicago now trailed 20 to 7, but there were still two and a half quarters left to play and their high-octane offense was capable of getting them quickly back into the game.

It never happened. The Giants took the kickoff and drove 72 yards downfield in just 5 plays. The highlight of the drive was a 50-yard pass from Conerly to Webster that left the Giants within striking distance of a score. Just 1 yard out, Conerly handed the ball back to Webster, who plunged across the goal line for his second touchdown of the day. Agajanian's leg was again true as the Giants increased their lead to 27 to 7.

Before the halftime gun the Giants were at it again. Ray Beck blocked Ed Brown's punt and substitute defensive back Henry Moore recovered the bouncing ball in the end zone for New York's fourth touchdown of the day. Another Agajanian's conversion left the halftime score at an overwhelming 34–7.

In the third quarter, Conerly hit Frank Gifford on a 67-yard pass to set up another New York score. As Gifford picked himself up, his mates rushed over to congratulate him.[5] On the next play, Conerly hit sneaker-clad Kyle Rote on a 9-yard route and the Giants' tally was now 40 to 7. Rote had taken a page out of Giants history and donned basketball shoes to help his footing on the frozen Yankee Stadium turf. With improved traction, Rote beat his man and was wide open as he leaped into the air, caught Conerly's pass with his arms outstretched and came down between the goal posts for the score. Amazingly, for the first time all season, Agajanian's kick failed and the score held at 40.

In the fourth quarter Gifford took another Conerly pass and carried it 14 yards into the end zone for the Giants' final score of the day. Ben Agajanian got back on track as he drove the conversion kick through the uprights for his eleventh point of the day. On the next New York possession, Conerly was removed to a thundering ovation and replaced by third-string quarterback Bobby Clatterbuck. The Giants led 47 to 7 and the Bears were content to just run out the clock. This was quite simply a day where it all came together for the Giants.

Conerly was effective as he led the Giants' offense to the one-sided victory. When called on for an aerial attack, he responded brilliantly. The nine-year veteran completed seven of ten passes for 195 yards and two touchdowns. The Giants' defense was also masterful. Sam Huff and the Giants' linebacking corps keyed on and almost completely shut down Chicago great Rick Casares and end Harlon Hill. The entire New York defense harried quarterbacks Ed Brown and George Blanda, and the Chicago receiving corps, to the point that the Bears completed only 8 of 19 passes; most of those came late in the fourth quarter when the game's outcome was no longer in any doubt. League-leading end Harlon Hill caught six balls, but each was in a contained and non-impactful scenario. "Those linebackers were terrific," said Hill. "No matter which way I turned, there was a linebacker on me. They played better than us. That's all."[6] But Bears' quarterback Ed Brown saw it another way. "We were overtrained. We had only one day off— Christmas Day — preparing for this. What the hell, the Giants got five days off. We were just too tied up."[7]

Len Elliott, sports editor for the *Newark Evening News*, wrote of the sub-par performance of the toothless Monsters of the Midway: "Suffice it to say that they couldn't run the ball (their grand total of 67 yards speaks for itself), they didn't block, they didn't tackle (five of them missed Mel Triplett on one run), their passing through the first half was terrible, their pass protection was atrocious, their deep backs were sucked in on simple fakes and let pass receivers get behind them."[8] Bears coach Paddy Driscoll summed up his frustration by stating, "Things that worked for us all year wouldn't go and everything they tried seemed to go to perfection."[9]

Giants coach Jim Lee Howell, understandably proud of his team, commented to reporters after the game, "It was a team victory." Howell continued, "I won't try to compare this club with the great Giant teams of 1940–41, but I feel it is the greatest Giant team I have been connected with and has more stars than any of them."[10] Howell did confide, however, that he was a bit anxious before the contest began. "The boys had me kinda worried before the game. Too much levity, I thought. They didn't seem serious enough. But they really showed me, didn't they?"[11] Howell went on to point out that this squad seemed to play better when they were relaxed.

Assistant coach Vince Lombardi agreed with Howell that the team had played well as a unit, but he pointed to one specific play that set the tone for the ball game. "That run by Gene gave the team its opening spark. From then on, it was a solid effort by each and every man."[12] Certainly, no one could disagree with that assessment.

SCORING

	1	2	3	4	Totals
Chicago Bears	0	7	0	0	7
New York Giants	13	21	6	7	47

1st Quarter: NYG — TD — Mel Triplett 17-yard rush (Agajanian kick). NYG — FG — Ben Agajanian 17 yards field goal. NYG — FG — Ben Agajanian 43 yards field goal. 2nd Quarter: NYG — TD — Alex Webster 3-yard rush (Agajanian kick). CHI — TD — Rick Casares 9-yard rush (Blanda kick). NYG — TD — Alex Webster 1 yard rush (Agajanian kick). NYG — TD — Henry Moore end zone fumble recovery (Agajanian kick). 3rd Quarter: NYG — TD — Kyle Rote 9-yard pass from Conerly (kick failed). 4th Quarter: NYG — TD — Frank Gifford 14-yard pass from Conerly (Agajanian kick).

STARTING LINEUPS

Chicago Bears		New York Giants
George Blanda	Quarterback	Don Heinrich
Rick Casares	Fullback	Mel Triplett
Bobby Watkins	Left Halfback	Frank Gifford
John Hoffman	Right Halfback	Alex Webster
Harlon Hill	Left End	Kyle Rote
Bill Wightkin	Left Tackle	Rosey Brown

Herman Clark	Left Guard	Bill Austin
Larry Strickland	Center	Ray Wietecha
Stan Jones	Right Guard	Jack Stroud
Kline Gilbert	Right Tackle	Dick Yelvington
Bill McColl	Right End	Ken MacAfee
Jack Hoffman	Left Defensive End	Walt Yowarsky
Fred Williams	Left Defensive Tackle	Dick Modzelewski
M.L. Brackett	Right Defensive Tackle	Rosey Grier
Ed Meadows	Right Defensive End	Andy Robustelli
Wayne Hansen	Left Linebacker	Bill Svoboda
Bill George	Middle Linebacker	Sam Huff
Joe Fortunato	Rightside Linebacker	Harland Svare
J.C. Caroline	Defensive Back	Jimmy Patton
McNeil Moore	Defensive Back	Ed Hughes
Ray Gene Smith	Defensive Back	Emlen Tunnell
Stan Wallace	Defensive Back	Dick Nolan

Head Coaches: Chicago: Paddy Driscoll; New York: Jim Lee Howell.
Game Officials: Referee: William Downes (Illinois Tech); Umpire: Samuel M. "Mike" Wilson (Lehigh); Back Judge: Don Looney (TCU); Linesman: Cleo N. Diehl (Northwestern); Field Judge: George Rennix (Minnesota)

TEAM STATISTICS

Chicago Bears		New York Giants
19	First Downs	16
79/314	Total Offense Plays/Yards	54/354
32	Rushing Attempts	34
67	Rushing Yardage	126
47	Pass Attempts	20
20	Pass Completions	11
42.5	Completion Percentage	55.0
247	Passing Yardage	228
0	Interceptions By	2
8	Punts	3
34	Punting Average	37
1	Punt Return Yards	46
2/1	Fumbles/Lost	3/2
4	Penalties	6
50	Penalty Yards	40

1957 NFL — A Long Day in Detroit

1957 NFL Championship — Cleveland Browns (14) vs. Detroit Lions (59)

DECEMBER 29, 1957 — BRIGGS STADIUM, DETROIT — 55,263
WEATHER CONDITIONS: BRILLIANT SUNSHINE, COLD, MID–30S.
FIELD CONDITION: DRY, FIRM.

Otto Graham was gone, but the Cleveland Browns were back in the championship game, where they had been ten of the previous eleven seasons. The Browns had had their usual stellar season, posting a 9–2–1 record, but one of those losses came late in the season to their championship game opponent, the Detroit Lions.

While the regular-season win was gratifying, the Lions were thrilled with the opportunity to get back at the Browns for the 56 to 10 shellacking they had received in the 1954 championship contest. Detroit's center Frank Gatski, who had been a member of the Browns from 1946 to 1956, was now lining up against his old mates.

The season had started in an odd fashion for the Lions. During training camp, they added a quarterback and lost their head coach. On July 25, Detroit traded for quarterback Tobin Rote of Green Bay to back up starter Bobby Layne. Rote, an 8-year veteran out of Rice, had become a good enough quarterback to win Green Bay's starting job. He turned out to be just the insurance policy the Lions needed. On July 25, no one could have known the crucial role that Tobin Rote would play in the Lions' run to the championship. He had been sharing the quarterback duties with Layne, but when Layne went down on December 8 with a broken ankle against these same Browns, Rote stepped in as the sole starter.

Obtaining a backup quarterback is somewhat common, but losing your head coach unexpectedly is not. On August 12, head coach Buddy Parker unexpectedly stepped down, stating, "I can't handle them. This is too big for me. I cannot take another losing season."[1] The next day, assistant coach George Wilson was named to the top spot.

The Lions had a slow start, losing to the Colts in Baltimore in their opener, and only holding a 3–3 record as late as November 9. But with six games to go, the Lions almost ran the table, losing only to the Bears on the Sunday before Thanksgiving. On the final Sunday of the regular season, however, the Lions managed a measure of revenge by beating the Bears in Chicago and eking out an 8–4 tie with the San Francisco 49ers for the Western Division lead.

A playoff was set for Sunday, December 22, in Kezar Stadium in San Francisco, to determine the Western Division champions. After trailing 27–7, the Lions came roaring back with an amazing second half resurgence to defeat the 49ers 31–27. Their confidence intact, the Lions headed home to host the Browns in the league championship contest the following Sunday.

For the Lions' faithful it was a great day all around, as the late December Michigan weather was, by Detroit standards, balmy. The sun shone brilliantly and made the 32-degree temperature feel even warmer and their beloved Lions were back in the championship contest and on a roll.

Rote wasted no time in getting the Lions on the scoreboard as he led a scoring drive that was capped by a 31-yard field goal by Jim Martin.

Rote put the finishing touch on their next possession by lugging the ball across the goal line as he scored on a 1-yard quarterback keeper. Martin increased the score to 10–0 with his first conversion of the day.

Later in the period, halfback Gene Gedman powered over goal on a 1-yard plunge. Again, Martin punched the ball through the uprights for the point after, and with the score now 17 to 0 in favor of the Lions, it looked like the day was going to be all Detroit.

Cleveland, however, was not quite ready to surrender and looked as if they might be awakening from their doldrums early in the second period. Rookie running sensation Jim Brown took the ball at the Detroit 29-yard line and powered his way into the end zone for the Browns' first points of the day. The always-reliable Lou Groza kicked for the point after and a ray of hope shone on the Cleveland sideline as the Browns pulled to within 10 points at 17–7.

On fourth down, Wilson called for a field goal to extend the Lions' lead by three. In the huddle, however, Rote had other ideas. He called for a fake and no one objected. After breaking the huddle, Rote took a knee at the Cleveland 33-yard line, ready to hold for an apparent field goal by Martin. As soon as center Frank Gatski snapped the ball, Rote was up and running to his right. A number of Browns reacted quickly to the fake kick and, thinking he was concentrating only on the first down, began closing in on Rote before he got to the line of scrimmage. Downfield, however, fullback John Henry Johnson and rookie end Steve Junker had sprinted for the goal line. Rote saw that the 6' 3" Junker, late of Xavier College, had broken free of defenders, and he lobbed a high, arching pass that Junker pulled in at the 5 and carried, untouched, into the end zone. Martin's third extra point of the day pushed the score to 24–7.

Before the half ended, the Lions scored again when halfback Terry Barr picked off a Cleveland pass at the Browns' 19-yard line and returned the ball for a touchdown. Jim Martin's kick made the score 31–7 in favor of the home team.

Still not ready to be counted out, the Browns opened the second half with a drive that ended in a 5-yard touchdown run by Lew Carpenter. Groza connected on his second point after kick of the day and Cleveland drew another breath of life as they cut the lead to 17.

The Lions, however, came back immediately. Just two plays after taking the ensuing kickoff, Detroit scored again. On third down, Rote connected on a touchdown pass to end Jim Doran, good for 78 yards. Jim Martin's kick put the Lions back on top 38–14, and snuffed out much hope of the Cleveland faithful for a second-half comeback.

One of the few miscues suffered by the Lions in the game came with Detroit facing a fourth down deep in their own territory. Yale Lary stood back ready to punt the Lions out of trouble. At the snap, center Charley Ane fired the ball back at Lary, but misfired low, leaving the ball bouncing in the backfield. Lary, who was always his coolest under pressure, ignored the oncoming Cleveland defenders, scooped the ball off the ground, and set a playoff record by booting away a 74-yard punt. Even the errors had happy endings for the Lions that day.[2]

Late in the third quarter, Rote again fired a touchdown pass, this time to rookie end Steve Junker for 23 yards. Jim Martin's kick increased Detroit's lead to 45–14.

As the fourth quarter began, the Browns had to be glad that time was winding down on this nightmare of a game. But the never-ending nature of that nightmare was to continue.

Detroit began another drive with Rote mixing runs and passes to help the Lions move down to the Cleveland 32-yard line. There, Rote called for another pass. He sent wide receiver Dave Middleton deep and connected with the former Auburn star for the touchdown. Jim Martin's seventh extra point kick increased Detroit's lead to a commanding 38 points.

With the game well in hand, Wilson replaced Rote at quarterback with backup Jerry Reichow. Rote left the game to a thundering ovation from the Briggs Stadium crowd with the score standing at a safe 52–14.

Even with Rote on the sidelines, the Lions were not finished growling that afternoon. End Howard "Hopalong" Cassady got into the act, taking a 16-yard pass from Reichow into the end zone for the Lions' last score on the day. Jim Martin's kick for conversion was good, putting the Lions on top 59–14. Martin was perfect on the day, scoring eleven points on a field goal and eight extra point kicks.

The beating was the worst ever suffered by the Browns. Coach Paul Brown tried to keep the battering in perspective. "I'm philosophical about it," said Brown to reporters after the game. Managing a smile, Brown continued, "The ball was just going to bounce that way and it did. The Lions were whetted to a fine competitive edge and we had been standing by waiting."[3] Brown was, of course, referring to the Lions' comeback playoff win over the 49ers the previous week, during which his Browns sat idle, having already sewn up the Eastern Division.

Detroit linebacker and team captain Joe Schmidt had another view of why the Lions whipped the Browns that day: "Cleveland isn't a hard team anymore," said Schmidt after the game. "They're not as tough as they used to be when they had Graham and some of those other guys. They don't hit as hard."[4]

Paul Brown spoke highly of the Lions' performance that day. "Rote and his receivers had a great day. They did everything right, guys diving and catching on their fingertips. I've got to give them credit." Brown even complimented the Detroit fans: "We couldn't hear our own signals. That crowd noise was terrific. There's something about that ballpark that makes the crowd noise drown our signals."[5]

SCORING

	1	2	3	4	Totals
Cleveland Browns	0	7	7	0	14
Detroit Lions	17	14	14	14	59

1st Quarter: DET — FG — Jim Martin 31 yards. DET — TD — Tobin Rote 1-yard rush (Jim Martin kick). DET — TD — Gene Gedman 1-yard rush (Jim Martin kick). 2nd Quarter: CLE — TD — Jim Brown 29-yard rush (Lou Groza kick). DET — TD — Steve Junker 26-yard pass from Tobin Rote (Jim Martin kick). DET — TD — Terry Barr 19-yard interception return (Jim Martin kick). 3rd Quarter: CLE — TD — Lew Carpenter 5-yard rush (Lou Groza kick). DET — TD — Jim Doran 78-yard pass from Tobin Rote (Jim Martin kick). DET — TD — Steve Junker 23-yard pass from Tobin Rote (Jim Martin kick). 4th Quarter: DET — TD — Dave Middleton 32-yard pass from Tobin Rote (Jim Martin kick). DET — TD — Howard Cassady 16-yard pass from Jerry Reichow (Jim Martin kick).

STARTING LINEUPS

Cleveland Browns		Detroit Lions
Tommy O'Connell	Quarterback	Tobin Rote
Jim Brown	Fullback	John Henry Johnson
Ray Renfro	Left Halfback	Gene Gedman
Lew Carpenter	Right Halfback	Howard Cassady
Pete Brewster	Left End	Jim Doran
Lou Groza	Left Tackle	Lou Creekmur
Herschel Forester	Left Guard	Harley Sewell
Art Hunter	Center	Frank Gatski
Fred Robinson	Right Guard	Stan Campbell
Mike McCormack	Right Tackle	Ken Russell
Preston Carpenter	Right End	Steve Junker
Bill Quinlan	Left Defensive End	Darris McCord
Bob Gain	Left Defensive Tackle	Ray Krouse
Don Colo	Right Defensive Tackle	Gil Mains
Len Ford	Right Defensive End	Gene Cronin
Galen Fiss	Left Linebacker	Bob W. Long
Vince Costello	Middle Linebacker	Joe Schmidt
Walt Michaels	Rightside Linebacker	Roger Zatkoff
Junior Wren	Defensive Back	Carl Karilivacz

Ken Konz	Defensive Back	Jack Christiansen
Warren Lahr	Defensive Back	Yale Lary
Don R. Paul	Defensive Back	Jim David

Head Coaches: Cleveland: Paul Brown; Detroit: George Wilson.
Game Officials: Referee: Ronald Gibbs (St. Thomas); Umpire: Joseph Connell (Pittsburgh); Linesman: Dan Tehan (Xavier); Back Judge: Cleo Diehl (Northwestern); Field Judge: Don Looney (TCU)

TEAM STATISTICS

Cleveland Browns		Detroit Lions
17	First Downs	22
59/313	Total Offense Plays/Yards	57/438
38	Rushing Attempts	36
218	Rushing Yardage	142
21	Pass Attempts	21
9	Pass Completions	13
42.8	Completion Percentage	61.9
112	Passing Yardage	296
0	Interceptions	4
2/17	Sacks/Yards Lost	0/0
3/85	Kickoff Returns/Yards	8/183
4	Punts	4
35.5	Punting Average	36.0
1	Punt Return Yards	13
2/2	Fumbles/Lost	3/1
4	Penalties	7
60	Penalty Yards	52

1958 NFL — Sudden Death

1958 NFL Championship — Baltimore Colts (23) vs. New York Giants (17)

DECEMBER 28, 1958 — YANKEE STADIUM, NEW YORK CITY — 64,185
WEATHER CONDITIONS: BRILLIANT SUNSHINE, COLD, 32°F.
FIELD CONDITION: DRY, FIRM.

The city of Baltimore was football crazy. They absolutely loved their Colts. The franchise's first incarnation was in the upstart All-American Football Conference in the late 1940s. The original Colts, who wore green jerseys rather than the now-familiar blue, were an AAFC replacement team in 1947. The team was a substitute for Miami's Seahawks, who had folded after just one season. With Y.A. Tittle at quarterback, the team made the AAFC playoffs in 1948, but fell to a losing record again the following year. The Colts were inexplicably accepted into the NFL along with two AAFC powerhouses — the Cleveland Browns and the San Francisco 49ers — for the 1950 season, but fell into bankruptcy, and the franchise was surrendered to the league by 1951. Left without a team, Colts fans still pined for the city's return to the NFL. The Colts' 127-member marching band even continued to practice in hopes of the team's eventual return. By loose connection, the franchise wound up for one season each in New York and Dallas, but neither of those teams was able to survive. In 1953, a group of investors led by businessman Carroll Rosenbloom purchased the defunct Dallas Texans franchise, returning the Colts to Baltimore and Baltimore to the NFL. After four losing seasons, the Colts posted a 7 and 5 campaign in 1957, and the patient and supportive but long-suffering Colts fans saw a ray of hope. In 1958, the support paid off and the wait was over. The Baltimore Colts were Western Division champions and playing the New York Giants for the NFL title.

Just three years earlier, Colts quarterback Johnny Unitas was playing football for six dollars a game for the semi-pro Bloomfield Rams. After a notable career at the University of Louisville, Unitas had been invited to try out with the Pittsburgh Steelers. Somehow the Steelers' coaching staff missed that little thing in Unitas's makeup called "superstar quarterback," and cut the future Hall of Famer before the 1955 season. Unitas kept his skills honed in Bloomfield while trying to catch on with another team. In 1956 he wrote to the Colts asking for a tryout, and the rest is history. During this game, Unitas would show those in the stadium, and the forty million tuned in on television across the country, just what a mistake the Steelers had made in 1955.

The Giants, too, were unsung during the 1958 season. They had notable stars such as Gifford, Conerly, Rote, Robustelli, and Huff, and were just two years removed from their last league title. Very few people, however, had chosen this team to be in the championship final when the season began. The Cleveland Browns were the pick to take the Eastern Division laurels, but on the strength of a 49-yard Pat Summerall field goal, the Giants defeated the Browns 13–10 in a swirling snowstorm during the final game of the regular season, forcing a playoff the following week. The Giants, playing inspired football, shut Cleveland out 10 to 0 to win the Eastern Division crown and a chance to meet the Colts in the championship final.

Early in the first quarter, Unitas sent flanker Lenny Moore sprinting down the sideline while the Colt quarterback patiently and coolly waited for Moore to slip past New York defender Lindon Crow and into the open. Unitas then fired a rope that Moore caught going full speed at the Giants' 40. No one caught up with the speedy flanker until the 25-yard line, where he was finally brought to earth. At this point, the New York defensive unit settled in and halted the Baltimore attack. Forced to try for a field goal, Baltimore place kicker Steve Myhra set up for the kick. At the snap, however, Colts lineman Art Spinney missed his block, leaving an open lane for New York linebacker Sam Huff. As Myhra kicked the ball, Huff arrived and smothered it, denying Baltimore the lead.

While the Colts had been denied by Huff's charge, the Colts' drive had been successful in one very significant way. The Giants' coaching staff determined that the Unitas — Moore combination was potentially so dangerous that they should permanently keep two men on Moore. That double coverage, however, left Colts end Raymond Berry with only one defender to beat on his pass routes, an equally dangerous prospect. It was really a matter of choosing their poison — both were deadly.

The Giants took over and immediately began moving the ball. Quarterback Charlie Conerly got things started by firing a short pass to Mel Triplett at the New York 31. Conerly then called Frank Gifford's number and the former USC star tore through the Baltimore defensive line and into the open field. With Gifford on the loose, the Colts' secondary began to close in. Baltimore defensive back Milt Davis dove at the elusive Giant and missed, but was able to slow Gifford enough that Davis's teammates were able to catch him as he sought to recover his balance and speed, but not until Gifford made it down to the Baltimore 31. Soon, Conerly went back to the air as he fired a perfect pass to Giant back Alex Webster, who had gotten loose in the Baltimore backfield. It looked like a sure touchdown pass, but as Webster cut to go for the ball, he lost his footing and slipped. By the time he recovered, the ball had sailed harmlessly over his head. The Colt defense now stiffened and stalled the New York drive. On fourth down, kicker Pat Summerall trotted onto the field and kicked a 36-yard field goal. They had missed on the touchdown, but New York had drawn first blood and now held a 3–0 lead.

In the second quarter, Baltimore's massive defensive tackle, Eugene "Big Daddy" Lipscomb recovered a Frank Gifford fumble on the New York 20. Finding themselves immediately in scoring position, Unitas handed off up the middle to Alan Ameche and Lenny Moore on the next two plays for a first down, but went to the well one too many times as the New Yorkers closed that route tightly on the third attempt. On second down, Unitas handed off to Moore, who swept around end on a graceful run that carried the drive down to the 2-yard line. On third down, Ameche got the ball and followed All-Pro tackle Jim Parker through the line. Parker blasted a hole in the New York defense by pushing the Giants' Rosey Grier several yards off the play, and Ameche bolted through the opening for the first Baltimore points of the afternoon. Grier was rumored to be injured and was clearly not on his game. Myhra's extra point kick put Baltimore up by a 7–3 margin.

Soon the Colts were back on offense and moving downfield. Starting on their own 14-yard line, Unitas and head coach Weeb Ewbank decided to travel mainly by the land route this go-around. The Baltimore runners shredded the New York line time and again, grinding out 4, 5, 6 yards at a time. Unitas only called two pass plays on the entire drive — both to Berry. The second pass was good for 15 yards and a touchdown. Myhra again kicked for the extra point and the Colts now led 14–3.

That was all the scoring for the rest of the half, but the teams continued to battle tooth and nail for yardage. The action was fierce, the hitting hard, and tempers on both sides began to flare. Late in the period, Huff hit Berry after a reception and tackled him hard out of bounds on the Baltimore sideline. Some of the Colts thought it was a bit too far out of bounds and said so. Weeb Ewbank shouted at Huff, "Leave my man alone!" To which Huff replied, "Do something about it!" Ewbank did. Although the New York linebacker towered over the Baltimore coach, Ewbank took a swing at Huff. Immediately, players, officials, and other coaches quickly intervened, but the tone was set for a raucous second half.[1]

At halftime Ewbank told his Colts that they could not afford to relax. The Giants were not going to quit and the lead was still too close for comfort against a talented outfit like this. In the Giants' locker room, Jim Lee Howell and his assistants Vince Lombardi and Tom Landry encouraged their men to keep fighting. The game was close and still very winnable.

As the second half began, the Giants' defense continued their fierce play. The Colts started off quickly, driving to the New York 3-yard line. Then the Giants' defense came alive. Four straight plunges yielded negative yardage. Most notably, on fourth down, linebacker Cliff Livingston invaded the Colts' backfield and dropped Alan Ameche for a 2-yard loss, giving the Giants possession on their own 5.

The successful goal-line stand seemed to change the complexion of the game for the Giants; indeed, the whole stadium's spirits seemed to pick up. Taking over the ball, the offense came alive. After Gifford gained 5 yards behind tackle and Webster plunged through the line for 3, Conerly, now standing at his 13, felt comfortable going back to the air. Conerly sent end Kyle Rote deep down the left sideline. Just past midfield, Rote cut sharply to his right, leaving his escort — Colt defensive back Milt Davis — several steps behind him. By this time, Conerly had launched a 47-yard strike that Rote grabbed at the Baltimore 40 on a dead run. Rote continued streaking downfield until he reached the 25, where he was hit hard and the ball popped out. For several seconds, each of which seemed like minutes, the ball bounced free until Alex Webster streaked over and scooped it up. Webster tucked the ball in and continued downfield for 24 yards before being brought down at the 1. On the next play, Mel Triplett carried for the touchdown as he dove over a mass of Baltimore defenders at the goal line. Pat Summerall's point after kick was good, bringing the Giants to within 4 points with a 14–10 score.[2]

As the fourth quarter began, the Giants still had the momentum and looked as if they might well catch Baltimore before the quarter was out. When New York got the ball back, Conerly picked up where he left off in the third. The Giants ran a fake reverse, off which the New York quarterback set up and fired a rocket to end Bob Schnelker that advanced the ball to the Baltimore 15-yard line.

From here, the Giants relied on a piece of first-half scouting by team secretary Wellington Mara to take the lead. Mara, son of team founder and owner Timothy Mara, was in his front-row seat in the upper deck at Yankee Stadium, from which he snapped Polaroids of enemy formations each week. The photographs were then placed in a rolled-up sock and thrown, by Mara or assistant coach Ken Kavanaugh, down to the field, where adjustments were made based on the aerial-view snaps. New York assistant coach Vince Lombardi said of the system, "It's a tremendous help to us. I have great faith in its value."[3] Mara's Polaroids showed that each time the Giants went to the line, the Colts would overstack their defense to the Giants' strong side, leaving only the outside linebacker to cover the weak side. Based on this information, Lombardi was sure that Frank Gifford, lined up alone on the weak side, could beat any bigger, slower linebacker that the Colts might leave to cover him.

Conerly sent Gifford to the left side and at the snap of the ball, he was gone, streaking down the sideline and past linebacker Steve Myhra. Gifford caught Conerly's pass at the 5, broke one tackle and sailed into the end zone, giving the Giants the lead. Pat Summerall extended that lead to 17–14. As Ewbank had warned his Colts at halftime, the Giants had not given up.

Unitas now tried to pull off some magic and save the day for his team. He drove the team to the New York 38-yard line, but could get no further. On fourth down, the Colts decided to try for a field goal, but the placement would put the kick at 45 yards. In that day of non-specialists, that was a tremendous distance. Myhra was deadly from short range, but not very reliable from more than about 30 to 35 yards. Instead of Myhra, the Colts trotted out Bert Rechichar, owner of the then-longest field goal in league history. Rechichar missed his attempt, however — the ball falling short — and the Colts still trailed by 3 points.

Baltimore quickly got the ball back after Giant fullback Phil King lost a fumble. Again, Unitas moved the Colts downfield, this time getting to the New York 27. There, the Giants' defense again rose to the occasion as Andy Robustelli and Jim Katcavage dropped Unitas for successive losses, dimming the Colts' chances as time was running out.

The Giants took over on downs and, with less than three minutes to play, moved the ball to their own 40-yard line. It was third down and 3 yards to go. A first down would probably put the game out of reach for the Colts. Conerly called a sweep right and handed off to Gifford, who slashed off tackle, ready to break into the clear. He made 2 yards and looked like he would make the third when Baltimore defensive end Gino Marchetti freed himself from a block by Schnelker and dove at Gifford, bringing him down. Big Daddy Lipscomb followed the pair down and landed on Marchetti's leg, breaking his ankle, but referee Charlie Berry spotted the ball just six inches short of the first down. To this day, Gifford insists that in the commotion over Marchetti's broken leg, Berry inadvertently placed the ball on the frozen turf well short of his progress. "I still swear on a stack of Bibles, I made it. I never made a habit of squawking, but I insist that the referee moved the ball back just far enough to cost us the first down."[4]

Marchetti's leg was badly broken. He was helped off the field, but refused to leave the sideline until the game was over. He sat on the sideline watching the game, with his legs stretched out in front of him, a royal blue Colts jacket draped over his shoulder pads, and towels covering his lap and broken right leg.[5]

The Giants' coaching staff now had to decide whether to punt or go for the six inches needed for a first down. If they went for it and missed, Baltimore would have the ball at the New York 40 with over two minutes to play. The Giants had one of the league's best punters in Don Chandler. The punt was the safe choice and Jim Lee Howell made it. Lombardi later recalled, "It was unquestionably the right call. I would've done the same thing in Howell's spot. Every time."[6]

Chandler's kick was a gem, traveling 46 yards and pinning the Colts back on their own 14. With 2:10 remaining, it looked bleak for Baltimore. Raymond Berry remembered jogging onto the field and saying to himself, "Well, we've blown this ball game." Little did he know that he would play a pivotal role in the game-tying drive.

While just about everyone else thought the game was as good as over, Johnny Unitas had other ideas. He immediately went to work reviewing the Giants' defensive setups, choosing plays that he thought would be effective, and set about getting his team in position to win the game. With the Giants still most concerned about a deep threat from Lenny Moore, Unitas again began throwing short to Berry. Three times he found Berry over the middle. On the second pass, Berry made a terrific leaping catch good for 35 yards. His third reception put the ball on the Giants' 13 with just seconds remaining in the fourth quarter. Berry's three catches were good for a total of 62 of the 73 yards gained during the Colts' drive the from their own 14 to the New York 13. Ewbank immediately called for the field goal and without a huddle, the Colts went to the line. Steve Myhra set up in his familiar spot, 8 yards behind center and two steps behind the holder, to await the snap.

With just seven seconds remaining, Myhra stared at the spot and drew several deep breaths. The Colts' entire season came down to this one kick. Make it and live on in overtime — miss it and the season is over. Doing his best to put the implications out of his head, Myhra concentrated on the task at hand. At the snap of the ball, he readied himself and as the point of the ball was placed on the ground, he stepped forward, swung his powerful leg in its familiar arc, and made contact, sending the ball sharply up, past the outstretched arms of the Giant defenders and through the uprights, tying the score as time ran out. With the score now tied at 17, the National Football League was to experience its first ever sudden-death overtime period.

After a brief rest period, the team captains met at midfield for the first coin toss to determine who would kick and receive in league history. The Giants won the toss, and elected to receive.

On first down from the 20, Conerly handed off to Gifford, who rushed for four yards. On second, Conerly threw an errant pass to Schnelker, who made a valiant dive for the ball, but came up short. On third and six, Conerly again called for a pass. As he dropped back and set, he scanned the horizon and saw nothing but well-covered receivers and Colt lineman heading his way. Left with little option, the 37-year-old Conerly took off on a dead run around right end, desperately seeking the 30-yard stripe. As he approached his target, he was hit by linebacker Bill Pellington and Don Shinnick and landed a mere foot short of the first-down marker. Again, Chandler came in to punt the Giants out of trouble. He did, and the Colts began their first overtime drive on their own 20.

Unitas went to work again, knowing that it was dangerous to risk returning the ball to the Giants. The defense had held on New York's first overtime possession, but if given another chance, the Giants' offense was likely to move the ball successfully. It was not something Unitas was willing to chance. He needed a quick score. The clock was not a factor and a touchdown was not necessary. All he had to do was get the ball close enough to the goal line for Myhra or Rechichar to kick a field goal. A drive of 55 or 60 yards would do the trick.

On the first play, Baltimore halfback L.G. Dupre ran around right end for 10 yards and a first down. Unitas then tried to break something open, throwing long to Moore, who was streaking along the sideline. As the ball approached its target, New York halfback Crow reached out and tipped the ball away.

With the Giants' defense now thinking about the pass, Unitas called a draw play. At the snap, the Colts' signal caller began to drop back as if to pass, but slipped the ball to Dupre for the delayed run. The play yielded only 3 yards, leaving a third and seven situation. Unitas called for a pass, hoping to find Berry downfield, but after dropping back, he saw New York linebacker Harland Svare covering Berry like a blanket. He saw Ameche open in the flat and quickly went to plan B. Unitas threw a dart to the fullback, who pulled it in and carried to the Baltimore 40 for another first down.

The Colts now went back to the ground, with Unitas again handing the ball to Dupre, who gained another six yards on an end sweep.

With the Colts moving the ball well, it was time for a big play by the New York defense. They got it when tackle Dick Modzelewski slipped by a couple of blockers and, moving like a freight train, hit Unitas as he was trying to pass. Unitas went down hard, but held onto the ball, after a nine yard loss. Again, the Colts faced a third and long situation and they were not anxious to give the Giants the ball back. In the huddle, Unitas called for a pass formation with both ends split six yards off tackle, and Lenny Moore as slot back a couple of yards behind the gap on the right side. At the snap, Unitas dropped back and surveyed the field. While Moore was his primary receiver, he noticed that Giant halfback Carl Karilivacz had slipped, leaving Berry open. Unitas fired a rocket deep and Berry caught it, and was finally brought down at the New York 42-yard line.

The Colts figured that another 20 yards or so would suffice. Unitas chose to catch Modzelewski and Huff on a trap play and chew up some of the precious yards up the middle. The play worked perfectly as Jim Parker tapped Modzelewski easily and then let him past and into the Baltimore backfield. Spinney, who had played a terrific game since his missed block in the first quarter, pulled behind center and leveled the Giants' tackle, taking him out of the play. Baltimore tackle George Preas sealed off Huff, who was playing back and to his left, and Ameche bolted through the seam down to the New York 21-yard line.[7]

Baltimore was now in field goal range, but with a new set of downs, Ewbank and Unitas decided to call some conservative plays and see if they could get just a little closer. On first down, Dupre hit a granite wall as the Giants' line stopped him cold at the line of scrimmage. On the next play, Unitas surprised everyone by throwing across the middle to Berry, who made another first down before being brought down at the New York 9.

As the chains were being moved and the teams began to huddle, the officials called a time out. The coaxial cable for the television feed had gone out, interrupting the television feed for millions of viewers across America at a critical juncture. NBC technicians quickly discovered the source of the television outage — fans crowding the field at the end of the game had jostled the power cable connection loose. Television screens across the nation went blank for two and a half minutes before the connection was restored. An NBC spokesman stated emphatically that the referee's time out that lasted for those same two and a half minutes, though it could not be attributed to anything else, had not been called to accommodate the television audience. Whatever the reason for the time out, the fans at home didn't miss the final play.

Both teams used the unscheduled break to huddle with their coaching staffs and review their options. Ewbank, no doubt thinking of the previous pass, told his quarterback to keep the ball on the ground and limit the risk of a turnover. Unitas did so on first down, handing off to Ameche, who gained a yard over the middle before being dropped by Huff in a violent collision. On second down, Unitas disregarded his coach by completing an aerial to end Jim Mutscheller that moved the ball to the one. Asked later about his decision to countermand Ewbank's order, Unitas stated, "I went against orders because I saw the Giants were overshifting and keying on Berry. Cliff Livingston was playing Mutscheller head to head, and I figured that Jim would have a step lead if he went for the corner." He was right and the play worked, good for eight yards. When Unitas was asked by reporters about the possibility of an interception, he responded coolly, "If I saw a danger of that, I would've thrown the ball out of bounds. When you know what you're doing, you're not intercepted." When Weeb Ewbank was asked about Unitas's brazen call, all he could say was, "What a mastermind."[8]

On third down, Unitas called a power play up the middle, with double teams on the tackle and the linebacker, and Lenny Moore leading fullback Alan Ameche through the resulting hole. At the snap, center Buzz Nutter and guard Alex Sandusky doubled up on tackle Dick Modzelewski and Mutscheller and George Preas sealed off Huff. The play worked as planned, with Unitas depositing the ball against the blue 35 on Ameche's jersey, and "The Horse" following Moore through a gaping hole in the New York line and into the end zone for a 23 to 17 victory. In thirteen plays, Unitas moved the Colts 80 yards and led the Baltimore franchise to their first championship.

And with that, it was over. It ended in an instant, one that was joyous for the Colts and heartbreaking for the Giants. But the Giants' feelings were summed up nicely by defensive end Andy Robustelli, who stated, "We played a good game against a great ball club. We have nothing to be ashamed of."[9] He was right: both teams played an all-out, full-speed, take-no-prisoners style of football that afternoon, but someone had to win and therefore, someone, by default, had to go down in defeat. Regardless of the game's outcome, no one on the field that day could be considered a loser.

The Colts were world champions and the Giants runners-up, but there really was more. The game was, of course, celebrated by fans in Baltimore, but it was also celebrated across the nation not for the Colts' victory, but for the impression it made on sports fans and the impact it would continue to have on professional football for years to come. Newspapers and news anchors across the country gave the contest unprecedented coverage. It seemed that professional football had finally arrived in the consciousness of the nation. Fifty years later, the 1958 NFL championship is still referred to as the greatest game ever played. Reflecting on the game years later, NFL Commissioner Pete Rozelle stated, "We didn't know it at the time, but it was the beginning for us. From that game forward, our fan base grew. We owe both franchises a huge debt."[10]

SCORING

	1	2	3	4	OT	Totals
Baltimore Colts	0	14	0	3	6	23
New York Giants	3	0	7	7	0	17

1st Quarter: NYG — FG — Pat Summerall 36 yards. 2nd Quarter: BAL — TD — Alan Ameche 2-yard rush (Myhra kick). BAL — TD — Raymond Berry 15-yard pass from Unitas (Myhra kick). 3rd Quarter: NYG — TD — Mel Triplett 1-yard rush (Summerall kick). 4th Quarter: NYG — TD — Frank Gifford 15-yard pass from Conerly (Summerall kick). BAL — TD — Steve Myhra 20 yards. OT: BAL — TD — Alan Ameche 1-yard rush.

STARTING LINEUPS

Baltimore Colts		New York Giants
Johnny Unitas	Quarterback	Don Heinrich
Alan Ameche	Fullback	Mel Triplett
L.G. Dupre	Left Halfback	Frank Gifford
Lenny Moore	Right Halfback	Alex Webster
Raymond Berry	Left End	Kyle Rote
Jim Parker	Left Tackle	Rosey Brown
Art Spinney	Left Guard	Al Barry
Buzz Nutter	Center	Ray Wietecha
Alex Sandusky	Right Guard	Bob Mischak
George Preas	Right Tackle	Frank Youso
Jim Mutscheller	Right End	Bob Schnelker
Gino Marchetti	Left Defensive End	Jim Katcavage
Art Donovan	Left Defensive Tackle	Dick Modzelewski
Gene Lipscomb	Right Defensive Tackle	Rosey Grier
Don Joyce	Right Defensive End	Andy Robustelli
Leo Sanford	Left Linebacker	Bill Svoboda
Bill Pellington	Middle Linebacker	Sam Huff
Don Shinnick	Rightside Linebacker	Harland Svare
Carl Taseff	Defensive Back	Jimmy Patton
Andy Nelson	Defensive Back	Lindon Crow
Ray Brown	Defensive Back	Carl Karilivacz
Milt Davis	Defensive Back	Emlen Tunnell

Head Coaches: Baltimore: Weeb Ewbank; New York: Jim Lee Howell.
Game Officials: Referee: Ronald Gibbs (St. Thomas); Umpire: Louis Palazzi (Penn State); Linesman: Charles F. Berry (Lafayette); Back Judge: Cleo N. Diehl (Northwestern); Field Judge: Charles Sweeney (Notre Dame).

TEAM STATISTICS

Baltimore Colts		New York Giants
27	First Downs	10
78/452	Total Offense Plays/Yards	49/266
38	Rushing Attempts	31
138	Rushing Yardage	88
40	Pass Attempts	18
26	Pass Completions	12

65.0	Completion Percentage	66.7
349	Passing Yardage	200
2	Interceptions By	1
4/35	Sacks/Yards Lost	3/22
2/2	Fumbles/Lost	6/4
3	Penalties	2
15	Penalty Yards	22

1959 NFL — A Brilliant Duel in Baltimore

1959 NFL Championship — New York Giants (16) vs. Baltimore Colts (31)

DECEMBER 28, 1959 — MEMORIAL STADIUM, BALTIMORE — 57,545
WEATHER CONDITIONS: BRILLIANT SUNSHINE, MILD, MID–50S.
FIELD CONDITION: DRY, FIRM.

The Giants had run through the NFL's Eastern Division with ease, posting a 10–1 record. They were now ready to face the Western champion Baltimore Colts in a rematch of the longest game ever played from one year earlier. The Colts were favored, but the Giants had a plan. Defensive coach Tom Landry summed the plan up by saying that the Giants would concede a couple of touchdowns to the Colts' running game, but they would double-team receivers Raymond Berry and Jim Mutschuller. "We knew that Charlie Conerly was in the middle of one of his finest seasons," Landry later recalled. "He was our quarterback and we knew with him in shape we could score at least two. We knew that with Pat Summerall [20 of 29 field goals that year] we had an edge in placekicking. We fully expected, therefore, to win a tight defensive battle."[1]

Early in the first quarter, the Colts drove 80 yards in six plays with Unitas completing four of five passes. Johnny Unitas pulled out a bit of deception by faking a handoff to Alan Ameche, then feinting twice to end Raymond Berry. Out of the corner of his eye, however, Unitas saw Lenny Moore streaking past defender Dick Nolan and breaking into the open. Redirecting, Unitas fired a 25-yard rocket that hit the speedy Moore in stride. Moore practically flew the remaining 35 yards to open the scoring on the day. Steve Myhra's conversion kick put Baltimore up 7 to 0.

Conerly answered quickly by moving the Giants down to the Baltimore six and what looked like a sure touchdown, but Baltimore's defense, led by Gino Marchetti and Art Donovan, not only held the Giants, but pushed them back ten yards. On fourth down, the Giants were forced to bring Pat Summerall in to try for a field goal. Summerall's kick was good from 23 yards and the Giants closed the gap to 7–3.

The Colts passed up a field goal opportunity in the second quarter when they chose to pass on fourth down on the New York 35. Giant defenders Rosey Grier and Andy

Robustelli swarmed into the Baltimore backfield and dropped Unitas for a three-yard loss, snuffing out a scoring opportunity. Baltimore head coach Weeb Ewbank accepted responsibility for that call. "Johnny was hitting his passes so well that I didn't hesitate letting him try for the first down. He ate the ball instead of throwing it away."[2]

In the second and third quarters New York began moving again. Twice, the Giants moved deep into Baltimore territory, but each time, the Colt defense refused to break and New York was forced to call on reliable Pat Summerall to salvage points out of the drive. Summerall hit on field goals of 37 and 22 yards in the second and third periods, respectively.

Late in the third period, the Giants began a drive from their own 44 and penetrated down to the Baltimore 27. On fourth and a foot, the Giants turned to Alex Webster to grind out a new set of downs. Webster headed through the middle of the line, but was stopped short by Ray Krouse and a host of Baltimore defenders. From that point on, the Baltimore defense, led by Gino Marchetti and Johnny Sample, were world-beaters. The tenor of the game began to change.[3]

"For a span of 10 minutes 21 seconds here in tension-packed Memorial Stadium — from midway of the third period to the third minute of the fourth — the outmanned, underdog Giants had the Colts whipped, three field goals to one touchdown. But they were living on borrowed time, hanging by their fingernails on the edge of a mighty cliff."[4] For the next 10 minutes, it was all Colts. During that span, Baltimore scored three touchdowns and a field goal to expunge a 9–7 lead the Maramen nursed heading into the final period.

After stopping Webster, the Colts drove 73 yards for the go-ahead touchdown. The ten-play drive was sparked by Lenny Moore's catch of a 36-yard pass from Unitas. As the fourth quarter began, Unitas rolled out and spun for the final 4 yards himself to put his team back on top. Myhra's point after made the score 14–9 in favor of the Colts. They would not trail again today.

The teams then traded punts, but on the ensuing Giants possession, Baltimore cornerback Andy Nelson intercepted a Conerly throw on the New York 31 and returned it 17 yards to the 14. After a two-yard plunge by Ameche, Unitas hit rookie end Jerry Richardson in the left flat for a 14-yard touchdown pass. Myhra again kicked for conversion and the rout was on.

The Colt defense kept up relentless pressure on Conerly for the remainder of the game, forcing him to scramble and hurry his throws. Conerly said after the game, "I was never rushed like that this year."[5] As a result, the Giants threw two more interceptions, both to cornerback Johnny Sample. On the first interception, Sample picked off an option pass from Frank Gifford and took the pigskin for a 41-yard ride into the end zone. Myhra's converted for a 28 to 9 lead. The second pick was made at midfield off Conerly and returned 24 yards to the New York 26, setting up a 25-yard Myhra field goal that stretched the score to 31–9.

With just minutes to play, New York got the ball back and refused to lie down. They drove down the field with Conerly finding Kyle Rote and Bob Schnelker each for 19 yards through the air. With a half minute to play, they scored on a 32-yard pass from Conerly to Schnelker, but at this point, it was only window dressing. Summerall's conversion brought the score to 31–16. The game ended with Don Chandler kicking off as time ran out.

The Giants' numbers on the day were respectable. The New York defense had played pretty well. The pass rush got to Unitas for six sacks, costing Baltimore 57 yards in losses. Andy Robustelli made four of those sacks. The front line held Baltimore rushers to just 73 yards rushing. The offense outgained Baltimore on the ground and had more first downs. Pass completions and yards through the air were similar. But once again, the Giants had made too many mistakes and failed to take advantage of their opportunities. Key turnovers had been costly and good scoring opportunities were wasted.

Defensive coordinator Tom Landry, coaching his last game with the Giants before heading to Dallas to take over the head coaching reigns for the expansion Cowboys, commented, "We decided to gamble on Lenny Moore. You can't cover all of the Colt offensive weapons. We wanted to stop their running game and provide double coverage on Raymond Berry and Jim Mutscheller. That meant we had to cover Moore with one man, Lindon Crow."[6] Landry said that the Giants were willing to concede a couple of touchdowns to Moore, but that the Giants' offense could more than get that back. "Lenny Moore is the fellow that beat us." Referring to Moore, Landry continued, "On both his big pass catches he was not the primary receiver. Unitas switched from Berry both times and Moore's execution was perfect, especially on the one he scored on."[7]

Both head coaches conceded that the other key play was the stopping of Alex Webster on fourth and inches in the third quarter. New York's Jim Lee Howell commented, "That was the turning point. From then on, we were on the defensive." Baltimore's Weeb Ewbank fully agreed as he complimented his vanquished opponents after the game. "Holding them to less than a yard on that play was the key," Ewbank said. "That was a great team that we beat."[8]

SCORING

	1	2	3	4	Totals
New York Giants	3	3	3	7	16
Baltimore Colts	7	0	0	24	31

1st Quarter: BAL — TD — Lenny Moore 60-yard pass from Unitas (Myhra kick). NYG — FG — Pat Summerall 23 yards. 2nd Quarter: NYG — FG — Pat Summerall 37 yards. 3rd Quarter: NYG — FG — Pat Summerall 22 yards. 4th Quarter: BAL — TD — Johnny Unitas 4-yard rush (Myhra kick). BAL — TD — Jerry Richardson 12-yard pass from Unitas (Myhra kick). BAL — TD — Johnny Sample 42-yard interception return (Myhra kick). BAL — FG — Steve Myhra 25 yards. NYG — TD — Bob Schnelker 32-yard pass from Conerly (Summerall kick).

STARTING LINEUPS

New York Giants		Baltimore Colts
Charlie Conerly	Quarterback	Johnny Unitas
Mel Triplett	Fullback	Alan Ameche
Frank Gifford	Left Halfback	Mike Sommer
Alex Webster	Right Halfback	Lenny Moore
Kyle Rote	Left End	Raymond Berry
Rosey Brown	Left Tackle	Jim Parker
Darrell Dess	Left Guard	Art Spinney
Ray Wietecha	Center	Buzz Nutter
Jack Stroud	Right Guard	Alex Sandusky
Frank Youso	Right Tackle	George Preas
Bob Schnelker	Right End	Jim Mutscheller
Jim Katcavage	Left Defensive End	Gino Marchetti
Dick Modzelewski	Left Defensive Tackle	Art Donovan
Rosey Grier	Right Defensive Tackle	Gene Lipscomb
Andy Robustelli	Right Defensive End	Don Joyce
Cliff Livingston	Left Linebacker	Bill Pellington

Sam Huff	Middle Linebacker	Dick Szymanski
Harland Svare	Rightside Linebacker	Don Shinnick
Dick Nolan	Defensive Back	Carl Taseff
Jimmy Patton	Defensive Back	Andy Nelson
Lindon Crow	Defensive Back	Ray Brown
Dick Lynch	Defensive Back	Milt Davis

Head Coaches: New York: Jim Lee Howell; Baltimore: Weeb Ewbank.
Game Officials: Referee: Ronald Gibbs (St. Thomas); Umpire: Louis Palazzi (Penn State); Linesman: Charles F. Berry (Lafayette); Back Judge: Cleo N. Diehl (Northwestern); Field Judge: Charles Sweeney (Notre Dame)

TEAM STATISTICS

New York Giants		Baltimore Colts
16	First Downs	13
63/368	Total Offense Plays/Yards	54/337
25	Rushing Attempts	25
118	Rushing Yardage	73
38	Pass Attempts	29
17	Pass Completions	18
44.7	Completion Percentage	62.1
250	Passing Yardage	264
0	Interceptions By	3
5/45	Sacks/Yards Lost	6/57
1/0	Fumbles/Lost	1/0
3	Penalties	4
23	Penalty Yards	20

1960 AFL — The George Blanda Show

1960 AFL Championship — Los Angeles Chargers (16) vs. Houston Oilers (24)

JANUARY 1, 1961 — JEPPESEN STADIUM, HOUSTON — 32,183
WEATHER CONDITIONS: OVERCAST, COOL, MID-40S.
FIELD CONDITION: DRY, FIRM.

The upstart American Football League had weathered their first season, and while there was a fair amount of red ink on the books, it had been a successful one. All eight teams that had started the year in the new circuit were still standing, and they planned on being back in 1961. The AFL had come a long way since its founding and things looked relatively good for the league as it completed its freshman year.

The Houston Oilers had also come a long way in one season. Their first training camp was Spartan, to say the least. Poor accommodations, triple-digit temperatures, humidity, and mosquitoes were all unwelcome factors. On August 6, the Oilers had played their first exhibition game in borrowed uniforms. The team was in Tulsa, Oklahoma, to play the exhibition game against the Dallas Texans when they discovered that roughly half of their Columbia Blue jerseys had been stolen.[1] They had to borrow 14 of the Texans' jerseys. The Texans ran onto the field looking impressive in their brilliant white uniforms. When the Oilers took the field, they were a mix of Columbia Blue and bright red jerseys. The game didn't go much better, as sloppy play and turnovers were common. But from there, the season would get considerably better, eventually leading them to the championship game. Before it, Houston coach Lou Rymkus told his team, "Gentlemen, after all we've been through, the heat, and the mud, and the mosquitoes, we deserve to be champions of the AFL. We do. They don't. Nobody is going to beat us."[2]

Houston boasted seasoned leadership at quarterback with longtime Chicago Bear George Blanda calling signals. The former Kentucky star[3] had retired from football following the 1958 season, but was coaxed back onto the playing field by Oilers owner Bud Adams for what he figured would be a few more seasons. "A few" turned into an amazing 16 more, with Blanda playing in his final game on January 4, 1976, at the age of 48. In that game, at Pittsburgh's Three Rivers Stadium, he kicked a 41-yard field goal and made one extra point as his Oakland Raiders lost to the Steelers 16–10 in the 1975 AFC Championship Game. During the 1960 season, Blanda had thrown for 2,413 yards and 24 touchdowns upon his return the gridiron. The 1960 Oilers' running game was sound, with 1959 Heisman Trophy winner Billy Cannon and Dave Smith posting similarly strong numbers. Wide receivers Bill Groman and Charley Hennigan and tight end John Carson were Blanda's go-to men in the passing game. As a unit, they were ranked first in passing in the AFL.

The Chargers entered the game on a four-game winning streak. They were on a roll and had a balanced offense. Los Angeles quarterback Jack Kemp was the AFL's leading passer in 1960. Kemp had a 52 percent pass completion average and had thrown for over 3,000 yards and 20 touchdowns during the regular season. Paul Lowe and Howie Ferguson shared backfield duties, with Lowe carrying for 855 yards and a 6.3 yards per carry average. Kemp distributed his passes fairly evenly among his backs and receivers, making it difficult for opposing defenses to know who to key on from week to week. Statistically, the team's leading receiver was Ralph Anderson, with 44 receptions for 614 yards and five touchdowns, but tragically, Anderson died on November 27 at the Los Angeles Coliseum, the result of a diabetic reaction following the Chargers' victory over the Oakland Raiders. Anderson's death weighed heavily on his teammates as they prepared for the first AFL championship contest. Both team's defenses were solid.

The game was originally scheduled to be held in Los Angeles at the Coliseum, but the league officials and owners had agreed to move it to Houston. The Chargers only averaged 15,000 fans per game in the cavernous L.A. Coliseum. The prospect of a national television audience seeing a stadium only 15 percent full for a championship game worried them enough that they chose to play in Houston's 36,000-seat high school field instead. The Oilers averaged over 25,000 fans a game. Based on the theory that a full small stadium was better than a nine-tenths empty huge venue, the owners — even Chargers owner Barron Hilton — agreed to head to Houston.[4]

The game was expected to be close and it was. Los Angeles started the scoring in what would be a back-and-forth struggle all day. The 41-year-old veteran kicker Ben Agajanian kicked two first-quarter field goals from 38 and 22 yards to put the Chargers up 6 to 0. The Chargers' second score was set up by a 30-yard Kemp to Lowe aerial that brought the ball to the Houston 18. Only gaining three more yards on the next three plays, the Chargers sent Agajanian in to kick his second field goal of the young contest.[5]

Blanda had been woefully off-target in the first quarter, but got the Oilers moving early in the second period.[6] Starting on his own 17-yard line, he completed eight consecutive passes to drive his team to a touchdown. The score came on a 17-yard pass to Dave Smith. Blanda, who had missed only one extra point in 47 attempts all season, tacked on another and put Houston up 7 to 6.

A pass interception by Houston's Bobby Gordon helped the Oilers increase their lead. Blanda took over, but could not crack the Los Angeles pass defense. Houston had to settle for a field goal, Blanda's first on the day, good from 18, putting the score at 10–6.

Late in the period, the Chargers fielded a weak punt from Houston's Charlie Milstead at the Oilers' 31, but with time running out, they were forced to bring in Agajanian again for a field goal of 27 yards, just nine seconds before the period ended to move the score to 10–9 in favor of the Oilers. The half ended with that slim one-point lead held by Houston due in large part to the Oilers' defense. The Houston defenders kept pressure on Kemp and the Chargers' receivers in the first half, helping to keep Los Angeles out of the end zone and forcing Agajanian's three field goals. Los Angeles head coach Sid Gillman told reporters after the game, however, that while the Oilers had defended well, his receivers were partly at fault for the lack of aerial productivity: "If we had been catching the ball in the first half, their pass defense wouldn't have looked so good."[7]

Billy Cannon returned the second-half kickoff 42 yards to spark the next Houston score. The Oilers' offense took advantage of the good field position and drove deep into Charger territory. Just minutes into the third period, Blanda found Bill Groman for a seven-yard flare pass for a Houston touchdown. Blanda's kick put the Oilers up 17 to 9.

The Chargers took the kickoff and countered quickly as Kemp found Dave Kocourek on a 33-yard strike into Houston territory to set up a score. Paul Lowe plunged for two yards off left tackle for the touchdown. Agajanian's conversion brought Los Angeles back to within one point of the Oilers at 17 to 16. Some question was raised as to why Gillman did not call for a two-point conversion try. A successful run or pass would have tied the score and a missed attempt would have still left the Chargers within a field goal of taking the lead. The decision may have become academic after the next Oiler possession, however.

Time was beginning to run out and Houston still maintained their tenuous one-point lead. Blanda then went to work. When Chargers cornerback Charlie McNeil followed Charley Hennigan on a sideline route, Billy Cannon broke into the open on a slant pattern. Blanda surveyed the field and saw the former LSU star in the open. He fired a long pass that Cannon caught on the dead run at the 35-yard line. Without breaking stride, Billy outraced Charger defensive back Jim Sears in covering the remaining distance to the goal line for the score.[8] The play covered 88 yards. Blanda added the extra point, and the Oilers now led by the score of 24–16.

Trailing by eight points, the Chargers began a last-chance drive to tie the game. Their only hope was a touchdown and a two-point conversion to send the game into overtime.

Aided by a defensive pass interference call, Kemp by air and Lowe on the ground drove the Chargers to the Houston 22-yard line, but that was as close as they would get. The Houston defense flexed their muscles and refused to give up any more precious ground.[9] A desperate fourth-down pass failed and the Oilers took over on downs. Having only to run out the clock, Blanda took a knee at the snap and the Houston Oilers were the new American Football League's first champion.

In the game, Paul Lowe ran for an astounding 174 yards. Kemp and Blanda had combined for 37 pass completions good for 472 yards on 73 attempts. Blanda had a hand in every point Houston scored, passing for all three touchdowns, kicking all three extra points, and kicking a field goal. Ben Agajanian accounted for ten of the Chargers' sixteen.

SCORING

	1	2	3	4	Totals
Los Angeles Chargers	6	3	7	0	16
Houston Oilers	0	10	7	7	24

1st Quarter: LAC — FG — Ben Agajanian 38 yards. LAC — FG — Ben Agajanian 22 yards. 2nd Quarter: HOU — TD — Dave Smith 17-yard pass from George Blanda (George Blanda kick). HOU — FG — George Blanda 18-yard. LAC — FG — Ben Agajanian 27-yard. 3rd Quarter: HOU — TD — Bill Groman 7-yard pass from George Blanda (George Blanda kick). LAC — TD — Paul Lowe 2-yard rush (Ben Agajanian kick). 4th Quarter: HOU — TD — Billy Cannon 88-yard pass from George Blanda (George Blanda kick).

STARTING LINEUPS

Los Angeles Chargers		**Houston Oilers**
Jack Kemp	Quarterback	George Blanda
Paul Lowe	Halfback	Billy Cannon
Howie Ferguson	Fullback	Dave Smith
Royce Womble	Flanker	Charley Hennigan
Don Norton	Split End	Bill Groman
Dave Kocourek	Tight End	John Carson
Ernie Wright	Left Tackle	Al Jamison
Orlando Ferrante	Left Guard	Bob Talamini
Don Rogers	Center	George Belotti
Fred Cole	Right Guard	Hogan Wharton
Ron Mix	Right Tackle	John Simerson
Maury Schleicher	Left Defensive End	Dalva Allen
Volney Peters	Left Defensive Tackle	Orville Trask
Gary Finneran	Right Defensive Tackle	George Shirkey
Ron Nery	Right Defensive End	Dan Lanphear
Ron Botchan	Left Linebacker	Al Witcher
Emil Karas	Middle Linebacker	Dennit Morris
Rommie Loudd	Rightside Linebacker	Mike Dukes
Charlie McNeil	Left Cornerback	Jim Norton
Dick Harris	Right Cornerback	Mark Johnston
Bob Zeman	Strong Safety	Bobby Gordon
Jimmy Sears	Free Safety	Julian Spence

Head Coaches: Los Angeles Chargers: Sid Luckman; Houston Oilers: Lou Rymkus.
Game Officials: Referee: John McDonough; Umpire: George Young; Head Linesman: Elvin Hutchison; Field Judge: Fritz Graf; Back Judge: Sonny Gamber.

TEAM STATISTICS

Los Angeles Chargers		**Houston Oilers**
21	First Downs	17
71/333	Total Offense Plays/Yards	72/401
30	Rushing Attempts	40
190	Rushing Yardage	100
41	Pass Attempts	32
21	Pass Completions	16

51.2	Completion Percentage	50.0
171	Passing Yardage	301
0/0	Interceptions	2/
3/28	Sacks/Yards Lost	0/0
2/0	Fumbles/Lost	0/0
3	Penalties	4
15	Penalty Yards	54

1960 NFL — Swan Song for the Dutchman

1960 NFL Championship — Green Bay Packers (13) vs. Philadelphia Eagles (17)

MONDAY, DECEMBER 26, 1960 — FRANKLIN FIELD, PHILADELPHIA — 67,325
WEATHER CONDITIONS: WARM, MID–TO UPPER 40S.
FIELD CONDITION: WET GRASS, HARD, PARTLY FROZEN DIRT,
SOME ICY SPOTS IN THE SHADOWS.

In a rarity of scheduling, the 1960 NFL title game was played on a Monday, since Christmas was on a Sunday. The decision was made not to play on Christmas Day, so Monday it was. Because Franklin Field had no lights, kickoff was scheduled for noon Eastern Time to make certain that the game would end well before the winter's early dusk.

Most people did not pick the Eagles and the Packers to be playing for the championship in 1960. Through most of the 1950s, both teams consistently finished at or near the bottom of their divisions. As recently as 1958, the Packers had posted an anemic 1–10–1 record, but with the arrival of Vince Lombardi in 1959, the turnaround had begun. Leading the team to a 7–5 record that year, Lombardi let it be known that his Packers would be competitive. "Nobody had expected the Packers to get there in the first place. But Green Bay, which hadn't won a division title since 1944, finished with a three game win streak to nose out the Colts for the 1960 Western Conference championship."[1]

Buck Shaw's Philadelphia Eagles knew that they had a daunting task before them. After years of mediocrity, the Green Bay Packers were back under second-year coach Vince Lombardi. He had taken a franchise with a long record of losing and, in two seasons, returned them to the league championship game. Lombardi's team was young, talented, and hungry. They had an intimidating defense, a strong passing corps, and a running game like a speeding freight train. There was nothing fancy about the Packers. They just played simple, hard-nosed football.

The weather was unseasonably beautiful in Philadelphia that Monday. With scattered clouds and temperatures climbing into the upper 40s, it was a perfect day for football. The weather did nothing to hurt attendance, as a crowd of 67,325 represented the second-largest gathering in championship game history.

The Packers kicked off to the Eagles to start the contest but wasted little time in establishing their credentials for being in the title game. On the Eagles' first play from scrimmage, Norm Van Brocklin threw a screen pass to halfback Billy Ray Barnes. The ball bounced off Barnes's hands and directly into the arms of Green Bay linebacker Bill Quinlan on the Philadelphia 14-yard line. Quinlan was tackled immediately, but the Packers had the ball a mere 14 yards from a score.

It was on this possession that Green Bay's offense set a tone for the afternoon — the inability to put points on the scoreboard. Calling on Taylor and Hornung to run the ball, the Packer offense failed to score or even get the 10 yards necessary for a first down. The Eagles took over on downs at the six.

The Eagles had dodged a bullet, but they were about to jump right back into the line of fire. On the third play of the possession, Green Bay's Bill Forrester recovered a Philadelphia fumble at the Eagles' 20, and the Packers had their next break of the day. Once again, however, Bart Starr and the Packer offense could not consistently move the ball. When the drive stalled at the 13, Hornung was able to put the Packers up 3–0 with a 20 yard field goal.

In the second period, Hornung hit on his second field goal of the day, this one also from 20-yards out, and the Packers now held a 6–0 lead.

Philadelphia began a drive that would yield the Eagles' first points of the day. After driving deep into Green Bay territory, Van Brocklin called for a pass play to Tommy McDonald. At the snap, McDonald got the jump on Hank Gremminger after the Green Bay defender slipped on an icy patch of turf. Now in the clear, McDonald took Van Brocklin's pass and sprinted into the end zone for a 35-yard score. Bobby Walston's point after kick gave Philadelphia their first lead of the day, at 7–6.

Green Bay responded by advancing the ball quickly into scoring range. With the ball at the Eagles' 13-yard line and just three seconds left in the half, the normally reliable Hornung tried for a go-ahead field goal, but this time he missed. The teams went into the intermission at 7–6 Eagles.

On the opening drive in the third period, the Packers took the ball deep into Philadelphia territory, but on fourth down on the Eagles' 26-yard line, instead of taking the field goal, Lombardi again chose to run the ball. Hornung took the ball, but was met by Chuck Bednarik, who slammed into the halfback like a hammer on an anvil. Hornung went down hard, landing short of the first-down marker. Again, the Packers came up short, and the Eagles took over on downs.[2]

Van Brocklin wasted little time in getting his club moving again. Passes to McDonald and Pete Retzlaff helped put the ball once again in scoring position. But as Van Brocklin went to the air once again, Green Bay safety Johnny Symank gambled on coverage, leaving his man open in the end zone, and sprinted over to snatch the ball away from an open McDonald. Symank had saved a touchdown and kept the Packers in the game.[3]

The Green Bay offense could do little with the gift from Symank and on fourth down were forced to punt. Max McGee made a freelance attempt to get the Packers back in the game when he defied Lombardi and ran for 35 yards on a fake punt. After Starr had missed on three straight passes, Max was standing on his own 19 awaiting the long snap and ready to punt Green Bay out of trouble. At the snap, he noticed the entire Philadelphia defense dropping back to set up the blocking for a return they were sure would come. "I catch the friggin' ball and all my instincts would not let me kick it," McGee recalled later. "I see these guys going back to set up their return. Normally they keep one guy to make sure you kick it. They didn't. I could see the first down."[4] Ignoring Lombardi's dictate that he was to punt on fourth down, not run, the All-Pro end took off for the first down and more. Max was finally wrestled down at the Philadelphia 46-yard line and the Packers had new life. Early in the fourth quarter, on the seventh play of the drive, McGee caught Starr's pass for 7 yards and a touchdown. With Hornung's kick, the Packers were now in front 13–10.

But the Eagles were not finished. With nine minutes showing on the game clock, halfback Ted Dean took the ensuing kickoff and returned it 58 yards before being driven out of bounds by Green Bay's Willie Wood, immediately putting the Eagles back in scoring position. Using Dean and Billy Ray Barnes, Van Brocklin moved the Eagles downfield. On a crucial third and eight, the Dutchman fooled the Packers and sent Barnes spinning for a vital first down at the Green Bay ten-yard line. Dean then ground out five more off tackle and on the eighth play of the drive, Dean carried around left end for five yards and a touchdown to reclaim the lead.[5] Walston's kick made the score 17–13 in favor of the Eagles.

After the teams exchanged punts, the Packers made a valiant attempt to reclaim the lead. Taking control of the ball on their own 37-yard line with 1:20 remaining, Starr put his offense to work. Mixing passes and runs, Starr kept the Eagles' defense on their heels as they frantically tried to adjust and stop Green Bay. Starr moved the Packers on completions to Gary Knafelc, Tom Moore, and Jim Taylor. Taylor picked up 9 yards on a sweep, but time was running out as the Packers found themselves on the Philadelphia 22-yard line, with time remaining for just one more play. Starr again called on Taylor to do the impossible. Jim ran around left end where Starr hit him with a short pass. Taylor grabbed the ball and cut back towards the middle, where he began to churn out the yardage towards the goal line. Taylor slammed off linebacker Maxie Baughan and now had just one man to beat — substitute back Bobby Jackson, who had just entered the game. The imposing sight of the big fullback coming at him and the knowledge that he was the only thing standing between a championship and a loss was not lost on the rookie, but Jackson managed to keep his head and grab Taylor at the 9-yard line as time was expiring. As Jackson was wrestling Taylor to the ground, Philadelphia linebacker Chuck Bednarik arrived in time to help ensure that Taylor went down and that the clock ran out. "I saw I had to get him," Bednarik said later. "I hit him high with a bear-hug tackle." And there, on the nine-yard line, the Packers' desperate title bid ended.[6]

Taylor lay on the turf, physically and emotionally spent. He had played a great ballgame, but had fallen just 9 yards short of his goal. The injured Hornung ran out to console his friend. As he was helping Taylor to his feet, Bednarik, the grizzled old veteran, approached the pair and embraced them. As the three walked off the field, arms around each other, and Bednarik between them, the Eagles' linebacker assured them that they were a great team who would be back in the championship contest the next year. Bednarik was right — the Packers were a great team, and they would be back to win championships in five of the next seven seasons.

For Green Bay, it was a day of missed opportunities. The Packers had outgained the Eagles, 401 yards to 296; registered 22 first downs to the Eagles' 13; completed more than twice as many passes; and controlled the clock, running 77 plays to Philadelphia's 48; but they had trouble translating yards into points. Twice in the first half they were within the shadow of the Philadelphia goal posts, but those two drives yielded only field goals. Starr's 7-yard pass to McGee was their only score in the second half.

There were tears and frustration in the Packers' locker room. Lombardi addressed his team in deliberate fashion by reminding them that they were a very good team, and that they would learn from this disappointment and improve from it. "Perhaps you didn't realize that you could have won this game," he said. "We are men and we will never let this happen again.... Now we can start preparing for next year."[7] Later, Lombardi told the press that the Packers had no excuses. "They outscored us. That's all that matters." But he added, "I'm very proud of our ball club."[8]

Scoring

	1	2	3	4	Totals
Green Bay Packers	3	3	0	7	13
Philadelphia Eagles	0	10	0	7	17

1st Quarter: Green Bay — FG — Hornung — 20 yards. 2nd Quarter: Green Bay — FG — Hornung — 20 yards. Philadelphia — TD — McDonald 35-yard pass from Van Brocklin (Walston kick). Philadelphia — FG — Walston 15 yards. 3rd Quarter: None. 4th Quarter: Green Bay — TD — McGee 7-yard pass from Starr (Hornung kick). Philadelphia — TD — Dean 5-yard rush (Walston kick).

Starting Lineups

Green Bay Packers		**Philadelphia Eagles**
Bart Starr	Quarterback	Norm Van Brocklin
Paul Hornung	Halfback	Billy Ray Barnes
Jim Taylor	Fullback	Ted Dean
Boyd Dowler	Flanker	Tommy McDonald
Max McGee	Split End	Pete Retzlaff
Gary Knafelc	Tight End	Bobby Walston
Bob Skoronski	Left Tackle	Jim McCusker
Fuzzy Thurston	Left Guard	Jerry Huth
Jim Ringo	Center	Bill Lapham
Jerry Kramer	Right Guard	Stan Campbell
Forrest Gregg	Right Tackle	J.D. Smith
Willie Davis	Left Defensive End	Joe Robb
Dave Hanner	Left Defensive Tackle	Jess Richardson
Henry Jordan	Right Defensive Tackle	Ed Khayat
Bill Quinlan	Right Defensive End	Marion Campbell
Dan Currie	Left Linebacker	Chuck Bednarik
Ray Nitschke	Middle Linebacker	Chuck Weber
Bill Forester	Rightside Linebacker	Maxie Baughan
John Symank	Left Cornerback	Jimmy Carr
Jesse Whittenton	Right Cornerback	Tom Brookshier
Emlen Tunnell	Left Safety	Don Burroughs
Hank Gremminger	Right Safety	Bobby Freeman

Head Coaches: Green Bay: Vince Lombardi; Philadelphia: Buck Shaw.
Game Officials: Referee: Ron Gibbs; Umpire: Joe Connell; Linesman: John Highberger; Back Judge: Sam Giangreco; Field Judge: Herman Rohrig.

Team Statistics

Green Bay Packers		Philadelphia Eagles
22	First Downs	13
77/401	Total Offense Plays/Yards	48/296
42	Rushing Attempts	28
223	Rushing Yardage	99
35	Pass Attempts	20
21	Pass Completions	9
60.0	Completion Percentage	45.0

178	Passing Yardage	197
1	Interceptions By	0
0/0	Sacks/Yards Lost	1/7
5	Punts	6
42.5	Punting Average	39.5
1/1	Fumbles/Lost	3/2
4	Penalties	0
27	Penalty Yards	0

1961 AFL — Blanda Bowl II

1961 AFL Championship — Houston Oilers (10) vs. San Diego Chargers (3)

DECEMBER 24, 1961 — BALBOA STADIUM, SAN DIEGO — 29,556
WEATHER CONDITIONS: WARM AND SUNNY, 67°F.
FIELD CONDITION: DRY, FIRM.

The second AFL championship game again featured the Houston Oilers and the San Diego (née Los Angeles) Chargers. The teams featured high-powered offenses and dominant defenses.

After a dismal start, Houston had posted a 10–3–1 record. The Oilers had pounded the Raiders in the season opener, but then proceeded to lose three straight. Following a 31–31 tie with the Boston Patriots in week five, the team turned it around and won nine straight, averaging 41 points per game. Quarterback George Blanda had thrown for 3,330 aerial yards and 36 touchdowns.

Blanda's professional career had started in 1949 with George Halas's Chicago Bears. Other than a brief stay with the 1950 Baltimore Colts, the Bears were his only team throughout the 1950s, but he was never happy there as he clashed regularly with Halas. Frustrated at his lack of playing time, Blanda retired after the 1958 season. He took a job at a trucking firm and prepared for life after football. In 1960, however, Bud Adams and the Houston Oilers of the new American Football League came calling. The offer was attractive. Blanda would be the starting quarterback in a new league that needed steady and tested leadership, he missed playing, and the pay was good. But there was something more — something unspoken. Here was a chance for Blanda to show his old boss George Halas that he was wrong about the former Kentucky star.

The Chargers, in their new home of San Diego, were 12 and 2 on the year. The Southern Californians had approached the season on a different tack. After abandoning the mostly empty Los Angeles Coliseum for the friendlier confines of San Diego's Balboa Stadium, with most of the 1960 team still intact, the Chargers seemed ready to return to the top of the AFL Western Division. Head coach and General Manager Sid Gillman had added three top-flight rookies to the already strong defense. Tackle Ernie Ladd, end Earl Faison, and linebacker Chuck Allen each made notable contributions throughout the season. The Chargers got off to a fast start, winning their first eleven games generally by comfortable margins. They boasted the number-one defense in the league, and quarterback Jack Kemp, along with halfback Paul Lowe and receivers Dave Kocourek and Don Norton, continued to light up the scoreboard. On December 3, however, they ran into their first roadblock — the Houston Oilers. While the Chargers had beaten the Oilers earlier in the season in a close struggle, they were beaten 33–13 in their second meeting. The Chargers rebounded nicely with a win over Buffalo the following week, but fell apart in the last week of the regular season in a 41–0 trouncing by the Patriots. Sid Gillman now had the task of getting his men's minds off the Boston debacle and in shape to compete for the championship against the red-hot Houston club.

In the second quarter, Houston safety Jim Norton hit Kemp as he rolled out and up the sidelines. The ferocious collision left Kemp with a broken finger on his left hand and Norton, also the Oilers' punter, with a slight concussion. It also brought about a Paul Maguire punt. Maguire, normally a reliable kicker, shanked this one, giving Houston good field position with which to start their next possession.[1]

Charley Hennigan was on his way to a huge game, having caught five passes from Blanda in the first quarter and a half before being knocked unconscious midway through the second period. He would not return until late in the second half. The Oilers continued the drive, but were slowed by the Charger defense at the San Diego 39. Blanda made good on a 46-yard field goal attempt and Houston led 3 to 0 at the half.

In the third period, Blanda, scrambling away from a heavy pass rush, lofted a 35-yard pass to Billy Cannon. The former LSU star caught the pass at the Chargers' 17-yard line and broke away from San Diego's Bud Whitehead for the touchdown. Blanda's conversion kick extended Houston's lead to 10 to 0.

In the fourth quarter, San Diego safety Charlie McNeil picked off Blanda deep in the Oiler end of the field. San Diego had a chance to score and, though it was getting late, to get back into the ball game. Tight end Dave Kocourek caught a screen pass from Kemp and carried to the Houston 12-yard line. The next three plays yielded only seven yards as the drive stalled, but George Blair, the Chargers' place-kicker, booted through a field goal from twelve yards out to make it a one-touchdown margin.

After the kickoff, Blanda drove his troops downfield. The Chargers were within one score of tying the game and the former Kentucky Wildcat was going to try to put it out of reach right now. As the Oilers neared the San Diego end zone, Blanda forced a pass to a receiver who was nearing the goal line. As the ball was coming down, Charger defensive halfback Bob Zeman had his eye on it. He began to sprint to the place where the ball was coming down and at the last second dove, making an outstretched, over-the-shoulder grab. Zeman had intercepted Blanda and stopped the Oiler from putting a bow on their victory. When he landed, aware that he was inside the two-yard line, Zeman intentionally rolled into the end zone for the touchback. Or so he thought. Instead of bringing the ball out to the twenty, the game officials ruled Zeman down at the two, leaving San Diego in terrible field position to mount a game-winning drive.[2]

The teams exchanged punts and San Diego got the ball back for one final possession with less than two minutes to play. Thanks to a defensive pass interference penalty, the Chargers were given a first down near midfield. The stadium was alive as the San Diego faithful began to hope against hope for an early Christmas gift from their Chargers. Once again, however, their hopes were dashed when Kemp was intercepted for the fourth time on the afternoon and Houston locked up their second straight league title. George Blanda could smile once again as he showed George Halas what he could really do when given the chance. Former teammate Al Jamison spoke of Blanda and his notoriously controversial personality: "George Blanda probably was the single most important factor in our winning those two championships. But he was irascible. We don't exchange Christmas cards."[3]

As is often the case with close contests, the game had been extremely hard fought and physical. More than a half-dozen gladiators needed medical assistance, most notably Charley Hennigan and Jim Norton for Houston, and tackle Ernie Ladd for San Diego. Game officials had called fifteen penalties for a total of 174 yards.

As the teams were leaving the field after the final gun had sounded, field judge John Morrow was knocked down as players, coaches, and a number of fans converged in the center of the field. It appeared that Morrow was knocked off his feet when jostled by a Charger defensive halfback, Bob Zeman. Later Zeman admitted that he moved into closer quarters when he saw his head coach, Sid Gillman, charging across the field toward the officials. Gillman was obviously enraged. His team had been penalized 10 times—7 in the last half—for a total of 106 yards. The coach said the officiating was the worst he had seen all season.[4]

SCORING

	1	2	3	4	Totals
Houston Oilers	0	3	7	0	10
San Diego Chargers	0	0	0	3	3

1st Quarter: None. 2nd Quarter: HOU—FG—George Blanda 46 yards. 3rd Quarter: HOU—TD—Billy Cannon 35-yard pass from George Blanda (George Blanda kick). 4th Quarter: SDG—FG—George Blair 12 yards.

STARTING LINEUPS

Houston Oilers		San Diego Chargers
George Blanda	Quarterback	Jack Kemp
Billy Cannon	Halfback	Paul Lowe
Charley Tolar	Fullback	Keith Lincoln
Charley Hennigan	Flanker	Dave Kocourek
Bill Groman	Split End	Don Norton
Willard Dewveall	Tight End	Bob Scarpitto
Al Jamison	Left Tackle	Ernie Wright
Bob Talamini	Left Guard	Ernie Barnes
Bob Schmidt	Center	Don Rogers
Hogan Wharton	Right Guard	Ron Mix
Rich Michael	Right Tackle	Sherman Plunkett
Dalva Allen	Left Defensive End	Earl Faison
George Shirkey	Left Defensive Tackle	Henry Schmidt
Ed Husmann	Right Defensive Tackle	Bill Hudson
Don Floyd	Right Defensive End	Ron Nery
Doug Cline	Left Linebacker	Emil Karas
Dennit Morris	Middle Linebacker	Maury Schleicher
Mike Dukes	Rightside Linebacker	Bob Laraba
Tony Banfield	Left Cornerback	Claude Gibson
Mark Johnston	Right Cornerback	Dick Harris
Jim Norton	Strong Safety	Bob Zeman
Fred Glick	Free Safety	Charlie McNeil

Head Coaches: Houston: Lou Rymkus; San Diego: Sid Gillman.

Game Officials: Referee: Jim Barnhill; Umpire: Anthony Veteri; Head Linesman: Bo McAllister; Back Judge: Jack Reader; Field Judge: Johnny Morrow.

TEAM STATISTICS

Houston Oilers		San Diego Chargers
18	First Downs	15
74/256	Total Offense Plays/Yards	52/256
33	Rushing Attempts	20
96	Rushing Yardage	79
41	Pass Attempts	32
18	Pass Completions	17
43.9	Completion Percentage	53.1
160	Passing Yardage	226
	Interceptions (Return Yards)	
0/0	Sacks/Yards Lost	6/49
5/1	Fumbles/Lost	2/2
5	Penalties	10
68	Penalty Yards	106

1961 NFL — The Pack Is Back

1961 NFL Championship — New York Giants (0) vs. Green Bay Packers (37)

DECEMBER 31, 1961 — CITY STADIUM, GREEN BAY — 39,029
WEATHER CONDITIONS: BRILLIANT SUNSHINE, COLD, 15°F.
FIELD CONDITION: DRY, FIRM.

The Green Bay Packers were back in the championship game for a second year in a row. This storied franchise with such a noble history was again on the verge of scaling to the peak of the professional football world. Back from the verge of bankruptcy and following a decade and a half of losing records, the team had been salvaged by a tough Northeasterner who arrived in Wisconsin in February 1959 to turn things around.

Third-year head coach Vince Lombardi hated to lose. Not since his early high school days at Cathedral Prep had he been associated with a losing team. Not after he transferred to St. Francis Prep in Brooklyn, nor at Fordham University, where he was one of the famed "Seven Blocks of Granite." Not as the head coach at St. Cecilia High School in New Jersey, nor as an assistant coach at Fordham, Army or with the New York Giants. Even his first basketball team at St. Cecilia finished with a 10–9 record.[1]

Lombardi immediately made wholesale changes in Green Bay. Backup quarterback Paul Hornung, who was used sparingly by the previous regime, became Lombardi's starting halfback. He brought an aging but still talented Emlen Tunnell with him from New York to help shore up the defensive secondary. He fully utilized fullback Jim Taylor and Max

McGee. He added players like Fuzzy Thurston and Willie Davis to further shore up already strong lines. He brought in new strategy and discipline to a team in desperate need of both. He believed in his players and told everybody who would listen. He loved to say about his quarterback Bart Starr, "He can't throw like Unitas or scramble like Otto Graham. All he can do is beat you."[2]

In 1959, Lombardi led the Packers to their first winning record in twelve years. In 1960, Green Bay won the Western Division crown and fought the Philadelphia Eagles to within nine yards of victory in the league championship game. In 1961, Lombardi's Packers, sporting a 9–3 record, were ready to claim victory.

The weather in Green Bay was a balmy 15 degrees on game day—balmy compared to the arctic-like 12 below zero that had been registered earlier in the week. Things were looking bright for the Packers in the personnel department as well. Paul Hornung, middle linebacker Ray Nitschke, and end Boyd Dowler were doing tours with their Army Reserve units, but each had been granted leave to play in this game. At full strength, the Packers fully believed in their chances to win.

Despite the bone-chilling air, 39,029 fans filled City Stadium for the city's first-ever championship contest. Of the Packers' five championship game appearances, none had ever been held in Green Bay. The 1936, 1938, 1944, and 1960 contests were all held in the Eastern Division winners' stadiums, and the 1939 game was held at the Packers' sometime home— the Wisconsin State Fairgrounds in Milwaukee.

A late first-quarter interception by Nitschke set up Green Bay's first touchdown. On first down Hornung carried around left end for four yards. On the next play, he caught a 26-yard pass from Starr that put the ball at midfield. Hornung and Taylor then alternated carries, grinding out yardage down to the New York six-yard line. There the clock ran out on the first period. On the first play of the second quarter, Hornung carried off tackle behind end Ron Kramer, and with New York defensive tackle Dick Modzelewski hanging on to his ankles, he scored the first touchdown of the contest. As the place-kicker, Hornung also kicked the conversion, and Green Bay led 7 to 0.

From there on, it was all Green Bay. "What had been billed as a mighty match between rushing power and aerial accuracy came apart at the seams in the second period as the Packers stormed to three touchdowns in the space of 10 minutes flat."[3]

The next Giant possession ended as badly as the last. Tittle went back to the air and Green Bay tackle Henry Jordan got his hand up and deflected the ball. This one too wound up in the hands of Nitschke and the Packers got the ball back at the New York 33. After Hornung and McGee failed to connect on a 13-yard halfback option pass, Starr overthrew McGee in the end zone. Undaunted, Starr went to the air again on third down, hitting Ron Kramer over the middle for a 15-yard gain to the 18. Taylor then ground out five yards over the next two plays, leaving a third and five situation. Starr decided to go for it all and hit flanker Boyd Dowler in the end zone for Green Bay's second touchdown. Hornung's kick made the score 14 to 0 in favor of the Packers.

Three plays after the kickoff, Green Bay's tenacious defense struck again. As Tittle dropped back to pass, Green Bay defensive back Hank Gremminger read his eyes and followed the ball perfectly, plucking it out of the air at midfield and returning it 13 yards to the New York 36. Again, Starr handed the ball to Hornung and Taylor, who drove the ball downfield to the 14. Starr then called for a Flood Right, a deception play designed to send a "flood" of receivers to the right side and pull the middle linebacker in that direction. At that point, tight end Ron Kramer would hit the open middle. The play worked, Kramer was wide open in the middle of the field, and he caught Starr's pass, dragging Sam Huff with him into the end zone for the score. Again, Hornung converted the kick and the Packers led 21 to 0.

Joel Wells returned the ensuing kickoff 27 yards to the New York 39. It was now late in the second quarter, and trailing 21 to 0, Giants coach Allie Sherman was anxious to put some points on the board before the half. He replaced the ineffective Tittle with another aging veteran, Charley Conerly. Conerly, who had led these Giants to the 1956 title over the Chicago Bears, was playing in the final game of his fourteen-year professional career. The wily veteran got New York on the move. A 35-yard pass from Conerly to Kyle Rote gave New York a first down on the Green Bay 15. Runs by Phil King and Alex Webster added nine more yards. On third down Joel Wells was stopped at the line for no gain and the Giants were faced with a fourth and short situation from the six. New York called a halfback option, and rookie Bob Gaiters took Conerly's pitch, swung wide to the right, but waited too long to pass. The young halfback out of New Mexico State, overthrew Kyle Rote in the right corner of the end zone. It was simply not the Giants' day. The drive ended on the six and Green Bay took over on downs. This was the only time the Giants would threaten to score all afternoon.

With less than two minutes remaining in the half, Green Bay's offense went back to work. Hornung started the Packers out with two carries good for 24 yards. Starr then found Ron Kramer on a 37-yard toss that moved the ball with lightning speed to the New York 15. The Giants then lined up offside, giving the Packers a five-yard gift. With time running out, Hornung kicked a 17-yard field goal on the last play of the half. The Packers went to the locker room at the break, up 24 to 0.

As the second half began, the Giants still could not get on track and mistakes continued to prove costly. In the third period, Joe Morrison fumbled while trying to catch Boyd Dowler's punt. The ball bounced off the Giant back and was recovered by Forrest Gregg on the New York 22-yard line. This time the Giants' defense held the Packers to just seven yards, but Hornung was able to boot a 27-yard field goal to extend the Green Bay lead to 27 points.

After the kickoff, the Giants stalled again and on the punt, Green Bay's Willie Wood called for a fair catch. Proving the theory that when it rains, it pours, New York's Joel Wells ran into Wood. The 15-yard penalty gave the Packers the ball on the Giants' 43, and once again, Starr went right to work. Working mostly through the air on this drive, Starr found Dowler on strikes of eleven and thirteen yards to move the ball to the New York 13. On second down Starr passed to Ron Kramer, who lugged the ball across the goal for another Green Bay score. Hornung's conversion made the score 34 to 0.

After Wells ran the kickoff back 25 yards to the Giants' 35, Tittle jogged back onto the field. Sherman wanted to see if his return to the game might spark something in his teammates. It seemed to, for in just four plays, the Giants had moved the ball to the Green Bay 30. But again, the magic ended abruptly. On the first play of the fourth quarter, Tittle threw an incomplete pass and on second down, he was sacked for a nine-yard loss by a host of Green Bay defenders. The Giants were stalled and chose to punt.

After a return punt by Green Bay, the Giants tried again. Morrison waved for a fair catch of Dowler's kick at the New York 21-yard line. Tittle, desperate to make something happen, immediately went deep for Del Shofner. Shofner, an All-American out of Baylor, took off down the field, but staying with him stride for stride was defensive back Jess Whittenton. As the pass came down at the Packer 38, the 6'3" Shofner reached up, but Whittenton, a fellow Texan, leaped high into the air at just the right instant to corral the ball over his shoulder, for the interception. Shofner immediately grabbed Whittenton and pushed him into the end zone as the officials blew the play dead.

Starr set about delivering the coup de grâce to the hapless Giants. He called for a draw play and handed the ball to fullback Jim Taylor, who was playing despite badly damaged ribs. The rugged fullback, showing no signs of his injuries, then broke through the line and shucking several would-be tacklers, made his way to the Giants' 14-yard line. There, the New York defense held, but Hornung kicked his third field goal of the day, bringing the score to 37 to nothing. That ended the scoring.

Green Bay's pass rush kept Tittle on the run all day, forcing the Bald Eagle into mistakes, including four interceptions. Three of those four resulted in Green Bay scores. Lombardi continually sent his linebackers and ends after Tittle. They swarmed into the backfield all day, causing Tittle to misfire on 14 of 20 passes on this frigid afternoon. Green Bay defensive end Willie Davis commented, "We've had it in our hearts to prove ourselves ever since the championship game last year."[4]

In summing up the Giants' frustration, head coach Allie Sherman said after the game, "We met a solid ball club, a very good football team and we don't have any alibis."[5] Sherman, in his first year at the helm in New York, said that the Giants' game plan was sound, it was turnovers and other mistakes that were killing them. He added that the coaching staff did not even change anything at the half. "We didn't even bother to use the blackboard at halftime. How do you fix a fumble or a dropped pass with a blackboard?"[6]

It's difficult to point out individual stars on a day when the entire Packer squad executed almost flawlessly. Many deserve some recognition: Starr, with his three touchdown passes; Nitschke, with his ball-hawking; the entire offensive line for the protection they provided; the entire defense for the pressure they kept on Tittle and Conerly. But Hornung, who collected a playoff game record 19 points, was truly amazing. Lombardi had high praise for his halfback: "Look at that guy over there. Positively the greatest competitor I ever saw. I don't know what it is inside a man like that, but the bigger the challenge is, the higher he rises to it."[7] Hornung received a car from *Sport Magazine* for being named the game's Most Valuable Player, but those words from Lombardi surely meant more to him. He was unstoppable that day, leaving both Giants and broken records in his wake. "Hornung beat the Giants in every imaginable way. He scored a touchdown, caught passes, kicked three field goals, and converted all four extra points."[8] He was truly the man of the hour on this New Year's Eve.

SCORING

	1	2	3	4	Totals
New York Giants	0	0	0	0	0
Green Bay Packers	0	24	10	3	37

1st Quarter: None. 2nd Quarter: GNB — TD — Paul Hornung 6-yard rush (Paul Hornung kick). GNB — TD — Boyd Dowler 13-yard pass from Bart Starr (Paul Hornung kick). GNB — TD — Ron Kramer 14-yard pass from Bart Starr (Paul Hornung kick). GNB — FG — Paul Hornung 17 yards. 3rd Quarter: GNB — FG — Paul Hornung 22 yards. GNB — FG — Ron Kramer 13-yard pass from Bart Starr (Paul Hornung kick). 4th Quarter: GNB — FG — Paul Hornung 19 yards.

STARTING LINEUPS

New York Giants		Green Bay Packers
Y.A. Tittle	Quarterback	Bart Starr
Joel Wells	Halfback	Paul Hornung
Alex Webster	Fullback	Jim Taylor

Kyle Rote	Flanker	Boyd Dowler
Del Shofner	Split End	Max McGee
Joe Walton	Tight End	Ron Kramer
Rosey Brown	Left Tackle	Bob Skoronski
Darrell Dess	Left Guard	Fuzzy Thurston
Ray Wietecha	Center	Jim Ringo
Jack Stroud	Right Guard	Forrest Gregg
Greg Larson	Right Tackle	Norm Masters
Jim Katcavage	Left Defensive End	Willie Davis
Dick Modzelewski	Left Defensive Tackle	Dave Hanner
Rosey Grier	Right Defensive Tackle	Henry Jordan
Andy Robustelli	Right Defensive End	Bill Quinlan
Cliff Livingston	Left Linebacker	Dan Currie
Sam Huff	Middle Linebacker	Ray Nitschke
Tom Scott	Rightside Linebacker	Bill Forester
Erich Barnes	Left Cornerback	Hank Gremminger
Dick Lynch	Right Cornerback	Jesse Whittenton
Joe Morrison	Strong Safety	John Symank
Jimmy Patton	Free Safety	Willie Wood

Head Coaches: New York: Allie Sherman; Green Bay: Vince Lombardi.
Game Officials: Referee: George Rennix; Umpire: James Beiersdorfer; Linesman: John Highberger; Back Judge: Charles Sweeney; Field Judge: Frank Luzar

TEAM STATISTICS

New York Giants		Green Bay Packers
6	First Downs	19
43/130	Total Offense Plays/Yards	63/345
14	Rushing Attempts	44
31	Rushing Yardage	181
29	Pass Attempts	19
10	Pass Completions	10
34.5	Completion Percentage	52.6
119	Passing Yardage	164
0	Interceptions	4
2/20	Sacks/Yards Lost	0/0
5/1	Fumbles/Lost	1/0
4	Penalties	4
38	Penalty Yards	16

1962 AFL — Sudden Death II

1962 AFL Championship — Dallas Texans (20) vs. Houston Oilers (17)

DECEMBER 23, 1962 — JEPPESEN STADIUM, HOUSTON — 37,981
WEATHER CONDITIONS: OVERCAST SKIES, MISTY RAIN, WINDY, COLD, 40°F.
FIELD CONDITION: DAMP, BUT RELATIVELY FIRM.

When the Dallas Texans took the field to face the Houston Oilers in Jeppesen Stadium on a cool, gray, misty late December day, no one could have anticipated the game that was about to unfold. Those present in the converted high school stadium, as well as those huddled around television sets across the country, saw an intrastate rivalry filled with action and excitement. They also saw what was to become the longest game in the history of professional football up to that time. Everyone settled in for a football game. Instead, they got a football game and a half.

While each team entered the contest with an 11–3 record on the season, the Oilers had the experience, and were 6-and-a-half point favorites coming into the game. They were veterans of the first two AFL championship contests, both times coming out on top. The Oilers were led by quarterback and placekicking veteran George Blanda and a running game that included hard-charging backs Billy Cannon and Charley Tolar, and a receiving corps of Bob McCleod, Charley Hennigan, and Willard Dewveall. Hank Stram's Texans were, however, not daunted by the opposition and set out to prove something to the rest of the league. Dallas made the decision to keep the ball on the ground much of the first half and take advantage of their running game, led by Curtis McClinton, Jack Spikes, and Abner Haynes. Haynes was playing flanker, due to an injury to Chris Burford. Quarterback Len Dawson only threw the ball seven times in each half.

Houston got things going first. Taking advantage of a short punt by Dallas kicker Jimmy Saxton, Blanda and his high-powered offense went to work. The Oilers' offense mixed runs by Tolar and Cannon with a pass to Hennigan that quickly moved the ball to the Texans' 9-yard line. On third down Blanda dropped back, looking for Hennigan in the end zone, but Dallas linebacker E.J. Holub stepped in front of the pass and intercepted it at the goal line. Holub returned the ball 43 yards before being wrestled down. The turnover provided a spark that resulted in a 17-point Dallas run.

Texan quarterback Lenny Dawson moved his team to the Oilers' 16-yard line, where the Houston defense finally held. On fourth down, Texans rookie tight end and field goal kicker Tom Brooker set up for a 23-yard field goal chance. Brooker connected on the kick, putting the Texans up 3–0.

In the second quarter, Dallas again began a sustained drive, this time for 80 yards. Dawson and his mates covered the distance in just four plays, the last of which was a 28-yard pass to Abner Haynes that, with the help of a Tommy Brooker conversion kick, increased the Texans' lead to 10.

Duane Wood intercepted Blanda in the second. Haynes took the ball for a 2-yard blast that, coupled with Brooker's second point after kick, put Dallas up 17–0.

During the halftime intermission the Oilers' coaches and Blanda huddled together, determined to devise a way to turn this game around.

Blanda came out in the third quarter and changed the momentum of the game by driving his club 67 yards to put the defending league champions on the board for the first time in the game. The touchdown came on a 15-yard Blanda to Willard Dewveall pass completion. Blanda, also Houston's placekicker, added the extra point and drew the Oilers to within 10-points at 17–7.

The Houston defense played inspired football after the kickoff. Dawson and the Texans could not move the ball and were forced to punt. The newly rejuvenated Oilers took the kick and began another drive deep into Dallas territory. This drive ended short, however, when Dallas's Johnny Robinson picked off Blanda in the end zone.

Early in the fourth quarter, Blanda again began to move the Oilers toward the Dallas end zone. Moving to the Texans' 31, the wily veteran threw to Cannon in the end zone for what looked to be a touchdown, but just as the former LSU star touched the ball, he was leveled by Dallas safety Duane Wood, and the ball fell to the turf for an incompletion. Unable to get closer, Blanda stepped into his placekicking role and made good a 31-yard field goal to make the score 17–10.

Once again, Dallas took the kickoff and failed to move the ball. Eddie Wilson, the Texans' backup quarterback, had replaced punter Jimmy Saxton after his first-quarter shank. Wilson had not fared much better than Saxton, averaging only 32 yards per kick on six tries. He did no better this time as another short kick put Houston on the Texans' 49-yard line with eight minutes to play.

Blanda went right back to the air, connecting with Cannon on the 33-yard line and later on the 10. Blanda passed to Hennigan at the one, and then he handed off to Charley Tolar, who broke through the line for the final yard and a touchdown. Blanda's conversion tied the score at 17, and the game was now either team's to win.

In an unhappy occurrence of déjà vu, Dallas took the Houston kickoff and was unable to move the ball, and, once again, Eddie Wilson punted short — this one good for just 23 yards, giving the Oilers the ball on the Dallas 41 with just short of three minutes remaining on the clock.

The Dallas defense allowed the Oilers just seven yards, so on fourth and three Blanda attempted a 42-yard field goal. It appeared as if the Houston comeback was about to be complete and the Oilers would win their third AFL championship. On the snap, Blanda stepped forward and swung his right leg upward, striking the ball and sending it on its journey through the uprights. The nearly 38,000 fans, players, and team officials held their collective breath as they watched the ball climb. As the ball lifted off Blanda's square-toed kicking shoe, however, Dallas middle linebacker Sherrill Headrick leaped up and got a hand on the ball, deflecting it away and saving the day for his team. Soon after, the gun signaled the end of regulation play with the score knotted at 17.

With faith in his defense, Dallas head coach Hank Stram decided to give the Oilers the ball, leaving him the choice of end zones to defend. Stram later said, "I wanted to kick off because our defense was playing much better than our offense and I thought we could hold them and get the ball back in good field position."[1] Stram also wanted to defend the goal that would leave the Oilers heading into the strong December winds. He relayed the message to team captains Abner Haynes and E.J. Holub as they trotted out for the coin toss. Holub recalls Stram's words, "We want to take the wind, and we'll kick off to them."

Waiting at midfield were referee Red Bourne, Houston captains Al Jamison and Ed Hussmann, and ABC announcer Jack Buck. Dallas won the overtime coin toss, but Haynes misstated Stram's wish to Bourne, stating that the Texans would kick. This left the Oilers with the choice of which goal to defend. Of course, they chose to have the wind at their backs. Stram later defended Haynes, saying, "The players were excited and tugging at Abner. He just didn't understand the options."[2] He also laid more of the blame directly at the feet of Bourne. "The official never gave Abner all the choices. That's what screwed it all up. The normal procedure is to ask if you want to kick, receive, or defend the goal. But the official said, 'What are you going to do, kick or receive?' Poor Abner's been taking the heat all these years, but that's really what took place."[3]

Kicking into the wind, Dallas's Tommy Brooker intentionally hooked a low squib kick, which Houston returned to their own 34-yard line to start their first overtime drive.[4] Most of the fifth period was a defensive struggle in which neither team could move the ball into scoring position. Houston and Dallas traded punts on their first two possessions, but at about the midpoint of the session, a short Dallas punt gave Houston the ball just short of midfield. With terrific field position, Blanda and the Oilers finally got something going. Closing to the Dallas 35-yard line, Blanda wanted to get just a bit closer before attempting another field goal. Blanda decided to try a safe pass, which with a time out remaining would still leave enough time set up for a field goal. But the kick would never come. Two plays before the fifth period came to a close, Blanda dropped back to search out Hennigan. Reading Blanda's intentions, Dallas's Bill Hull dropped back from his defensive end position and into pass coverage. As the Houston quarterback let go the pass, Hull, a 6'8" rookie out of Wake Forest, read it perfectly and leaped high into the air, pulling in the ball at the Texans' 27. Hull then returned the ball 23 yards to midfield. It was the fifth time the former Kentucky great was picked off that day, but this one proved fatal. The Texans burned the last play of the period and the teams got ready for another.

On the first play of the sixth period, Dawson sent Spikes downfield, and hit the former TCU star at the Houston 38-yard line. On the next play, Dawson again looked to Spikes, this time calling his number on an off-tackle play to the left that netted 19 yards. The Texans were now in field goal range at the Houston 19. Stram and Dawson played it conservatively with straight hand-offs up the middle. Any additional yardage at this point was nice to have, but not necessary. The Oilers' defenders knew that too, and they punched and clawed at the ball on every play, trying to force a fumble. The Texan backs held on tightly with both hands, digging out just one more yard in the next three plays.

The end finally came when Dawson, kneeling at the Oilers' 25-yard line, took the long snap from center and placed the ball on the ground in front of Brooker. The rookie's right leg swung forward, launching the pigskin on a trajectory that would carry it just over the outstretched arms of the Oiler defenders and allow it to split the uprights, thus ending the Oilers' 2-year hold on the championship.[5]

The teams struggled for almost seventy-eight minutes, the longest professional football game on record. There were many who were pleased to see someone other than the Oilers win, to avoid the possibility of a dynasty like the Browns had had in the old All-American Football Conference in the late 1940s. The Texans were obviously happy to dethrone the champions, but no one more so than Abner Haynes. "My mother and dad were in tears the way the TV guys had dogged me and how stupid I was. If the Oilers had taken the kick and scored, I'd have had to leave the country."[6]

To say that Hank Stram was extremely proud of his Texans' performance that day is almost an understatement. "I never saw a bunch of guys fight so hard for a win — never. Not anywhere, not in all of football."[7]

SCORING

	1	2	3	4	OT1	OT2	Totals
Dallas Texans	3	14	0	0	0	3	20
Houston Oilers	0	0	7	10	0	0	17

1st Quarter: Dallas — FG — Tommy Brooker 16 yards. 2nd Quarter: Dallas — TD — Abner Haynes 28-yard pass from Len Dawson (Tommy Brooker kick). Dallas — TD — Abner Haynes 2-yard rush (Tommy Brooker kick). 3rd Quarter: Houston — TD — Willard Dewveall 15-yard pass from George Blanda (George Blanda kick). 4th Quarter: Houston — FG — George Blanda 31 yards. Houston — TD — Charley Tolar 1-yard rush (George Blanda kick). OT1: None. OT2: Dallas — FG — Tommy Brooker 25 yards.

STARTING LINEUPS

Dallas Texans		Houston Oilers
Len Dawson	Quarterback	George Blanda
Abner Haynes	Halfback	Billy Cannon
Curtis McClinton	Fullback	Charley Tolar
Frank Jackson	Flanker	Charley Hennigan
Tommy Brooker	Split End	Bob McLeod
Fred Arbanas	Tight End	Willard Dewveall
Jim Tyrer	Left Tackle	Al Jamison
Marvin Terrell	Left Guard	Bob Talamini
Jon Gilliam	Center	Bob Schmidt
Al Reynolds	Right Guard	Hogan Wharton
Jerry Cornelison	Right Tackle	Rich Michael
Curt Merz	Left Defensive End	Gary Cutsinger
Paul Rochester	Left Defensive Tackle	Ed Culpepper
Jerry Mays	Right Defensive Tackle	Ed Husmann
Mel Branch	Right Defensive End	Don Floyd
E.J. Holub	Left Linebacker	Doug Cline
Sherrill Headrick	Middle Linebacker	Gene Babb
Walt Corey	Rightside Linebacker	Mike Dukes
Duane Wood	Left Cornerback	Tony Banfield
Dave Grayson	Right Cornerback	Bobby Jancik
Bobby Hunt	Strong Safety	Jim Norton
Bobby Ply	Free Safety	Fred Glick

Head Coaches: Dallas: Hank Stram; Houston: Lou Rymkus.

Game Officials: Referee: Harold Bourne; Umpire: Bob Finley; Head Linesman: Bo McAllister; Back Judge: Hugh Gamber; Field Judge: Ben Dreith.

TEAM STATISTICS

Dallas Texans		Houston Oilers
19	First Downs	21
68/237	Total Offense Plays/Yards	76/359
54	Rushing Attempts	30
199	Rushing Yardage	98
14	Pass Attempts	46
9	Pass Completions	23
64.3	Completion Percentage	50.0
88	Passing Yardage	261
5	Interceptions (Return Yards)	0
6/50	Sacks/Yards Lost	0/0
	Kickoff Returns — Yards	
8	Punts	3
31	Punting Average	39
2/1	Fumbles/Lost	0/0
6	Penalties	6
42	Penalty Yards	50

1962 NFL — One That Got Away: Tales of the Wind and Jimmy Taylor

1962 NFL Championship — Green Bay Packers (16) vs. New York Giants (7)

DECEMBER 30, 1962 — YANKEE STADIUM, NEW YORK CITY — 64,892
WEATHER CONDITIONS: BRILLIANT SUNSHINE, FRIGID COLD, 20°F. AT GAME TIME,
17°F. DURING THE SECOND HALF, WIND GUSTS UP TO 40 MPH.
FIELD CONDITION: FROZEN, FIRM.

It was New York in late December and it was supposed to be cold, but even by Gotham standards, this was ridiculous. "The day began cold, but calm. By game time, however, the temperatures had fallen to 19 degrees, with wind gusts of 40 miles per hour and a reported wind chill of minus 25 degrees."[1] The bitter cold did not keep the crowd down, however, as 64,892 hardy souls filled Yankee Stadium to see if the Maramen could gain a measure of revenge for the shellacking they had received in Green Bay a year earlier.

New York coach Allie Sherman wanted his team ready with their minds on this game, but he wanted them all to keep the memory of the 1961 championship contest alive in their minds as well. Every Giant had a large envelope waiting in his dressing locker before the game. Each contained a duplicate of last year's headlines: Packers 37 Giants 0.[2]

The weather conditions did not affect the turnout, but it did affect the passing game as New York's explosive aerial assault was largely impeded and the ground game tested by the frozen conditions. Throughout the contest, the wind continually changed direction and swirled throughout the stadium. First it was from the north, then the west, and then northwest. Both coaches agreed after the contest that the wind was more bothersome than the cold. The swirling wind "littered the Yankee Stadium turf with newspapers, swirled dust clouds in player's faces and lifted hats through the cold air. But most important, it sent Y.A. Tittle's passes nose diving like a dying duck."[3] Even the opening kickoff was affected by the high winds as Green Bay's Earl Gros had to hold the ball for Willie Wood in order to keep it from blowing off the kicking tee.

The first Green Bay score came on their very first possession, the result of a 10-play, 60-yard drive that moved the ball into scoring position. NFL rushing leader Jimmy Taylor led the charge with runs of 9 and 14 yards, and two pass receptions from Bart Starr good for 14 and 7 yards. Tasked with being the workhorse fullback once more on third down, Taylor came up just inches short of a new set of downs. The Packers took the lead on Jerry Kramer's 26-yard field goal. Kramer stepped into the placekicking role when Paul Hornung went down to injury during the fifth game of the season. The officials signaled that the kick was good, having sailed just inside the right goal post, but many in the stadium questioned the call. New York's defensive captain Andy Robustelli made a violent protest to the game officials. Later Robustelli would remark, "That kick missed by at least three feet to the right. I watched that one and I know it wasn't good."[4] Despite Robustelli's protests, the call stood and Green Bay took a 3 to 0 lead.

The Giants came right back on a tear of their own. Sam Horner returned Kramer's kickoff 25 yards and the Giants were off. On the strength of three passes from Y.A. Tittle, the Maramen moved to within 16 yards of the end zone. The Tittle aerials were good for 38 yards and landed in the hands of Phil King and twice to Del Shofner. After King carried for 1 yard, Tittle went back to the air. As the Bald Eagle let go of the pass, linebacker Ray Nitschke deflected the ball into the arms of teammate Dan Currie, who had an open field in front of him. The former All-American from Michigan State rumbled 39 yards before his injured knee buckled. He fell and was downed at the New York 39.

The Packers could only move to the 30 on three plays and Kramer set up for another field goal try. This one was blocked by New York defensive back Erich Barnes and the score remained 3 to 0.

Midway through the second period Nitschke and Currie struck again. Currie made a hard tackle on King, forcing a fumble that Nitschke fell on at the Giants' 28. After Taylor gained one yard on first down, Paul Hornung took a handoff from Starr, ran wide, pulled up and threw for a 20-yard gain to end Boyd Dowler on the seven. On the next play, Taylor blasted through the middle of the line and past linebacker Sam Huff, virtually untouched, for a touchdown. Years later, Taylor recalled one play early in the scoring drive in which Huff had tackled him hard. "I was hauling myself up from the ground when Huff said, 'Taylor, you stink.'" Taylor headed back to the Packers' huddle without saying a word, but several plays later, after scoring on his seven-yard bolt, he had his response. "From the end zone, I yelled to Huff, 'Hey, Sam, how do I smell from here?'"[5] Kramer's point after kick made the score 10 to 0 in favor of Green Bay. Huff told reporters after the game, "Call it a mistake in execution, a confused defense or what have you, but it was my fault." New York's All-Pro middle linebacker continued, "I didn't play position. I thought Jim was off on a slant to the right and I moved over to that side. That left it up to Grier, and Taylor was inside just far enough to miss being grabbed by Rosey."[6] King one-upped Huff in the blame department, referring to his fumble that set up Taylor's touchdown: "I lost the game. I have no excuse. Dan Currie tackled me hard, but I should have held on to the ball."[7]

The Giants had one more scoring opportunity in the first half. After New York drove to the Green Bay 40, the Packer defense held firm, forcing a Giants' fourth down situation. In trotted Don Chandler to attempt a long, 47-yard field goal. It was not an easy kick on the best of days, but with strong winds gusting around the cavernous concrete stadium in the Bronx, it was anyone's guess which way this ball might fly. Chandler swung his dependable leg in its familiar arc and the ball sailed upward toward the goal, but as if on cue, the wind whipped up, sweeping the ball away to the right as easily as a man sweeps away a fly on a summer day. The kick had failed and Green Bay's lead was secure at 10 to 0 going into the locker room for the intermission.

New York took the kickoff opening the second half, but could do nothing to advance the ball. Chandler punted into the end zone for the touchback and Green Bay took over on their 20. The Giants' Bill Winter broke into the backfield and spilled Hornung for a five-yard loss on first down. Starr then threw two unsuccessful passes. On fourth and fifteen, Max McGee stood on his five-yard line waiting to punt the ball away. At the snap, defensive halfback Erich Barnes sprinted in to the Green Bay backfield and blocked McGee's punt into the end zone where New York's Jim Collier dropped on the loose ball for the score. Chandler then kicked the extra point, bringing the Giants to within three points of the Packers.

With the game close again, the Yankee Stadium crowd roared its approval. Maybe this break was enough to get the Giants moving again and on the road to the championship. The New York defense held the Packers on the next series of downs, and things seemed to be looking up for the home club. McGee came in to punt and booted a low knuckleball kick in the direction of Horner. The New York return man then tried to field the bouncing ball, fumbled it, and lost possession when Nitschke again recovered the loose pigskin on the Giant 42-yard line.

Taylor again ground out yardage, picking up 20 yards and getting the Packers close enough for another Kramer field goal attempt, this one good from the 29. The Packers were now up by six points, at 13 to 7. Not a comfortable lead, but at least with the Giants now down by more than a field goal, they were safe from Don Chandler's accurate leg.

After the ensuing kickoff, Tittle turned red hot. Four short completions produced a first down at the Packers' 46. On the next play, Packer defensive halfback Willie Wood was called for interference on New York's Joe Walton. Irate about the call, Wood hit back judge Tom Kelleher, knocking him to the ground. In a statement, Kelleher stated, "In my opinion Wood made an overt act of striking me that called for his expulsion from the game."[8]

Wood pleaded his innocence after the game. "It was an accident. I didn't interfere with Shofner on that pass. I played the ball and managed to touch it. As I was falling to the ground, I saw Kelleher's flag calling it interference. As I got up he was running past me and I tried to grab his arm. But he ran into it and was knocked down. He didn't give me a chance to explain before he ordered me off the field. I only wanted to protest the call, but there was nothing I could say after he ordered me off the field. That was the first time I was ever thrown out of a game in my life." Lombardi refused to comment on Wood's actions after the game, simply telling reporters, "Ask the commissioner."[9]

New York now had a first down at the Green Bay 18-yard line. Three plays and two holding penalties later the Giants faced a fourth and long, just short of midfield. Having lost 28 yards in three plays, the Giants had managed to blow an excellent opportunity to score, and by shooting themselves in the foot here, they managed to virtually end their chances for the afternoon.

The Giants managed one more drive midway through the final quarter, moving the ball to their own 45-yard line. On third and three, Tittle, running wide on an option play, and with an open field ahead of him, slipped, fell to the turf, and wound up two yards short of the marker. Chandler punted the ball away with just inside of seven minutes to play.

Green Bay started their last drive of the day on their own 28-yard line. Still up by just six points, and with Y.A. Tittle and company on the other side of the field, Lombardi and his troops knew that they could finally breathe easier if they scored again. Starr and Taylor ground out yardage for almost five minutes, getting the ball down to the New York 23. On fourth down, Kramer stepped off the line and readied himself for a kick that could put the game beyond New York's reach. With just inside two minutes to play, the snap came back, Kramer kicked and the ball sailed through the uprights. The Packers now led by nine and the game was a lock.

Tittle fought valiantly to the last play, hitting Joe Walton at the Green Bay seven for a 25-yard completion on the last play of the game. As the final seconds ticked off the clock, The Packers headed for the warmth of their locker room, while the Giants and their faithful could only think ahead to next season.

New York quarterback Y.A. Tittle later explained that the swirling winds in Yankee Stadium adversely affected nearly every pass he threw. He completed just 18 of 41 passes on the day, well below his usual average, and he was probably lucky to get some of those. His normally accurate throws veered away from intended targets, into the frozen turf, and even into the stands. "The wind didn't hurt them because they're a running team, but it killed our offense. I could throw short, but when I went long the ball would drop, swirl or just take off."[10] Bart Starr's aerial numbers were similar as the Green Bay helmsman completed only 10 passes of the 22 he threw.

Jimmy Taylor played a great game, gaining 85 yards on an amazing 31 rushes. The former LSU star took a tremendous amount of punishment, not the least of which came when he bit his tongue in the first quarter. It bled for much of the rest of the game, causing Taylor to swallow blood for the entire contest. The exhausted fullback commented to reporters as he limped out of the shower, "This was the toughest. I can't remember getting hit as hard before. They came to play."[11] In the Giants' locker room, Sam Huff agreed with the Green Bay star and said, "Taylor isn't human. No human could have taken the punishment he got today."[12]

Summing up the grit and heart that the Giants displayed throughout the hard-fought contest, a disappointed Kyle Rote, now a New York assistant coach, commented after the game, "I never saw a team that tried so hard and lost."[13]

SCORING

	1	2	3	4	Totals
Green Bay Packers	3	7	3	3	16
New York Giants	0	0	7	0	7

1st Quarter: GNB — FG — Jerry Kramer 26 yards. 2nd Quarter: GNB — TD — Jim Taylor 7-yard rush (Jerry Kramer kick). 3rd Quarter: NYG — TD — Jim Collier recovered blocked punt in end zone (Don Chandler kick). GNB — FG — Jerry Kramer 29 yards. 4th Quarter: GNB — FG — Jerry Kramer 30 yards.

STARTING LINEUPS

Green Bay Packers		New York Giants
Bart Starr	Quarterback	Y.A. Tittle
Paul Hornung	Halfback	Phil King
Jim Taylor	Fullback	Alex Webster
Boyd Dowler	Flanker	Frank Gifford
Max McGee	Split End	Del Shofner
Ron Kramer	Tight End	Joe Walton
Norm Masters	Left Tackle	Rosey Brown
Fuzzy Thurston	Left Guard	Darrell Dess
Jim Ringo	Center	Ray Wietecha
Jerry Kramer	Right Guard	Greg Larson
Forrest Gregg	Right Tackle	Jack Stroud
Willie Davis	Left Defensive End	Jim Katcavage
Dave Hanner	Left Defensive Tackle	Dick Modzelewski
Henry Jordan	Right Defensive Tackle	Rosey Grier
Bill Quinlan	Right Defensive End	Andy Robustelli
Dan Currie	Left Linebacker	Bill Winter
Ray Nitschke	Middle Linebacker	Sam Huff
Bill Forester	Rightside Linebacker	Tom Scott
Herb Adderley	Left Cornerback	Erich Barnes
Jesse Whittenton	Right Cornerback	Dick Lynch
Hank Gremminger	Strong Safety	Allan Webb
Willie Wood	Free Safety	Jimmy Patton

Head Coaches: Green Bay: Vince Lombardi; New York: Allie Sherman.
Game Officials: Referee: Emil Heintz (Pennsylvania); Umpire: Joseph Connell (Pittsburgh); Linesman: George Murphy (Southern California); Back Judge: Thomas Kelleher (Holy Cross); Field Judge: Fred Swearingen (Ohio)

TEAM STATISTICS

Green Bay Packers		New York Giants
18	First Downs	18
68/254	Total Offense Plays/Yards	67/291
46	Rushing Attempts	26
148	Rushing Yardage	94
22	Pass Attempts	41
10	Pass Completions	18
45.4	Completion Percentage	43.9
106	Passing Yardage	197
1	Interceptions By	0
1/10	Sacks/Yards Lost	0/0
2/0	Fumbles/Lost	3/2
5	Penalties	4
44	Penalty Yards	62

1963 AFL — Keith Lincoln's Big Day

1963 AFL Championship — Boston Patriots (10) vs. San Diego Chargers (51)

JANUARY 5, 1964 — BALBOA STADIUM, SAN DIEGO — 30,127
WEATHER CONDITIONS: BRIGHT SUNSHINE, WARM, 72°F.
FIELD CONDITION: DRY, FIRM.

The San Diego Chargers were often referred to as one of the best teams in the American Football League, a team that could stand up to the best teams in the National Football League. The Chargers had, however, been to the AFL championship game each of the previous two seasons and lost. They were now out to prove that they could stand up to the best AFL squads as they squared off against the Boston Patriots on January 5, 1964.

The sun shone brightly over San Diego on that January day as the mercury rose to the low 70s. It was a perfect day for football. 30,127 fans filled Balboa Stadium to near capacity on this sun-drenched Sunday. The fans hoped to see the Chargers, twice league runners up, finally win the big game.

In the preseason the Chargers' head coach Sid Gillman had hired a strength coach and held preseason training camp at the remote Rough Acres Ranch in California. The team had little to do but practice, get stronger by lifting weights and doing isometrics, and become a closely bonded team.[1] Many of the players, however, were less than enthusiastic. Fullback Keith Lincoln once described Rough Acres this way: "If it wasn't the end of the world, you could see it from there."[2]

During the offseason, San Diego had lured strong-armed quarterback Tobin Rote back from the Canadian Football League's Toronto Argonauts to take over the reigns of the Charger offense. Actually, lured is too strong a word. In reality, they won him in a coin toss with the Denver Broncos. The 35-year-old Rote was a former passing leader in the NFL and the CFL, and had a championship with the 1957 Detroit Lions under his belt. He began to pay immediate dividends for the Chargers, soon becoming the only player to win the passing championship in the NFL, the CFL, and the AFL.

The offense also boasted the power running duo of Keith Lincoln and Paul Lowe. Lincoln, who lined up at fullback for San Diego, ran like a halfback and caught passes like an end. Rushing 128 times in 1963, the former Washington State star had averaged an impressive 6.5 yards per carry. Lowe, a fleet-footed halfback, had been even busier, lugging the pigskin 177 times for 1,010 yards and a 5.7-yard average. Lowe, who seemingly could go from zero to sixty in 3.4 seconds, was often employed as a man in motion. He would take a pitch from Rote and swing wide around end for big yardage. Lincoln was a power back who would hit the line or follow, pulling guards Sam Gruneisen, Pat Shea and Sam DeLuca on sweeps.[3] The offense also boasted a promising young receiver by the name of Lance Alworth. Alworth, in his second year as a professional, was already beginning to show signs of the greatness that would land him in the Hall of Fame. With an offensive line anchored by tackles Ron Mix and Ernie Wright, the Chargers' offense was the real deal.

The Patriots were also formidable, with a gut-busting, blitz-minded defense that had held the Chargers' high-octane running game to only 97 yards in the season's two previous encounters. They were arguably the best defense in the four-year history of the league. Veteran signal caller Babe Parilli, who had once shared the quarterback duties with Rote in Green Bay, ably led the offense. Against this masterful but blitz-minded defense, Gillman decided to keep his backs in motion and run traps, quick pitches, and draw plays to control and confuse the Boston defense.[4]

Lincoln started out with an offensive explosion to put San Diego on he victory road. On the Chargers' first play from scrimmage, the 200-pound back took a swing pass from Rote, shucked a couple of would be tacklers and rolled for 12 yards. Rote then called on Lincoln again. This time, taking a handoff, Lincoln cut to the right, found a hole in the Boston line and bolted 56 yards before being brought down to earth at the Patriots' four. Two plays later, Rote snuck across the goal line from the Boston 2-yard line, and just 89 seconds into the contest, the Chargers took a lead they would never relinquish. George Blair's kick made the score 7–0.

After receiving the ensuing kickoff, quarterback Babe Parilli and the Patriots' offense could do little with the ball. The San Diego defensive unit, led by tackle Ernie Ladd and linebacker Chuck Allen, forced Boston to punt. With possession returned, the Chargers were off again and less than three minutes after his 56-yard outburst, Lincoln took a quick pitch from Rote, avoided a blitzing linebacker, leapt over another fallen defender, and sprinted 67 yards around right end for a touchdown.

A 14–0 deficit was not enough to daunt the Patriots. Parilli led his team back on a 7-play, 67-yard scoring drive to tighten the game at 14–7. Larry Garron smashed 7 yards for the touchdown. Gino Cappelletti made the conversion kick and the Patriots were back in the game — for a few minutes at least.

San Diego immediately answered back on their next possession, with Paul Lowe taking a pitchout from Rote and taking off on a 58 yard touchdown jaunt to put the Chargers up by two touchdowns. With the game less than 11 minutes old, the teams had already posted a remarkable 28 points. And amazingly, the Chargers had scored three touchdowns while running just ten offensive plays.

Early in the second period, the Chargers had a rare event occur: an offensive drive stalled as they neared the end zone and they were forced to bring in placement kicker George Blair. Blair kicked for three from eleven yards out to increase the San Diego lead to 24–7.

The Patriots made an attempt to keep the game in reach with a second-quarter drive, but the San Diego defense stalled the drive inside the Chargers' 20, forcing a field goal attempt. Gino Cappelletti kicked successfully from 15 yards out to make the score 24–10. That was the end of the Boston scoring on the day.

The Chargers were not finished with their first-half fireworks. With just forty-eight seconds remaining in the half, Rote connected with Don Norton on a 14-yard pass for yet another touchdown. Blair's extra point kick made the score at halftime 31–10.

The San Diego management had arranged for a halftime show featuring Grambling University's fabulous band. Things were going so well for the Chargers that when Gillman finished his halftime preparations early, he told his team that he was going back onto the field to see the show, saying, "I want to watch the band." Gillman's confidence was not misplaced. The second half would be all San Diego as they put an exclamation point on their first championship.[5]

In the third quarter, Alworth wrestled a Tobin Rote pass away from Patriots defender Bob Suci at the Boston 20, and took the ball the rest of the way in for the touchdown. Again, Blair kicked for the extra point and the Chargers increased their already impressive lead to 28 points.

With a 38–10 lead, Gillman sent in backup quarterback John Hadl to command the offense the rest of the way. Hadl, San Diego's quarterback of the future, went to work showcasing his considerable skills. Hadl led the Chargers to two more scores in the fourth quarter, one a 25-yard pass to Lincoln for the game MVP's second touchdown of the day. The extra point failed. Hadl wasn't finished yet. On the Chargers' next possession, he directed his team on a 66-yard drive that also yielded a score. Hadl carried for a 1-yard touchdown plunge in the final quarter. Blair's extra point kick made the final score 51–10 in favor of the Chargers.

Lincoln had a remarkable day, rushing for 206 yards, adding 123 more on seven receptions, and scoring two touchdowns. He also threw for 20 yards as a passer. San Diego head coach Sid Gillman marveled at Lincoln's play that afternoon and called him "the best all-around back we've had on the squad." He continued, "And that Tobin Rote called a great game. I didn't call any of the plays. Rote calls plays better than I could ever hope to call them."[6]

Boston head coach Mike Holovak told reporters in a somber Patriots clubhouse, "They were a great club today ... a great club. I thought we were ready, but they just beat us at everything. I don't know how a back could be any better than Lincoln was against us."[7] Holovak continued by placing the blame for his team's poor performance squarely on his own shoulders: "They left nothing untouched. Give them all the credit in the world and give me hell for not getting them ready. I thought we were ready."[8]

SCORING

	1	2	3	4	Totals
Boston Patriots	7	3	0	0	10
San Diego Chargers	21	10	7	13	51

1st Quarter: San Diego — TD — Rote 2-yard run (Blair kick). San Diego — TD — Lincoln 67-yard run (Blair kick). Boston — TD — Garron 7-yard run (Cappelletti kick). San Diego — TD — Lowe 58-yard run (Blair kick). 2nd Quarter: San Diego — FG — Blair 11 yards. Boston — FG — Cappelletti 15 yards. San Diego — Norton 14-yard pass from Rote (Blair kick). 3rd Quarter: San Diego — TD — Alworth 48-yard pass from Rote (Blair kick). 4th Quarter: San Diego — TD — Lincoln 25-yard pass from Hadl (pass failed). San Diego — TD — Hadl 1-yard run (Blair kick).

STARTING LINEUPS

Boston Patriots		**San Diego Chargers**
Babe Parilli	Quarterback	Tobin Rote
Ron Burton	Halfback	Paul Lowe
Larry Garron	Fullback	Keith Lincoln
Jim Colclough	Flanker	Lance Alworth
Gino Cappelletti	Split End	Don Norton
Tony Romeo	Tight End	Dave Kocourek
Don Oakes	Left Tackle	Ernie Wright
Charley Long	Left Guard	Sam DeLuca
Walt Cudzik	Center	Don Rogers
Billy Neighbors	Right Guard	Pat Shea
Milt Graham	Right Tackle	Ron Mix
Larry Eisenhauer	Left Defensive End	Earl Faison
Jess Richardson	Left Defensive Tackle	Henry Schmidt
Houston Antwine	Right Defensive Tackle	George Gross
Bob Dee	Right Defensive End	Bob Petrich
Tom Addison	Left Linebacker	Emil Karas
Nick Buoniconti	Middle Linebacker	Chuck Allen
Jack Rudolph	Rightside Linebacker	Paul Maguire
Dick Felt	Left Cornerback	Bud Whitehead
Bob Suci	Right Cornerback	Dick Harris
Ross O'Hanley	Strong Safety	George Blair
Ron Hall	Free Safety	Gary Glick

Head Coaches: Boston: Mike Holovak; San Diego: Sid Gillman.

Game Officials: Referee: Harold Bourne; Umpire: Gil Castree; Head Linesman: Tony Veteri; Back Judge: Ken Gallagher; Field Judge: Al Huetter.

TEAM STATISTICS

Boston Patriots		**San Diego Chargers**
14	First Downs	21
64/261	Total Offense Plays/Yards	69/620
27	Rushing Attempts	43
75	Rushing Yardage	328
37	Pass Attempts	26
17	Pass Completions	17
45.9	Completion Percentage	65.3
186	Passing Yardage	292
0	Interceptions By	2
7/47	Punts	2/44
/0	Fumbles/Lost	/1
3	Penalties	4
18	Penalty Yards	30

1963 NFL — One More
for Papa Bear

1963 NFL Championship — New York Giants (10) vs. Chicago Bears (14)

DECEMBER 29, 1963 — WRIGLEY FIELD, CHICAGO — 45,801
WEATHER CONDITIONS: BRILLIANT SUNSHINE, BITTER COLD, 11°F. AT GAME TIME,
SLIPPING TO 5°F. IN THE FOURTH QUARTER.
FIELD CONDITION: FROZEN TURF, HARD, FIRM.

The New York Giants were back in the title game for the sixth time in eight years. The perennial Eastern Division champions had only missed the 1957 and 1960 contests during that run, but had not won one since defeating the Chicago Bears at Yankee Stadium in 1956. On this cold but sunny December day in Chicago, the Maramen were ready to put their persistent bridegroom status behind them against the same Bears they had defeated seven years earlier.

Led by the ageless Y.A. Tittle, and his 36 touchdown passes, the Giants were the league's leading scorers, putting up 448 points in 1963, but they were up against the league's best defense. George Halas's Bears had only given up 144 points all season.

The Giants' passing game featured Tittle's favorite receiver, speedy Baylor alumnus Del Shofner, whose 1,181 receiving yards was the third-highest total in the league in 1963. Flanker Frank Gifford could still do it all — run, catch, and throw. Phil King, Joe Morrison, and Alex Webster mainly held down the running game. The aging but still dangerous Hugh McElhenny gave the Giants an assist in all offensive categories. He touched the ball a combined 85 times in 1963 as a runner, receiver, and kick returner.

The Giants' defense was again formidable. Sam Huff, and Andy Robustelli continued to anchor the defensive line and linebacking corps, while defensive back Dick Lynch tied for the league lead in interceptions with nine.

The Bears boasted a powerful defense led by a strong corps of linebackers that featured Larry Morris and Joe Fortunato. Doug Atkins and Ed O'Bradovich anchored the line on either end. The defensive backfield was studded with stars such as Rosie Taylor, Bennie McRae, Richie Petitbon, and an aging but still notable J.C. Caroline. In two meetings in 1963, Johnny Unitas had been shut down without a single touchdown pass, and the mighty Green Bay Packers only managed one touchdown in two games. The game was touted to be entertaining, but New York was the 10-point favorite of most odds makers going into the contest.

While the winter sun was brilliant over Wrigley Field that day, it was a bitter cold nine degrees at noon, when New York's Don Chandler kicked off to the Bears to start the contest. Robustelli reflected that his most vivid memory of the game was "cold, cold, cold."[1]

The Bears began their first possession with a series of screen passes and runs. Willie Galimore, Joe Marconi, and quarterback Bill Wade moved the ball to the Chicago 41. It was there, on the next play, that the Giants got an early break when New York's Dick Lynch leveled Wade after the Chicago quarterback had gained 12 yards, causing a fumble. Giant defensive back Erich Barnes fell on it immediately, giving New York the ball.

Blessed with terrific field position, the Giants began hammering out yardage. Tittle called a series of draw plays up the middle for short yardage gains by Hugh McElhenny, Joe Morrison and Phil King. Morrison carried five times on the ground for 13 yards and took one screen pass from Tittle for eleven more. The final play in the drive was a 14-yard pass to Frank Gifford in the corner of the end zone. The sneaker-clad Gifford beat defensive back Bennie McRae by a step and caught the ball, putting the Giants on the scoreboard. Don Chandler kicked the extra point and the Giants were up 7 to 0.

The scoring pass was, however, a mixed blessing. Expecting a pass, the Bears put on a full rush, sending Joe Fortunato, Doug Atkins, and Larry Morris into the New York backfield. As Tittle dropped back and set himself to throw, the trio was quickly upon him. Morris, coming full speed, was tripped up by Morrison in the backfield. Morris, instead of falling and being excluded from the play, began to roll in an effort to get to the quarterback. As Tittle threw the ball, Morris crashed into the signal caller's planted left leg, bending the knee inward at a grotesque angle. Tittle went down like a rock, having suffered several torn ligaments. In tremendous pain, "Yat" picked himself up off the frozen turf and limped off the field. Upon reaching the sideline, he assured coach Allie Sherman that it was minor and that he was fine. All during the Bears' next offensive series, Tittle walked the sidelines attempting to shake off the injury.

Tittle returned to the field after New York cornerback Dick Pesonen recovered a Willie Galimore fumble at the Chicago 31-yard line. Again, the Giants were blessed with terrific field position. As Tittle jogged onto the field with his offensive unit, he was in great pain, but he ran without a limp, determined not to show the Bears that he was injured. On the first play from scrimmage, Tittle sent Del Shofner deep. The fast and crafty end got a couple of steps on Bear defender Dave Whitsell and was open. As Tittle set up, he saw Shofner open and streaking toward the end zone. The Bald Eagle let loose a long pass to the spot where Shofner was heading. The missile was dead on target and it looked like a sure touchdown. Shofner went up and got his left hand on the ball, but could not hold on, dropping an easy six in the end zone. The usually sure-handed receiver had jumped an instant too late and he knew it. Shofner kicked the ground as he headed back to the huddle, fully realizing that he could have increased his team's lead to fourteen. Shofner refused to make excuses, telling the press after the game, "It was just a miserable attempt to make a catch. I should have had it."[2]

On second down Tittle called for another pass, with his primary receiver being Joe Morrison on a screen to the right side. At the snap, Gifford ran a down and out pattern, taking defenders Richie Petitbon and Bennie McRae with him. Aaron Thomas and Phil King were well covered on down and out and flare patterns, respectively. With pass coverage blanketing the receivers downfield, and a strong block by offensive tackle Jack Stroud on Bear end Ed O'Bradovich, Morrison was wide open as he ran to his right for the screen. Tittle set up, looked to Morrison on his right, and waited briefly. For a few seconds, but what must have seemed like minutes, Yat looked at his wide-open running back and thought, "C'mon, Joe, turn around." By the time Morrison did, Tittle was looking to his left and he forced a pass to King. King also turned to the ball too late. Larry Morris, guarding the outside, saw the ball coming and headed straight for it. Catching it in full stride, he took off down the sideline, traveling 61 yards before being brought down at the Giants' five. It was a tough blow to the New Yorkers, who were so close to a quick and potentially devastating second touchdown.

The Bears took full advantage of their good fortune. After gaining three yards on first down, Wade called a keeper and snuck it over from the two. Bob Jencks's kick for conversion tied the score at seven.

The Giants were stunned. Instead of assuming a 14–0 lead, they were now tied with the Bears, 7–7. It's pointless to play what-if, but had the Giants scored during that series, the rout might well have been on and the outcome of the game very different. Rather than a commanding lead, the Giants were back to square one, and Tittle's knee was getting stiffer and the pain worse.

In the second period, the Giants began yet another drive and it looked like they might get into the end zone again. On a crucial third and one situation, Tittle threw to Thomas for 36 yards on a slant pattern. Then King, behind superior blocking by the New York interior linemen, carried up the middle three times, depositing the ball at the three-yard line. But the Giants suddenly could do nothing. On first down, Morrison moved toward right end for no gain. On second, he broke for the other end and was dropped by O'Bradovich in the backfield for a three-yard loss. On third down, King dropped a screen pass. After three attempts at goal, the Giants had to settle for three as Don Chandler pushed a 13-yard field goal through the uprights to put New York back on top 10 to 7.

Later in the second quarter, Chandler, kicking into a 14 mile an hour wind, missed on a 36-yard try that would have had a big impact in the final minute of the game. Like so many other "what ifs" on this day, a field goal here might have changed the outcome of the contest. Had Chandler's kick been good, the Giants would have trailed by just one point in the final half-minute of the game. Another field goal at that point would then have won it for New York and Tittle's Hail Mary end zone pass that was picked off by Richie Petibone would never have needed to be thrown.

After the ensuing kickoff, the Giants' defense again stymied Chicago, and the Bears were forced to punt. On the Giants' next series, runs by King and Alex Webster netted 25 yards on three carries. On the next play, Tittle threw an incompletion intended for Gifford. During that play, Morris, again on the pass rush, hit Tittle while the quarterback was in his passing motion, further injuring his already brittle knee. Yat confessed later, "That second shot, it really hurt. I felt the knee pop."[3] He finally got off the turf with the help of his longtime teammate Hugh McElhenny, but he could barely stand. Tittle was in such bad shape after this hit that he had to leave the game. As Tittle was helped off the field, Sherman sent backup Glynn Griffing to replace Yat at quarterback. The Giants had no seasoned backup to put in, having traded Ralph Gugliemi away during the season. With the Bald Eagle out for the next two New York possessions, the Giants' offense struggled, gaining just a few yards in total. The Giants' struggles on the last possession before the half were due in large measure to the punting of Chicago's Bobby Joe Green, who pinned New York down at their own two with a terrific kick. Sherman, his troops unable to move the ball, chose to punt out of trouble on third down. Things were looking a bit problematic for the Giants in the waning minutes of the second period, but the score at halftime remained 10 to 7 in favor of the Maramen.

In the Giants' locker room during the intermission, trainers worked on Tittle to see if he could go in the second half. It took a minor medical miracle, but after the application of yards of tape and injections of painkillers, the aging veteran was on his feet and boldly ready to return to the fray. Team doctor Anthony Pisoni explained, "We shot him at halftime. We put both Novocain and cortisone in his leg."[4] The injury, however, would continue to affect his mobility and passing motion for the rest of the day. Passing off his back foot, Tittle's accuracy was off and this had dire consequences for the Giants.

With about seven minutes left in the third period, Bears defensive end Ed O'Bradovich made a huge play that set up Chicago's final score of the day. "Fortunato had just warned us in our defensive huddle to look for the screen," O'Bradovich said. "[Jack] Stroud blocked me, but when he released to the inside, I knew it was a screen, looked up and there was the ball. It meant Morrison was behind me."[5] Tittle dropped back, "avoided the lunge of a large citizen named Fred Williams and lofted the ball gently toward his right."[6] O'Bradovich put his left hand out and pulled it in, returning it 10 yards to the Giants' 14 before being tackled by Stroud. Again, the Bears' defense had given the offense a gift.

On the first play from scrimmage, Wade threw to Joe Marconi and the ball was almost intercepted by New York's Jerry Hillebrand. After dodging that bullet, Wade stood his ground and went to the air again, finding tight end Mike Ditka over the middle with a bullet, good for twelve yards. On the final play of the series, the Bears found themselves inside the New York one. Wade called another keeper and the former Vanderbilt star lugged the ball for the final few inches and a score. Bob Jencks's second point after kick was good and the Bears led 14 to 10.

Tittle gamely tried to get his team back into the lead. Try as he might, it just wasn't in the cards that day. The Giants continued to turn the ball over, ending the next two drives on a fumble and Yat's third interception of the game. The Bears, however, failed to take advantage of either New York miscue. Stalled by New York's tenacious defense, the Bears were left to try field goals, but kicker Roger LeClerc missed on tries of 28 and 34 yards in the third and fourth quarters, respectively.

Following the second errant kick, the Giants took over on their own 20-yard line with just five minutes to play. Again, Tittle limped onto the field. He knew he had time to put together one final drive and pull this game out. He began moving his team downfield and after two first downs, the Giants were across midfield. Trailing by four points, they would need a touchdown to win. He still had half a field to go, but the veteran signal caller knew this was doable. Every eye in Wrigley Field was on Tittle. Everyone in the stands, in the press box, on the sidelines, and on both sides of the ball knew that Yat could do this, too. The air in the frozen ice box on Waveland Avenue was electric. Making use of a screen to Morrison, a run by Webster, and a pitchout to McElhenny, Yat moved the ball to well inside Chicago territory. On third and five, Yat dropped back looking for an open receiver. He saw Gifford open in the end zone and he stepped forward to throw. As he did, a sharp pain went through his knee, jolting the man and causing the ball to fly just off target. Instead of finding Gifford for the go-ahead touchdown, the ball landed in Bennie McRae's hands for Tittle's fourth interception of the contest. For a man of Tittle's usual accuracy, this was unbelievable.

After dodging yet another bullet, the Bears only had to hold onto the ball for the final three minutes of the game. Attempting to eat up the clock, Wade directed Chicago to a first down on two running plays. On the third play of the new set of downs, fullback Ronnie Bull headed into the line for the first down. After a tremendous crash of bodies, the officials spotted the ball and measured Bull's progress. He had missed a first down by inches. The Giants would get the ball back one more time. On fourth down, Bobby Joe Green got off a towering punt that finally rolled dead at the New York 16-yard line. With only 90 ticks left on the game clock, the Giants would have to earn a touchdown the hard way.

One last time Tittle made his way back to the New York huddle. He had one more chance. He had been in tougher spots before and he knew he could manage the clock and get this done. He started with two pass completions to Aaron Thomas, good for ten and eight yards. A pass to Morrison then yielded twelve more, moving the ball to the New York 46-yard line. There was just inside a minute remaining and 54 yards to travel for the winning touchdown. The tension in Wrigley Field again began to grow.

A pass to McElhenny fell incomplete, but stopped the clock at 39 seconds. On the next play a sideline pass to Gifford was ruled out of bounds. Back in the huddle Yat called for Gifford to run the same play, but this time to cut in to catch the Chicago defenders off guard. He did, and Gifford carried the ball to the Bears' 39. Immediately calling time out, Tittle and Sherman met to discuss their next move. With less than ten seconds remaining, and the ball on the Chicago 39, the brain trust decided to go for it all. They would flood the Chicago secondary with Giant receivers and throw a bomb into the end zone with Shofner as the primary target. At the snap, Tittle dropped back for one last-ditch throw — a Hail Mary on which all of the hopes of Tittle and his teammates rested. Chicago sent only three men on the rush, leaving more pass defenders back to guard against the bomb they knew was coming. Tittle dropped back and, seeing Shofner, heaved the wobbly pass downfield and into the end zone, hoping against hope that someone in a white jersey would catch it. But once again, fate intervened and Chicago halfback Richie Petibone caught the ball as teammate J.C. Caroline looked on, icing the game for the Bears. The ball came out to the New York 20-yard line, where Wade took a knee on first down and the game was over. The Bears were league champions for the first time since 1946.

Y.A. Tittle suffered one of the worst days he ever had, throwing for five interceptions. He played the entire second half on an injured left knee. He recalled later, "Larry Morris tackled me — and I couldn't move well. I was just a sitting duck back there. It took so long for me to drop back and set up, I ended up throwing balls I didn't want to throw because I had to get rid of the ball."[7] His teammates agreed that it was just a tough situation. Sam Huff recalled years later, "Y.A. Tittle was hurt, and that was what caused a lot of turnovers. He just couldn't move or maneuver like he normally could, and so he had to get rid of the ball quicker than he wanted to on various plays."[8]

Looking up from the trainer's table after the game, Yat summed up the fifth and final interception by Petibone. "We had only seven seconds, no sense sitting back and eating it, so you throw it up there and hope someone will catch it." He then lowered his head and, fighting emotion, said, "It was just a bad day."[9] Giant head coach Allie Sherman had nothing but praise for his quarterback: "He's a hell of a man. He played on one leg. It's too bad. I think we would have cut them up a little better if he had not been hurt."[10]

It had been a physical contest. In addition to Tittle's knee, the Giants suffered several other injuries. Linebacker Tom Scott broke his forearm, King sprained his ankle in the second period, offensive guard Bookie Bolin was helped from the field with a concussion in the fourth quarter, and Morrison took a considerable beating throughout the contest, having to come out of the game in the fourth quarter. Sherman noted that his running game was thin by the end of the day. "I was down to two reasonably healthy backfield men, Hugh McElhenny and Alex Webster."[11]

A beaming George Halas, still on top of the league he had helped create 44 years earlier, sat back in his office after the game and told reporters, "This has to be my biggest personal satisfaction. It was as great as 73–0."[12] Halas's reference was to the Bears' 1940 title victory over the Washington Redskins. He continued, "We had a number of things that we felt we had to do today to win, but our primary objective was stopping the screen." Halas praised Tittle's passing ability, stating that he and defensive coordinator George Allen impressed upon their defenders that if they could shut down the outside flat completely, the Bears would be "halfway home."[13] The Chicago defense rose to the occasion and honored Allen by presenting him the game ball.

Chicago's offense never clicked. Wade completed 10 of 38 passes for 138 yards and Ronnie Bull was the only notable ground gainer with 42 yards. Sam Huff recalled, "What I remember most about that game was that the Bears never crossed the 50-yard line offensively. Our offense turned the ball over to the Bears seven times in that game. Two of the turnovers — interceptions — set up their two touchdowns, both on quarterback sneaks by Billy Wade. We outgained them, we got more first downs than them, we just didn't get more points."[14]

Huff was right in his assessment. The Giants led in every offensive category, but unfortunately, they also led by a wide margin in turnovers. The statistics were of scant consolation for the Giants, "who had made such a gorgeous beginning as they slammed their way to a quick, first-quarter touchdown on a seven-play, two-pass sequence punctuated by the Bald Eagle's 14-yard TD pitch to his old reliable, Frank Gifford."[15]

Sports journalist Cameron Snyder wrote this bittersweet truth following the game: "If it were possible to do so, the goat of this game would also wear the hero's mantle, because Tittle, ageless veteran, was both a goat and a hero, carrying on despite a left leg he could hardly stand on."[16]

The Giants had been both blessed and cursed. Over the past eight seasons, they had been to the heights, but had also been dashed upon the rocks. The team had won the league championship in 1956, and had played in five of the last six championship games, but had lost all five. They had come so close to defeating the Colts in 1958, they had come within a few breaks of defeating Green Bay in 1962, and surely they did not deserve to lose this one. But New York defensive end Andy Robustelli, having just played the final game of his Hall of Fame career, put it this way: "There's a lot of things in life you don't deserve, but you get. That's it. You take the good with the bad."[17]

Scoring

	1	2	3	4	Totals
New York Giants	7	3	0	0	10
Chicago Bears	7	0	7	0	14

1st Quarter: NYG — TD — Frank Gifford 14-yard pass from Y.A. Tittle (Don Chandler kick) 7:22. CHI — TD — Billy Wade 2-yard rush (Bob Jencks kick) 14:44. 2nd Quarter: NYG — FG — Don Chandler 13 yards 5:11. 3rd Quarter: CHI — TD — Billy Wade 1-yard rush (Bob Jencks kick) 12:48. 4th Quarter: None.

Starting Lineups

New York Giants		**Chicago Bears**
Y.A. Tittle	Quarterback	Billy Wade
Phil King	Halfback	Willie Galimore
Joe Morrison	Fullback	Joe Marconi
Frank Gifford	Flanker	Johnny Morris
Del Shofner	Split End	Bo Farrington
Joe Walton	Tight End	Mike Ditka
Rosey Brown	Left Tackle	Herman Lee
Darrell Dess	Left Guard	Ted Karras
Greg Larson	Center	Mike Pyle
Bookie Bolin	Right Guard	Roger Davis
Jack Stroud	Right Tackle	Bob Wetoska
Jim Katcavage	Left Defensive End	Ed O'Bradovich

New York		Chicago
Dick Modzelewski	Left Defensive Tackle	Stan Jones
John LoVetere	Right Defensive Tackle	Fred Williams
Andy Robustelli	Right Defensive End	Doug Atkins
Jerry Hillebrand	Left Linebacker	Joe Fortunato
Sam Huff	Middle Linebacker	Bill George
Tom Scott	Rightside Linebacker	Larry Morris
Erich Barnes	Left Cornerback	Bennie McRae
Dick Lynch	Right Cornerback	Dave Whitsell
Dick Pesonen	Strong Safety	Richie Petitbon
Jimmy Patton	Free Safety	Rosey Taylor

Head Coaches: New York: Allie Sherman; Chicago: George Halas.
Game Officials: Referee: Norman Schacter; Umpire: Ralph Morcraft; Linesman: Dan Tehan Back Judge: Ralph Vandenberg; Field Judge: Fred Swearingen

Team Statistics

New York Giants		Chicago Bears
17	First Downs	14
89/268	Total Offense Plays/Yards	60/222
38	Rushing Attempts	31
128	Rushing Yardage	93
30	Pass Attempts	28
11	Pass Completions	10
36.6	Completion Percentage	33.3
147	Passing Yardage	138
0	Interceptions By	5
1/7	Sacks/Yards Lost	1/9
2/1	Fumbles/Lost	2/2
3	Penalties	5
25	Penalty Yards	35

1964 AFL — Jack Kemp's Revenge

1964 AFL Championship — San Diego Chargers (7) vs. Buffalo Bills (20)

DECEMBER 26, 1964 — WAR MEMORIAL STADIUM, BUFFALO — 40,242
WEATHER CONDITIONS: GRAY SKIES, HEAVY FOG HANGING, DAMP, MID–30S.
FIELD CONDITION: FIRM, MUDDY PATCHES.

Jack Kemp, the future congressman, cabinet secretary, and vice-presidential nominee, came into Buffalo's War Memorial Stadium the day after Christmas with a single focus: to win a league championship. In winning, he planned to prove something to his opponents, the reigning AFL champion San Diego Chargers. Following an early season hand injury in 1962, the Chargers' GM and coach Sid Gillman had placed Kemp on the injured-deferred list. The quarterback-starved Bills, not believing their good fortune, immediately claimed

Kemp and paid San Diego the $100 claiming fee. Gillman, realizing that he had made a monumental error, tried to circumvent league rules, but it was no use, Kemp was a member of the Buffalo Bills. Kemp, a Southern California native, was miffed that the Chargers had made such a mistake, and he was ready to make them pay for it.

Cookie Gilchrist, Buffalo's troubled freight train of a fullback, would help his quarterback by rumbling for 144 yards against the Chargers. Like Kemp, Gilchrist arrived in Buffalo in 1962. Bypassing the college route, Cookie had signed with the Toronto Argonauts of the Canadian Football League, and had starred there for several seasons. He then brought his swift and punishing style of running south of the border and picked up where he had left off in Canada, by gaining 1,096 yards in his first season in Buffalo.

The Chargers were dinged up going onto the game and it got worse as the contest progressed. Lance Alworth had been injured against the Oakland Raiders the week before. The running game was more of a gimping game as star fullback Keith Lincoln, San Diego's leading rusher that year, had to leave the game early, and Paul Lowe in uniform but ailing. Veteran quarterback Tobin Rote had battled pain in his throwing arm and shoulder for much of the season. Still, Gillman felt that if the Chargers could throw short flares and screens to take advantage of the Bills linebackers' playing back and control the ground, they could win a second straight championship.

Braving the elements, 40,242 fans filed into the stadium on a gray, misty Saturday. The weather was not ideal, but by late December standards for Buffalo, New York, it was better than it could have been. The temperature was just above freezing, and the fog hung low in the air, but at least it was not snowing. To help prepare the field, tarps were left on much of the time before the game, 60 tons of sand was spread in two separate intervals, and helicopters were flown in to hover over the surface to help dry it out. When the tarps were removed on Saturday after an early morning rain, the field was in remarkably dry and firm condition.[1]

San Diego coach Sid Gillman looked to Rote to lead this injury-riddled team to a second straight title. Rote got right to work. On the first play from scrimmage after the opening kickoff, Rote called on Lincoln through the middle of the line on a draw play, and the injured but game fullback tore off 39 yards. On the next two plays, Lincoln hit the line for four yards and caught a pass from Rote for another eleven. Then, Rote found tight end Dave Kocourek in the end zone for a 26-yard touchdown pass. Lincoln's kick for conversion put the Chargers up 7–0, with little more than three minutes elapsed from the game clock. But that was it. The Chargers' offense was spent and they could muster up little else all afternoon.

The Bills got the ball and stalled out quickly on their first drive, but soon the tide would turn decidedly in Buffalo's favor. On San Diego's next possession, Rote began to move the team, again trying for a two-score lead. Rote, scheduled to retire and to have surgery to remove calcium deposits from his right elbow, launched a 60-yard pass to receiver Jerry Robinson. Robinson, Alworth's replacement, could not hold onto the ball, but the play showed that Rote could still air out the long pass. The drive stalled due principally to Bills linebacker Mike Stratton. Two plays had a major impact not only on the drive, but the outcome of the game itself. On the first play, Stratton dropped into pass coverage and picked up San Diego's Paul Lowe. The 6-foot-3, 240-pound linebacker ran stride for stride with Lowe and got his hands up in time to knock away a long pass from Rote that looked like a possible score. On the next play, Stratton saw Rote searching futilely for a receiver downfield. Knowing that the veteran signal caller would now look next for something short, he sprinted over to the left flat, where San Diego fullback Keith Lincoln had quietly arrived. Rote fired a flare pass into the left flat in the direction of Lincoln. The Bills' linebacker read the play correctly and was quickly closing in as the ball approached its target. Then Stratton, traveling at full speed, put a devastating hit on Lincoln as the fullback went up for the ball. Stratton's wallop left Lincoln laid out on the turf with broken ribs and seriously damaged the Chargers' chances of successfully defending their league championship. With Alworth out, the Chargers could scarcely afford to lose their All-League fullback. Lincoln lay on his back as the team trainers and physician huddled around him. When he finally got to his feet, Lincoln was helped to the Chargers' locker room. It looked like he was done for the day. "Gosh, I didn't think I hit him that hard," Stratton said after the game. "I just saw him out there, and when Rote couldn't find a man open downfield I knew Lincoln was mine, and I went for him. One second sooner, it was interference. One second later, I would have missed him."[2]

It was soon Buffalo's turn to get on the board. After Kemp led a drive down to the San Diego 12-yard line, the Chargers' defense stiffened, forcing the Bills to try a field goal.

Onto the field trotted the Bills' rookie placekicking specialist, Pete Gogolak. Gogolak was a Hungarian soccer-style kicker out of Cornell University who started a trend that would spell the end of the head-on kickers who stepped off the line or out of the backfield and wore flat-toed shoes. Gogolak later recalled, "I basically made the team because I kicked a 57-yard field goal in the first exhibition game, against the Jets in Tampa, Florida. I think Ralph Wilson said, 'We're going to keep this guy. He might bring some people to the stadium.'"[3] Gogolak and his holder Daryle Lamonica set up. At the snap the kicker came forward at the soccer-style angle that is now so familiar to football fans, but in 1964 was such a curiosity. As his right leg swung forward, the ball exploded off the side of his foot and sailed easily through the uprights to tighten the score at 7–3.

In the second quarter, another Buffalo drive ended in a touchdown as Wray Carlton, with Chargers Kenny Graham and Chuck Allen holding onto his legs, carried over right tackle from the 4-yard line. Gogolak kicked for the conversion and the Bills took their first lead of the day 10–7. The only other scoring in the first half came when Gogolak's second field goal of the afternoon, this one good for 17 yards, extended the Bills' lead to 13–7 at the half.

Rote suffered from poor field position during much of the first half, twice starting from inside his own ten, but on this kickoff, San Diego rookie Jim Warren, who had averaged 27.2 yards on 13 carries in the regular season, set up the Chargers on their own 33 to start the next possession. With just under three minutes to play in the half, Rote wanted to get downfield to at least field goal range. Choosing to get there by air, Rote had his first pass of this possession was picked off by Stratton. Game officials, however, called defensive interference, and the Chargers had new life with a new set of downs and the ball on their own 43. Rote used the break to keep his team marching downfield. A short pass completion and a ten-yard sweep by Lowe moved the ball past midfield. Rote then dodged another bullet when Buffalo cornerback Charley Warner dropped what looked like an interception. Unfazed, Rote picked up another eleven on a pass to Don Norton that put the ball on the Buffalo 15. The clock showed 59 seconds and it looked like San Diego would score easily before the half. But the ever-present Mike Stratton, denied an interception earlier in this drive, had other ideas. Rote's next pass fell directly into the linebacker's hands and the drive was ended. A dejected Rote walked off the field with his head down.

In the locker room at halftime, Lincoln had his ribs taped and pleaded with Gillman to put him back into the game in the second half. Gillman, on the advice of the team physician, determined that it was not in Lincoln's best interests to play.[4]

Rote, who was playing in his final game as a Charger, was still unable to get anything going, and late in the third quarter, he was pulled in favor of John Hadl. Hadl, the Chargers' future quarterback, had actually played more during the regular season than Rote, but had been denied the start today when Gillman chose experience over youth. But nothing made any difference as the Buffalo defenders simply shut down everything the Chargers tried. Hadl's first pass of the afternoon was picked off.

By the fourth quarter, the already dark day was getting darker, and the fog that had shrouded the stadium all day was dipping lower and lower into the stands. The game was bruising and even the rugged Cookie Gilchrist was forced out in the final period with injured ribs.

Kemp, behind excellent blocking, hit Glenn Bass on a 15-yard slant pass that Bass carried to the San Diego one. The next play yielded only about a half-yard, so on second and goal, Kemp called a keeper and carried for the final few inches himself. Gogolak's kick made the score 20–7 in favor of the hometown Bills. That was the end of the scoring on the day and the Bills had locked up their first league championship.

The Bills boasted several stars this afternoon. Kemp had a brilliant game, completing 10 of 20 passes for 188 yards. Gilchrist, even missing most of the fourth quarter, gained 122 yards on sixteen carries. His longest runs of the day were of 39 and 32 yards. Carlton carried eighteen times for 70 yards and a touchdown. But Buffalo's biggest star today had to be Mike Stratton. The linebacker was all over the field when San Diego had the ball, disrupting Rote's timing, breaking up and intercepting passes, and his devastating hit on Keith Lincoln may well have changed the tenor of the game.

Tobin Rote sat in the locker room after the game. It was an inglorious ending to a career that had seen two championships and three leagues. His right arm was iced and painful, but he refused to make any excuses. "My arm didn't bother me today," he said. "They didn't shoot it. They haven't shot it all year. I wish we could have had Lincoln and Alworth, but there's no use in making excuses. I'm just sorry I couldn't have gone out a winner."[5]

SCORING

	1	2	3	4	Totals
San Diego Chargers	7	0	0	0	7
Buffalo Bills	3	10	0	7	20

1st Quarter: San Diego — TD — Dave Kocourek 26-yard pass from Tobin Rote (Keith Lincoln kick). Buffalo — FG — Pete Gogolak 12 yards. 2nd Quarter: Buffalo — TD — Wray Carlton 4-yard rush (Pete Gogolak kick). Buffalo — FG — Pete Gogolak 17 yards. 3rd Quarter: None. 4th Quarter: Buffalo — TD — Jack Kemp 1-yard rush (Pete Gogolak kick).

STARTING LINEUPS

San Diego Chargers		**Buffalo Bills**
Tobin Rote	Quarterback	Jack Kemp
Paul Lowe	Halfback	Wray Carlton
Keith Lincoln	Fullback	Cookie Gilchrist
Jerry Robinson	Flanker	Elbert Dubenion
Don Norton	Split End	Glenn Bass

Dave Kocourek	Tight End	Ernie Warlick
Ernie Wright	Left Tackle	Stew Barber
Pat Shea	Left Guard	Billy Shaw
Don Rogers	Center	Walt Cudzik
Walt Sweeney	Right Guard	Al Bemiller
Ron Mix	Right Tackle	Dick Hudson
Earl Faison	Left Defensive End	Ron McDole
George Gross	Left Defensive Tackle	Jim Dunaway
Ernie Ladd	Right Defensive Tackle	Tom Sestak
Bob Petrich	Right Defensive End	Tom Day
Ron D. Carpenter	Left Linebacker	John Tracey
Frank Buncom	Middle Linebacker	Harry Jacobs
Chuck Allen	Rightside Linebacker	Mike Stratton
Jimmy Warren	Left Cornerback	Charley Warner
Dick Westmoreland	Right Cornerback	Butch Byrd
Kenny Graham	Strong Safety	Eugene Sykes
Bud Whitehead	Free Safety	George Saimes

Head Coaches: San Diego Chargers: Sid Gillman; Buffalo Bills: Lou Saban.
Game Officials: Referee: Bob Findley; Umpire: Walt Parker; Linesman: Al Sabato; Back Judge: Hugh Gamber; Field Judge: Frank Rustich

Team Statistics

San Diego Chargers		Buffalo Bills
15	First Downs	20
54/273	Total Offense Plays/Yards	61/407
18	Rushing Attempts	41
124	Rushing Yardage	219
36	Pass Attempts	20
13	Pass Completions	10
36.1	Completion Percentage	50.0
149	Passing Yardage	188
0	Interceptions By	3
2/14	Sacks/Yards Lost	2/20
5	Punts	5
36	Punting Average	46
1/0	Fumbles/Lost	0/0
3	Penalties	3
20	Penalty Yards	45

1964 NFL — Ambush by the Lake

1964 NFL Championship — Baltimore Colts (0) vs. Cleveland Browns (27)

DECEMBER 27, 1964 — MUNICIPAL STADIUM, CLEVELAND — 79,544
WEATHER CONDITIONS: GRAY SKIES, COLD, 32°F., SCATTERED
SNOW FLURRIES, WIND GUSTS UP TO 20 MPH.
FIELD CONDITION: DRY, FIRM.

The Baltimore Colts and their formidable offense were the heavy favorites to come into Cleveland's Municipal Stadium on this late December afternoon and lay it on the hometown Browns. At the end of that evening, the Colts would be winging their way back to Baltimore licking their wounds after a completely one-sided affair on the shores of Lake Erie.

The Colts were the number-one offense in the NFL in 1964. With the incomparable Johnny Unitas at quarterback, a solid ground attack, and receivers like Raymond Berry, Lenny Moore, and John Mackey, the offense was high-octane. The Baltimore defense had allowed the fewest overall points and the fewest touchdowns, and led the league in quarterback sacks. They were certain that all they needed to do was key on Cleveland's great fullback Jim Brown and the game would be in the bag. Baltimore head coach Don Shula, however, tried to keep his players from listening to talk of a rout. Shula knew Cleveland coach Blanton Collier well. He had played under him when Collier was an assistant with the Browns in the 1950s and he had coached under him when Collier was the head coach at the University of Kentucky. He appreciated Collier's astute coaching style and insights and he knew that his old boss would have his troops ready.

Collier did. "We had all of the psychological edges going for us," Collier said. "We were put down. Johnny Unitas was going to eat us alive.... Now, I hated to be told I couldn't do something, and I didn't like being told my team couldn't win the game. The more we prepared for the Colts in the two weeks before the game, the stronger the feeling got."[1] The Browns truly believed that the Colts could not beat them. If the defensive backs could blanket Unitas's primary receivers, they would force him to look to his second and third man on each play, buying a valuable second or two for the pass rush to get to the quarterback.

The Browns had not put up impressive defensive statistics in 1964. They were, in fact, rated last in total defense. Still, the Browns defense boasted a strong front line that featured former Giant Dick Modzelewski, who had been traded west during the off season, as well as Paul Wiggin, Jim Kanicki, and Bill Glass. These men would put a heavy rush on Colts quarterback Johnny Unitas all day, causing the future Hall of Famer nightmares as he was harassed throughout the contest.

Just six minutes after the opening kickoff, Unitas, under extreme pressure while attempting to pass, escaped out of a collapsing pocket and ran for seven yards. It was a sign of things to come. Cleveland's pass rush would stay on Unitas all afternoon, taking away the passing game and making him scramble. Veteran Browns linebacker Galen Fiss said after the game, "When he started to run, I knew we would win. He can't beat you with his legs."[2]

Cleveland did manage to get a good drive going late in the first period as quarterback Frank Ryan mixed runs with aerials. On third and long, Ryan passed to Jim Brown over the middle. Brown made a terrific one-handed grab, moving the ball for a first down just past midfield. It looked like the Browns might get on the scoreboard. This drive, however, ended too when Baltimore's defense stiffened and forced a Cleveland punt.

Regardless of the terrific defense put up by Cleveland, Unitas and company managed a drive into Cleveland territory early in the second quarter. With the ball at the Cleveland 22, the Brown defense finally stood their ground, and on fourth down, Baltimore's trusty left-footed kicker Lou Michaels set up for a 29-yard field goal attempt. The snap from center was high and holder Bob Boyd was unable to corral the ball and get it down for the kick. This ended the Colts' only legitimate chance for points in the entire contest.

But Baltimore did begin to get some rhythm. On the next possession, again driving successfully, the Colts were showing some signs of life. Then fate struck again. Unitas threw a hard pass to John Mackey that deflected off the great end's hands and caromed directly into the arms of Cleveland's Vince Costello. Another miscue had cost the Colts a chance to take the lead.

The first half ended in a scoreless tie, prompting columnist Red Smith to paraphrase Winston Churchill and write, "Never had so many paid so dearly to see so little."[3] The half was clearly a defensive struggle and characterized by most sportswriters as "spectacularly dull" and "a throwback to the early days of pro football." Tex Maule wrote, "Neither team seemed willing to gamble for a long gain; Unitas and Ryan played with all the flair of a pair of elderly clubwomen in a Sunday afternoon croquet match."[4]

During the break, however, Collier, ever the planner, was busy making adjustments to his team's game plan. Collier and his strategists noticed one important thing: "The Colts were covering Paul Warfield so thoroughly that we just couldn't take the chance of throwing to him. But that coverage left Collins open many times, so we thought it was time to make him the primary target."[5] That switch broke the game wide open.

The complexion of the game began to change as the third period began. Collier said, "The wind was a decisive factor in this game." The wind also affected the kicking game. Two forgivably short punts into the gusting wind off the lake, by Baltimore's Tom Gilburg, gave the Browns good field position.

The Colts took the second-half kickoff, but could do nothing to move the ball and were forced to punt from their own 23-yard line. Gilburg set himself, took the snap, and kicked. The ball sailed up, but was caught in the swirling winds and redirected, traveling only 25 yards and giving the Browns the ball at the Colts' 47. On first down, Ryan called for a flare pass to Jim Brown that was good for 11 yards. Then Baltimore's defenders began to stiffen. Two more passes fell incomplete, forcing a fourth down. Collier decided to try for three. The oldest man in the league, 40-year old Lou Groza, with the wind at his back, boomed a 43-yard field goal to break the scoreless deadlock.

Groza then kicked off and again, thanks to the wind at his back, his kick sailed into the end zone for a touchback. Baltimore started at their 20. The Cleveland defensive backs played back when Unitas had the wind behind him and dropped in close when he was throwing into the gale. This time he was facing the wind, so knowing that he couldn't throw long, the Browns pulled in tight to cut off the short passes. On first down Unitas missed his receiver. On second he was under too much pressure to get a pass away and wound up running for a yard. On third down he hit Tony Lorick on a short screen, but Galen Fiss played it beautifully, dropping Lorick for a short gain.

Gilburg's second punt was longer, this one for 38 yards, but again left Cleveland with decent field position at their own 32-yard line. Ryan noticed that the Colt linebackers were cheating in towards the middle and the defensive backs on the left side were playing too far back. He decided to exploit this gap. On second down, Jimmy Brown took a pitchout from Ryan and ran wide to his left. With three blockers ahead of him, broke loose on a 46-yard sprint. He looked as if he might score until he was chased down from behind by the Colts' Jerry Logan at the Baltimore 18.

On the next play, receiver Gary Collins, running a down and in pattern, weaved his way between Baltimore defenders Bob Boyd and Jimmy Welch and leaped into the air to catch the first of three second-half touchdowns he would claim that afternoon. The tall and lanky Collins recalled that he ran "a hook post pattern. I just got out there and took off."[6] He was supposed to go down and out into the corner of the end zone, "but I couldn't shake the safety, so I cut behind the goal posts. Frank spotted me and fired a perfect waist-high pitch."[7] This pass from Ryan covered 18 yards. Groza's conversion put the score at 10 to 0 Cleveland.

Collins's second touchdown came on a broken pattern on which the former Maryland star managed to break loose and was spotted by Ryan as he was breaking downfield. Groza's point after kick gave Cleveland a 17-point edge.

In the fourth quarter, the Browns were moving again. Following a slashing 21-yard run by Brown and two passes by Ryan to Paul Warfield and Johnny Brewer, Cleveland wound up with the ball on the Baltimore one. There the Colts' defense came alive and held fast, forcing a 10-yard field goal try by Groza. Groza and holder Bob Franklin set up, completely aware of what the wind was doing to the kicking game, but the snap came, Franklin set, and Groza kicked the ball through the uprights for his second three-pointer of the contest. The score now stood at 20 to 0 in favor of the Browns.

Collins scored a third time on a 51-yard strike on which he left Baltimore's Bob Boyd behind at the ten. Collins made a masterful catch in heavy traffic. "I caught it right here," he said, pointing to the crook of his right arm.[8] Once more, Groza lined up for the conversion kick and, when Franklin placed the ball, stepped forward and booted it successfully through the uprights. The Browns now led the Colts 27 to 0.

The Cleveland defense played a masterful game. The front four of Modzelewski, Glass, Kanicki, and Wiggin kept Unitas on the run and only allowed 110 rushing yards all day. Modzelewski and Wiggin recovered fumbles by Jerry Hill and Lenny Moore, respectively, to help stop Baltimore drives in the first half. Veteran Galen Fiss led the linebacking corps, smashing through the line time and again to nail the ball carrier. The secondary bottled up Moore, Mackey, and Hill. Raymond Berry managed three catches for 38 yards, but they were insignificant to the game's outcome.

Brown was a bulldozer all afternoon, gaining 114 yards on 27 carries. Ryan said after the game, "They just couldn't stop Jimmy Brown and that slowed up their rushing me. If Jimmy wasn't human, I would have run him on every play."[9] Ryan himself played a terrific game, completing 11 of 18 passes for 206 yards.

Often overlooked when considering factors in the victory is rookie Paul Warfield, who caught only one pass for 13 yards, but his contribution was huge. Warfield played decoy much of the time, with the Colts frequently playing double coverage on the speedy end out of Ohio State. This freed up Collins to wreak havoc. A smiling Warfield pointed out after the game, "They couldn't afford to have single coverage on Gary."[10]

A half dozen Baltimore miscues were deadly to the Colts. The four turnovers stopped drives and the two short punts set up Cleveland scores. The Colts got very little going offensively in the first half and virtually nothing in the second. Shula was frustrated with the whole affair. "Their defense did a heck of a job," the coach conceded, "but when you say that, you also have to mention our complete lack of offense. We couldn't get anything done." Shula refused, however, to lay blame on anyone. "We had zero points on the scoreboard. I wasn't satisfied with anyone."[11] It was simply not the Colts' day. Johnny Unitas wrapped up the Baltimore disaster concisely when he said, "They just beat the hell out of us. That sums it up."[12]

SCORING

	1	2	3	4	Totals
Baltimore Colts	0	0	0	0	0
Cleveland Browns	0	0	17	10	27

1st Quarter: None. 2nd Quarter: None. 3rd Quarter: CLE — FG — Lou Groza 43 yards. CLE — TD — Gary Collins 18-yard pass from Frank Ryan (Lou Groza kick). CLE — TD — Gary Collins 42-yard pass from Frank Ryan (Lou Groza kick). 4th Quarter: CLE — FG — Lou Groza 10 yards. CLE — TD — Gary Collins 51-yard pass from Frank Ryan (Lou Groza kick).

STARTING LINEUPS

Baltimore Colts		Cleveland Browns
Johnny Unitas	Quarterback	Frank Ryan
Lenny Moore	Halfback	Ernie Green
Jerry Hill	Fullback	Jim Brown
Jimmy Orr	Flanker	Gary Collins
Raymond Berry	Split End	Paul Warfield
John Mackey	Tight End	Johnny Brewer
Bob Vogel	Left Tackle	Dick Schafrath
Jim Parker	Left Guard	John Wooten
Dick Szymanski	Center	John Morrow
Alex Sandusky	Right Guard	Gene Hickerson
George Preas	Right Tackle	Monte Clark
Gino Marchetti	Left Defensive End	Paul Wiggin
Guy Reese	Left Defensive Tackle	Dick Modzelewski
Fred Miller	Right Defensive Tackle	Jim Kanicki
Ordell Braase	Right Defensive End	Bill Glass
Steve Stonebreaker	Left Linebacker	Jim Houston
Bill Pellington	Middle Linebacker	Vince Costello
Don Shinnick	Rightside Linebacker	Galen Fiss
Bobby Boyd	Left Cornerback	Bernie Parrish
Lenny Lyles	Right Cornerback	Walter Beach
Jerry Logan	Strong Safety	Larry Benz
Jim Welch	Free Safety	Ross Fichtner

Head Coaches: Baltimore Colts: Don Shula; Cleveland Browns: Blanton Collier.
Game Officials: Referee: Norm Schachter; Umpire: Joe Connell; Head Linesman: George Murphy; Back Judge: Tom Kelleher; Field Judge: Mike Lisetski.

TEAM STATISTICS

Baltimore Colts		Cleveland Browns
11	First Downs	20
45/187	Total Offense Plays/Yards	59/348
25	Rushing Attempts	41

92	Rushing Yardage	142
20	Pass Attempts	18
12	Pass Completions	11
60.0	Completion Percentage	61.1
95	Passing Yardage	206
1	Interceptions By	2
2/6	Sacks/Yards Lost	1/9
2/2	Fumbles/Lost	0/0
5	Penalties	7
48	Penalty Yards	59

1965 AFL — Trampled by a Thundering Herd

1965 AFL Championship — Buffalo Bills (23) vs. San Diego Chargers (0)

DECEMBER 26, 1965 — BALBOA STADIUM, SAN DIEGO — 30,361
WEATHER CONDITIONS: SUNNY, 59–60°F.
FIELD CONDITION: DRY, FIRM.

On a typically beautiful late December day in San Diego, the Buffalo Bills came calling on the hometown Chargers. Jack Kemp and company were in town, determined to hold onto their American Football League championship, won just a year before on a foggy day in Buffalo, against these same Chargers.

The Bills were truly a team in the sense that no one on squad put up huge numbers in 1965. Jack Kemp was still a stable leader at quarterback, throwing for 2,368 yards, but only ten touchdowns and only a 45.8 percent completion average. Cookie Gilchrist had gone to Denver. Wray Carlton led the club in rushing, but it was with only 592 yards. Bo Roberson and Paul Costa were the reception leaders, but neither had as many as 500 yards through the air. The team was very good, but no one player really stood out in 1965. Lineman Al Bemiller made the point when he said, "We didn't have any big stars. Jack Kemp was probably the biggest star."[1] Defensive end Ron McDole summed the squad up well when he said that he and his teammates never could figure out why some teams had several players in the Hall of Fame, but the Bills had no one until Billy Shaw went in. "It dawned on me, that's probably the way our team was. We had a good defense, good offense, but everybody had to play to make it work. Every week, somebody else got the job done."[2]

The Chargers took the Western Division championship with a 9-2-3 record. Despite a less than sterling record, they possessed the number-one offense and defense in the league. John Hadl had done a respectable job at quarterback, throwing for 2,798 yards, a 50 percent completion average, and 20 touchdown passes. Paul Lowe was the big ground gainer with a league-leading 1,121 yards and an average of 5.0 yards per carry. Lance Alworth, Don Norton, and Dave Kocourak were Hadl's primary receivers. Hadl, Lowe, and Alworth were named All-Pro. San Diego was favored by the odds makers by six and a half points.

Bills head coach Lou Saban knew he had to have his team blunt the threat presented by the Chargers' star receiver Lance Alworth. He set a permanent double team up on the All-Pro flanker, increasing the traffic in the middle of his defense to take away the middle pass routes. He also called for Kemp to throw sparingly and control the ball on the ground to keep it out of the Chargers' hands. As a result, the Bills ran nearly twice as much as they threw.

Buffalo suffered a tough blow when they lost 252-pound All-Pro guard Billy Shaw to an injury on the opening kickoff.

After a scoreless first quarter, Buffalo struck for two quick touchdowns in the second period. Kemp got the scoring started early in the second period as he directed the Bills for 60 yards in six plays. Fullback Wray Carlton got things revved up with two blasts through the vaunted Charger defensive line. Each carry was good for eight yards. Kemp then went to the air, connecting with Paul Costa for 22 yards to put Buffalo in scoring position. On the final play of the drive, Kemp found Ernie Warlick in the end zone on an 18-yard bullet that passed through the goal posts, past cornerback Speedy Duncan, and into the tight end's hands. Warlick had turned in time to see the ball hurtling toward him, caught the perfectly placed missile, and then lost his footing, tumbling to his left and rolling, but hanging onto the ball for the score.[3] The 6'3", 235-pound Warlick, playing in the final game of his four-year professional career, had only eight receptions and one touchdown all season, but caught three balls in the championship game. Pete Gogolak kicked the conversion and the Bills led 7 to 0.

The second touchdown came on a spectacular 74-yard punt return by defensive back Butch Byrd, who took John Hadl's 40-yard kick on his own 26 and took off looking for an open seam. Byrd saw some daylight along the San Diego sideline and sprinted as fast as he could go all the way into the Chargers' end zone. Gogolak again tacked on the extra point and the underdog Bills now led by fourteen.

In the third quarter, Kemp fired a long pass to Bo Roberson good for 49 yards and a first down on the San Diego 24. The Bills kept driving to the four, but were stopped cold there by the Charger defense. On fourth down Pete Gogolak came in for an 11-yard chip shot field goal which he nailed, and the Bills were now on top 17 to 0.

On the next Charger possession, Butch Byrd struck again. As Hadl tried to get his team on the board, he threw a pass that Byrd snagged at the San Diego 47-yard line. The All-Pro cornerback then returned the ball 24 yards to the Charger 23. When the Bills' offense could do nothing with the ball, Gogolak kicked his second field goal of the game to extend the Buffalo lead to 20 to 0.

In the fourth quarter Gogolak kicked his third field goal from 32 yards out, to tie Ben Agajanian's record and finish the scoring on the day. The tally now stood at 23 to 0.

Buffalo's defensive unit played a tremendous game with Tom Day and Tom Sestak stopping the run, and blitzing safety George Saimes hurrying Hadl all day. On the offense, Lowe was Buffalo's leading rusher with 57 yards, but 47 of those came on one run. Kemp completed 8 of 19 passes for 155 yards through the air. Gogolak scored eleven points in the game on three field goals and two extra points. He actually missed on another 32-yard try that would have put him alone in the record books.

Unbelievably, San Diego's high-powered offense did not score a single point. In fact, they didn't even pass the Buffalo 24-yard line all day. It was the first time the Chargers' offense had been shut out since 1961.

Scoring

	1	2	3	4	Totals
Buffalo Bills	0	14	6	3	23
San Diego Chargers	0	0	0	0	0

1st Quarter: None. 2nd Quarter: BUF — TD — Ernie Warlick 18-yard pass from Jack Kemp (Pete Gogolak kick). BUF — TD — Butch Byrd 74-yard interception return (Pete Gogolak kick). 3rd Quarter: BUF — FG — Pete Gogolak 11 yards. BUF — FG — Pete Gogolak 39 yards. 4th Quarter: BUF — FG — Pete Gogolak 32 yards.

Starting Lineups

Buffalo Bills		San Diego Chargers
Jack Kemp	Quarterback	John Hadl
Wray Carlton	Halfback	Paul Lowe
Billy Joe	Fullback	Gene Foster
Bo Roberson	Flanker	Lance Alworth
Charley Ferguson	Split End	Don Norton
Paul Costa	Tight End	Dave Kocourek
Stew Barber	Left Tackle	Ernie Wright
George Flint	Left Guard	Ernie Park
Al Bemiller	Center	Sam Gruneisen
Joe O'Donnell	Right Guard	Walt Sweeney
Dick Hudson	Right Tackle	Ron Mix
Ron McDole	Left Defensive End	Earl Faison
Jim Dunaway	Left Defensive Tackle	George Gross
Tom Sestak	Right Defensive Tackle	Ernie Ladd
Tom Day	Right Defensive End	Bob Petrich
John Tracey	Left Linebacker	Dick Degen
Harry Jacobs	Middle Linebacker	Chuck Allen
Mike Stratton	Rightside Linebacker	Frank Buncom
Booker Edgerson	Left Cornerback	Jimmy Warren
Butch Byrd	Right Cornerback	Speedy Duncan
Hagood Clarke	Strong Safety	Kenny Graham
George Saimes	Free Safety	Bud Whitehead

Head Coaches: Buffalo Bills: Lou Saban; San Diego Chargers: Sid Gillman.

Game Officials: Game Officials: Referee: Jim Barnhill; Umpire: Walt Parker; Line Judge: Harry Kessel; Field Judge: Ben Dreith; Back Judge: Jack Reader; Head Linesman: Elvin Hutchison

Team Statistics

Buffalo Bills		San Diego Chargers
23	First Downs	12
56/275	Total Offense Plays/Yards	52/268
36	Rushing Attempts	27
108	Rushing Yardage	104
20	Pass Attempts	25
9	Pass Completions	12
45.0	Completion Percentage	48.3
167	Passing Yardage	164
2	Interceptions By	1
2/15	Sacks/Yards Lost	5/45
1/0	Fumbles/Lost	1/0
2	Penalties	3
21	Penalty Yards	41

1965 NFL — A Win for the Walking Wounded

1965 NFL Championship — Cleveland Browns (12) vs. Green Bay Packers (23)

SUNDAY, JANUARY 2, 1966 — LAMBEAU FIELD, GREEN BAY — 64,185
WEATHER CONDITIONS: CLOUDY, SNOW SHOWERS THAT TURNED TO LIGHT
DRIZZLE JUST BEFORE KICKOFF, COLD, LOW 30S.
FIELD CONDITION: LIGHT DUSTING OF SNOW, INTERMITTENT PATCHES
OF FROZEN AND SLOPPY, MUDDY TURF.

The Green Bay Packers were back in the championship game after a two-year absence. Vince Lombardi's men posted a 10–3–1 record to tie the Colts for first place in the Western Division. The deadlock forced the teams to meet in a division playoff game on the day after Christmas, to determine a titlist to go on to meet the Eastern Division champion Cleveland Browns. The Packers beat the Colts, winning a physical contest 13–10. The Packers had fought injuries all year and this game was to be no exception with reserve quarterback Zeke Bratkowski ably filling in for Bart Starr, who went down early in the contest with a rib injury. Starr was injured on the Packers' first play from scrimmage while trying to bring down the Colts' Don Shinnick, who had recovered a fumble and was rambling downfield for a 25-yard touchdown. "The Packers came limping out of the sudden death playoff with Baltimore. Bart Starr winced along with aching ribs, Jimmy Taylor had a severe muscle pull and Boyd Dowler had a bad ankle and two damaged ribs."[1]

On the day of the game, the snow was falling in Green Bay, and by mid-morning, five inches had fallen. "Crews were busy inside Lambeau Field removing not only the snow, but 40 tons of marsh hay that had been put on the field to keep it from freezing."[2] The Browns were staying at a hotel in nearby Appleton, but the roads were a mess and it took their team bus almost two hours to cover the 30 miles to the stadium.[3] Even Wisconsin governor Warren P. Knowles was affected by the storm when his plane could not land at Green Bay's Austen Straubel Airport due the severe weather conditions. He was forced to fly back to Madison and watch the game on television.[4]

Green Bay struck first on their opening drive as Bart Starr connected with Carroll Dale on a 47-yard pass for the first touchdown. Dale, who had made a diving touchdown catch on a Zeke Bratkowski pass the previous week, made this one look easy. He went deep down the left sideline and beat two defenders, taking Starr's pass at the 16. Dale cut back toward the center of the field and outran a couple of defenders to cross the goal line for the score. With Starr holding, Don Chandler kicked for the conversion and Green Bay was up 7 to 0.[5]

Cleveland quarterback Frank Ryan responded quickly, picking up where he left off in last year's title game by throwing a 30-yard strike to Jim Brown down the right side of the field. Brown was almost in the clear, but was slowed by the unsure footing and brought down near the sideline by Ray Nitschke. Next, Ryan completed a 19-yarder to Paul Warfield and a 17-yard touchdown pass to Gary Collins in the corner of the end zone. Lou Groza then trotted onto the field for the conversion attempt. Groza, who had kicked 96 consecutive extra points, never got the chance to try on this one. The center snap was wide and beyond the reach of holder Bob Franklin. As the ball was rolling around in the Cleveland backfield, the old tackle Groza gave chase and picked it up in time to see the entire Green Bay defensive unit bearing down on him. Just then Groza saw Franklin in front of him and threw a pass to his teammate. Franklin caught the ball at the six, but was tackled immediately by a host of Packers. The botched extra point attempt left the Browns still trailing by one point, 7 to 6.

On the next Cleveland possession, Ryan, with Nitschke coming at him at full speed, got a pass off to Warfield, who made his way to the Green Bay 24-yard line, moving the Browns within scoring position. The Green Bay defense then stiffened, yielding only seven more yards. On fourth and three, the 42-year-old Groza connected on a 24-yard field goal to put Cleveland in the lead 9 to 7.

Chandler and Groza did all the scoring in the second period as field goals reigned. Green Bay started out with a drive deep into Cleveland territory. The key play was a 35-yard bolt around left end by Paul Hornung to the 19. The Packer offense stalled and on fourth down from the Browns' eight, they turned to Don Chandler for a field goal. Chandler had come to Green Bay from the New York Giants before the season. He had played in New York since 1956 and was now participating in his seventh league championship contest. As usual, Chandler was dead on target and the Packers retook the lead 10 to 9.

On Cleveland's next possession, Green Bay defensive back Willie Wood picked off a Ryan pass at the Cleveland 30 and returned it 20 yards. But Green Bay's offense was unable to get the ball any closer than the Cleveland six, and the Packers again called on Chandler to put up the three-pointer. Chandler kicked his second field goal of the day from the 13 to put his team on top by a score of 13 to 9.

The Cleveland defensive unit returned the favor late in the second period when Starr was picked off by Cleveland safety Walt Beach. The former Central Michigan star caught the ball at the sideline and was carried out of bounds by his momentum at the Green Bay 30. The Browns could only manage nine yards on the Packers' stingy defense, but drew within one point again, as Groza hit on a 28-yard field goal in the final seconds of the first half.

The Packers' offensive line began to establish superiority over the Browns' defense in the second half. Behind the powerful blocking of the Green Bay offensive line, Hornung and Taylor moved the ball 90 yards in eleven plays. Early in the drive, the Cleveland defense held and on fourth down, Green Bay was forced to punt, but as Don Chandler got the ball away, he was hit by Cleveland's Ralph Smith. The roughing the kicker penalty gave new life to the Packers, who wasted little time in taking advantage of their good fortune.[6] Jim Taylor took a short pass from Starr and carried the ball to just inside the Cleveland 35-yard line. Several short gains put the ball on the 13. On the final play of the drive, the Packers would score on what had become the symbol of the Green Bay offense, the Packer Sweep. At the snap, Hornung took the handoff from Starr and followed linemen Jerry Kramer and Bob Skoronski to the left side of the line on the sweep. When his linemen's blocks sealed an alley, Hornung cut through the hole and bolted for the final 13 yards to increase the Packers' lead. Don Chandler's kick for conversion was good, giving the Packers a 20 to 12 lead.

The only scoring in the fourth quarter came when Starr drove Green Bay deep into

Cleveland territory, mixing runs by Hornung and Taylor and passes to Dowler and Dale. Don Chandler extended the Packers' lead by three as he kicked a 29-yard field goal to make the score 23 to 12.

"The Browns' attack was choked off in the air by a good Packer secondary and a slippery ball, and on the ground by a good Packer defense and the slippery field."[7] Between the Packers' tough defense and the muddy field, Jim Brown was slowed and gained only 50 yards. The muddy field didn't slow down Taylor and Hornung, who gained 201 yards between them. Packer placekicker Don Chandler tied a playoff game record by kicking three field goals.

The Packers had weathered a difficult season with some key midseason setbacks and several key injuries. Through it all, however, the players had kept their composure and stepped in to fill holes in the roster. All season long, including during the championship contest, the team overcame adversity and played like true champions. After the game, a clearly proud and jubilant Lombardi told reporters, "This team has more character than any other team I've had."[8]

This game was the last NFL title game to be played before the Super Bowl era began. Although it was the first of the three straight championships that Lombardi's Packers were to register from 1965 to 1967, it is almost a footnote in the annals of professional football. Author Dave Maraniss called it "both unfair and fitting in a sense, because the game was best considered on its own, a faded dream played in the mist and slop, a transitory moment between football's past and future."[9]

SCORING

	1	2	3	4	Totals
Cleveland Browns	9	3	0	0	12
Green Bay Packers	7	6	7	3	23

1st Quarter: GNB — TD — Carroll Dale 47-yard pass from Bart Starr (Don Chandler kick). CLE — TD — Gary Collins 17-yard pass from Frank Ryan (kick failed). CLE — FG — Lou Groza 24 yards. 2nd Quarter: GNB — FG — Don Chandler 15 yards. GNB — FG — Don Chandler 23 yards. CLE — FG — Lou Groza 28 yards. 3rd Quarter: GNB — TD — Paul Hornung 13-yard rush (Don Chandler kick). 4th Quarter: GNB — FG — Don Chandler 29 yards.

STARTING LINEUPS

Cleveland Browns		Green Bay Packers
Frank Ryan	Quarterback	Bart Starr
Ernie Green	Halfback	Paul Hornung
Jim Brown	Fullback	Jim Taylor
Paul Warfield	Wide Receiver	Boyd Dowler
Gary Collins	Flanker	Carroll Dale
Johnny Brewer	Tight End	Marv Fleming
John Brown	Left Tackle	Bob Skoronski
John Wooten	Left Guard	Fuzzy Thurston
John Morrow	Center	Ken Bowman
Gene Hickerson	Right Guard	Jerry Kramer
Monte Clark	Right Tackle	Forrest Gregg
Paul Wiggin	Left Defensive End	Willie Davis
Dick Modzelewski	Left Defensive Tackle	Ron Kostelnik
Jim Kanicki	Right Defensive Tackle	Henry Jordan
Bill Glass	Right Defensive End	Lionel Aldridge
Jim Houston	Left Linebacker	Dave Robinson

Vince Costello	Middle Linebacker	Ray Nitschke
Galen Fiss	Rightside Linebacker	Lee Roy Caffey
Bernie Parrish	Left Cornerback	Herb Adderley
Walter Beach	Right Cornerback	Doug Hart
Ross Fichtner	Strong Safety	Willie Wood
Larry Benz	Free Safety	Tom Brown

Head Coaches: Cleveland: Blanton Collier; Green Bay: Vince Lombardi.

Game Officials: Referee: George Rennix; Umpire: Tony Sacco; Head Linesman: George Murphy; Back Judge: Stan Javie; Field Judge: Mike Lisetski; Line Judge: Bill Schleibaum.

Team Statistics

Cleveland Browns		Green Bay Packers
8	First Downs	21
36/179	Total Offense Plays/Yards	38/351
18	Rushing Attempts	47
64	Rushing Yardage	204
18	Pass Attempts	19
8	Pass Completions	10
44.4	Completion Percentage	52.6
115	Passing Yardage	147
4	Punts	3
46.0	Punting Avg.	38.3
1	Interceptions By	2
2/18	Sacks/Yards Lost	2/19
0/0	Fumbles/Lost	0/0
2	Penalties	3
20	Penalty Yards	35

Professional Football Champions Prior to the 1933 Title Game

1919 Canton Bulldogs (Ohio League)
1920 Akron Pros
1921 Chicago Staleys (Bears)
    Buffalo All-Americans*
1922 Canton Bulldogs
1923 Canton Bulldogs
1924 Cleveland Bulldogs
    Frankford Yellow Jackets*
    Chicago Bears*
1925 Chicago Cardinals
    Pottsville Maroons*
1926 Frankford Yellow Jackets
    Chicago Bears*
1926 Philadelphia Quakers (AFL)
1927 New York Giants
1928 Providence Steamrollers
    Frankford Yellow Jackets*
1929 Green Bay Packers
    New York Giants*
1930 Green Bay Packers
    New York Giants*
1931 Green Bay Packers
    Portsmouth Spartans*
1932 Chicago Bears**

*Denotes runners up who were considered in the voting for the title. NFL unless otherwise noted.
**Unofficial "championship game" played; Bears defeat Portsmouth Spartans 9–0

Chapter Notes

1926 AFL — The First Championship Games

1. Gary Andrew Poole, *The Galloping Ghost: Red Grange, an American Football Legend* (Boston: Houghton Mifflin Harcourt, 2008), pp. 228–229.
2. *New York Times*, November 26, 1926.
3. *Philadelphia Public Ledger*, November 26, 1926.
4. Poole, pp. 228–229.
5. *Philadelphia Record*, November 28, 1926.
6. *Philadelphia Public Ledger*, November 28, 1926.
7. *Philadelphia Public Ledger*, November 28, 1926.
8. *Philadelphia Public Ledger*, November 28, 1926.
9. *Philadelphia Public Ledger*, November 28, 1926.
10. *Philadelphia Evening Bulletin*, November 29, 1926.
11. *Philadelphia Public Ledger*, November 29, 1926.

1926 AFL — The NFL Challenge

1. Robert W. Peterson, *Pigskin: The Early Years of Pro Football* (New York: Oxford University Press, 1997), p. 99.
2. *New York Times*, November 28, 1926.
3. Charles E. Parker, *Philadelphia Record*, December 13, 1926.
4. Charles E. Parker, *Philadelphia Record*, December 13, 1926.

1932 NFL — In from the Snow and the Cold

1. Bob Hooey, *Columbus State Journal*, December 8, 1931.
2. *Portsmouth Times*, December 5, 1932.
3. *Milwaukee Journal*, December 13, 1932.
4. *The Coffin Corner* 2, no. 10 (1980).
5. *Portsmouth Times*, December 14, 1932.
6. *The Coffin Corner* 2, no. 10 (1980).
7. *The Coffin Corner* 2, no. 10 (1980).
8. Wilfrid Smith, *Chicago Tribune*, December 18, 1932.
9. George S. Halas, *Halas by Halas* (New York: McGraw-Hill, 1979), p. 168.

10. "Joe Kopcha Recalls the1932 Title Game," *The Coffin Corner* 8, no. 1 (1986).
11. *Nashville Banner*, December 19, 1932.
12. *The Coffin Corner* 2, no. 10 (1980).
13. *The Coffin Corner* 2, no. 10 (1980).
14. Carl M. Becker, *Home & Away* (Athens: Ohio University Press, 1998), p. 286.
15. Richard M. Cohen et al., *The Scrapbook History of Pro Football* (Indianapolis: Bobbs-Merrill, 1979), p. 51.
16. Doug Warren, *Roar Report*, LionsFans.com, August 2, 2003.
17. Richard Whittingham, *The Bears: A 75-Year Celebration* (Dallas: Taylor, 1994), p. 122.
18. Halas, p. 169.
19. Wilfrid Smith, *Chicago Tribune*, December 19, 1932.
20. *The Coffin Corner* 2, no. 10 (1980).
21. National Football League Properties, Inc., *75 Seasons* (Atlanta: Turner, 1994), p. 48.
22. Lynn A. Wittenburg, *Portsmouth Times*, December 19, 1932.
23. NFL Properties, *75 Seasons*, p. 42.
24. *The Coffin Corner* 2, no. 10 (1980).

1933 NFL — Number One

1. Jerry Izenberg, *Championship: The NFL Title Games Plus Super Bowl* (New York: Associated Features, 1971), p. 4.
2. *Football Digest*, January 1974.
3. *Newark Evening News*, December 18, 1933.
4. *Newark Star-Eagle*, December 18, 1933.
5. Richard Whittingham, *What a Game They Played* (New York: Simon & Schuster, 1984), p. 25.
6. Tim Klass, *Seattle Times*, July 14, 1998.
7. *Football Digest*, January 1974.
8. Richard Whittingham, *Giants in Their Own Words* (Chicago: Contemporary Books, 1992), pp. 191–192.
9. *Pro!*, December 9, 1973.
10. Jeff Davis, *Papa Bear* (New York: McGraw-Hill, 2005), p. 120.
11. *Newark Evening News*, December 18, 1933.

1934 NFL — MVP: Abe Cohen

1. *Chicago Tribune*, January 4, 1986.
2. Dave Anderson, *New York Times*, December 31, 1985.
3. Whittingham, *Giants in Their Own Words*, pp. 259–260.
4. Cohen et al.
5. Whittingham, *Giants in Their Own Words*, pp. 259–260.
6. Robert F. Kelley, *New York Times*, December 10, 1934.
7. *Newark Evening News*, December 10, 1934.
8. *Newark Star-Eagle*, December 10, 1934.
9. *New York Daily News*, December 10, 1934.
10. *New York Daily News*, December 10, 1934.
11. Cohen et al.
12. *Pro!*, October 1973.
13. Izenberg, *Championship*, p. 14.
14. Lewis Burton, *New York American*, December 10, 1934.

1935 NFL — The Lions Roar

1. Whittingham, *What a Game They Played*, p. 76.
2. Whittingham, *What a Game They Played*, p. 63.
3. *Newark Evening News*, December 16, 1935.
4. John Drebinger, *The New York Times*, December 16, 1935.
5. Whittingham, *What a Game They Played*, p. 63.
6. *Newark Star-Eagle*, December 16, 1935.

1936 NFL — The First Neutral Site

1. Thom Loverro, *Washington Redskins: The Authorized History* (Dallas: Taylor, 1996), pp. 11–12.
2. Loverro, p. 12.
3. Bob Curran, *Pro Football's Rag Days* (Englewood Cliffs, NJ: Prentice Hall, 1969), p. 135.
4. David S. Neft and Richard M. Cohen, *The Football Encyclopedia* (New York: St. Martin's, 1991), p. 127.
5. Arthur J. Daley, *New York Times*, December 14, 1936.
6. *Newark Star Eagle*, December 14, 1936.
7. *Newark Star Eagle*, December 14, 1936.
8. Myron Cope, *The Game That Was: The Early Days of Pro Football* (New York: World Publishing, 1970), p. 118.

1937 NFL — Enter Sammy Baugh

1. National Football League, *The First 50 Years* (New York: Simon & Schuster, 1971), p. 175.
2. Oliver E. Kuechle, *Milwaukee Journal*, December 13, 1937.
3. National Football League, *The NFL's Official Encyclopedic History of Professional Football* (New York: Macmillan, 1973), pp. 102–103.

1938 NFL — The Gridiron Sport at Its Primitive Best

1. Arthur J. Daley, *New York Times*, December 12, 1938.
2. Arthur J. Daley, *New York Times*, December 12, 1938.
3. *Newark Star-Eagle*, December 12, 1938.
4. *Newark Star-Eagle*, December 12, 1938.
5. *Newark Evening News*, December 12, 1938.

1939 NFL — Curley's Perfect Packers

1. R.G. Lynch, *Milwaukee Journal*, December 11, 1939.
2. *Newark Star-Eagle*, December 11, 1939.
3. *Newark Evening News*, December 11, 1939.
4. Cohen et al. *The Scrapbook History of Pro Football*. p. 73.
5. *Newark Star-Eagle*, December 11, 1939.

1940 NFL — The Wrath of the Bears

1. Peterson, pp. 130–131.
2. NFL, *Official Encyclopedic History*, p. 104.
3. Phil Berger. *Great Moments in Pro Football* (New York: Grosset & Dunlap, 1969), p. 26.
4. Berger, pp. 26–27.
5. Berger, p. 27.
6. Berger, p. 27.
7. Izenberg, *Championship*, p. 44.
8. Berger, p. 28.
9. Berger, p. 30.
10. Shirley Povich, *Washington Post*, December 9, 1940.
11. NFL Properties, *75 Seasons*, p. 68.
12. Loverro, p. 30.
13. Whittingham, *What a Game They Played*, pp. 176–177.
14. Arthur J. Daley, *New York Times*, December 9, 1940.

1941 NFL — Storm Clouds on the Horizon

1. *Newark Evening News*, December 22, 1941.
2. *Newark Star-Ledger*, December 22, 1941.
3. *Newark Star-Ledger*, December 22, 1941.

1942 NFL — The Redskins' Revenge

1. Neft and Cohen, p. 152.
2. Michael Richman, Redskins.com, July 14, 2009.
3. The third was Eddie Hare, who was the punter for the 1979 New England Patriots.

4. *Nashville Banner*, December 14, 1942.
5. National Football League, Play by Play, December 13, 1942.
6. Izenberg, *Championship*, p. 56.
7. *Nashville Tennessean*, December 14, 1942.

1943 NFL — Bronko's Back!

1. Jack Cuddy, *Nashville Banner*, December 20, 1943.
2. Jim Dent, *Monster of the Midway* (New York: St. Martin's, 2003), p. 236.
3. Halas, p. 213.
4. Davis, p. 187.
5. Davis, p. 188.
6. Cohen et al., p. 87.
7. Cohen et al., p. 87.
8. Izenberg, *Championship*, p. 58.
9. Davis, p. 188.
10. Cohen et al., p. 87.

1944 NFL — A Hidden Jewel

1. Bob Considine, *Nashville Tennessean*, December 18, 1944.
2. Jim Ogle, *Newark Star-Ledger*, December 18, 1944.
3. Jim Ogle, *Newark Star-Ledger*, December 18, 1944.
4. Fred J. Bendel, *Newark Evening News*, December 18, 1944.
5. Fred J. Bendel, *Newark Evening News*, December 18, 1944.
6. *New York Daily News*, December 18, 1944.
7. *Pro!* New York Giants Edition, October 24, 1976.

1945 NFL — Of Cold and Crossbars

1. Jack Clary, *Pro Football's Great Moments* (New York: Bonanza Books, 1985), p. 9.
2. Curran, pp. 152–153.
3. Richard Whittingham, *Sunday's Heroes* (Chicago: Triumph Books, 2003), p. 151.
4. Cohen et al., p. 93.
5. Clary, p. 11.
6. Clary, p. 12.
7. Shirley Povich, *Washington Post*, December 17, 1945.

1946 AAFC — The Browns Take Center Stage

1. *New York Times*, December 23, 1946.
2. Andy Piascik, *The Best Show in Football: The 1946–1955 Cleveland Browns* (Dallas: Taylor Trade Publishing, 2007), p. 65.

1946 NFL — A Dark Day in Gotham

1. Peterson, p. 159.
2. Dave Anderson, *New York Times*, December 31, 1985.
3. Hy Goldberg, *Newark Evening News*, December 16, 1946.
4. *New York Daily News*, December 16, 1946.
5. *Newark Evening News*, December 16, 1946.
6. Peterson, p. 160.
7. Peterson, p. 160.
8. Sprinkle, *Newark Star Ledger*, December 16, 1946.
9. Whittingham, *What a Game They Played*, pp. 205–206.
10. "Football or Mayhem?," *Time Magazine*, December 23, 1946.
11. *Newark Star-Ledger*, December 16, 1946.
12. Hy Goldberg, *Newark Evening News*, December 16, 1946.
13. *Newark Evening News*, December 16, 1946.
14. Stanley H. Teitelbaum, *Sports Heroes, Fallen Idols* (Lincoln: University of Nebraska Press, 2005).
15. *New York Times*, April 18, 1947.
16. Bob Braunwart, Bob Carroll and Joe Horrigan, "The Peregrinations of Frankie Filchock," *Professional Football Researchers Association Annual 1981*.

1947 AAFC — The Browns Repeat

1. Cohen et al., p. 103.
2. Neft and Cohen, p. 197.
3. Piascik, pp. 81–82.
4. Piascik, p. 81.

1947 NFL — This One's for Charlie

1. Joe Ziemba, *When Football Was Football: The Chicago Cardinals and the Birth of the NFL* (Chicago: Triumph Books, 1999), p. 351.
2. Ziemba, p. 351.
3. Ziemba, p. 352.
4. *Green Bay Press Gazette*, December 29, 1947.
5. Curran, p. 57.
6. Ziemba, p. 351.
7. Curran, p. 57.
8. Cohen et al., p. 104.
9. *Philadelphia Inquirer*, December 29, 1947.
10. Cohen et al., p. 104.
11. Cohen et al., p. 104.
12. Ziemba, p. 359.

1948 AAFC — Perfect

1. Piascik, p. 121.
2. Cohen et al., p. 111.
3. Cohen et al., p. 103.

1948 NFL — Snowbirds

1. Ziemba, p. 364.
2. Ziemba, p. 364.
3. Zander Hollander, ed., *More Strange but True Football Stories* (New York: Random House, 1973), p. 75.
4. Whittingham, *Sunday's Heroes*, pp. 131–132.
5. NFL Properties, *75 Seasons*, p. 79.
6. Ziemba, p. 364.
7. Izenberg, *Championship*, pp. 88–89.
8. Ziemba, p. 364.
9. Ziemba, p. 364.
10. NFL Properties, *75 Seasons*, p. 80.
11. National Football League, Play by Play, December 19, 1948.

1949 AAFC — Four for Four!

1. *The Coffin Corner* 18, no. 2 (1996).
2. Cohen et al., p. 117.
3. This does not include the Shamrock Charity Bowl, the AAFC All-Star Game played in Rice Stadium in Houston, Texas, on December 17, 1949. In the game, the AAFC All-Star team defeated the Browns 12–7.
4. Buck Shaw.
5. Andrew O'Toole, *Paul Brown* (Cincinnati: Clerisy Press, 2008), p. 153.

1949 NFL — Are You Sure This Isn't Seattle?

1. Clary, p. 16.
2. Izenberg, *Championship*, p. 93.
3. Izenberg, *Championship*, p. 93.
4. Clary, p. 18.
5. Izenberg, *Championship*, p. 93.

1950 NFL — Look, Elmer, We've Got a Ball!

1. John Thorn, *The Coffin Corner* 22, no. 6 (2000).
2. NFL, *Official Encyclopedic History*, p. 109.
3. NFL, *Official Encyclopedic History*, p. 109.
4. Clary, pp. 28–29.
5. Berger, p. 49.
6. Clary, pp. 28–29.
7. Clary, p. 29.
8. Clary, p. 29.
9. Piascik, p. 182.
10. Berger, p. 49; Izenberg, *Championship*, p. 100.

1951 NFL — How to Stop a Freight Train?

1. Harold Sauerbrei, *Cleveland Plain Dealer*, December 23, 1951.

2. Clary, p. 33.
3. Clary, p. 34.
4. Harold Sauerbrei, *Cleveland Plain Dealer*, December 23, 1951.
5. Cohen et al., p. 127.

1952 NFL — The Lions' Texas Connections

1. Cohen et al., p. 131.
2. NFL Properties, *75 Years*, p. 108.
3. Patricia Zacharias, "Bobby Layne and the Lions' Glory Days," *Detroit News*, July 30, 1996.
4. Harold Sauerbrei, *Cleveland Plain Dealer*, December 28, 1952.
5. Harold Sauerbrei, *Cleveland Plain Dealer*, December 28, 1952.
6. Harold Sauerbrei, *Cleveland Plain Dealer*, December 28, 1952.
7. Piascik, p. 254.

1953 NFL — The Lions Repeat

1. Harold Sauerbrei, *Cleveland Plain Dealer*, December 28, 1953.
2. Harold Sauerbrei, *Cleveland Plain Dealer*, December 28, 1953.
3. Harold Sauerbrei, *Cleveland Plain Dealer*, December 28, 1953.
4. Izenberg, *Championship*, p. 113.
5. *Nashville Banner*, December 28, 1953.

1954 NFL — Goodbye, Otto

1. Izenberg, *Championship*, p. 117.
2. *Sports Illustrated*, January 3, 1955.
3. Chuck Heaton, *Cleveland Plain Dealer*. December 26, 1954.
4. Associated Press, December 26, 1954.
5. *Sports Illustrated*, January 3, 1955.

1955 NFL — Goodbye, Otto ... Again

1. Cohen et al., p. 139.
2. Cohen et al., p. 139.
3. *Sports Illustrated*, January 2, 1956.
4. Cohen et al., p. 142.
5. Izenberg, *Championship*, p. 121.
6. Piascik, p. 340.
7. Piascik, p. 341.
8. Izenberg, *Championship*, pp. 121–122.

1956 NFL — Gene Filipski's Giant Day

1. Izenberg, *Championship*, p. 124.
2. Herb Jaffe, *Newark Star-Ledger*, December 31, 1956.
3. Jim Terzian, *New York Giants* (New York: Macmillan, 1973), p. 56.
4. Hy Goldberg, *Newark Evening News*, December 31, 1956.
5. *New York Daily News*, December 31, 1956.
6. *Sports Illustrated*, January 7, 1957.
7. *Sports Illustrated*, January 7, 1957.
8. Len Elliott, *Newark Evening News*, December 31, 1956.
9. *Newark Evening News*, December 31, 1956.
10. *Newark Evening News*, December 31, 1956.
11. Lud Duroska, *Newark Star-Ledger*, December 31, 1956.
12. Terzian, p. 59.

1957 NFL — A Long Day in Detroit

1. Izenberg, *Championship*, pp. 128–129.
2. Mickey Herskowitz, *The Golden Age of Pro Football: NFL Football in the 1950s* (Dallas: Taylor, 1990), p. 135.
3. Cohen et al., p. 152.
4. Tex Maule, *Sports Illustrated*, January 6, 1958.
5. Cohen et al., p. 152.

1958 NFL — Sudden Death

1. Berger, pp. 81–82.
2. *New York Daily News*, December 29, 1958.
3. Dick Young, *New York Daily News*, December 14, 1957.
4. Berger, p. 84.
5. Tex Maule, *Sports Illustrated*, January 5, 1959.
6. Berger, p. 84.
7. Berger, p. 87.
8. Berger, p. 88.
9. *Baltimore Sun*, December 29, 1958.
10. Jerry Izenberg, *New York Giants: 75 Years* (New York: Time-Life Books, 1999), p. 63.

1959 NFL — A Brilliant Duel in Baltimore

1. Izenberg, *Championship*, pp. 138–139.
2. *Newark Evening News*, December 28, 1959.
3. *Baltimore Sun*, December 28, 1959.
4. *New York Daily News*, December 28, 1959.
5. Ed Friel, *Newark Evening News*, December 28, 1959.
6. Tex Maule, *Sports Illustrated*, January 4, 1960.
7. *Newark Evening News*, December 28, 1959.
8. Jack Cavanaugh, *Giants Among Men: How Robustelli, Huff, Gifford, and the Giants Made New York*

a *Football Town and Changed the NFL* (New York: Random House, 2008), pp. 207–208.

1960 AFL — The George Blanda Show

1. Wells Twombly, *Blanda: Alive and Kicking* (New York: Avon Books, 1972), p. 184.
2. Twombly, p. 187.
3. Author's note: My father, Tom Page, and his brother Bob played against Blanda in the late 1940s while they were linemen at Vanderbilt. As we watched Blanda play for the Oilers and then with the Oakland Raiders, my dad always enjoyed remembering when he had tackled the Kentucky star.
4. David Steidel. *Remember the AFL: The Ultimate Fan's Guide to the American Football League* (Cincinnati: Clerisy Press, 2008), p. 61.
5. Cohen et al., p. 172.
6. Don Schiffer, *1961 Pro Football Handbook* (New York: Pocket Books, 1961), p. 158.
7. *Sports Illustrated*, January 9, 1961.
8. Cohen et al., p. 172.
9. Schiffer, p. 158.

1960 NFL — Swan Song for the Dutchman

1. Bud Lea, *Milwaukee Sentinel*, December 27, 1960.
2. *Sports Illustrated*, January 9, 1961.
3. *Sports Illustrated*, January 9, 1961.
4. David Maraniss, *When Pride Still Mattered: A Life of Vince Lombardi* (New York: Simon & Schuster, 1999), p. 263.
5. Schiffer, p. 156.
6. Bud Lea, *Milwaukee Sentinel*, December 27, 1960.
7. Michael O'Brien, *Vince: A Personal Biography of Vince Lombardi* (New York: William Morrow, 1987), p. 156.
8. O'Brien, p. 156.

1961 AFL — Blanda Bowl II

1. Jeff Miller. *Going Long: The Wild 10-Year Saga of the Renegade American Football League in the Words of Those Who Lived It* (New York: McGraw-Hill, 2003), p. 53.
2. *Sports Illustrated*, January 1, 1962.
3. Miller, p. 54.
4. Cohen et al., p. 178.

1961 NFL — The Pack Is Back

1. O'Brien, p. 56–57.
2. Izenberg, *Championship*, p. 147.
3. *New York Daily News*, January 1, 1962.
4. *Sports Illustrated*, January 8, 1962.
5. *Newark Star-Ledger*, January 1, 1962.

6. *Green Bay Post-Gazette*, January 1, 1962.
7. Berger, p. 103.
8. *Newark Star-Ledger*, January 1, 1962.

1962 AFL — Sudden Death II

1. Miller, p. 63.
2. Jack Horrigan and Mike Rathet, *The Other League: The Fabulous Story of the American Football League* (Chicago: Follett, 1970), p. 70.
3. Miller, p. 64.
4. *Sports Illustrated*, December 31, 1962.
5. *Nashville Banner*, December 24, 1962.
6. Miller, p. 66.
7. Horrigan and Rathet, p. 68.

1962 NFL — One That Got Away

1. *New York Daily News*, December 31, 1962.
2. *Newark Evening News*, December 31, 1962.
3. *Newark Star-Ledger*, December 31, 1962.
4. *Newark Evening News*, December 31, 1962.
5. Paul Hornung and Billy Reed, *Lombardi and Me* (Chicago: Triumph Books, 2006), p. 128.
6. *Newark Evening News*, December 31, 1962.
7. *Newark Evening News*, December 31, 1962.
8. *Newark Evening News*, December 31, 1962.
9. *Newark Evening News*, December 31, 1962.
10. Phil Cocco, *Newark Star-Ledger*, December 31, 1962.
11. Tex Maule, *Sports Illustrated*, January 7, 1963.
12. *Green Bay Post Gazette*, December 31, 1962.
13. *New York Daily News*, December 31, 1962.

1963 AFL — Keith Lincoln's Big Day

1. Steidel, p. 152.
2. Miller, p. 77.
3. Horrigan and Rathet, pp. 77–79.
4. Steidel, p. 158.
5. Gilbert Rogin, *Sports Illustrated*, January 13, 1964.
6. *Nashville Banner*, January 6, 1964.
7. *Nashville Banner*, January 6, 1964.
8. Cohen et al., p. 198.

1963 NFL — One More for Papa Bear

1. Whittingham, *Giants in Their Own Words*, pp. 116–117.
2. *Newark Evening News*, December 30, 1963.
3. Terzian, p. 95.
4. Chuck Slater, *Newark Star-Ledger*, December 30, 1963.
5. Bob Riger, *Best Plays of the Year* (New York: Prentice Hall, 1963), p. 94.
6. Jerry Izenberg, *Newark Star-Ledger*, December 30, 1963.

7. Whittingham, *Giants in Their Own Words*, pp. 63–64.
8. Whittingham, *Giants in Their Own Words*, p. 75.
9. Riger, p. 96.
10. Riger, p. 96.
11. *Newark Evening News*, December 30, 1963.
12. *Newark Evening News*, December 30, 1963.
13. Riger, p. 94.
14. Whittingham, *Giants in Their Own Words*, p. 75.
15. *New York Daily News*, December 30, 1963.
16. Cameron C. Snyder, *Baltimore Sun*, December 30, 1963.
17. Riger, p. 96.

1964 AFL — Jack Kemp's Revenge

1. Edwin Shrake, *Sports Illustrated*, January 4, 1965.
2. Edwin Shrake, *Sports Illustrated*, January 4, 1965.
3. Miller, p. 132.
4. *Nashville Tennessean*, December 27, 1964.
5. Edwin Shrake, *Sports Illustrated*, January 4, 1965.

1964 NFL — Ambush by the Lake

1. Clary, p. 87.
2. Izenberg, *Championship*, p. 171.
3. *Nashville Banner*, December 28, 1964.
4. Tex Maule, *Sports Illustrated*, January 4, 1965.
5. *New York Times*, December 28, 1964.
6. *Nashville Tennessean*, December 28, 1964.
7. *New York Times*, December 28, 1964.
8. *Nashville Tennessean*, December 28, 1964.
9. *Nashville Banner*, December 28, 1964.
10. *Nashville Tennessean*, December 28, 1964.
11. *Nashville Tennessean*, December 28, 1964.
12. *New York Times*, December 28, 1964.

1965 AFL — Trampled by a Thundering Herd

1. Miller, p. 141.
2. Miller, p. 141.
3. Edwin Shrake, *Sports Illustrated*, January 3, 1966.

1965 NFL — A Win for the Walking Wounded

1. *Milwaukee Sentinel*, January 3, 1966.
2. *Milwaukee Sentinel*, January 3, 1966.
3. Maraniss, p. 382.
4. Cohen et al., p. 216.
5. *Sports Illustrated*, January 3, 1966.
6. Tex Maule, *Sports Illustrated*, January 10, 1966.
7. Cameron Snyder, *Baltimore Sun*, January 3, 1966.
8. O'Brien, p. 174.
9. Maraniss, p. 382.

Bibliography

Books

Becker, Carl M. *Home & Away*. Athens: Ohio University Press, 1998.

Berger, Phil. *Great Moments in Pro Football*. New York: Grosset & Dunlap, 1969.

Carroll, Bob, Michael Gershman, David Neft, and John Thorn. *Total Football II*. New York: Harper-Collins, 1999.

Cavanaugh, Jack. *Giants Among Men: How Robustelli, Huff, Gifford, and the Giants Made New York a Football Town and Changed the NFL*. New York: Random House, 2008.

Clary, Jack. *Pro Football's Great Moments*. New York: Bonanza Books, 1985.

Cohen, Richard M., Jordan A. Deutsch, and David S. Neft. *The Scrapbook History of Pro Football*. Indianapolis: Bobbs-Merrill, 1979.

Cope, Myron. *The Game That Was: The Early Days of Pro Football*. New York: The World Publishing, 1970.

Curran, Bob. *Pro Football's Rag Days*. Englewood Cliffs, NJ: Prentice Hall, 1969.

Davis, Jeff. *Papa Bear*. New York: McGraw-Hill, 2005.

Dent, Jim. *Monster of the Midway*. New York: St. Martin's, 2003.

Grange, Red, and Ira Morton. *The Red Grange Story*. Champaign: University of Illinois Press, 1993.

Halas, George S. *Halas by Halas*. New York: McGraw-Hill, 1979.

Herskowitz, Mickey. *The Golden Age of Pro Football: NFL Football in the 1950s*. Dallas: Taylor, 1990.

Hollander, Zander, ed. *Great Moments in Pro Football*. New York: Random House, Inc./Scholastic Book Services, 1971.

_____. *More Strange but True Football Stories*. New York: Random House, 1973.

_____. *Strange but True Football Stories*. New York: Random House, 1967.

Hornung, Paul, and Billy Reed. *Lombardi and Me*. Chicago: Triumph Books, 2006.

Horrigan, Jack, and Mike Rathet. *The Other League: The Fabulous Story of the American Football League*. Chicago: Follett, 1970.

Izenberg, Jerry. *Championship: The NFL Title Games Plus Super Bowl*. New York: Associated Features, 1971.

_____. *New York Giants: 75 Years*. New York: Time-Life Books, 1999.

Jarrett, William S. *Timetables of Sports History: Football*. New York: Facts on File, 1993.

Lazenby, Roland. *The Pictorial History of Football*. New York: Gallery Books, 1987.

Loverro, Thom. *Washington Redskins: The Authorized History*. Dallas: Taylor, 1996.

Lowry, Philip J. *Green Gridirons*. North Huntington, PA: Professional Football Researchers Association, 1990.

Maher, Tod, and Bob Gill. *The Pro Football Encyclopedia*. New York: Macmillan, 1997.

Maraniss, David. *When Pride Still Mattered: A Life of Vince Lombardi*. New York: Simon & Schuster, 1999.

Maule, Tex. *The Game*. New York: Random House, 1963.

Miller, Jeff. *Going Long: The Wild 10-Year Saga of the Renegade American Football League in the Words of Those Who Lived It*. New York: McGraw-Hill, 2003.

National Football League. *The First 50 Years: The Story of the National Football League*. New York: Simon & Schuster, 1971.

_____. *The NFL's Official Encyclopedic History of Professional Football*. New York: Macmillan, 1973.

National Football League Properties, Inc. *75 Seasons*. Atlanta: Turner, 1994.

_____. *Fifty Years of NFL Excitement*. New York: NFL Productions, 1986.

Neft, David S., and Richard M. Cohen. *The Football Encyclopedia*. New York: St. Martin's, 1991.

O'Brien, Michael. *Vince: A Personal Biography of Vince Lombardi*. New York: William Morrow, 1987.

O'Toole, Andrew. *Paul Brown*. Cincinnati: Clerisy Press, 2008.

Peterson, Robert W. *Pigskin: The Early Years of Pro Football*. New York: Oxford University Press, 1997.

Piascik, Andy. *The Best Show in Football: The 1946–1955 Cleveland Browns*. Dallas: Taylor Trade Publishing, 2007.

Poole, Gary Andrew. *The Galloping Ghost: Red Grange, an American Football Legend*. Boston: Houghton Mifflin Harcourt, 2008.

Rathet, Mike, and Don R. Smith. *Their Deeds and Dogged Faith*. New York: Bantam, 1984.

Riger, Bob. *Best Plays of the Year (First Annual Edition 1963)*. New York: Prentice Hall, 1963.

_____. *The Pros: A Documentary of Professional Football in America*. New York: Simon & Schuster, 1960.

Rosenthal, Harold, ed. *American Football League: Offi-*

cial History 1960–1969. St. Louis: Sporting News, 1970.

Schiffer, Don. *1961 Pro Football Handbook.* New York: Pocket Books, 1961.

Steidel, David. *Remember the AFL: The Ultimate Fan's Guide to the American Football League.* Cincinnati: Clerisy Press, 2008.

Teitelbaum, Stanley H. *Sports Heroes, Fallen Idols.* Lincoln: University of Nebraska Press, 2005.

Terzian, Jim. *New York Giants.* New York: Macmillan, 1973.

Treat, Roger. *The Encyclopedia of Football.* 2nd, 9th, & 13th revised editions. New York: 1961, 1971, 1975.

Twombly, Wells. *Blanda: Alive and Kicking.* New York: Avon Books, 1972.

Whittingham, Richard. *The Bears: A 75-Year Celebration.* Dallas: Taylor, 1994.

_____. *Giants in Their Own Words.* Chicago: Contemporary Books, 1992.

_____. *Sunday's Heroes.* Chicago: Triumph Books, 2003.

_____. *What a Game They Played.* New York: Simon & Schuster, 1984.

Ziemba, Joe. *When Football Was Football: The Chicago Cardinals and the Birth of the NFL.* Chicago: Triumph Books, 1999.

Newspapers and Periodicals

Baltimore Sun
Chicago Tribune
Cleveland Plain Dealer
The Coffin Corner (Professional Football Researchers Association)
Columbus State Journal
Detroit Free Press
Detroit News
Football Digest
Gameday
Green Bay Press Gazette
Los Angeles Times
Milwaukee Journal
Milwaukee Sentinel
Nashville Banner
Nashville Tennessean
New York American
New York Daily Mirror
New York Daily News
New York Times
Newark Evening News
Newark Star-Eagle
Newark Star-Ledger
Philadelphia Evening Bulletin
Philadelphia Inquirer
Philadelphia Public Ledger
Philadelphia Record
Portsmouth Times
Pro!
Redskins.com
San Francisco Chronicle
San Francisco Examiner
Seattle Times
Sports Illustrated
Time Magazine
Washington Post

Index